The Routes
of Modernity

The Bucknell Studies in Latin American Literature and Theory
Series Editor: Aníbal González, *Pennsylvania State University*

The literature of Latin America, with its intensely critical, self-questioning, and experimental impulses, is currently one of the most influential in the world. In its earlier phases, this literary tradition produced major writers, such as Bartolomé de las Casas, Bernal Díaz del Castillo, the Inca Garcilaso, Sor Juana Inés de la Cruz, Andrés Bello, Gertrudis Gómez de Avellaneda, Domingo F. Sarmiento, José Martí, and Rubén Darío. More recently, writers from the U.S. to China, from Britain to Africa and India, and of course from the Iberian Peninsula, have felt the impact of the fiction and the poetry of such contemporary Latin American writers as Borges, Cortázar, García Márquez, Guimarães Rosa, Lezama Lima, Neruda, Vargas Llosa, Paz, Poniatowska, and Lispector, among many others. Dealing with far-reaching questions of history and modernity, language and selfhood, and power and ethics, Latin American literature sheds light on the many-faceted nature of Latin American life, as well as on the human condition as a whole.

The aim of this series of books is to provide a forum for the best criticism on Latin American literature in a wide range of critical approaches, with an emphasis on works that productively combine scholarship with theory. Acknowledging the historical links and cultural affinities between Latin American and Iberian literatures, the series welcomes consideration of Spanish and Portuguese texts and topics, while also providing a space of convergence for scholars working in Romance studies, comparative literature, cultural studies, and literary theory.

Titles in Series

César Augusto Salgado, *From Modernism to Neobaroque: Joyce and Lezama Lima*

Robert Ignacio Díaz, *Unhomely Rooms: Foreign Tongues and Spanish American Literature*

Mario Santana, *Foreigners in the Homeland: The Latin American New Novel in Spain, 1962–1974*

Robert T. Conn, *The Politics of Philology: Alfonso Reyes and the Invention of the Latin American Literary Tradition*

Andrew Bush, *The Routes of Modernity: Spanish American Poetry from the Early Eighteenth to the Mid-Nineteenth Century*

Alice A. Nelson, *Political Bodies: Gender, History, and the Struggle for Narrative Power in Recent Chilean Literature*

Santa Arias and Marieselle Meléndez, *Mapping Colonial Spanish America: Places and Commonplaces of Identity, Culture, and Experience*

http://www.departments.bucknell.edu/univ_press

The Routes of Modernity

Spanish American Poetry from the Early Eighteenth to the Mid-Nineteenth Century

Andrew Bush

Lewisburg
Bucknell University Press
London: Associated University Presses

Associated University Presses
440 Forsgate Drive
Cranbury, NJ 08512

Associated University Presses
16 Barter Street
London WC1A 2AH, England

Associated University Presses
P.O. Box 338, Port Credit
Mississauga, Ontario
Canada L5G 4L8

The paper used in this publication meets the requirements of the American National Standard for Permanence of Paper for Printed Library Materials Z39.48-1984.

Library of Congress Cataloging-in-Publication Data

Bush, Andrew, 1954–
    The routes of modernity : Spanish American poetry from the early eighteenth to the mid-nineteenth century / Andrew Bush.
        p.   cm.—(The Bucknell studies in Latin American literature and theory)
    Includes bibliographical references and index.
    ISBN 0-8387-5514-3 (alk. paper)
    1. Spanish American poetry—To 1800—History and criticism.   2. Spanish American poetry—19th century—History and criticism.   I. Title.   II. Series
PQ7082.P7 B87   2002
861'.40998—dc21   2001052731

PRINTED IN THE UNITED STATES OF AMERICA

For my parents, my roots
And my brothers, my wings

The idea of life and afterlife in works of art should be regarded
with an entirely unmetaphorical objectivity.

—Walter Benjamin

. . . whatever returns from oblivion returns to find a voice

—Louise Glück

Contents

Preface

SPANISH AMERICAN LETTERS OF THE EIGHTEENTH CENTURY DIED AN
entirely unmetaphorical death; the subsequent period, extending up
to the mid-nineteenth century, has known but few survivors. The
decade in which I have been at work on this study has witnessed
the first signs of an afterlife, although the poetry of that century and
a half has not yet participated in the incipient revival of interest to
the same, albeit still limited, extent as prose. It is my hope that the
following pages dedicated to that poetry will contribute to a return
from oblivion and the finding of a voice long absent from the study
of Spanish American literature.

My own scattered interests in the period were beginning to con-
geal as a monograph on the Cuban poet José María Heredia—a
project that still shows forth in the present book—when I received
an invitation from Roberto González Echevarría and Enrique Pupo-
Walker to contribute a chapter on the lyric poetry of the eighteenth
and nineteenth centuries to their *Cambridge History of Latin American Literature*. It is to them, therefore, that I owe the great debt of
a broader challenge. When the initial draft exceeded the dimensions
of their design, their encouragement led to the writing of this book
as well as a new and separate chapter for their excellent composite
history. My father, Arthur Bush, also read that first draft, and his
comments have been crucial to the evolution of the final version.
The interest and unflagging support of Aníbal González has carried
me forward from there.

So long a project has many friends. Where possible they are
acknowledged in parenthetical citations and notes. Others have contributed in ways that lie beyond bibliography. Olga Bush has been
the incisive respondent to every stage of the work; her assistance
has been incalculable in the discovery of a voice for the text and in
sustaining that voice. Important support at crucial moments has
also been forthcoming from dear colleagues near and far, especially
Reinaldo Ayerbe-Chaux, Inés Azar, Ruth El Saffar of blessed memory, Mary Gaylord, John Ochoa, Lisa Paravisini, Randolph Pope,

9

the poet Mercedes Roffé, and Douglas and Diana Wilson. And still closer to the project, I have benefited from the profound intellectual stimulation of constant conversation with Daniel and Sasha Bush, as well as Linda Bush, Andrew Davison, Anne Gardon, Charles Geiger, Mihai Grünfeld, Maria Hoehn, Peter Leonard, Deborah Dash Moore, MacDonald Moore, Nicholas Rand, Nedra Rosen, and David Selenkow.

My dedication looks back to my earliest intellectual training; my epigraphs point forward to my future field of research.

Acknowledgements

CONSCIENTIOUS EFFORTS HAVE BEEN MADE TO COMMUNICATE WITH publishers of materials from which extended quotations have been reprinted. Regrettably, in many cases it has been impossible to establish contact. All sources are duly acknowledged through notes and bibliography.

The author gratefully acknowledges permission to reprint extended quotations from the following published texts:

Werner Guttentag for use of material from Yolanda Bedregal, *Antología de la poesía boliviana* (Cochabamba: Editorial "Los amigos del Libro," Werner Guttentag, 1991); and from Adolfo Cáceres Romero, *Nueva historia de la literatura boliviana,* vol. 1. *Literaturas aborígenes (Aimara-Quechua-Callawaya-Guariní)* (Editorial "Los Amigos del Libro," Werner Guttentag, 1987).

Professor Yolanda Salas de Lecuna, for use of material from Salas de Lecuna, *Bolívar y la historia en la conciencia popular,* with the collaboration of Norma González Vitoria and Ronny Velásquez (Caracas: Universidad Simón Bolívar/Instituto de Altos Estudios de América Latina, 1987).

The University of Texas Press for use of material from Victoria R. Bricker, *The Indian Christ, the Indian King: The Historical Substrate of Maya Myth and Ritual* (Austin: University of Texas Press, 1981).

Introduction: Mapping the Routes

1

IN 1735 FELIPE V REVERSED TWO CENTURIES OF SPANISH COLONIAL closed-door policy by authorizing the La Condamine scientific expedition to visit Spanish America. The voyage would inaugurate a new "planetary consciousness," according to Mary Louise Pratt, "marked by an orientation toward interior exploration and the construction of global-scale meaning through the descriptive apparatuses of natural history" (Pratt 1992, 15). The universal knowledge that was the purported scientific goal of this and subsequent international expeditions to Spanish America in the eighteenth century was irremediably compromised by its grounding in geo-politics, both European hegemony throughout the world and inter-European rivalries, as Pratt has amply demonstrated. In the case of the La Condamine expedition, this political cast was manifest in the assignment of Spanish captains Jorge Juan and Antonio Ulloa to the French expeditionary party. In the interests of Spanish colonial security, Juan and Ulloa's task was to limit the information made available to the world. Thus, their own public account of the voyage, published in 1747, was shadowed by the report on matters of strategic value that they delivered to the king, the now famous *Noticias secretas de América* (1826).

The open secret of that report, long before it became widely available after reaching British hands in the first years of the nineteenth century, was the Spanish will to monopolize the economic exploitation of America. A chief cause of consternation for Juan and Ulloa, therefore, was the evidence of unchecked contraband traffic by which precious metals, in the form of monies for illicit payments, were constantly escaping the imperial economy and, thus, the imperial coffers. Nearly half a century later, Adam Smith would explain that so long as the wealth of nations was measured by the accumulation of precious metals, the problem was insoluble. Gold and silver, being "much as the furniture of the kitchen," he

13

claimed, ought to be no greater in quantity "than what use requires": "Were they ever to be accumulated beyond this quantity, their transportation is so easy, and the loss which attends their lying idle and unemployed so great, that no law could prevent their being immediately sent out of the country" (Smith 1961, 1.462). This theoretical formulation corresponds to the economic reality that Juan and Ulloa encountered. Rather than leave their capital idle while awaiting the arrival of the official flotillas, those in America with money to expend were disregarding the law and investing in contraband.[1]

The solution ultimately proffered by Juan and Ulloa would be in keeping with the political economy that characterized the Spanish colonial regime over its three centuries of rule. They recommended more frequent official flotillas as "the only means of destroying the coastal trade" (Juan and Ulloa 1985, 222). Yet at one moment in the *Noticias secretas* they themselves suggest another means, when they frame the problem of contraband in terms of the possibility of an alternative investment:

> Certainly one can raise the well-founded objection that having local goods, such as cloth, baize and linen manufactured in Quito, in which to employ the resources that they continually convert into cash out of a greater inclination toward the profits from prohibited goods than from those that are not [prohibited]. The cause of this preference is that commerce in goods from Europe must always be considered as independent from internal commerce, leading to a division of resources, of which one *must assume* that one part is applied to the merchandise from Europe and the other part to local [merchandise]. Trade in the latter goes on ceaselessly, since the people wear them, that is the mestizos, mulattos, Indians and poor people use no other, and so they have the same consumption at the time of the official flotilla as at other [times]. (Juan and Ulloa 1985, 218, emphasis added)[2]

A planetary consciousness oriented toward internal exploration, including internal commerce, will come to challenge this assumption by midcentury. The French physiocrats under the leadership of François Quesnay would emphasize the value of a self-sufficient agriculture; and Smith would broaden their critique of mercantilism stressing manufacture as well.[3] But limited by a more restricted interest in precious metals, and by racial and class prejudice, it seems not to have occurred to Juan and Ulloa, nor to the American aristocracy under their observation, that instead of dressing themselves—and, I add, their poetry—in imported finery, they might have capitalized on the local American products in constant supply and demand.

As concerns the commerce of letters, the invariable charge leveled against Spanish American poetry of the eighteenth and nineteenth century—unoriginal, derivative of European models, which were often adulterated, moreover, by their passage through Peninsular Spanish filters—might be reconsidered in the light of this rejected glimpse at an alternative, internal commerce. The predominantly maritime orientation of scholarship in the areas of Spanish American economic history, perpetuating the assumption, if not to say the prejudices of Juan and Ulloa's report, has undergone a shift in the current generation.[4] The growing body of knowledge concerning the production and distribution of popular textiles of the *obrajes* of Quito, Puebla and elsewhere, as well as other forms of local trade (e.g. Semprat Assadourien 1983; Macleod 1984 and Deustua 1994), hints at a parallel history for popular texts, traveling the same routes and amidst the same castes and classes.[5] The songs of the open road, whether originating in or passing through the oral tradition, represent a poetry that has been held of little account and now calls for study. It will be one of my purposes to investigate that road less traveled by literary scholarship, and to integrate the study of popular poetry and the poetry of mestizos, mulattos and Indians into the discussion of the general literary problematics of the period. More broadly, I hope to expand the reading list beyond the handful of "central names."[6] I might add, however, that simply to insist on the place of eighteenth- and nineteenth-century poetry in the curriculum of Spanish American literature is already to expand that list in the face of general neglect.[7]

Juan and Ulloa's derogation of internal commerce was not overcome by the shift from a royalist to a revolutionary politics. Witness the great Precursor, Francisco de Miranda in the rhetorical tour de force of his "Propuesta fundamental a William Pitt en consecuencia de la conferencia tenida en Hollwood el 14 de febrero de 1790." Applying to the British prime minister for aid in his quest to drive the colonial regime from America, Miranda admits that the *criollos* might have been expected to oust the Spanish on their own:

But if one considers the size of that continent, and the great distances between one capital and another, if one observes that there are no roads for inter-communication by land, so that it is necessary to go by sea from one place to another, and furthermore, the absence in all the Spanish dominions of that hemisphere of a single gazette through which to communicate the events of one province to another; one sees that it is impossible to work in harmony, and that in consequence a maritime force that might preserve free communication and resist the [forces] that Spain might deploy in order to obstruct these designs is indispensable. (Miranda 1938, 15:116–17)

Although current historiography corroborates the assertion of "poor overland communication" (Mörner 1984, 211), Miranda nonetheless exaggerates to make a case for a dependency model. Since that model predominates in the understanding of the literary history no less than the military, political and economic history of Spanish America, and especially of the literary period under study here, it is well to recall that his view of American roads is inconsistent with his declared interest in the Incas who, in fact, had built them (see Hyslop 1984). Thus, the Precursor's precursor, José Gabriel Condorcanqui, Túpac Amaru (1742–81), communicated his designs and fomented his rebellion almost a decade prior to Miranda's proposal to Pitt, by the agency of muleteers whose experience in internal commerce had made land routes familiar (O'Phelan 1988, 232–33; see also Hyslop 1984).

Miranda does not simply negate the possibility of a network of internal intercommunication; such lanes of communication, to conflate his references to both roads and periodicals, remain an implicit desideratum. Nevertheless, his preference for British naval intervention over the exploration of interior routes to revolution anticipates not so much the independence for which he struggled, as the neocolonial dependence that would come to vitiate his dream. This short-sightedness on the part of one of the great visionaries of the independence movement provides a context in which to revisit the acute and influential condemnation of Hispanic culture of the eighteenth and nineteenth centuries enunciated by Octavio Paz in *Los hijos del limo*:

The eighteenth century was a critical century, but criticism was prohibited in Spain. The adoption of the French neoclassical aesthetic was an act of external imitation that did not alter the profound reality of Spain. The Spanish version of the Enlightenment left intact psychic as well as social structures. Romanticism was the reaction of the bourgeois consciousness to and against itself—against its own work of criticism: the Enlightenment. In Spain the bourgeoisie and the intellectuals did not undertake the criticism of the traditional institutions or, if they did, that criticism was inadequate: How were they going to criticize a modernity that they did not have? (Paz 1974, 121)

This view of the situation in Peninsular letters has been reinforced by Philip Silver, who rejects all critical positions that discover a revolutionary, high Romanticism in Spain in the nineteenth century, in favor of a view that Spain experienced an accommodating, Biedermeier reaction to "an absent romanticism" (Silver 1994, 298): "a Biedermeier reaction is possible even where there is no domestic high romanticism, as in Spain [w]here the insecurity caused by wars at home and revolutions abroad awakened real fears about the viability of the status quo" (Silver 1994, 298).[8] One may recall the strong, initial attractions of the French Revolution in the formation of Romanticism in England and Germany, and in that light, note that despite the long historiographic tradition of framing the uprising against Napoleonic occupation in 1808 as a War of Independence, Spain was fighting to restore its monarchy, that is, in Silver's terms, already accommodating in reaction to an absent revolution. The vicissitudes of modernity on the Peninsula, therefore, would appear to turn upon those "real fears." But one may then pose a further question about the years prior to the French Revolution in which Russell Sebold (1974) finds the first glimmerings of Romanticism in the Salamanca school. If, for poetry, the hallmark of modernity is epiphany, as Silver suggests (Silver 1994, 299), then does Peninsular poetry know epiphanic moments before the fears for the status quo were raised by revolution in France, the War of Independence in North America and the crisis of the monarchy at the beginning of the nineteenth century? Where other national poetries in Europe take a sublime turn, Spanish poetry turns back.[9]

Silver's proposal of a Spanish Biedermeier that preempted Romanticism leads him on to a second proposal of a " 'trickle-down' effect" that he links explicitly to the position of Paz in *Los hijos del limo*: "the dissemination in Spain (and Spanish America too), throughout the nineteenth century, of the detritus of European high romanticism" (Silver 1994, 299).[10] As in Reaganomics, the theoretical construct results in the rich (i.e. the twentieth-century poets of Silver's preference) getting richer and the poor (the nineteenth-century poets whom he disparages), poorer. Silver offers the following examples: "Heredia's indebtedness to *Ossian*, Foscolo, and Lamartine, Larra's and Esproncedas's to Heine, Bécquer's to Chateaubriand and Heine, in our own century there is Jiménez's and Salinas's debt to Shelley and Keats, and Cernuda's to Keats, Hölderlin, and Leopardi" (Silver 1994, 299). It is clear that in the case of Jiménez, Salinas and Cernuda, and in their wake, Claudio Rodríguez, Silver sees that their contact with the poetry in other languages allowed these poets to circumvent the roadblock of Spanish Biedermeier and so to write epiphanic poetry (see Silver 1994, 299–300). It is less clear why the reading habits of Heredia, Larra, Espronceda and Bécquer should have been less salutary by this account, unless their choices, Heine, et al., are themselves to be discounted as detritus, and a different status accorded to Keats and Shelley, Hölderlin and Leopardi. (But, then, what of Echeverría, who read Wordsworth and Hugo?) The distinction is clarified for Spanish American poetry at least in Paz's corollary to his assessment of the situation in Spain: "Hispanic American Romanticism was even poorer than that of Spain: the reflection of a reflection" (Paz 1974, 122), which he extends to the work of the revolutionaries in Miranda's wake: "our armies defeated the Spanish monarchists and the day after Independence was consummated, republican governments were established in our lands. Nevertheless, the movement failed: it did not change our societies nor did it liberate us from our liberators" (123).

Carlos J. Alonso (1996) has addressed the differential results of the "trickle-down effect" ("rippled and delayed expansion," for C. Alonso 1996, 228) directly—and Paz, indirectly—by considering the ideological tensions in the relation of Spanish American culture to European modernity.[11] Keats and Shelley, too, read *Ossian*, without that preventing them from becoming Keats and Shelley. But for the "postcolonial cultural condition" of Spanish America, in which access to the modern world of international exchange, whether economic or cultural, was limited to neocolonial dependence, "the rhetoric of modernity was both the bedrock of Spanish American cultural discourse and the potential source of its most radical disempowerment" (C. Alonso 1996, 229). Whether Spanish American poets read *Ossian* or Shelley, Lamartine or Leopardi, in so doing they demonstrated at once their modernity and their backwardness. "At the center of every Spanish American text, then, lies a turning away," writes Alonso (229), in an especially bold formulation of his thesis, which offers an explanatory mechanism for the real fears and consequent shying away from epiphany, the sublime, Romanticism and modernity, noted in relation to Peninsular poetry. At the same time, it is to return to the argument of Paz, for whom the rhetoric of modernity itself is just such a turning away, a "tradition of rupture." Paz's oxymoron meant to capture the dialectical balance he discerned between critical ironies that disrupt continuity and so free the present from the past, and metaphorical analogies that rediscover linkages in the synchronic field. For Alonso that "radical ambivalence" (229) is directed at the present, called "modernity," rather than the past.[12] As a metacritique of modernity, Alonso positions his own discussion as postmodern, with a corresponding shift from temporal coordinates to the characteristically postmodern spatiality of center and periphery and the related critical metaphor of "distancing" (231). That postmodern geography follows the secularizing expectations of modernity in accounting well for a culture embedded in a political economy. The map of center and peripheries, however, is complicated by the alternative modernity of Spanish America, in which religion refused to wither away. The center, for Catholic America, has always been where the host is, in the local churches in the very midst of geographically far-flung places. And though there have been peripheries—especially the unassimilated indigenous communities and a variety of syncretisms—the encroaching frontiers of religious orthodoxy were not on the other side of the Atlantic in Spain or Rome. In this light, I shall presently contend that the modernity of Spanish American culture manifests itself paradigmatically in an effort to claim the space of churches for the present against the past in late eighteenth-century discussion of burial reform. But it is the temporal, not the spatial relation that predominates, and in so saying, I return to Paz's dialectical "tradición de la ruptura," which sets the question of modernity in temporal terms, even if I contest his view of an absent modernity arriving belatedly by railroad as a Biedermeier accommodation to positivism.[13]

No less influential than his brilliant illumination of the dialectical temporality of modernity, Paz's specific comments excising Hispanic culture on both sides of the Atlantic from modern literary history has provided a theoretical foundation for the longstanding consensus that Spanish American poetry of the eighteenth and nineteenth centuries before the advent of modernismo constituted a mere succession of artistic styles rather than a fundamental rupture. Witness, for instance, that when the Valencian Manuel Tolsá arrived in Mexico in 1791 to become the director of sculpture at the

recently founded Academia de San Carlos, he took an active role in
the dissemination of neoclassicism, and he was celebrated there by
a poet of the new aesthetic, Manuel Gómez Marín (1761–1850):

> Praxiteles sin duda varió nombre
> Ausentóse de Atenas y Rodas,
> Y tocando en la América, ha querido
> Vivir oculto con llamarse Tolsa.
>
> (Gómez Marín 1981, 35)

> No doubt Praxiteles changed his name,
> He left Athens and Rhodes behind,
> And reaching America, made up his mind
> To live incognito as Tolsá.

But whereas in France, neoclassicism was enmeshed in the philosophical promotion of reason over religious authority (allegorized
in aesthetics as Greco-Roman antiquity over the Christian Middle
Ages), Tolsá did not partake in this project of criticism. On the contrary, his own chief monuments, the Colegio de Minería (1797–
1813) and the equestrian statue of Carlos IV (cast in 1803), if
progressive in their moment from the point of view of style, represent rather a reactionary ideology. The Colegio, of which Tolsá was
the architect, may express a new dedication to Enlightenment
developments in the mechanical arts, but it is above all a rededica-
tion of the mining industry as the economic raison d'être of the
colonial regime, long since the physiocrats and the early theorists
of capitalism had turned the course of economic thinking.

Tolsá's equestrian statue is still more militant. Its art historical
referents all argue for the continuity of monarchy against the dis-
ruptions of the age. The neoclassical style generally recalls the preceding reign of Carlos III in which it was introduced to Spain, and
thus reinforces the political legitimacy of the new king with an aesthetic link to his father. The immediate model for Tolsá's work,
according to Manuel Toussaint (1967, 434), was François Girardon's equestrian statue of Louis XIV, thereby extending the continuity by relating the Spanish Bourbons to their French roots. But
Girardon's statue had been destroyed in the revolutionary year of
1793, and it is to that threat that Tolsá's statue responds as a work of
restoration. The equestrian pose reaches back through Renaissance
sources to Roman antiquity. Carlos IV *is* Trajan, much as Tolsá *is*
Praxiteles, and not merely like him, according to Gómez Marín's

epigram. The statue justifies monarchy, and not only the monarch; Spanish sovereignty in America is marked aesthetically as a contemporary enactment of an eternal and immutable paradigm, even when colonial authority had already been successfully challenged to the north and monarchy itself in France. Tolsá ended his career, it almost goes without saying, casting cannons for the defense of colonial rule against the criollo revolutionaries, making it "possible to terrorize Your Majesty's enemies and to contain within bounds the deadly torrent ready to spread about us its devastation," in the words of the Conde de Heras on behalf of the Academia in 1817 (Charlot 1962, 48).

Yet if neoclassical expression in poetry and the arts fails here to undertake the modern project of criticism, much as Paz expects, one may nonetheless find evidence of that modernity by extending the reading list. An anonymous corrido—a popular verse form sung to accompaniment and often printed and sold on the streets in illustrated broadsides—was occasioned by the same equestrian statue and, one surmises, the rumor that Carlos IV might come to America (perhaps to escape Napoleon):

> Ya con cabeza de bronce
> lo tenemos en la Plaza,
> venga y lo tendremos con
> cabeza de calabaza

> (Vázquez Santa Ana 1925, 217)

> We've already got him
> with a bronze head in the square
> let him come and then we'll have him
> with a head that's made of squash.

The patent political criticism is of special interest for the testimony it gives of popular antiroyalist sentiment in the urban milieu, which is to say far removed from the setting of Padre Hidalgo's rural uprising.[14]

The unexpectedly modern, which is to say, in Paz's terms, critical poetry is not restricted to popular forms and anonymous poets. The verse "Discurso de economía política" originally published in the volume, *La vacuna,/canto/dirigido á los jóvenes/por D. Simón Bergaño y Villegas./con una silva/de economía política,/del mismo autor* in Nueva Guatemala, 1808, for instance, undertakes a far-ranging critique of American consumption, of working conditions

in American mines (compared to his idealized understanding of
English factories), of scholastic education in the colonies, and, in
general, of the short-sightedness of imperial Spain's political economy that left America prey to foreign incursions. It may be no more
than the late royalist concern for the interests of the Spanish crown
that leads Bergaño y Villegas (1781–1828) to the sceptical stance
toward British intentions found wanting in Miranda's address to
Pitt:

> . . . si tú no despertares
> La reina del comercio y de los mares
> Te asaltará dormida, y de tu sueño
> Volverás cuando tengas ya otro dueño.
> (Bergaño y Villegas 1959, 42)

> . . . if you don't wake faster
> The queen of commerce and the seas
> Will take you in your sleep, and from your dream
> You'll wake to find you have another master.

Yet in his awareness of the value of internal commerce in goods of
local manufacture as a bulwark against imperialist designs, Bergaño y Villegas gives evidence of a modern, critical outlook in both
economics and politics.[15]

Reliance on precious metals from what we now refer to as extractive industries does not provide a secure channel for colonial
wealth, as Bergaño y Villegas observes in a play on words: "Y tú
sacas millones anuales [out of the mines]/Que te sabe *extra*er el
*extra*njero" (Bergaño y Villegas 1959, 42; emphasis added) (And
yearly you take millions [from the mines]/That foreigners forsake
not to take from you). The chief mode of that expropriation is the
sale of foreign textiles:

> Ningún hombre en la calle se divisa
> Que sea mi paisano en la camisa,
>   Porque en cuanto le cubre
> Ser inglés, o francés solo descubre.
>   Y ¿dirán que no es tacha
> No traer de su tierra ni una hilacha?
>   En mi Patria querida
> La industria soberana está perdida,
> La industria, de los vicios destructora,

La industria, que es del oro la señora.
No hay géneros, ni aspiran a tejerlos,
Temiendo no encontrar donde venderlos . . .
(Bergaño y Villegas 1959, 44–45)

No man in the street might I declare
To be my countryman by what he wears,
    As far as his clothing goes
British or French himself he shows.
    And will they say it is no crime
To be threadbare of cloth from their own clime?
    In my beloved land
Sovereign industry has been banned,
Industry, destroyer of all vice from times of old,
    Industry, the mistress of all gold.
There are no stuffs, nor weavers who would make them,
For fear there are no customers to take them.

The *Patria* of these lines remains imperial Spain, and thus the call for a better national industry, with improved quality and less expensive goods, is aimed most squarely at the Peninsula. The recommendation of Bergaño y Villegas' "Cierto quidán" (Certain Señor), the criollo aristocrat who is the poem's principal speaker, therefore, is to compete with the British by investing in Peninsular Spanish industry. The dictates of capital, as Smith explained, make colonial realignment the price of failure:

    Y, según su discurso,
Parece no tenía otro recurso
    Para evitar pobreza
Y conservar intacta su riqueza,
    Que declarar la guerra
A su patria, en favor de la Inglaterra
(Bergaño y Villegas 1959, 50)

    And, as he said in his own voice
It seems he had no other choice
    to escape impoverishment
And preserve his wealth without diminishment,
    Than declare war on his homeland,
And take up sides with England

The certain Señor provides a critical light for the reading of Miranda's proposal to Pitt; a potential British alliance now appears as the consolidation of class interest across national boundaries. The poem thus gives evidence of a self-conscious bourgeoisie capable of bringing developments in Enlightenment thinking to bear critically upon an outmoded colonial political economy.

Despite the loyalist orientation of the poem, Bergaño y Villegas also expresses a specifically American alienation:

> Todo lo remediara
> Si mis buenos proyectos realizara,
> Mas ellos con mis fuerzas no se miden,
> 　　Pues requieren y piden
> 　　Ejecución más alta,
> Que aunque tenga instrucción poder me falta;
> Y por más que los dice la experiencia
> Do no hay autoridad no vale ciencia.
> 　　　　　　　　　　(Bergaño y Villegas 1959, 48)

> 　　All would be remedied
> Were I to realize my fond designs,
> But these are greater than my strength,
> 　　Hence, they require and demand
> 　　Execution at a higher station,
> For although I may have learning, I lack power
> And for all that experience may teach,
> Knowledge avails not without authority.

The final twist on the relation of knowledge to authority expresses a politically enlightened critique of the Enlightenment. From the point of view of the disempowered—here, the colonial subject—the ideology of the Age of Reason merely covers over the translation of the Heavenly City of the medieval church to the metropolitan capital of modern imperial rule.[16] This frank self-awareness provides the perspective whereby a still more sharply critical expression of the interests of a different class may enter into the the geopolitical breach. Between the colonial competitors, that is, Bergaño y Villegas raises the possibility of fomenting local manufacture, dismissed by Juan and Ulloa, as an alternative recommendation to solve the economic problem of the flight of precious metals:

> Y todos redoblaron
> 　　Su codicia y dinero
> Con el triste sudor del jornalero.
> ¿En cuánto ganará para un vestido

Aunque sea de jerga? En quince días
Si no salieron mal las cuentas mías.
Y si tiene familia ¿qué partido
Tomará el infeliz?—Andar desnudo,
O disponerse para ser cornudo.
    Pues la industria casera,
Que la paz y abundancia le trajera
Si los hijos y esposa se entregaran
    A ella, y le ayudaran;
La veo en decadencia lastimosa,
Sin que alguno se aplique a proveerla,
    Aunque para ejercerla
    El pueblo esté dispuesto.
¡Quién pudiera decir la cause de esto!
                (Bergaño y Villegas 1959, 48)

And everybody multiplied
    Their money and their greed
By the sad sweat of the worker's hide.
How much time will he need
To earn some decent clothes,
Though they be of coarse cloth, God knows?
A fortnight, if I'm not mistaken.
And what choice has he, if he has a family,
    unhappy man?—To go naked,
or prepare himself for cuckoldry.
    As for domestic industry,
which would bring him prosperity
and peace, were his wife and offspring
    to help him manage it;
I see it in woeful decadence,
with no one committed to its repair,
    though the people be willing
    to work their share.
Oh who could tell the cause of it!

This critical perspective on the colonial economy, moreover, opens onto a critical response to the dependency model of Spanish American poetry of the period within the poem itself. The Enlightenment represented a modern criticism of traditional authority—e.g. of the unquestioned priority of the economic interests of the crown—in the name of experience, alias ciencia. Thereupon, to continue to follow Paz's outline, the bourgeoisie undertook a criticism of that very modernity, as here, when Bergaño y Villegas further questions the Enlightenment premise that knowledge equals power. The result, in and for the poem, is the climactic passage in which the self-defeating decorum of instruction is abandoned in favor of an oppositional and popular voice:

> "Venda yo, gane, y sea como fuere,
>   Y caiga el que cayere:
> Mas di: ¿y el patriotismo? . . . ¡Dale bola!
> ¡Me he de ver pereciendo! ¿Sí? ¡mamola!
>   El daño es muy profundo
>   Mas primero soy yo que todo el mundo,
> Y mientras corta el acerado filo,
> Que, como rueda de amolar, afilo,
>   Estos terribles daños,
> En fuerza de funestos desengaños,
> Implore el buen patriota al santo cielo
> Destierre el egoísmo de este suelo;
>   Y que su gran clemencia
> Arranque de los pechos nacionales
> Este genio infernal de la indolencia
> Que origina a mi patria tantos males."
>   (Bergaño y Villegas 1959, 49, text emended)

> Let me sell and profit as I may,
>   It's every man for himself:
> But say: and patriotism? . . . Enough's enough!
> Should I watch myself perish? Yes? No way!
>   The pain is very deep
>   But I come first of all,
> And while the sharpened blade cuts,
> Which, like a grinding wheel, I whet,
>   These terrible pains,
> On account of these awful disillusionings,
> Let the good patriot implore high Heaven
> To exile egotism from this world;
>   And that its great clemency
> Tear from the nation's breasts
> This infernal gift for indolence
> That is the source of my country's ills.

Caught between the apparent alternatives of colonial and neocolonial power, legal and illegal trade in European textiles, the certain Señor reintroduces the *jerga*, now in the alternative sense of "jargon," that is, coarse speech rather than coarse cloth. Where Enlightened discourse finds itself cut off from the realization of its projects, American interests are preserved as popular speech—or, to make a point tendentiously, as popular poetry. In the same period, Wordsworth pronounces a similar turn to "the very language of men" in the preface to the 1800 edition of the *Lyrical Ballads* (Wordsworth and Coleridge 1963, 250); but in England, popular diction and conversational poems are an experiment in nostalgia for a world of cottage industry overwhelmed by factories and mechanization. The fractiousness of Bergaño y Villegas' jerga is not a quiet recollection of domesticity lost, but a rebellious cry against the smothering of regional interests in the making.

In this strategy for resistance to colonial power, Bergaño y Villegas writes a surprisingly modern poem. On the one hand, the sudden shift in the level of the diction and the turn to dialogue anticipates the tone and structure of the *poesía gauchesca*. And on the other, the certain Señor takes advantage of this unbridled popular speech to articulate a thoroughly Romantic posture, the outcry of the Byronic self: "Mas primero soy yo que todo el mundo" (But I come first of all).

The narrator hastens to reimpose the social order. Patriotism dictates that one must choose colonial rule over American interests, including one's own, and from that point of view, the encroachment of contraband on metropolitan trade is ultimately less menacing than a self-sufficient American economy. The certain Señor acquiesces. But his silence is obtained by recourse to literary history rather than economic argument: an allusion to Horace's *Ars poetica* in the image of the whetstone, unacknowledged here, but cited and translated as an epigraph to the text.[17] Neoclassicism cuts short both proto-Romantic self-aggrandizement and the diction of conversational poetry, two routes to poetic modernity found and lost in Bergaño y Villegas's poem.

A modernity arising unexpectedly out of Central America nearly a century before Darío? My point in examining the "Discurso de economía política" is not to promote the individual talent, but to begin to reconsider the poetic tradition—not the originality of Bergaño y Villegas and his election to a new canon of central names, but quite the contrary, the characteristic features of a minor poet.[18] Miranda's proposal to Pitt outlines, in the negative, the very lanes of communication that were routes to modernity: the internal circulation of people and newspapers. In that light, Bergaño y Villegas's career may be read as an exemplary tale. Briefly sketched, in his youth, he had made his way from the province of Escuintla in the Reino de Guatemala to Mexico City, returning to his native region in the personal service of a Captain José Jiménez, whom he met in Veracruz (Carrillo Ramírez 1960, 36). After his return, he came to be the editor of the *Gazeta de Guatelmala*. In other words, the impediments to intercommunication decried by Miranda a decade earlier did not prohibit a considerable movement of persons, both in commercial trade, as I have remarked already, and within the imperial "ciudad letrada," as defined by Angel Rama (1984a), the conglomerate of lettered careers, military power and administrative bureaucracy.

As regards more particularly the commerce of letters, the intervening years since Miranda's proposal to Pitt had seen important developments in the periodical press. Bergaño y Villegas' *Gazeta de Guatemala*, for instance, had been founded in December 1729, but suspended publication in April 1731, due to a paucity of subscribers, according to Salomón Carrillo Ramírez, "since only a small minority knew how to read" (Carrillo Ramírez 1960, 28). But now, in 1794, the paper resumed publication, the new editor, Ignacio Beteta (1785–1827), having petitioned the government for permission by referring to his determination to imitate the *Mercurio Peruano* (57). In sum, against the various, but in each case dismissive positions of Juan and Ulloa, Miranda and Paz, I assert that the conditions existed by the close of the eighteenth century for both a Spanish American modernity and a network of Spanish American intertextuality. A coherent and autonomous tradition of modern Spanish American poetry may find its roots there.

2

As Aníbal González has remarked (1983, 12), Paz's term "criticism," definitive of the initial break between modernity and tradition, calls for further precision. González himself substitutes philology in his theoretical framework for the study of modernismo, a discipline that enacts Paz's dialectical balance in the demonstration of both continuities and ruptures in the diachronic course of language. Looking ahead to modernismo from the unaccustomed vantage point of the eighteenth century, I note that Spanish America does not wait to encounter philology in a late nineteenth-century scene of instruction at the Biblioteque National, where a young and overawed González Prada took a seat near Ernst Renan, paradigmatic though the moment may have been for modernismo (A. González 1983, 38–39).

The disciplinary history of philology reaches back to eighteenth-century disquisitions on the origins of language in the writings of Rousseau, Herder and Vico, of course, as well as the linguistic studies of Wilhelm von Humboldt. The allied researches by Spanish Americans are less familiar. Nevertheless, at the moment when European neoclassicism was asserting its short-lived predominance in Mexico, as the towers of the Mexican-born student of the Academia de San Carlos, architect José Damián de Ortiz, brought the centuries-long work on the edifice to completion in 1791, an autochthonous classicism was newly in the public eye. A civil engineering project in that same year unearthed two of the most important extant pieces of Aztec stone carving not far from the cathedral: the giant statue of the snake-skirted goddess Coatlicue and the Aztec calendar stone of Paz's own *Piedra del sol* (1957) (see Bernal 1980, 81). The hieroglyphs on these monuments spurred philological studies in Mexico by Ignacio Borunda (n.d.) and Antonio de León y Gama (1735–1802). The impulse, as González argues with regard to the later period (A. González 1983, 25) and León y Gama himself testifies for the late eighteenth century, is closely related to the Enlightenment institution of the museum.

León y Gama undertakes his philological decoding, he explains, "to illuminate antique literature which has been greatly fomented in other countries, and which . . . [Carlos III], while King of Naples, promoted with his celebrated Museum, which, at the cost of enormous sums of money, he founded in Portici, from the excavations that he ordered undertaken for the discovery of the ancient cities of Herculaneum and Pompeii" (León y Gama 1832, 4). On assuming the throne of Spain, the same Carlos extended his gaze from Pompeii to America. An undated document from late eighteenth-century Guatemala explains:

> that the king, being informed that on the outskirts of the town of Palenque . . . certain buildings have been discovered whose ruins show themselves to be those of a destroyed city so ancient that the passing of many centuries have erased them from the memory of men; he ordered that the most illustrious Sr. President of the Real Audiencia of this Realm [of Guatemala] arrange to inspect the ruins of that city by the most

> opportune means, to map the palaces that once ennobled it, to copy the
> unknown characters . . . and, finally, to undertake . . . other new and
> more exact investigations. (Castañeda Paganini 1946, 17)

Other documents in Ricardo Castañeda Paganini's compilation
concerning the eighteenth-century explorations of Palenque indicate that in addition to transcriptions, Carlos III required the collection and shipment of artifacts to Spain—"you will also remit pieces
of plaster . . . pots and whatever other utensils or tools are found,"
reads the Royal Order of March 15, 1786 (Castañeda Paganini
1946, 45).

We are reminded, then, that the museums, laboratories and philology against which modernismo would define its project, were
themselves founded upon Enlightenment "voyages into substance"
(see Stafford 1987). A reenactment, in the mode of criticism, of the
voyages of conquest, the scientific expedition—recording travels,
tracing roads and canals, opening transport and communication—is
the originary topos, both in theory and practice, of modernity in
Spanish America, beginning already in the eighteenth and nineteenth centuries. And in the Spanish American context I would
underline, taking now my own turn at philology, that while Spanish
expedición leans to dispatching legal or, more important to my discussion, commercial affairs; the Latin etymology, *expedire*, speaks
of liberation, an unfettering of the feet. The former sense has
already and will continue to inform my study; as regards the latter,
I would recall here the philological labors of Borunda in which the
liberating implications of the expeditionary impulse were realized.
Borunda discerned ideological design in philological ignorance
when he explained that "the Colonists were unaware of the allegorical and composite sense of the language in which ancient testimonies concerning the local monuments were preserved in New
Spain" (Borunda 1898, 64). His own philological reconstruction
was intended not only to unfetter the hieroglyphs from their colonialist misreadings, but moreover, to unfetter the colonies themselves. He argued that the hieroglyphs give evidence that the
apostle Thomas had preached to the indigenous peoples long before
the arrival of the Spaniards, thereby undercutting the evangelical
justification of conquest and colonization. The separatist implications were clearly grasped by colonial authorities when Friar Servando Teresa de Mier (Mexico 1763–1827) drew upon Borunda's
philological disquisitions to declare in a sermon of 1794: "*One*

*thousand seven hundred and fifty years ago the image of Our Lady
of Guadalupe was already well-known and venerated by Indians
[who were] already Christian"* (Mier 1981, 1:238; I follow the italics of that edition).[19]

The expeditions of the late eighteenth and early nineteenth centuries invent the American interior of their explorations in a writing
of the earth's surface—of geography, botany and zoology, and of
Enlightenment economics with its physiocratic emphasis on agriculture.[20] Thus, they respond critically to the colonial emphasis on
mining the earth's depths. To choose another sign of that critical
dialogue, I note that in 1790, José Longinos Martínez opened the
first public *Gabinete de Historia Natural* in Mexico, displaying scientific books and instruments as well as specimens that he had collected. Xavier Lozoya cites a contemporaneous newspaper account
of the opening from the *Gazeta de México*, wherein it was related
that "hardly had [Longinos] set foot on the ground in Veracruz
when he found the precious shellfish *Estalacta*, for whose exquisite
shell certain sovereigns have given enormous sums" (Lozoya 1984,
104). Although the chronicle goes on to describe Longinos forming
his collection by searching "the surfaces of the earth as well as the
concavity of its entrails" (104), I would contend that the narrative
of his first step in America transforms that conjunction into a critical question. The assignment of a financial value of "enormous
sums" to Longinos's discovery upon the surface makes the competition between the new expeditionaries and the old mining industry,
soon to be housed in Tolsá's Colegio de Minería, especially clear.

The attention to surfaces manifest in the expeditions and translated into literature primarily in the form of landscape poetry will
eventually be contested by a return to depths, as the human individual comes to be increasingly understood as a subject with a psychic
interior calling for poetic exploration and expression. As it is my
intention to pursue the routes of modernity from the eighteenth century into the nineteenth, I would broaden the theoretical frame
beyond the topos of the scientific expedition. José Antonio Maravall remarks in this regard, "If the eighteenth century took a passionate interest in physics, grounding the hopes for the progress of
human societies upon it"—where, I add, physics stands for the various natural sciences flourishing in the period—"one must recognize no less the inauguration in that century of a clear historical
consciousness that will open the road to the comprehension of
human phenomena, in precisely those aspects in which it is appar-

ent that they cannot be simply reduced to pure natural phenomena" (Maravall 1991, 113). It is the historical consciousness inaugurated in the eighteenth century, of which philology is but one disciplinary expression, that I offer in place of Paz's "criticism" as the keystone of modernity.

Before proceeding to a theoretical account of historical consciousness as it comes to orient my readings of poetry, I would follow Maravall further in his assessment of Hispanic culture in this respect: a more nuanced view of the Spanish Enlightenment than that of Paz. Throughout Europe, critical historiography, according to Maravall, provided the basis from which the eighteenth century *mentalité*, committed to the rational induction of universal laws, could construct a philosophical anthropology (Maravall 1991, 126). Comparing the incipient bourgeoisie of Spain to that of England as the exemplum of the class whose historical consciousness was reconceiving the world in its own image in that period, Maravall notes the contrasting "weakness and insufficiency of a historiography in which the mentality of a group, quite weak and vacilating in [Spain], did not succeed in expressing itself fully" (119). He adds, however, "that does not mean that there was no analogy . . . between Enlightenment historiography in Spain and that of the other countries of western Europe" (119). It is not my purpose to investigate historiography here, but in considering the historical consciousness manifest in Spanish American poetry of the eighteenth and nineteenth centuries, I hope to discover a means by which that poetry may be seen as analogous to the emerging modernity of other European and American literatures. On the other hand, I hope to provide a theoretical framework within which the vicissitudes of the Spanish American historical consciousness and its poetry may be understood critically and yet without recourse to the charge of insufficiency (Maravall) or inadequacy (Paz).

The implicit measure of adequacy or sufficiency in Maravall's remarks, as well as those of Paz, is the efficacy of criticism, or more specifically, critical historiography, as a means toward social reform. The present is therefore judged in relation to the future that they prepare. My own concern with the historical consciousness emerging in the eighteenth century and pervading, not without significant reorientation, the nineteenth, centers on the will to accomplish the rupture that Paz details, and so focuses rather on the relation of the present to the past. To elucidate that relation, I key my theoretical account of historical consciousness to the work of mourning. Taking the dead as the embodiment of the past, I ask what relation their survivors maintain to them.

I draw my theoretical model primarily from psychoanalysis, especially the elaboration of the distinction between the process of *introjection* and the fantasy of *incorporation* as articulated by Nicolas Abraham and Maria Torok. Their work on these topics enables them to return to Freud's crucial article in this area, "Mourning and Melancholia," rewriting his conjunction as a distinction; "Mourning *or* Melancholia," they say.[21] Abraham and Torok's theoretical contributions are of special interest here for two reasons. First, their understanding of melancholia allows one to reconsider a topos long since recognized as central to the period, but also long since consigned to the tired cataloging of undetermined angst by moonlight in many literatures of the late eighteenth and nineteenth centuries (see esp. van Tieghem 1970). Marshall Brown (1991) has recently reinvigorated the related and equally worn designation of preromanticism, powered by theoretical developments in British and Continental studies; a refined concept of melancholia may carry discussion further.[22] Abraham and Torok are especially useful in this regard for the aid they offer in reconceiving the felt inadequacies or insufficiencies of historical consciousness as it is manifest in Spanish American poetry of the eighteenth and nineteenth centuries. Their work is of further interest in their explication of intergenerational transmissions in which the idiolect of the sons and daughters is riddled by the gaps in the language of their forebears.[23]

The terminology of introjection and incorporation is fraught with difficulties, as Torok herself points out (Abraham and Torok 1994, 110–12), due to their varied and unsystematic usage in the history of psychoanalytic thought. Returning to Sandor Ferenczi's "On the Definition of Introjection" of 1912 (Ferenczi 1980), Abraham and Torok emphasize that introjection is the process of psychic growth by the extension of the ego to include objects; the model for introjection is transference. Ferenczi himself illustrated the point by reference to the fairy tale of the fisherman's wife whose hasty use of magic wishes causes a sausage to grow on her nose: she "felt any contact with the sausage as if it were her own skin, and had to protest violently against any suggestion of cutting off the unpleasant growth: so we feel all suffering caused to our loved object as our own. I used the term introjection for all such growing on to, all such including of the loved object in the ego" (Ferenczi 1980, 316).

Abraham and Torok enlarge this view of introjection by postulating that the transference can also be made onto words:

> Without going into detail, suffice it to say that the initial stages of intro-jection emerge in infancy when the mouth's emptiness is experienced alongside the mother's simultaneous presence. The emptiness is first experienced in the form of cries and sobs, delayed fullness, then as call-ing, ways of requesting presence, as language. . . . Finally, the early satisfactions of the mouth, as yet filled with the maternal object, are partially and gradually replaced by the novel satisfactions of a mouth now empty of that object but filled with words pertaining to the subject. (Abraham and Torok 1994, 127)

Having achieved the "successful replacement of the object's pres-ence with the self's cognizance of its absence" (128), the final stage of introjection is attained when the ego enters a language commu-nity, or "community of empty mouths" (128).

The presence of the mother, who can decode the linguistic substi-tution of sobs or infantile words and respond by providing their real object, the breast, to fill the mouth again, normally prevents the experience of the empty mouth from becoming traumatic. The mother, in this breast-feeding model, is thus "the guarantor of the meaning of words" (128), and her tutelage leads the infant on to new introjections and participation in the language community.[24] Nevertheless, introjection can face vicissitudes that disrupt the process of "*giving figurative shape* to presence" (128; authors' ital-ics). In cases of traumatic loss, the infant or adult may deny the experience of the "mouth's emptiness" and refuse to introject, pre-ferring instead to produce and cling to a fantasy of fullness. Incor-poration is such a fantasy.

By way of clarification, I add, with Ferenczi, that displacements are a form of introjection (not incorporation), and even when neu-rotic in nature, are grounded in the normal processes of growth. To say "milk" is an introjection, and so is to drink a glass of scotch. In either case—your mother has weaned you, your spouse has left you—the "mouth-work" follows upon an acknowledgement of emptiness and proceeds as a displaced, figurative substitution. In either case, therefore, the ego is adjusting itself to reality. Fantasies adjust reality instead. The specificity of the fantasy of incorporation is two-fold. First, "[i]ncorporation results from those losses that for some reason cannot be acknowledged as such" (Abraham and

Torok 1994, 130). The blockage is not due to the potential damage to the ego of a disclosure, as in the situation of dynamic repression, where subjects thwart their own desires. Rather, some secret blemishes the lost love-object, particularly one who has been an ego-ideal. It is the secret of the other that must be kept—Abraham and Torok theorize the agency of an alternative "preservative repression" (135)—and the very loss of the other will be denied, if acknowledgement would compromise the secret. Second, incorporation proceeds by means of *antimetaphors*, Abraham and Torok's figure for the destruction of figuration itself—"the annulment of figurative language"; "the active destruction of representation" (132)—that is, "by implementing literally something that has only figurative meaning" (126). Above all, incorporation *demetaphorizes* introjection itself, making the words that have served to fill the empty mouth into objects to be ingested. I offer an example from Abraham and Torok's extension of Freud's complex case study of the Wolf Man.[25] The Wolf Man's sister suffered a seduction by their father when she was a child. The father gained satisfaction by having her "rub" him. The Wolf Man himself learned of the scene, but his testimony was anulled. The word *tereet*, to rub, in their native Russian, becomes the pathogenic hub of the psychological disturbances that led Freud to a variety of theoretical formulations (e.g. the primal scene, the splitting of the ego, inter alia). Freud's analysis of the Wolf Man and that of Abraham and Torok are long to retell. But the sister's fate may be related thus: she eventually committed suicide by swallowing mercury, *rtout*, that is by making an antimetaphor of the "magic word" *tereet*, and literally incorporating it (Abraham and Torok 1994).

Introjection expands the ego by expanding language. The ego "includes" objects by naming them. Incorporation disrupts language by making some word or words into objects that are then withdrawn from language and buried within the ego in an intrapsychic crypt. I stress the topographic distinction. What is held in the unconscious by dynamic repression strains for expression, and finds it in the classical Freudian understanding of dreams, parapraxes and symptoms. The crypt, on the contrary, preserves its contents; there is no corresponding drive to express the cryptic words, only to ingest them. The intergenerational haunting that Abraham and Torok investigate under the heading of the *phantom* prevails where the subject learns language (has the efficacy of linguistic substitution guaranteed) by a person who bears such a crypt. The subject acquires a language already riddled by the gaps left behind by the incorporated words. The result is a language strangely deformed, with some words altogether missing and others—homonyms, allo-semes, anagrams of the missing word—oddly over-charged.

From this brief exposition, I would turn to the intersection of introjection and incorporation with historical consciousness. British analytic philosopher Michael Oakeshott delineates historical con-sciousness through the relation between the historical record and the historical past. The record is constituted by survivals: "Each fragment, damaged, perhaps mutilated, often detached from its transactional relationship with others or trailing relationships no less opaque than itself" (Oakeshott 1983, 32). The landscape of the present, to deploy important metaphors of the eighteenth and nine-teenth centuries, is littered with ruins of the past. These survivals or ruins do not inevitably incite a historical consciousness. As Oakeshott points out, the ruins may be perceived simply as pertain-ing to the present, in which case "they are *legenda*, what is 'read' and what may be read with advantage to ourselves in our present circumstances" (17). The skull of the *memento mori*, for instance, need not recall the life of some poor Yorick; rather it may be per-ceived strictly with respect to its moral lesson for the present. The historical consciousness comes into play, according to Oakeshott, only when the past is conceived of as lost to the present; "a histori-cally understood past," he asserts, is "a past which has not itself survived" (33). The task of critical historiography is the reconstruc-tion of the past by dint of an inferential reading of its ruins.

Oakeshott illustrates the difference between the indefinitely expanding present of *legenda* and the historical consciousness in a brief parable:

> [I] perceive a man with a wooden leg hobbling by; and if this is all I perceive, present is not significantly qualified. . . . On the other hand, if what I perceive is a man who has lost one of his legs and acquired a wooden one in its place, then present has been qualified by past. And this awareness of past is evoked, not by neglecting present, but in a read-ing of present which evokes past expressed in the word "lost." Past, then, is an understanding of the present in terms of a change it may be perceived to record or to conserve. (8)

A parable of detachment: first, the past is envisioned as severed from the present. But also the I of the historian is set at a distance from the hobbled man of his observation; this latter detachment is not simply rhetorical, but rather would pertain even were the picture of the hobbled man a self-portrait.

Nicolas Abraham tells the parable of detachment otherwise: "Let us imagine a man having lost his right arm. Precisely what might then happen in him?" (Abraham 1978, 397). The question Abraham poses is how the subject internalizes the loss of the arm. He suggests three possibilities. First, "he can deny the loss of his member and he will then be the very unity of that negation" (397), in which case he will feel ghost pains in the missing limb. Reading his parable in terms of historical consciousness I would say that the missing arm continues a legendary life, remaining legible as an external source of pain *in the present*. In short, the path of denial is marked by an absence of historical consciousness.

The goal of therapy would be to make a historian of this amputee by means of introjection. The amputee would be led to relinquish the fantasy in the name of the reality principle, and to complete the work of mourning. For Freud this work begins, once again, as a parable of detachment. The bereaved must withdraw the emotional investment in the love-object (the deceased, the amputated arm), restore that investment to the ego in a revivified narcissicism, and finally establish new attachments in the world. Abraham and Torok note that the work of mourning is a process of introjection, where loss—the real diminishment of the body in the case of the amputee—becomes the basis for the expansion of the ego. "The transition from a mouth filled with the breast to a mouth filled with words occurs by virtue of the intervening experiences of the empty mouth," they recall.

Reading empty sleeve for empty mouth, the loss of limb might yield to the substitutions of language, and the members of the language community would then "grow onto" the place of the missing limb. Abraham illustrates the path of introjection by reference to the founding of "a sect entitled, 'My Right Arm' " (Abraham 1978, 398) by several amputees: "Thus from then on the lost member will acquire a symbolic existence by the very means of this appellation, in which the members (and this is not an empty word here) of a society will be able to commune. One could go further and imagine the life of such a society, from the erection of its emblem, a huge right arm, brandished periodically, initiation ceremonies consisting of inscribing in a book the circumstances of the loss of the precious member, a liturgy consisting of its public recitation or its symbolic repetition" (398). The relating of histories transforms the amputees from incomplete members of their various social worlds to full members of an imagined community (Anderson 1983). The language community of introjection may thus be viewed at once as a burial society and as a historical society. The members admit that the past is lost and bury it, but through the rituals of communal mourning they constitute a new society, even a new national identity, and reconstitute themselves through the workings of the historical consciousness.

These first two paths of fantasy and introjection correspond to Oakeshott's ahistorical reader of legends and his historical observer with respect to the relation between present and past: on the one hand, a past that has never passed away and on the other a past that the present buries and survives.[26] But between these two poles, Abraham positions a third possibility, which is the route of melancholia: "the amputee, instead of denying [the loss], will undertake to incorporate the trauma. He will reissue it within himself, either by the resistance to healing, or by the sensation of pain in the stump (and not in the lost member as above) or again, by a paralysis of the opposite member, etc. This will define yet another, new unity. To remain alone with his lost member, to reconstitute it by the reissuing of the moment of the loss" (Abraham 1978, 397–98). Recognizing in each "reissuing" the force of a compulsion to repeat that carries the subject beyond the pleasure principle, one might say that from the perspective of Freud's work, the relation between mourning and melancholia is analogous to that between his life instincts and death drive as they came to be articulated several years later. The melancholic shuns a potentially saving fantasy, but succumbs to the power of the death drive, repeating self-inflicted wounds rather than accept detachment. The melancholic knows that the past has passed and that the present is therefore significantly altered; but, no historian, the melancholic sacrifices a place in the present in order to live in the past. To this Freudian reading I would apply Abraham and Torok's theoretical amendment: the self-sacrifice is made in order to allow the past to live in the melancholic, to preserve the past, buried alive, in the crypt. Again, an illustration from the analytical couch: "one of us," write Abraham and Torok, "analyzed a boy who 'carried' inside him his sister, two years older than he." They continue:

This sister, who died when the boy was eight, had "seduced" him. Several years of analytic relationship and a providential slip of the tongue—in which the boy gave as his own the age his sister would have been, had she lived—led to the reconstruction of the boy's internal situation and also revealed the motivation behind his kleptomania. "Yes," he said, explaining his thefts, "at fourteen she would have needed a bra." This boy's crypt sheltered the girl "alive" as he unconsciously followed her maturation. (Abraham and Torok 1994, 130–31)

The metapsychology of the crypt, formed by incorporation, allows Abraham and Torok to replace the death instinct of the melancholic subject with a dialogue between the living and the dead, or rather the bereaved ego and the encrypted love-object. It is a dialogue that reverses the subject positions as presented by Freud. "We consider it useful," they explain, "to complement Freud's metapsychological formula, in " 'Mourning and Melancholia'—which shows 'the ego in the guise of the object'—by its opposite, in order to signal an initial clinical finding: *the 'object,' in its turn, carries the ego as its mask*" (Abraham and Torok 1994, 141; authors' italics). In this endocryptic identification, the suffering expressed by the melancholic does not represent the subject's bereavement for the loss of the object—for the object is not lost, metapsychologically, only incorporated—but instead the grief of the encrypted object for its loss of the subject. It is as though the melancholic has died, leaving the object to mourn. The more excessive the expressions of suffering (on the part of the encrypted object), the greater the confirmation that the melancholic has been and continues to be loved. The melancholic recognizes the past as past and the present as the result of prior change, yet he maintains his dialogue with the dead, conjuring his absent limb by the black magic of his antimetaphors, unable to achieve sufficient detachment from the past to enter the language community of survivors. He is burdened with a story he cannot tell.

From the point of view of modernity, melancholia is only a failure of the work of mourning to be dismissed as historical masquerade or cured by an education in historical consciousness. But conceived as a dialogue, melancholia may be judged, in premodern terms, as a form of symbolic exchange. In this light Jean Baudrillard has argued that it is an "*imaginary* disjunction between life and death that is at the origin of the *reality* of death" (Baudrillard 1976, 226). To accept that disjunction is a sign of mental health in the modern world; it is the fundamental step of the work of mourning and its life-affirming introjections. In poetry, it is the grounds for the strategy of elegy (see Sacks 1985). But there are other poems where, rather than enter the historical society in which the dead are buried for the sake of the living, the poet makes imagistic self-sacrifice to keep alive a symbolic exchange with the dead. Are such poems merely inadequate or insufficient elegies, which, failing to achieve a fully historical consciousness, fall short of literary modernity? I believe, rather, that the melancholic poem is a distinct category, and that it is crucial to the formation of modern Spanish American literature.

3

The melancholic poem, I shall argue, was the central poetic form of José María Heredia (Cuba 1803–39), the strongest poet—which is to say most influential, in Bloom's antithetical sense—of the period from Sor Juana to Darío. Through the perspicacious reading of the melancholic strain in the Salamanca school on the part of Spanish American poets, Heredia included, the melancholic poem came to represent a point of resistance to a historical consciousness that would sever the symbolic exchange with the dead and so free the present from the past—this latter project embodied particularly for poetry by Andrés Bello (Venzuela 1781–1865). I will presently offer introductory illustrations of the melancholic poem and of an elegiac expression of modern historical consciousness in Spanish America. In the face of Paz's objections, however, I would first provide some evidence for the awareness of the theoretical issues within the period itself. Paz is helpful in setting a broad Hispanic frame. Spanish American literary history of the eighteenth and nineteenth centuries requires some reflection on contemporaneous developments in Spain. In this light, I turn to the leading figure of the Peninsular Enlightenment, Gaspar Melchor de Jovellanos. His reception address to the Academia de Historia of 1780, "Discurso sobre la necesidad de unir al estudio de la legislación el de nuestra historia y antigüedades" (1987), may be read as a manifesto for Hispanic modernity a full century before José Martí wrote his prologue to Juan Antonio Pérez Bonalde's *Poema de Niágara* in 1882, a text often cited as modernismo's inaugural address (e.g. Zavala 1988, 283–86; the important poem appeared previously in Pérez Bonalde 1880).

Jovellanos's goal is educational reform. He would end the exclusive study of Roman law as the curriculum of legal training, integrating the history of the laws promulgated in the Peninsula (Hechavarría y O'Gavan's satire of 1819 attests to the same complaint in America [1879]). The historical "we" (Castro 1977) of his title, repeated throughout the address—"our legislation," "amongst ourselves," "our national laws" (Jovellanos 1987, 81, 83 and 95, respectively)—grounds a continuous national identity in the distant period of the Visigoths: "Let us go up, then, to the primitive fountainhead of our rights," he exhorts the academy, "and let us discover the ancient source of the laws that govern us, and that having had their origin under the domination of the Visigoths from the fifth to the eighth century, are still obeyed by the Spaniards of the eighteenth century" (Jovellanos 1987, 76). This extended retrospective program brings together many elements of Jovellanos's intellectual milieu, some of them in unresolved opposition. The special interest in the Visigoths, for instance, strikes an epochal note with resonance long beyond the boundaries of Spain in the broad "gothic" revival that swept European art and letters in the late eighteenth and early nineteenth centuries. The ideological slant is perspicuous here. Jovellanos champions the Visigoths for their independence: "ill at ease with the scarce fortunes offered them by the decadence of the lords of the world [i.e. the Romans], they decided to seek another [fate] less dependent, and to owe it to their efforts and triumphs alone" (76), a position that might well be described as a postcolonial critique of Rome's enduring intellectual hegemony. Jovellanos is pleased to find precursors of the modern nation in that first postimperial period and to trace the Visigothic heritage from the seventh-century *Fuero Juzgo* to the thirteenth-century *Fuero Viejo*, the latter but recently edited (1771) as he addressed the academy. Nevertheless, the nationalist impulse runs athwart Jovellanos's clear awareness that the political economy of the Visigoths could not stand as a model of Enlightenment. Thus he posits against their *independencia*, the counter-value of *libertad*, missing, he argues, from the Visigothic polity (93). And liberty, understood in legal terms as "the best principles of equality and justice," is instituted rather by Alfonso X's thirteenth-century *Partidas*. Jovellanos complains that the *Partidas* are doubly foreign to the fundamentally Visigothic national character, because they introduced "not only the laws of Rome, but also the opinions of the jurisconsults of Italy" (95). But he asserts nonetheless that they represent "an enlightenment worthy of more cultivated centuries" (96), and principally because they establish "uniformity" (93), a first step toward bureaucracy.[27]

Jovellanos thus delineates a mixed inheritance for Spanish law. Moreover, he lays emphasis on the pertinence of the early strata of legislation to the contemporaneous code, so as to promote the utility of his curricular reform, true to the pragmatic interests of the Enlightenment. That is, where the directors of the standard course of study in Roman law "looked upon other studies, including that of history, as devoid of practical value" (72), Jovellanos "fleeing from sloth and dissipation" (71), hopes to prove that "the science of history is, as I believe, altogether necessary to the jurisconsult" (72). But in thus defending the discipline of history from the accusation of a vain antiquarianism—a conception of the past which remains forever past with no contact whatsoever with the present—he commits historical study to that "practical present" which, in Oakeshott's analysis, is never really past at all ("let us discover the source of the laws that govern us," i.e. in the present). In this respect—and it is in fact the explicit intent of the address— Jovellanos does not speak for a historical consciousness, much as he also does not speak for the distinctive (postcolonial, as it were) strain in the national character.

Even so, in this transitional period, Jovellanos speaks in other respects as well, and against the straightforward utility of his curricular reform and the implicit cry of liberty, equality, bureaucracy, he articulates a historical consciousness in a minor key. And he does so with particular reference to the history of language and within the narrative frame of a miniature Bildungsroman.

The past does reach the present in the Spanish legal code, but it does so, Jovellanos observes, as maimed speech: "The words and phrases that constitute it are almost exiled from our dictionaries, and the preferential study that our jurisconsults have made of foreign laws [i.e. Roman law], written in a foreign language [i.e. Latin], have caused them to be entirely forgotten. Their meanings have either been completely lost or have been changed and strangely disfigured" (88). He then goes on to enumerate the disjecta membra, a few dozen Castilian legal terms that render the body of the law illegible. He concludes his list with a rhetorical question that underlines once more the disfigurement of the legal code: "Who, finally, will be able to understand countless other nouns, verbs, phrases, idiomatic expressions of that language, whose meanings have been lost or disfigured by the pretentious culture of our century?" (89). It is a historical consciousness that finds language riddled by survivals.

A pervasive metaphor in the address, borrowed from Montesquieu, to whom Jovellanos refers explicitly, articulates that consciousness: the spirit of the law—alluding of course to *De l'esprit des lois* (1748), whose closing books represent a foundational text for modern history. Like Montesquieu, Jovellanos would have read in II Corinthians 3:6 that "the letter kills, but the spirit gives life." But the historical consciousness alters this eternizing conception to remark that if the spirit lives, its life is manifest in letters that do not kill but rather are themselves dead (see Hollier 1993): dead letters that disfigure the correspondence between signifier and signified. The student of history, faced with "legal codes . . . written in an enigmatic language" (Jovellanos 1987, 73), will learn to "penetrate their spirit" (73). The implicit image of a textured language, layer upon layer, available to the penetration of historical understanding, widens the breach in signification, such that words may become lost to their meanings. In sum, language itself gains an interiority inhabited by the spirits of waylaid desires. Language has already become, for Jovellanos, the double, if not the template, of the modern self.

That self is visible in Jovellanos's "Discurso" through the autobiographical references that open and close the text, and in particular, in the initial inflection of the modesty topos: "The embarrassment with which I look at myself adorned with a title of which I do not judge myself worthy, would diminish my present satisfaction, if I did not contemplate that when you give me the right to seat myself among you, you do not so much take into consideration what I am as what I wish to be" (Jovellanos 1987, 71). The address itself becomes the self-conscious staging of the transition from one state to the other, and, much as Mikhail Bakhtin (Bakhtin 1986, 23–25) claims as a characteristic of the Bildungsroman, the world emerges with and through the self: "my good wishes" (Jovellanos 1987, 71) become "the public wishes" (101), of which Jovellanos's *yo* is but "the organ" (101).

Jovellanos tells his developmental tale as a melancholic passage. He reports that having completed the course of Roman law in school, he began to read the Spanish legal code that "I would have to execute one day": "the same difficulties that I found in penetrating its spirit made me desire the knowledge of its origin; and this desire in itself guided me naturally [me guiaba ya naturalmente] to the historical sources" (Jovellanos 1987, 73). The critique of the old curriculum maintains that it left no place for desire, whose epistemological object is historical knowledge; to express this critique in terms of natural inclinations (ya naturalmente) is to verge upon the idiom of Romanticism. Desire is itself unmediated (ya) and natural (naturalmente) but also, youth in all its intellectual innocence finds its way untutored to historical sources. Jovellanos continues: "But in this state I saw myself suddenly elevated to the magistrature" (73). I stress that the idyll between youth and history is disrupted suddenly, that is in the mode of trauma. Bereft of the knowledge that would give the opaque language of the law historical depth, Jovellanos offers a self-portrait of the lawyer as a young man wandering amidst the letters of the law, unable to express its lost spirit. The address to the academy, then, becomes his opportunity to revisit the trauma, to recollect the history from which he was debarred by his legal training and practice, and to repeat his story. He becomes a member of a *société de mon bras*—or *de notre—droit*, by instituting a new entrance requirement: the recitation of his moment of loss as an exemplary tale; and by articulating, through that tale, a new social purpose: the writing by the academy of "a civil history that might explain the origin, progress and alterations of our constitution, our political and civil hierarchy, our legislation, our customs, our glories and our miseries" (101). The therapy for the melancholic self: a national history.

If Jovellanos demonstrates an ample and sophisticated self-awareness of the vicissitudes of historical consciousness, the burden of proof remains to show that a modern severance of symbolic exchange, thus unfettering the present from the past, was in fact accomplished in the Hispanic world at this early date. To this end I pursue an area of concern of Jovellanos, the reform of burial practices, across to the Spanish American milieu as it appears in a local polemic in the periodical literature of the day.[28] I refer to an article in the first volume of the *Mercurio Peruano* dated 17 February 1791, "Razones físicas, que reprueban la costumbre de enterrar en las Iglesias." The article is unsigned, but attributed in the index to "Hesperióphylo," which would make the author Jacinto Calero y Moreira. He presents "a monument of . . . enlightenment": "In Spain they have begun to adopt the laudable and necessary custom of rural cemeteries. Lima, ever disposed by inclination and by wisdom to receive all that relates to public welfare, may join the number of those famed nations and cities that have raised a cemetery as a monument of its enlightenment and orderliness (*buena policía*)" (Calero y Moreira 1964f, 127).

The debate concerns the traditional practice of interment beneath the church floor. The *Mercurio Peruano* aligns its position with Enlightenment opinion in Spain against that custom. The Enlightenment stance finds grounds in Roman law, which, Calero y Moreira points out, had always opposed intramural burial, as well as a long history of ecclesiastical pronouncements against interment in church.

To these arguments, themselves altogether traditional in their appeal to authority and especially to the authority of classical antiquity and the church, Calero y Moreira adds two lines of attack that are more strictly products of modern times. The more straightforward and more self-consciously modern approach is highlighted in the second article in the series. Calero y Moreira's premise in this respect is the principle of modern science, with the pragmatic bent of the Enlightenment: "Nature has its general laws, complete knowledge of which appears to be prohibited to human beings; but they continually enlighten themselves in proportion to their efforts in studying them, and applying those that they know to practical cases" (Calero y Moreira 1964f, 124). The practical case in point is, as it were, air pollution. As Calero y Moreira recalls, Alfonso X was already aware of the noxious effect of the air in churches wherein burial was permitted. Nevertheless, scholastic authority and peripatetic philosophy, which still predominated the curriculum in the sciences in Spanish America until the final decades of the eighteenth century (see Lanning 1956, 173), were unable to reveal the general laws governing the particular case. Modern science, however, could make larger claims: "The epidemics, the plagues, . . . in the moral sphere are punishments from Heaven," Calero y Moreira admits, marking the boundaries of the Enlightenment in a social context of religious orthodoxy; but he continues, "in the physical sphere [they] are almost always the effects of a corrupt air" (Calero y Moreira 1964f, 124–25). He then cites several less controversial instances which point to his more polemical conclusion: "These are truths proven with infinite series of experiments. All of them demonstrate that it is extremely prejudicial to the health of the citizens to bury the dead within the Church, and even in populated areas" (125). Experiments are distinguished from recourse to classical authority, for the series is infinite in that the experiments may be repeated by the doubtful with the same corroborating results.

The second and still more innovative approach to the debate is introduced under the heading of history. One may return to the 1790 Prospectus for the *Mercurio Peruano* that Calero y Moreira signed in his own name for an outline of the two principal orientations that the periodical will give to historical investigation. First, history is to be local in its focus. The topic of burial practices, for instance, enters the *Mercurio Peruano* in an article dedicated to the "Erección de un Campo-Santo en la villa de Tarma, y otro en el Pueblo de Late" (Calero y Moreira 1964b). The "reduced place" that Peru occupies in world history is due, Calero y Moreira declares, to "the scarcity of news that we have of the very country in which we live, and from the interior; and the absence of vehicles that are available to spread our ideas in the literary World"; hence, "The repair of this fault is the primordial object of the Mercurio, to which I dispose myself (me dispongo)" (Calero y Moreira 1964e). History is at the service of national identity, and reciprocally, national identity is dependent on historical consciousness. I anticipate matters in referring to a nation in 1790, though not with respect to an identification with the region, which Calero y Moreira describes, furthermore, in the period terms of natural history as "well favored by nature in the benignity of the Climate and in the opulence of the Soil" (ibid.). The emphatic I (*me dispongo*) is both the agent of the corresponding historiography, i.e. the filter of national identity, and a participant in the imagined community.

The second theoretical consideration enunciated by Calero y Moreira delimits historical practice in terms of Enlightenment pragmatism. The enlightened historiography of the *Mercurio Peruano* will restrict itself to a past that forms part of the practical present. The goal will be to further the projects of the present by reference to the past, rather than the more fully historical aim, in Oakeshott's understanding, of reconstructing what is lost in the past by inference from what survives in the present. In this sense, the *Mercurio Peruano* stands firmly rooted in the emerging historicism of the eighteenth century, but also already aware of the enigmatic quality of the present riddled by the past: "those things that surround us, and that, in a manner of speaking, we are constantly touching with an uncertain hand and in the dark as to any positive notion" (ibid.).

Calero y Moreira's history presses against these limits. He initiates his series of articles with what he calls a historical overview, but verges on comparative ethnography, noting the burial practices of the Hebrew bible and the ancient Mediterranean, but also ranging beyond the European classicism to present the evidence of China and—a distinctive note—of "the ancient Peruvians" (Calero y Moreira 1964c, 120). "Pain," Calero y Moreira explains, "that sentiment that appears the most invariable, since it always presupposes an effective and mortifying cause, would hardly be recognizable if we were to analyze it in all of its parts" (117). A history of pain is a more daring project than the Prospectus anticipates and it is ultimately reined in by the utilitarian designs of the issue at hand. But even within these constraints, Calero y Moreira's incipient historical consciousness speaks against a conception of the past as a source of stable, universal laws—i.e. distinguishes human sciences from the natural sciences of his own "Razones físicas." The immediate thrust of this historical argument would establish that church burial is neither natural nor foreordained. The broader import will require two centuries of meditation before its consistent articulation in our time: pain has a history, mourning is culturally specific and death itself, as Baudrillard asserts, is a cultural determination rather than a biological fact (Baudrillard 1976, 202).

The implications for the modernity of Calero y Moreira's historiography may be drawn out by contrasting the related concerns of Benito Jerónimo Feijóo (Spain 1676–1764), the fountainhead of the Enlightenment in Spain. Feijóo addresses the topic of premature burial, recounting cases—"I neither affirm that they are frequent, nor that they are extremely rare" (Feijóo 1928, 19)—and condemning attending physicians for their ignorance of vital signs and of his own warnings in the *Teatro Crítico*. Feijóo's advocacy of an improved medical semiotics forms part of his larger critique of superstition in the name of direct observation. But I would suggest that the extreme situation of premature burial, which Feijóo understands as a problem for biology, speaks to the question of ritual definition as well. For the practice of church interment implies that all burials are premature: the dead participate in the congregation of the living, whose ritual practices confer benedictions upon the deceased who have been gathered to the altar. The dead, in turn, may benefit the living, whether as intermediaries before heaven or, more concretely, as ever-present reminders of the proximity of death and the vanity of life. In this light the institutional reform promoted by the *Mercurio Peruano* would segregate the dead from the community of the living. I would then allegorize to make a broader point about Calero y Moreira's modernity. Taking the dead as the representatives of the past, church burials marked a reciprocal relation: the past sheltered by the continuing reverence of the present, the present founded upon a past that is never dead and gone. The later assertions of physics only concretize an ideological change whereby the past comes to represent a mortal threat to the present, a threat that demands control (*buena policía*). The cemetery may thus be ranged alongside Foucault's prison and asylum, but also alongside Carlos III's archaeological museum. The cemetery may be taken as a paradigm for the Enlightenment collection: the past laid out and labeled, walled in and walled out, amputated from and policed by the present (see Baudrillard 1976, 197–200). A past thus collected, organized and displayed is a past historically understood. The *Mercurio Peruano* advocates entry into the modern world.

4

Both the historical consciousness that underwrites the formation of the burial society and an active self-awareness of the vicissitudes that block the routes of modernity are manifest in the poetry of Spanish America beginning in the late eighteenth century. For introductory illustrations of these formations, I begin with a reading of certain elegiac responses to the death of one of Argentina's founding fathers, Manuel Belgrano (1770–1820), gathered as a funereal tribute within the larger anthology *La Lira Argentina, o colección de las piezas poéticas dadas a luz en Buenos Ayres durante la guerra de su independencia* (1824). Among the contributors, Juan Crisóstomo Lafinur (Argentina 1797–1824) would have been but thirteen years old when independence was proclaimed in 1810 and thus represents a generation that comes of age in the revolutionary period, which is to say under Belgrano's tutelage. Lafinur makes the point in both of his elegies in praising the war hero as a patron of Enlightenment education in Argentina: "Ora al genio se presta y lo engrandece:/corre la juventud, y a la natura/la espía en sus arcanos" (Now he serves genius [in its Enlightenment and not yet romantic sense; here, intellect] and enlarges it:/youth hastens near, and nature/espies in its mysteries), to which he appends an autobiographical note referring to his own education in the Academica de Matemáticas of Tucumán founded by Belgrano (Barcia 1982, 400 and 400 n. 1).

As a personal beneficiary, then, and as an embodiment of just that future of which Belgrano was the precursor, Lafinur takes on the quintessential task of elegy. He would consign Belgrano to the past, introject the latter's voice to fortify his own, and establish a new society around the grave through the commemorative act of mourning. He begins with a question directed to a personified Virtue:

> ¿A dónde alzaste fugitiva el vuelo
> robándote al mortal infortunado,
> virtud, hija del cielo?

(Barcia 1982, 392)

> Whither hast thou, fugitive, raised thyself
> in flight, absconding with the unfortunate mortal,
> Virtue, daughter of heaven?

The paradox of a thieving virtue alerts the reader that the question is more than rhetorical. The poetic voice is grieved to confusion. But the crime touches literary history. Pedro Luis Barcia recognizes the theft of a line from Fray Luis de León's "A don Pedro Portocarrero" in his notes to the text (Barcia 1982, 392). The syntactic equivocation that plays the feminine "fugitiva" against the masculine "vuelo" stands as evidence of a prior lifting from Góngora's "Soledad primera": "Ni isla hoy a su vuelo/fugitiva"—a verse made familiar to readers of Spanish American literature by Roberto González Echevarría (1983). I stress this unacknowledged echo in a poem whose tone and rhetoric are thoroughly neoclassical in order to recall the persistence of the Baroque to the very close of the period that supposedly buried it in oblivion. Lafinur's elegiac task, therefore, has this literary historical variant: the need to detach himself from the Spanish poetry of the past in order to write a new poetry for this distinctly American moment.

Virtue itself does not respond to Lafinur's opening question, but rather one further "eco pavoroso" (terrifying echo) intervenes: *"Olvidó para siempre al mundo injusto;/al túmulo volóse, allí se esconde"* ([Virtue] forgot forever the unjust world;/flew off to the tomb, and there hides herself) (Barcia 1982, 393; Lafinur's italics distinguish this echo from the narrating voice of the text). A melancholic virtue has attached itself too intimately to Belgrano and has failed to detach itself upon his death, reinvesting the world that survives him with justice.

Lafinur will prosecute this virtue, flying after her, and rewriting that echo, first as an "oráculo espantoso" (horrifying oracle), italicized as the voice of "los huecos de la tumba" (the emptiness of the tomb). Finally, he will gain poetic control through the detailed narration of the death scene that preceded the entombment:

> cárdeno el labio, trabajosa el habla
> al cielo alzando las deshechas manos,
> se rindió a un parasismo. . . . Americanos,
> un cuadro tan terrible y tan sublime
> os faltó ver; entonces clamaríais:
> Nuestra patria no vuelve a los tiranos.
> Vuela el tiempo sus alas empapando
> del excelso vivir en las corrientes
>   hasta secarlas todas;
> Belgrano ya no alienta; ¡oh!, ¡qué elocuentes
> son sus miradas lánguidas, sus formas
> escuálidas y tristes!
>
> (Barcia 1982, 396–97)

> purple the lip, labored the speech
> lifting to heaven his beaten hands,
> he was lost in a paroxysm. . . . Americans,
> a scene so terrible and so sublime
> you required; thus you would proclaim:
> Our country shall not return to tyranny.
> Time flies soaking its wings
> in the currents of insuperable life
>   until it has dried them all;
> Belgrano no longer breathes; oh!
> how eloquent his languid looks, his forms
>   so squalid and so sad!

The emphasis on dying lips and speech provide an image of Belgrano's voice just in the moment when the hands that once wrote out that voice as text are now engaged, like fugitive virtue, in raising his soul to heaven. By his expiration Belgrano may acquire grace, but his body remains as a ruin; terrible and sublime in dying, in death it has the eloquence of its own corruption. Decay has set in immediately, but so, too, a burden has passed, a voice has been recovered.

The words that might have formed Belgrano's postrevolutionary, and altogether prosaic motto are now assigned to a *vosotros*, the community of the survivors, a burial society which must rifle the tomb where the corpse lies enshrouded in a runaway virtue, and reinter the hero in the text of history. Thus Lafinur specifies in the second elegy:

¡Oh! ¡quién puede
describir su piedad inmaculada,
su corázon de fuego, su ferviente
anhelo por el bien! Solo a ti es dado,
historia de los hombres: a ti que eres
la maestra de los tiempos. La arca de oro
de los hechos ilustres de mi héroe,
en ti se deposita; recogedla,
y al mundo dadla en signos indelebles.
(Barcia 1982, 400–401)

Oh! who can
describe his immaculate piety,
his fiery heart, his fervent desire
for good! To you alone, history
of mankind is it granted: you who are
the mistress of time. The golden arc
of my hero's illustrious deeds
is deposited in you; recover it,
and give it to the world in indelible signs.

A closing image counterbalances the flight of virtue to its hiding place in Belgrano's grave of the other elegy. Here a feminine society (*vosotras*) is formed of "vírgenes tiernas" (tender virgins) with the instruction to visit Belgrano's tomb, transforming their playful floral crowns into funeral wreaths, the flowers of a bucolic rhetoric into pastoral elegy.

Lafinur himself would not accomplish the task of history, dying but shortly thereafter. It is more than biographical contingency, however, that blocks the route of elegiac history. The independence movement celebrated through the homage to Belgrano had been stained by a mark no less indelible than the record of Belgrano's achievements: "la muerte,/y el crimen, y el destino de consuno,/ deshacen la obra santa" (death,/and crime and destiny together/ undo the holy work) (Barcia 1982, 399). As Lafinur remarks fleetingly and Esteban de Luca (Argentina 1786–1824) at considerable length in his elegies on the same occasion, Belgrano's death occurs in the midst of civil war: "anuncio horrible/fue de su muerte la Discordia impía" (horrible presage/of his death was the impious Discord) writes Luca (Barcia 1982, 372). If Belgrano himself remains untarnished, the ideal of a postrevolutionary American unity that he represented does not survive him and the break with Spain, neither here nor throughout the newly independent former colonies. One might deny the loss and pursue the path of political fantasy—the fate of Bolívar, perhaps. One might bury recent revolutionary ideals, along with the more remote colonial past, so as to form postindependence societies of political amputees: the national identities of the new republics. Or one might incorporate the dead, repeating the trauma, but now from the point of view of the lost ideal, such that the present is perceived as the ghost of a past greater than itself. Whether the lost—and blemished—ideal was a revolutionary vision or, for royalists, imperial glory, the result could be a melancholic poem.

One may look to "La ronda," by Manuel Zequeira y Arango (Cuba 1764–1846) for an early expression of that poetic melancholia in a burlesque tone. For as Bahktin teaches, textual innovation may often take place in carnivalesque forms, and in "La ronda" the sublime is shoved, slapstick, to the ridiculous—or to the grotesque, as Victor Hugo (1802–85) would expound to a self-consciously romantic readership a generation later in his preface to *Cromwell* (Hugo 1867, 33). Zequeira is neither widely read today nor entirely unknown—his neoclassical ode "A la piña" being regularly anthologized—and in this sense his literary fortunes are typical of most of the poets who will receive notice in the pages to follow. The focus on "La ronda," however, permits me to make a further point about reading habits, namely, not only might we look beyond the better-known texts of lesser-known poets, but also, we need to expand the horizons of the critical tradition: beyond the lucidity of Octavio Paz, for instance, to the conundrums of José Lezama Lima, perhaps Spanish America's best reader of eighteenth- and nineteenth-century verse.[29] In focusing on "La ronda," then, I am following Lezama's unorthodox critical assessment: "It is for me one of the most veridical moments that our poetry can offer and I would be disposed to affirm that if a selection were made of our twenty best poems [in Cuba], 'La ronda' would have to be included among them" (Lezama 1977b, 1009).

Zequeira inaugurates his burlesque with a disfiguration, self-making becoming a self-unmaking. The initial metaphor describes a skinny military officer: "Soy militar a lo vivo/Y esqueleto a lo viviente" (I am a lively soldier/And a living skeleton) (Zequeira 1964, 237). He then enacts this metaphor, i.e. demetaphorizes the figure, by making his rounds of military checkpoints on a blustery night, only to be mistaken for the wandering spirit of a dead man. Bakhtin's observation (Bakhtin 1984, 7) that there are no footlights in carnival time to divide the stage from the world, actors from general public, is particularly germane, as the officer invades the safe haven of the watch. In fact, there are no lights at all much of the time. The wind extinguishes the officer's lantern, and with it the visible evidence of his corporeal existence, such that giving the *qui vive* (Zequeira 1964, 238, 243) takes on a new meaning. When the frightened guard whom he addresses is unconvinced that a voice alone is a certain sign of life, he sets another test: "Para afirmar mi existencia/Tuve que implorar a un Santo" (238) (To affirm my existence/I had to implore a Saint). The ability to pronounce the holy name acts as the guarantor that the officer is not a soul in torment, condemned and excommunicate. A wily examination: the guard would hear him do things with words.

The officer is exasperated by the breach in military protocol: "Y el cabo lleno de espanto/Sin mirar a mi respeto,/Quiso viéndome esqueleto/Soplarme en el Campo-Santo" (240) (And the corporal in his anxiety/Without respect for my station/Seeing but a skeleton/He'd turn me over [literally, he'd blow me into] to the cemetery). But this corporal and the other guards do not so much wish him in his grave as hear him issuing from it, his "muchas voces" (240) (here, great shouting, but literally "many voices" or "many words") hardly distinguishable from "tanto viento" (240) (so much wind). His principal speech act, then, both from a military and a poetic point of view, will be to name himself, thereby reestablishing the authority of his voice: he signs the log at each checkpoint as the mark of his passing. Bakhtin crosses swords with Derrida: in the carnivalesque atmosphere of this topsy-turvy night, the scene of writing is inverted. Voice is disembodied and betokens absence, while writing is the sign of presence. The colonel's ambulatory signature, however, proves as troubled and turbulent as the weather: "Dejé allí la firma mía,/Que no la conociera," he confesses, "La pluma que la parió" (241) (There I left my signature/That would be unrecognizable/To the very pen that gave it birth). So writing too has been disfigured, an errant script, opaque and enigmatic.

The irate officer is a ghost writer. A voice beyond his own has disturbed his control of the pen. A full and patient reading of "La ronda," of which I will offer here but a hasty review, would listen for that voice where it puts most pressure on the text:

> Después que entregué el marrón,
> Vi sirviendo de tintero
> Un casco como mortero,
> Y por pluma había un cañón:
>   Al firmar, sin dilación
> Mi pluma luego se excita,
> Y en la espesura infinita
> Que el cañón tenía en su talla,
> Una rígida metralla
> En vez de tinta vomita.

> After handing over the *marrón*
> I saw serving as an inkwell
> A casque like a mortar
> And for a pen there was a cannon:
>   Signing without vacillation,
> My pen then becomes excited,
> And in the infinite thickness
> That makes up the cannon's measure,
> My pen vomits a rigid round
> Instead of simply issuing ink.

Facile recourse to the Freudian skeleton key to open the metaphoric chain of excited pen and turgid cannon as phallic references would be no more than a trap. This streetwalker offers more than a begrudging sublimation of impure night thoughts—though a mockery of the popular Edward Young (England 1683–1765) or his Hispanic followers may not be altogether unintended. I would suggest rather that the disruption to—or eruption of—the image of writing is a misleading figuration for the prior image of voice.[30] The enigma resides in the *voz marrón*. What had the poet *incorporated* at the outset of the décima that his imagistic surrogate must vomit at the close?

The *marrón* was a "piece of metal used in military positions on which the hours of an officer's duty are inscribed, and which they leave at the posts that they review during the night" (M. Alonso 1958), that is a text. Zequeira disfigures that text in the following *décima* by repeating the rhyme, but transforming the word: marrón—

cañón becomes borrón—cañón (ink blot—cannon). The text is rendered illegible, a *borrón*, but the voice continues to speak. Zequeira pronounces marrón anew, calling explicit attention to it through a play on words:

> Un capitán hallo aquí
> Que extranjero parecía,
> Y fue tal la algarabía
> De su rara explicación,
> Que por pedirme el marrón
> El macarrón me pedía.

(Zequeira 1964, 243)

> I find a captain here
> Who strikes me
> As a foreigner
> And such was the gibberish
> Of his strange explanation
> That asking me for the *marrón*
> The macaroon is what he asked for.

The engima may now be restated. As text, the marrón is understood to be a borrón, a ruined script that calls for a conjectural decipherment. The foreign guard initiates interpretation by giving the misshapen text a voice. His faulty Spanish recalls that marrón, like his rhyming lapsus *macarrón*, is a loan word; an alloseme of the metal military symbol, it is also the color maroon, which, even as late as 1925, Darío Rubio would still emphatically mark as "a gallicism through and through." Here the trail divides.

The interests of political history discover the cryptonym *cimarrón*, the native criollo coinage behind the foreign loan. Zequeira encrypts his desire: "entregué [a]l [ci]marrón" (I handed over the runaway slave). So color, skin color, was at issue after all in marrón. Whatever titular duties are inscribed on his marrón, Zequeira's officer makes his rounds to guard against the threat from within, from the cimarrón in the interior, not the foreigner without, whether under Spanish or some other flag. The officer's subsequent excitement betrays him. The excess points beyond his duties to the subversive energies of the slaves in what Agnes I. Lugo-Ortiz describes as the *fiesta de los muertos* of slave resistance (Lugo-Ortiz 1997, 57–58). "When the slaves, in their nocturnal rituals, in a parenthesis in their workday labors, and in the uncontainable frenzy of the drumbeat," writes Lugo-Ortiz, "defied . . . the enforcement of non-being, anxiety and bewilderment were released in the masters" (58). Zequeira's officer would keep the rebellious slaves inside, in the interior of the island, in the crypt of the poem, by incorporating their subject position, literally enacting a nocturnal ritual of the living dead. Thus he transforms anxiety into the longed for satisfaction of his class: to arrest the perceived threat of slave rebellion that especially preoccupied white Cubans after revolution in Haiti, even at the cost of aborting political independence.[31]

An immanent literary history might take another fork in the linguistic path. The gibberish of the guard suggests as well that marrón disguises a macaronic Latin. Has Zequeira swallowed too much Virgil—Publius Vergilius Maro, in Spanish, Virgilio or Marón? The intertext for these poetic wanderings with their pretensions to military history—witness the specificity of the subtitle of the poem, "La ronda/Verificada la noche del 15 de enero de 1808"—is Book 6 of the Aeneid: the hero's visit to the world of the dead and the proleptic history of Rome pronounced as prophecy by his father Anchises. In this respect Zequeira may be seen to respond *avant la lettre* to Bello's call for "algún Marón americano" (some American Vergil) in the "Alocución a la poesía" of 1823 (Bello 1979, 24)

Here I might pause to note the parallel development in Spanish American prose romances, which, according to Sommer, "look relentlessly forward" (Sommer 1991, 46). "Without a proper genealogy to root them in the Land," Sommer explains, "the creoles had at least to establish conjugal and then paternity rights, making a *generative* rather than a *genealogical* claim" (15; Sommer's emphases).[32] Aeneas finds himself in quite the same bind, and Anchises' prophecy provides much the same solution, forecasting his son as a "revolutionary departure" (17) and progenitor of Rome, and so "imagining the nation through a future history, like a desire that works through time and yet derives its irresistible power from feeling natural and ahistorical" (39). Whether or not Zequeira consciously employed his marrón as a debased golden bough, shoring up his poetic vision with the authority of transumptive allusion, as did other Spanish American poets before him and after, "La ronda" engages the *projectional* poetics of the foundational fictions in the mode of defense. The *mestizaje* that the prose fictions tended to idealize in their construction of national identity, was, for Zequeira, a blemish on the national ideal that he would incorporate, obstructing the national project. In enunciating the discourse of the criollo elite, "La ronda" offers a reminder that not all expeditions unfetter. In Spanish America in the eighteenth and nineteenth centuries, expeditionary forces and their poetry, including the independence movements themselves, as Paz remarked, were most often compulsive repetitions of the Conquest rather than successful introjections of a multiracial American identity. A historical consciousness that buries the past to make way for progress can lead to ethnic cleansing on the pampas; and melancholic incorporations that resist the Enlightenment project can preserve voices buried alive by Conquest and nation-building, even against the intentions of the authors.

5

In the chapters that follow I will examine the emergence of the historical consciousness and the resistances of melancholia in the poetry of Spanish America's "middle period" (Szuchman 1989), tracing the roots and routes of modernity. I divide that period in accordance with the chronological outline suggested by Miguel Lerdo (Mexico 1812–61) for an economic history written in 1853:

> To avoid the confusion that might arise from presenting together without any distinction the diverse information from the whole era to which this little work is dedicated, it has seemed convenient to me to divide it into three periods that are marked by just those noteworthy transformations that commerce underwent with respect to the mode and established rules for its conduct, to wit: that which runs from the time of the Conquest embracing the system of the official flotillas up to 1778; that which began with the regulation of that year, known by the name of the Ordinance of Free Trade, until this Colony separated from its former metropolis in 1822, and that which has transpired from Independence up to today. (Szuchman 1989, 88)

The today of that outline, the mid-nineteenth century, will be my endpoint, for which Lerdo himself may stand as a characteristic figure. A determined liberal in confusing times, associated both with Juárez and with Santa Anna, Lerdo is best known for his role in promulgating laws intended to increase internal circulation of property, including the property of the church, to foment the domestic economy; his promotion of the railroad (see Lerdo 1985) enhances the same picture of a thoroughly modern man. One sees

Lerdo and his times at the end of a trajectory imagined by Miranda: an enlightened nation-state; and at the beginning of another, imagined by Paz: a positivist culture against which modernismo will react. With few exceptions, I will not pursue analyses of texts beyond the 1850s.

In addition to the convenience of adopting Lerdo's key dates, I cite his authority as a reminder that the history of commerce from Juan and Ulloa to Miranda to Lerdo's own times provides the implicit context of my study of poetry. Indeed, I contend that a Spanish American poetry may only be said to exist as anything other than Menéndez y Pelayo's adjunct to the literary history of Spain insofar as an internal commerce of letters comes to form a Spanish American network of intertextuality, a process greatly accelerated by the rise of print culture in the wake of independence. Spanish America does not wait for independence to discover printing, of course, but Miranda's complaint accurately reflects the fact that there were virtually no presses outside the centers of viceregal power until well into the eighteenth or even the early nineteenth century in much of Spanish America: e.g. Quito 1760, Buenos Aires 1780, Veracruz 1794, Puerto Rico and Caracas 1808 (Martínez Baeza 1985). Thus, much as Benedict Anderson proposes in his analysis of nationalism, war against Spain may be viewed in terms of the struggle for control of the press and for the constitution of a print culture in Spanish America. For a characteristic minor expression of that struggle, I would refer to the Prospectus of the *El Ilustrador Nacional*, which José María Cos (Mexico, died 1819) wrote in the midst of Mexico's War of Independence on 11 April 1812. There he recounted the obstacles met and overcome in the publication of his insurgency periodical: "A press put together with our own hands amidst the agitation and uproar of the war and always on the move, without devices, without tools, with no more instruction than that which reflection and necessity have given us, it is irrefutable proof of American ingenuity, always so fertile in resources and tireless in its extraordinary efforts to shake the yoke of degradation and oppression" (Cos 1984, 4). Speaking on behalf of "American ingenuity" Cos presents an allegory for the construction of its voice, and his proposal—"The press limits itself for now to giving evidence of the *internal relations* of the nation" (4; emphasis added)—may be read as a declaration of Miranda's vision: a separatist statement determined to foment a national consciousness precisely by establishing free lanes of communication.

At the same time, Cos works at the threshold of the new period, though he did not live to see it, and his autobiographical allusions already invoke the coming figure of individual genius as the unmediated expression of nature ("without devices, without tools"). That threshold marks the division of my study into its two parts.

Part I is dedicated to the two periods in Lerdo's outline in which poetry is not yet predominantly a form of print culture in Spanish America. In chapter 1 especially, I am attentive to poetry produced as oral literature or in the context of the restricted dissemination of manuscript. I introduce this poetry by way of a discussion of prose, following the structure already employed above, where the articles from the *Mercurio Peruano* frame the issues investigated in the poetry of Lafinur and Zequiera. The prose sample is drawn from the documents of a Jesuit mission to Baja California at the turn of the eighteenth century, which allow me to present two points. First, quite simply, the Conquest was still in progress in the period. Second, in focusing upon an interrupted language lesson, I take note of the manner in which the Christian mission, which coincides with the discourse of power, incorporates, in Abraham and Torok's sense, the indigenous voice. A partial restitution of such voices (Abraham and Torok would say their introjection) becomes an important focus of the chapter. The readings of poetry of the period from 1700–78, following Lerdo's dates, repeatedly touch upon the relation of religious devotion, especially as expressed in a dogmatic humility that inhibits the formation of the self, to the master narrative of the Conquest. The discourses of power are consolidated when the Conquest is read ahistorically within a providential Christian scheme in early eighteenth-century epic poetry. For the Jesuits, however, the wedding of Christian mission and imperial expansion ends in divorce with their expulsion from all Spanish domains. That split is manifest in poetry in the text with which I close the chapter—not coincidentally a text that enters the print culture and its commerce as contraband, that is a pirated edition—a Christian epic of sorts in which the providential scheme is explored but the overlay of the Conquest is stripped away.

Chapter 2 begins once again with a discussion of prose texts, here selected from the manuscripts of the Mopox expedition to Cuba, now at the turn of the nineteenth century. These selections introduce several points to frame the subsequent reading of poetry in the period between Lerdo's key dates of 1778 and 1822. First, one sees the hegemonic relation of center and periphery that governs the colonial system replicated in the relations between American locales. I concentrate attention on the manner in which this internalization of colonial relations is contested intermittently in the poetry of the period, which gives evidence of the periphery breaking into literature, especially in the mode of satire. Yet in the most famous case, Olmedo's "Victoria de Junín," the introjection of the indigenous voice is mere ventriloquisim; criollo independence at the periphery and in the service of a new, more local center. A second area of interest introduced by the manuscripts of the Mopox expedition concerns the Enlightenment penchant for scientific observation and its application in engineering projects for the benefit of commerce. Here as elsewhere in the frequent expeditions of the period, these interests combine to foster a reevaluation of the land that carries over into landscape poetry. I close the chapter at a point of confluence between these two issues in a poem wherein the land itself provides an image of voice for the overthrow of metropolitan hegemony in Luca's less famous song to San Martín.

The projection of landscape as the poetic mode of Spanish American independence is more customarily associated with the subsequent "Alocución" of Andrés Bello, the outstanding figure in establishing the ascendancy of print culture in Spanish America in the period to which I turn in part II. Chapter 3 is devoted in its entirety to providing a frame from prose, circa 1823—remembering that the triumph of print will also be the triumph of prose over poetry. The publication of *Facundo*, strictly contemporaneous with Lerdo's day, would be another point to mark an end to my study. I concentrate on the promulgation of constitutions, real and imaginary, with particular interest in the role of labor in changing land into property and dwellers on the land into citizens. I also focus on the mode of dialogue as a generic feature of the political fiction of constituting America. For it is the critical dialogue of poems that will constitute the internal commerce of a truly Spanish American poetry.

The following two chapters are devoted to that dialogue. Chapter 4 takes up the relation between the poetry of Bello and Heredia. The predominant view of literary history holds that Bello had the best of this agon and that the literary currents of Spanish American modernity find their source in his "Alocución." While I too will examine Bello's impact on Heredia in mapping the progress of poetry, I will nevertheless read against the current.[33] For I am most interested in a crucial moment when Bello himself looks back to his sources in the poetry of the Salamanca school and his own progress vacillates. It is that moment to which Heredia responds in his misreading of Bello. The result, for Heredia, is a melancholic countersublime, which, if not triumphant over Bello in the constitution of Spanish American modernity, opens an alternative route in which the past is a debacle at which the present lingers, a trauma from which the present cannot recover. Chapter 5 then pursues that alternative route to modernity by examining the dialogue of two subsequent poets with Heredia, namely Esteban Echeverría and Gertrudis Gómez de Avellaneda, customarily considered the first Spanish American Romantic and the best, respectively.

The conclusion addresses the text that marks the self-conscious achievement of an internal commerce of Spanish America poetry and stands as the very constitution of an *América poética*: Juan María Gutiérrez's Pan American poetic anthology covering the period from Independence to its present moment of publication from 1846 to 1848 in Valparaiso. Focusing discussion on a selection of minor poets from the anthology—the relatively central names included by Gutiérrez having been treated already in the preceding chapters—I undertake to read this constitution of Spanish American poetry as a unified text in which one finds the routes of an emerging historical consciousness. The last word, however, is given to an alternative modernity: a conscious articulation, hence an introjection, but an introjection of history conceived as incorporation, of the buried past that pronounces its undying grip upon the present.

The Routes
of Modernity

I
Historical Consciousness and Its Vicissitudes

1

Religious Persuasions, 1700–1778

1

A SET OF LETTERS FROM THE RECENTLY ESTABLISHED JESUIT missions in Baja California and printed in Mexico City in 1699 show that news of the illness of Carlos II, the Hapsburg king of Spain, had spread throughout the empire. "God grant a long life to our king," writes Juan María de Salvatierra (born Giovanni de Salvaterra in Milan, 1648–1717), adding, by way of sagacious political commentary, "may he put an end to the threat of civil wars which can break out in so many of his dominions because of the succession" (Salvatierra 1971, 195).[1] Carlos II died the following year, leading to the ascension of the Bourbon Philip V in 1700, and, as Salvatierra feared, a war of succession. In his letter to the Jesuit General Tirso González, dated 29 August 1701, Salvatierra once again attests that he is abreast of political events. His new missions in California had never received adequate financial support from the crown nor the viceroyalty of New Spain in the waning days of Hapsburg rule, whereas, he relates in this letter and often elsewhere, "From the Emperor Charles to King Charles II, vast sums were expended to get a foothold here" (204). And the only firm foothold, he makes clear, is his own. Hence, in seeking funding anew, either from the viceroy in Mexico or the king, he calls for the support of the Jesuit general: "Possibly through the influence Your Paternity has on the royal officials in Madrid—yes, and possibly with the change at the court there—things here may also change" (205). The renewed petition proves successful. The new king grants an annual subsidy of 6000 pesos, beginning in 1702, according to Salvatierra's letter of 9 October 1706 (218). But even Salvatierra's considerable acumen does not extend so far that he might see that the change at court would, in time, bring a change in Jesuit influence as well. By the end of the period under study in this chapter,

Philip V's successor, Carlos III will have expelled the Jesuits from all his lands.

Salvatierra's letter to Tirso González speaks primarily to the issue of funding for the California missions, a concern which may be restated in a more general scope as an attempt to redirect economic relations. Previous expeditionaries had failed to discover precious metals on the peninsula, nor had pearl fishing succeeded in the gulf. The chief interest of the crown in the colonization of Baja California, therefore, remained the project for a harbor for the Manilla Galleon on the Pacific coast. A waning maritime power continued to dream the old dream of an uncompromising and impregnable flotilla system, whose official demise three quarters of a century later would mark the beginning of the end of the colonial regime. The westward progress of the Jesuit missions across the peninsula would facilitate that project, though of course Salvatierra himself presents his petition in strictly evangelical terms—"the good news that I can give to Your Paternity" (Salvatierra 1971, 207)—tabulating the numbers of the converted as a return on the initial investment of funds.

The close of the letter strikes a different chord. Salvatierra reports a discovery: "I should also like to inform Your Paternity that I crossed over to the mainland and traveled northward along its coast until I learned for certain from the Indians that there is a land passage by which the natives of California communicate with those in New Spain" (Salvatierra 1971, 209). Salvatierra's companion in discovery, Father Eusebio Kino (1644–1711), will make a fuller report of the expedition to the Jesuit general, but in this brief anticipation, Salvatierra already sketches the significance. "This discovery," he writes,

> may now seem of little practical value inasmuch as we are down in California at about 26 degrees latitude and the land passage is at the head of the Gulf at about 32 degrees or a little more; but this land route may, within a few years, prove to be the lifeline of this realm. And hence I beg Your Paternity to encourage all to persevere in helping these missions of Nuestra Señora de Loreto de Californias." (210)

The missions were not agriculturally self-sufficient, and the gulf crossing had always been treacherous, obstructing the shipment of supplies from Sinaloa and Sonora. Now that the long-standing hypothesis that California was an island had been decisively disproved, Salvatierra held out new hope for the missions—and thus a better base for fund raising: the increased circulation to be afforded by new roads.

I stress that the internal traffic between American provinces that Salvatierra foresees is based upon a prior communication. First, as Pratt (1992) points out in other latitudes with respect to voyages to the interior (though she associates such travels primarily with a later age), "discovery" by Europeans depends upon the preexistent knowledge of native informants. To note as much is to diminish European presumptions with respect to their originality of vision. But this is only a concern for a self enmeshed in history—the self of such later explorers as the Mungo Park or Dr. Livingston of Pratt's illuminating discussions, whose fundamental belief in historical continuity and the concomitant notion of development are given metaphoric expression in the very goals of their voyages, i.e. to reach a source.

Salvatierra, on the contrary, does not manifest such a historical consciousness, which is to say, in the terms outlined in the introduction, that his is not a modern expedition. He is aware, as noted, of the colonizing efforts that preceded him, and indeed, in their first sally, he and his group come upon the ruins of San Bruno, base camp of the prior Kino-Atondo expedition of 1684 to 1685. But these remains are immediately abandoned. the place is overgrown and dilapidated, the water brackish, and even the Indian who met them there, calling himself Francisco, registers the impact of the past on the present in name only. Salvatierra declares in his first extensive report from California, dated 27 November 1697, "he could speak a word or two of Spanish, but knew nothing about our faith" (Salvatierra 1971, 103). Here is Oakeshott's man hobbling by on a spiritual wooden leg, from the point of view of the Jesuit mission, and yet Salvatierra gives no evidence that he perceives the present to be "significantly qualified" by these fragments of colonization and conversion. His relation to the past is modeled rather on the figurative pattern of Christian exegesis. His mission will repeat *sub gratia* the steps of his predecessors. They had traveled "with eyes blinded by earth," Salvatierra declared (160), and so, as Kino himself wrote in his diary entry of 13 January 1685, during the earlier expedition, "I certify and attest that all of the lands which we discovered . . . are not appropriate for planting nor settling because all are mountain ranges so rugged that almost all of the hills are landslides and steep" (Kino 1969, 55). Whereas now, to those whose vision is "cleared by the pure air of heaven" (Salvatierra 1971, 160), the same land reveals its promise: "a valley suddenly came into view, extensive and delightful to behold, with groves and streams. All were overjoyed" (162). Salvatierra's published report of 9 July 1699 is a new testament.

Thus, the fact that the indigenous peoples had communicated between the interior of Baja California and its coast, or between the peninsula and the mainland is as much a matter of indifference to Salvatierra, with respect to the workings of grace and the meaning of revelation, as the prior experience of other expeditions, motivated by temporal interests. Others had looked, but only he had seen, and what he saw was the intervention of the Virgin of Loreto. Insofar as the propagation of that vision was his mission, communication is the crucial issue, if not in the same sense of internal traffic (i.e. commerce amongst the indigenous peoples themselves or between the missionaries and Christians on the mainland and in Europe). And the communication between the as yet unconquered and their would-be conquerors is obscured by the language of conversion, including that of the rhetorical conversion of conquest into religious mission. Salvatierra lays bare that rhetorical conversion when he declares in his letter of 27 November 1697 that the first pitched battle—harquebuses triumphing over arrows—and not the prior procession of the Virgin from shipboard to shore, "marks the real beginning of the enterprise" (Salvatierra 1971, 128).

Such issues have become a cornerstone of the increasing literary scholarship devoted to the colonial period, particularly in the reading of bicultural chroniclers like El Inca Garcilaso and Guaman Poma. It bears reiterating in this context, however, since that scholarship rarely extends forward into the eighteenth century, even though conquest and colonization proceeded, when new lands, as Salvatierra attests, appear on the horizon. It bears reiterating here, that is, because the Conquest remains the backdrop of the poetry of Spanish America at the outset of the eighteenth century, wherein the indigenous voice already riddles texts as an unspoken and unspeakable secret.

I pause, therefore, to listen for the submerged indigenous voice in Salvatierra's account, for he records it. He depicts a scene of language instruction shortly after his arrival. As tensions grew in the days leading up to his first military victory, he relates that he attempted to maintain the calm by carrying out the daily chores unvaryingly: cooking and distributing food to the indigenous people who came to the camp and offering them religious instruction. Thereafter, Salvatierra recounts:

> I walked about and then sat down on a stump to practice language. In the meantime, with greater curiosity than usual, more natives gathered about me than on similar occasions. One of the natives standing by the cauldron pointed out to me the largest bags of maize and ordered me to give him one and said that if I refused he would kill us. (Salvatierra 1971, 116)

Salvatierra had at his disposal "the notebooks of Father Juan Bautista Copart" (109), compiled during the Kino-Atondo expedition, including a "catechism and other linguistic materials" no longer extant according to Ernest J. Burrus's excellent notes (see Salvatierra 1971, 109, nn. 54–55; see also Barco 1981). He is further aided on this occasion by the gesture of pointing to the maize. But the key to correct understanding here, a language teacher marvels, is the proper comprehension of the word "kill," unaccompanied by gestures, according to the brief account. Salvatierra further explains:

> In order to say "kill," they use the expression "lui lui." I pretended not to understand him—easy enough for one to do who is just beginning to learn a language and is receiving instruction in it. I pretended to understand "Luis" or "Luisillo," the name of a California Indian, a relative of these natives. At the time of Don Isidro de Atondo, Luis left this country with two other little California lads in company of Father Juan Bautista Copart before California was abandoned. (Salvatierra 1971, 116)

Salvatierra includes a brief aside here, noting that he had tried unsuccessfully to recruit the two of those three boys who were still alive for his expedition, without specifying if one of them was Luis. In any case, he narrates that he assured the hostile group that Luisillo was alive and that he would be returning to California, and "by holding their attention with this recital, I retreated gradually from them and retired within the entrenched area" (117).

A ready wit has saved his life, or so Salvatierra believes. His version of the tale is coherent and compelling, fitting neatly into a narrative of increasing and unmotivated animosity on the part of his indigenous interlocutors that culminates in the detailed description of the battle. But as Abraham (1978, 416–17) suggests when he returns to the all-too-familiar syllables, *o-a*, of Freud's *fort-da* game, from the child's point of view, the very comprehensiveness of a theoretical reconstruction may be evidence of tendentious interpretation. A novice in a new language in a moment in which he was fearing for his life and the well-being of his mission, did Salvatierra hear "lui lui"? Is this oral comprehension or simply projection?

I raise the shadow of this doubt in order to cast Salvatierra's cryptic procedure in higher relief. The indigenous word sets the intercalated narrative of Luisillo in motion across the bridge of the interlinguistic pun. That story is plainly and self-consciously a fiction, if not to say a lie. All the more so if, as one may suspect, the reason that Luisillo is not named as one of the two surviving boys is that Salvatierra knows him, or at least believes him to be the third, that is the one already dead. Is this what leads Salvatierra to conflate the word he takes to mean "kill" with the name of the missing Luis? Conjecture may be vain after nearly two centuries, but the alternative is to leave the ghost of the conquistadors, that is *their* texts, to guard the crypt of the cultures that they buried alive.

The text is altogether explicit in stating that the purpose of the story of Luisillo as told to the indigenous listeners and to the reader—"that he was alive, that he would come, and that they would see him" (Salvatierra 1971, 117)—was to distract attention from the indigenous *voz*. The tales of the Conquest, whether here in prose or elsewhere in verse, may be understood to undertake, wholesale, the same task through a process that leads from the indigenous voice to a falsified history cast—as Salvatierra does—as prophecy. In that process the encrypted originary word is left to stalk the imagination of the text. I might speculate, for instance, that where Salvatierra pretends to hear in Castilian what he understands to be the threat "to kill," the native speakers were in fact joining in his language lesson, speaking the "word or two of Spanish" of the unconverted, that word being none other than Luis, Luis. The better-understood pre-Columbian cultures of mainland Mexico, then, might underwrite an expectation that the sacrifice of Luisillo would be made good in a symbolic exchange for maize.[2] The equivalence of Luis and maize—the pointing of the Indians: there, that is Luis—would be a barbarous hallucination from the Jesuit perspective. But had the Edues of Baja California, like the Aztecs, a myth of the return of the god, sailing west to them across the sea, a teacher of the arts of cultivation? And what gifts might they expect from him in return for their submission, the loss, if not of Luis, then of their lands, their language, their culture? Perhaps the gift of maize, which did not grow in their peninsula.

I desist. My reconstruction of the language of a myth-motif in formation—the introduction of maize into the indigenous cultures of Baja California—is also a conscious fiction. The text, I confess, is more apt to yield up the mechanisms of Salvatierra's psychic defenses than the secrets of his indigenous interlocutors. Within the narrower compass of Salvatierra's literary imagination, however, it is also possible to detect a symbolic exchange at its inauguration. It was Father Copart, Salvatierra had noted, who had carried off Luisillo and the other two indigenous boys. Father Copart, too, provided the notebooks of Salvatierra's language lesson. Translating with Borges's sinologist Stephen Albert, I would suggest that these two events are one, or more precisely, that they constitute a transaction. Salvatierra neither hallucinates the presence of Luis; nor, acknowledging his absence as definitive, does he creates a new, transcultural community of mourners, bound to retell, bound by the retelling of his death. Instead, he *incorporates* Luis into the language of conversion. The present is viewed as incomplete, but a history is projected in which the missing member will return—and the Edues are to swallow his tale of Luis's coming in place of the maize. A melancholy story on several counts: both Salvatierra and Luis's relatives are compelled to repeat the loss in displaced form (the loss of a potential bilingual interpreter is reenacted as the interruption of the language lesson for the one and as the loss of maize for the others); the true history of the loss (Luis' inability or his unwillingness to return to his native people) becomes the tale that cannot be told; and, finally, the stories that take its place are riddled by a cryptic word. Incorporating "Luis" as "lui" makes the announcement of his future presence—Luis will be here—into a prediction of slaughter—*lui* will be here, there will be killing. The abiding melancholia of Spanish American modernity enters the literature through the text of Conquest.

Salvatierra is driven to the brink of a historical consciousness by a moment of crisis. But the crisis passes and the consciousness recedes. The killing does come presently in the familiar military history of the Americas. The first mission is established at Loreto. Luis is not mentioned again. But in the ensuing process of transculturation, the indigenous peoples too learn the art of misleading. At the outset of his letter from Loreto of 9 July 1699, Salvatierra had announced that "the [missionary] enterprise was extended through an expedition to the settlements around Viggé, which means 'highland' " (Salvatierra 1971, 155). He returns to the account of that expedition some pages later, now narrating second-hand, for he remained behind in Loreto. He tells of balking soldiers and of the inspirational force of Father Francisco María Píccolo (Sicily, 1654–1729) whose exhortation in the name of "the Blessed Virgin, *La Conquistadora*" so moved the military escort "that they resolved not to turn back until they reached the settlements *on the mountain heights*" (Salvatierra 1971, 161; emphasis added). I lay stress on an interlinguistic crux. Salvatierra continues: "The next day, after hearing Mass, they trudged on foot over terrifying cliffs. They advanced a considerable distance along the arroyo, where they found a patch of wild grapes which extended for a full league" (161), and which he assesses with respect to their agricultural potential. He then relates:

> That afternoon, guided by the natives, they found the mountain ascent most exhausting. It was all due to a misunderstanding; the natives thought that we did not want to visit the settlements but rather the high mountain cliffs. Finally, when the missionary asked José [an indigenous guide] where the natives lived, he answered that no one lived up there, although the natives did go occasionally there for *mescales*. These mountain heights are called Viggé, the source of the mix-up. The word means "land high above the valleys." Along the coastal areas, the term is used to designate all the high or mountainous regions of California; and the natives on such heights are referred to as "people of Viggé." (Salvatierra 1971, 161–62)

Salvatierra seems as convinced that the natives' misunderstanding was ingenuous as he was that his own had been cunning and feigned. But whose the exhaustion, and whose, perhaps, the sense of triumph when the Spaniards completed the ascent only to find no peoples to subjugate? And what did the indigenous guides understand when they heard the Spaniards shouting as they descended to the populated valley, "vega, vega" (162, n.19; Burrus translates "meadows, meadows"): a mispronunciation of their own word "Viggé" (as Salvatierra heard or misheard lui-Luis) or a deliberate and menacing metonymy whereby the living presence of a people is effaced in their geography? *Viggé, vega*: if you can see the contours of the land and not the culture of the people, then in self-defense we will show you what you're looking for, the deserted heights.

Piccolo sent word back by native couriers to Salvatierra at Loreto telling him of the establishment of a second mission, San Francisco Javier de Viggé Biaundó, and receiving thence new supplies. "All these interchanges," Salvatierra writes, "were carried out quite faithfully by the California natives, who would leave one point in the morning and reach the other fairly early in the afternoon. This rapidity," he adds, though he does not suspect that the joke may be on him, "caused our men to conclude that they were using a shorter route" (Salvatierra 1971, 164). Salvatierra then adds:

> After Father Francisco María Píccolo had set up the Holy Cross and built an arbor [i.e. a make-shift place of worship], he returned with the soldiers, traveling along a route which was shorter but which also ran through such sheer crags that it seemed impassable for horses. En route they came across the California Indians who had been alone four days attending to the horses and saddles. This encounter seemed to be a miracle performed by the holy Madonna of Loreto and the Apostle of the Indies, Saint Francis Xavier. It took them only one day to return over this route. (164)

The encounter will seem less miraculous, of course, if we imagine that the same native couriers of the preceding paragraph were present to guide Píccolo on what was, for them, the customary route of their own internal traffic through the Viggé. Their omission in the present context serves the missionaries' greater purpose: the aggrandizement of the Madonna of Loreto.

In the Spanish chronicles, needless to say, the Spaniards have the final word and the final way. Within a month, Píccolo and a body of soldiers, accompanied, explicitly once again, by native guides (Salvatierra 1971, 176), return to the impassable site. There, aided by metal tools and the advice of a native guide who shows them a route that obviates the need to bridge a stream—a service repaid by christening him Angel, "as it was the work of an angel rather than that of any human" (177)—the party quickly succeeds in constructing a road that the Spaniards could travel on horseback: "Such was their delight that even the animals seemed to share in it on seeing such fine pasturages on those highlands" (177). The whole of the episode is then adjusted to the calendar of saints' days and punctuated by a devotional exercise. The captain of the troops makes a promise to the Virgin to ascend once more to the heights, which, dutifully accomplished, is recompensed with a view of the two seas, to the east and west of the peninsula, and "an intense joy for a discovery desired for nearly two centuries and not attained by so many persons, but realized only in the shadow of the Holy House of Mary and her Saturday devotions" (179). A historical consciousness has faded altogether from so auspicious a view. The preceding centuries are now as naught—indeed, as Burrus points out (Salvatierra 1971, 179, n. 66), the assertion overlooks the discoveries made in the Atondo-Kino expedition, which had already crossed the peninsula (see Kino 1969). The present differs from the past by dint of miraculous intervention. In the task of road-building, "Heaven helped the men. . . . All invoked Our Lady of Loreto" (Salvatierra 1971, 176). "With such *sublime* assistance," Salvatierra declares, "every blow of the crowbar or pick helped break down the impeding boulders" (176 emphasis added). A sign of the times a century before Humboldt ascends Chimborozo, and a benchmark against which to measure the trajectory of the period here in question, from 1700 to 1778. In the heights of the Viggé, the cliffs are "terrifying" and the crags "sheer," but sublimity remains as yet preeminently a theological, rather than an aesthetic category for Spanish American letters. Yet one may already note that from the theological high ground thus staked out, an ideological slant inclines expeditionary writing toward natural history beneath which a cultural history lies buried in an unmarked grave.

2

An unknown poet copies out a satire of some sixty-nine *cuartetos* relating an incident of illegal traffic, would-be conquest, and failed expeditionary forces in Mexico in 1703. A certain Don Domingo Tagle, having already announced his matrimonial intentions to one woman, is off across Mexico City to marry another. To do so he must free her from the custody of the Convent of San Lorenzo. José Miranda and Pablo González Casanova identify the object of Tagle's desire as Ignacia Cruzat, daughter of the viceroy of the Philippines, thus setting the affair in the highest echelons of colonial society. The anonymous poet, however, deflates colonial pretensions with popular diction, denominating Don Domingo "el sacadamas" ["the lady snatcher"] (Miranda and González Casanova

1953, 64), and relating how his myrmidons turned tail and ran when they met with opposition to their seige:

> Unos se van por acá,
> otros por allá se parten,
> otros van a la baluca,
> de otros aún no se sabe.
>   (Miranda and González Casanova 1953, 63)

> Some of them head out this way,
> others take off over there,
> others head for the hills,
> and some, we still don't know where.

The scattering prefigures the fate of a century of poets to come. Indeed of many, like this satirist himself, nothing is known. He disappears, leaving behind as his mark a verbal curiosity, "baluca," otherwise unattested by the principal lexicographers, but redolent of a certain milieu and its sociolect, which have receded with him.

The predominant forms of poetry and culture that held their ground while popular voices evanesced speak against the premise of the satire, even in its mock-epic mode. There was no pitched battle between the colonial aristocracy and the institutions of the church. Hence, cultivated poetry, which served both of those centers of power, can easily penetrate the convent, where the ruffian-poet failed to gain entrance. It may be that the indigenous voices of Baja California, at best, can be reconstructed from the historical record of their conquerors' tendentious misunderstandings. But for the voice of one "enjaulada con las Madres" ["caged with the Mothers"] (Miranda and González Casanova 1953, 5), as the Mexican satirist might have it, one may turn directly to the poets.

An anonymous poem directed "Al virrey Castelldosrius, suplicando vuelva a visitar un convento de monjas" and discovered in a manuscript by Ramón Vargas Ugarte, provides an example from early in the period that deploys the trope of conquest through the image of fettering as a linkage between willing partners in the dialogue of colonial authority. The poem may be dated to the years 1707 to 1710, the period of Castell-dos-Rius's tenure as viceroy of Peru. The text gives ample evidence of a poet well-schooled in the forms and rhetoric of baroque verse. Castell-dos-Rius is known to have been a congenial patron of the same, for he maintained a literary academia at the viceregal court, a model of the pre-modern institution of literature characterized by a narrow circulation of manuscripts in an elite society under personal patronage.[3] The nun who authored the supplication would have been removed by gender and by religious profession from the immediate setting of the academia, but her poem contributes to its larger context. Her invitation pulls at the common but uneasy yoke of wit and deference:

> Con blasones tan grandes
> muy bien venido seas,
> que tus prendas ilustres
> saben hacer las almas prisioneras.
> Mas están ciertas,
> que no es yerro el atarse
> de esta cadena.
>
> (Vargas Ugarte 1951, 61)

> With such a coat of arms
> you are most welcome here,
> for your illustrious charms
> souls prisoners take.
> But they are sure,
> for to be bound is no mistake
> by such a chain.

Acknowledgment of the viceroy's elevated station must make the poet meek, but her purpose—to incline his will to make the desired visit—requires that she be bold. To take the role of suitor in this chaste seduction raises the potential accusation of impropriety. The poet herself hints at arrest, only the better to display her dexterity in slipping free of the charges. Against her own trope of imprisonment and chains, she breaks the implicit *hierro* (iron, i.e. of shackles) with the leverage of a homophonic pun: "que no es yerro" (for it is no error) (Vargas Ugarte 1951, 61). The rhetorical conundrum is resolved as a minor poetic victory by the characteristically baroque device of word play.

Maravall has argued that such a compromise is the cornerstone of baroque culture in Spain. An embattled throne wins the nobility to its side by granting greater power; the nobility, in turn, affirms their loyalty to the king at the same time that they assert their own rising position through ostentatious display. The nun's supplication conforms to the pattern; her deferential acknowledgement of the viceroy is the occasion for the performance of her own rhetorical strength. Her role in this power play is dictated more generally by the overarching paradigm of the willing obedience that poet and viceroy, nobles and kings, all owe to God. Indeed, as Father Salvatierra's reading of the poem *lui, lui,* kill, kill, demonstrated, a heterodox critique of submission and of the associated trope of conquest as the chains that set peoples free, is itself understood as the mark of paganism.

Religious, social and poetic orthodoxy express themselves repeatedly in the eighteenth century in the ample current of devotional verse. But even the most orthodox devotion is affected by the epistemological uncertainty of baroque sensibility. Representation, including poetry, pertains more to illusion than to a realm of eternal verities. This problem, too, is visible in the supplication. The viceroy is represented by *blasones*; and even *prendas* could be duplicitous, inducing error, as they often do in courtly love lyrics. The trope of fetters, in this regard, defends against error by staying or fixing the mutabilty of signs.[4]

Where love is directed above temporal (and therefore transient) authority to an immutable God, the opposition between illusion and truth is heightened. Both that devotion and that poetic predicament find especially compelling expression in the small extant body of verse of María Francisca Josefa de la Concepción of the Order of Saint Clare, born Francisca del Castillo y Guevara (Colombia 1671–1742) and known as Madre Castillo. In her posthumously published autobiography, she noted that in her childhood, "My mother read the books of Santa Teresa de Jesús and her foundations, and that gave me a very great desire to be like one of those nuns" (Castillo 1968, 1:5). And like her illustrious model, she, too, wrote a vademecum of the mystical path, her *Afectos espirituales*, also published posthumously (see Castillo 1968). Nevertheless, as Kathryn McKnight explains in her excellent study, *The Mystic of Tunja* (McKnight 1997), the Council of Trent, with its insistence upon perpetual enclosure, separates Madre Castillo from her precursor. In this regard, McKnight lays emphasis on the fact that it was the *Fundaciones* to which Madre Castillo referred as her earliest literary model, a work in which Santa Teresa "is not constrained to judge her own life but rather free to write the history of a reform movement as a nun who has successfully negotiated her right to work on either side of the convent walls" (148). In contrast, asserts McKnight, Madre Castillo "patterns her behaviors and desires after those of Saint Teresa, but shows the impossibility of working out a positive role in the world and in the position of leadership [that she attained in her own convent of Poor Clares] by marking these consistently with scandal and sin" (148). The chief sin, as concerns the role of authorship and, more generally, of subjectivity, is pride. McKnight comments:

> By positing pride and humility as the primary axis of sin and virtue with which the (female monastic) self must be concerned, Church ideologies seek to contain (female) individuation. Official discourse locates the principal damage perpetrated by the sin of pride in its division of the community, masking the threat the Church itself feels to its authority from the assertion of female individuality by saying that it is the women themselves who are hurt. (163)

The championing of divisiveness, in the mode of the *tradición de la ruptura*, for instance, will be a hallmark of modernity, whose agent will be the individuated self. The self becomes the fixed point of authenticity about which the mutable world of experience revolved. Madre Castillo, as an author and as a woman, is a self at the brink of modernity, hemmed in by the counter-reformation. McKnight presents her as a woman intent on the expeditions into the two worlds of secular and sacred power: deeply involved in the financial and commercial affairs of her convent and related power struggles, on the one hand, and daring to offer independent exegesis of Scripture, on the the other. Nevertheless, Madre Castillo restrains her boldness. The *Vida* continually shows the mark of that restraint—the insinuation of self-control in the burgeoning interiority where institutional control could not reach—in the narration of sufferings explained as just punishment for her sinful pride.[5]

Generic distinctions between the *Vida* and the *Afectos* resolve the burden in part in the latter, and so open a route to a severely qualified subjectivity. McKnight underlines the rhetorical strategy whereby Madre Castillo presents herself not as an author, but as "God's amanuensis" (McKnight 1997, 169). Her "Deliquios del divino amor en el corazón de la criatura, y en las agonías del huerto," a poem included as a chapter of the *Afectos*, exemplify the role of amanuensis in compositional technique and in its figuration. The poem is composed by the *enlace* of passages from the Song of Songs, molded to the shape of her heptasyllabic line and rhyme scheme.[6] In addition, where the romantics will take the self as its own source out of which expression flows,[7] Madre Castillo is a receptacle for divine expression:

Su melíflua palabra
Corta como rocío
Y con ella florece
El corazón marchito.
    Tan suave se introduce
Su delicado silbo,
Que duda el corazón
Si es el corazón mismo.

(Castillo 1968, 2:124)

His mellifluous word
Cuts like dew,
And with it the withered heart
flourishes anew.
    Its delicate whistle
Enters so gently
That the heart wonders
If it is itself the heart.[8]

The word of the allegorical lover is a divine breath, and as such will return, magnified, in the final stanzas as the gentle south wind (Castillo 1968, 2:125–26). But in its introduction, the image of the divine voice derives from the "whistle of the shepherd" in *Las moradas* of Saint Teresa (McKnight 1997, 57).[9] The allusion is a crucial reminder that however unmediated her experience of the divine may have been as a mystic, as a writer Madre Castillo is embedded in literary history. Here, too, she is an amanuensis in the most literal sense. Several of the poems traditionally attributed to her were identified as transcriptions of poetry by Sor Juana Inés de la Cruz after the publication Madre Castillo's works at the head of a series of *Clásicos Colombianos* in 1942.[10] There is no hint that Madre Castillo ever intended that the poems she copied from Sor Juana be attributed to herself, any more than, say, the verses of San Juan de la Cruz that McKnight found copied in Madre Castillo's hand. Hence I recall the misattribution not to demean her contribution, but rather to emphasize the manner in which Madre Castillo herself bracketed the question of originality, which will be the proof the modern self will offer in support of its authenticity. Moreover, one finds in these transcriptions evidence of an internal commerce of American letters within the conventual orders, and, in Madre Castillo's predilection for Sor Juana, an example of the persistence of the baroque, which carries over to the stanzas interpolated into Sor

Juana's texts that appear to be of her own composition. A text combining verses from Sor Juana's *letrillas*, for instance, includes the image of the whistling:

> Aquel que te salva silba
> y te da mil veces voces,
> y de amor con llama, llama
> para que en sus horas ores
>
> (Castillo 1968, 2:495))

> That which whistling reclaims,
> with redoubled voice invokes,
> and involving in love's flame,
> calls you hourly to oraisons.

Stylistically, the verses stand at a great remove from "Deliquios," but once again, the fundamental image is one of a spiritual revitalization that enters into the self from without in the form of inspiration. The disproportion of divine breath to human receptacle is then manifest when the poet breathes out her own poem. In the highly wrought sound play, the poetic self is compelled to repeat, as though stammering, unable to articulate distinctly what is, after all, an experience of the ineffable.

   This high poetic striving beyond rational limits informed even the secular experience of the baroque and the expression of even the minor poets of the period:

> Que palabras, que elocuencia,
> que retórico artificio
> podrá dejar figurado,
> lo que aun no se ha comprendido.
>
> (Vargas Ugarte 1951, 73)

> What words, what eloquence,
> what rhetorical artifice
> will be able to leave a figure
> for what remains incomprehensible.

Thus, the anonymous poet of the "Rasgo histórico sobre la ruina de Lima e inundación del Callao 1746" states in simple terms the poetic challenge Madre Castillo inherited from Sor Juana. All poetry, of course, is threatened by its own figurative limitations. But baroque poetry courts that danger assiduously by its stylistic hubris, its massive, self-conscious overvaluations by which the worldly objects of ideological disdain are tripped out in luxury.

The baroque lyric will frequently take up the related didactic labor of correcting those *yerros* in epitaphic poetry, whose traditional interpellation from the grave—*sta viator*—is a chief subtext of baroque *fijeza*. An anthropology of eighteenth-century poetic occasion, therefore, will be particularly interested in interment. In this regard, the Baroque offers an especially clear backdrop against which one may distinguish the emergence of modernity, characterized in turn, as I have suggested in the introduction, by distinct burial practices.

The *pira* (pyre) for María de Uresti on the anniversary of her death, celebrated in 1727 in San Luis Potosí, provides a characteristic minor expression. A set of sixteen anonymous poems, along with the memorial sermon and a description of the pyre were published in Mexico City that same year. As was the custom for such funerary games, the poems all develop a single conceit, in this case the metaphor, "Quebrado racional espejo" (Broken rational mirror): broken, because dead; rational, because human; doubly a mirror, because her good deeds in life reflected God's glory and her death reflects the impending fate of the living. The poems take on a lyrical cast through the use of a first-person point of view— "Temporal vida acabé/morí . . ." (I finished temporal lifc/I died . . .) (Peñalosa 1988, 254)—though in fact this technique is the extension of the sepulchral epitaph. The deceased speaks primarily in *décimas*:

> Si de verme respirar
> luces en mis mismas sombras
> acaso, oh mortal, te asombras,
> nada tienes que admirar
> si llegas a contemplar
> en este espejo quebrado;
> pues notará tu cuidado
> que me quebré, mas no dejo
> por eso de ser espejo
> en que enmiendes si has errado.
>
> (Peñalosa 1988, 257)

> If seeing me respire lights
> in my own expired shade
> perhaps, oh mortal, you are stunned,

> you have nothing at which to wonder
> if you come to reflect
> upon this broken mirror;
> for your care will note
> that I'm broken, but I'm not
> for that reason less a mirror
> in which, having erred, you may yourself correct.

As the closing rhyme indicates, concern for the breaking of the body is an error (cuidado-errado). The shattering of the mirror is rather a figure for the impaired perception of the living. The spirit remains intact to preach that death is gain: "nueva mejor vida hallé" (new, better life I found) (Peñalosa 1988, 254). This resolute negation of loss excludes any historical consciousness. Despite the potential intimacy of the first-person voice, the speaking I of the poetry is as universalized as the "mortal" to whom the verses are addressed. The I does not depict the concrete personal experience of life. Despite the common metatextual figure of the mirror, the poetry is not mimetic, but didactic. And the baroque teaching on the occasion of funerary rites is based upon the conception of the past as legendary, in Oakeshott's sense. The past is legible as a lesson to the present precisely because the present is understood not to differ from, but rather to repeat the past.

This relation to death and to the past is pervasive, but there is also a poetry in which death is itself a rhetorical figure, anticipating the more common stance of the nineteenth and twentieth centuries. The anonymous Quechua poem "Manchay Puitu," for instance, explores the transformation of the voice of the living into the voice of the dead that is elided in the pira to María de Uresti. Known with variants in both Peru and Bolivia, it is considered by both Jesús Lara and Adolfo Cáceres Romero (Cáceres Romero 1987, 174) as the foremost lyrical poem of the eighteenth century in the extant *supérstite* literature, defined as "that which survives the Spanish conquest and which, in some form, remains faithful, in language and thought, to pre-Columbian tradition" (149). The surrounding legend relates that a priest has come to lament his illicit lover, who has died in his brief absence. Weeping over the grave, he narrates:

> Voy arañando la tumba en que duerme
> Mientras cae mi llanto como lluvia sin fin.
>
> (Cáceres Romero 1987, 178)[11]

I go on scratching at the grave in which she sleeps
While my mourning song falls like an endless rain.

The anonymous poet returns, as it were, to the crossroads between the funereal and love elegies, there where Garcilaso once promoted the forms in Castilian poetry in his "Elegía II." But this poet's classical tradition is altogether distinct, as is his situation, writing in the language of a vanquished culture. His solutions will be different, too.

"Manchay Puitu" is animated by a steady transmutation of the figure of the wind. Having conjectured that "¿Algún viento maligno tal vez se la ha llevado?" ["Perhaps some malign wind has borne her away?"] in the opening stanza, the mourner would restore his beloved to life with a breath, "el calor más tierno de mi lamento" ["the most tender warmth of my lament"], which would include the breathing of his poem. Failing that, he desires death, and to that end he invokes the cyclone, which Lara explicates as "the overpowering breath with which Pachamama, a goddess representing the Earth, manifested her anger for some misconduct of men," according to ancient beliefs (Lara, 1947, 133). But death does not come, nor the consolation that customarily resolves elegiac grief, persuading the poet to accept separation and join the *Société de Mon Bras Droit*. Instead, the conclusion is a stunning disfiguration. First, the metaphor: "Yo soy la propia carne de la angustia" ["I am the very flesh of anguish"]. But if he is figuratively the flesh, she is literally the bone:

> . . . le arrancaré siquiera un hueso
> Y lo tendré en mi seno tal si fuera ella misma.
>
> Se convertirá en quena entre mis manos
> Y llorará mis propias lágrimas.
> Desde la eternidad
> Desde el origen de la luz.
> ¿Es tal vez ella quien me está llamando?
> ¡No! . . . ¡Es tan solo el lamento de mi quena!
>
> (Cáceres Romero 1987, 179)

> . . . I will at least remove a bone from her
> And I will hold it in my bosom, as though it were she herself.
>
> It will turn into a quena [an indigenous flute] in my hands
> And it will weep with my own tears.

From eternity
From the origin of light.
Perhaps it is she who is calling me?
No! . . . It is but the lament of my quena!

Although the poet speaks of eternity, here, as opposed to the pira, the expression is a hyperbole, aimed at conveying a concrete, individual experience. Rather than the consolations of dogma attributed to the broken mirror of María de Uresti, the voice of the dead will repeat the poet's grief, threatening an endless reissuing of loss. He defends himself, therefore, with a final negation that would lead the menacing hallucinatory prosopopeia back to the reality principle of the elegy: you are gone (stay gone!), and I remain. But this, too, may be read as a ruse, the melancholic hiding in the guise of mourning. A historical consciousness has taken hold. He knows the beloved not as she was and eternally is, like María de Uresti in God's grace and whole despite her shattering, but rather as she has become through the transformative experience of death, an amputee, shorn of this bone. Yet he maintains a relationship of symbolic exchange with the remnant. The quena weeps with the poet's tears, but speaks with the beloved's voice. In sum, he acknowledges loss, but does not accept separation. He continues to press her literally to his lips.

Death as an occasion for didactic preaching highlights the gulf in sensibilities that separates the baroque poetry of the pira from modern readers. The melancholia of "Manchay Puitu," on the other hand, still proved accessible late in the following century, when Ricardo Palma included the legend and even some of the verses in his *Tradiciones peruanas* (Lima, 1872–83) under the title "El Manchay-Puito" (Palma, 1980, 187–90). His version presents a notable alteration. The protagonists are now Hispanized under the names of Don Gaspar de Angulo y Valdivieso and Ana Sielles, and further Christianized: he is a priest and she has a "little smile" that is equated to *Gloria in excelsis Deo* ("una sonrisita de *Gloria in excelsis Deo*," Palma 1980, 187). After a salacious narration of the priest's corruption and Ana's untimely and unexplained death, Palma relates that Angulo exhumes his beloved from her burial place in the sacristy floor and carries her off to his rooms, where he serenades the corpse with his quena, improvising the song preserved as "Manchay Puitu." When the music ceases on the third night, the neighbors break into the room and discover Don Gaspar in the throes of death, clutching the cadaver of his lover.

Lara assails Palma's version on various counts, not least for errors in the translation and for Palma's commentary on the verses, "arising, no doubt, from his ignorance of Quechua" (Lara 1947, 30–31)—and, I would speculate, from his knowledge of Peninsular literary history. For it may be that Palma has transposed the Quechua legend as an American version of José Cadalso's *Noches lúgubres* (1789–90), accentuating the piquancy of a perverse eroticism. Far more fundamental, however, is the musical transposition practiced by Palma. He narrates that the distraught lover "held [his quena] inside a jug and made it produce lugubrious sounds, true echoes of an anguish nameless and infinite" (Palma 1980, 189), a point that he reiterates in the brief envoy to the tale, where he relates that the church has pronounced excommunication on "those who sing the Manchay Puitu or play the quena inside a jug" (190). This detail transfers the special funereal quality of the music from the quena itself to the cántaro, displacing the indigenous character of the song. Furthermore, we read a posthumous letter from Ana in plain Castilian prose (188), but the quena is no longer her bone, nor its music her voice. The tendentiousness of Palma's version suggests in retrospect that the melancholic preservation of the literal bone and figurative voice of the beloved in the eighteenth-century Quechua lyric pointed through personal loss to the wider experience of indigenous culture. It may well be that the occasion for all *supérstite* literature is the conquest, that the beloved lost but not yet abandoned is also the culture itself, and the quena, therefore, the fragmentary cultural vestige which is the poetry.

3

The Conquest is also a theme, or indeed a problem, for the Spanish language poets of the eighteenth century, though the poetic occasion has shifted significantly since the time of Balbuena's *Grandeza mexicana* (Mexico 1604) and the early chroniclers. A vision of indigenous grandeur, crucial to the exaltation of the conquerors, is no longer a pressing demand. The need to define the transplanted European culture against the native peoples had waned, replaced by the growing desire to promote a criollo culture, Hispanic and yet distinct from the Peninsula. In the humanist hierarchy of poetic genres an epic poem was still required, and the proper model was clearly Virgil, whose Aeneas speaks far less for the Troy he left behind than for the Rome he was to found.

Returning to the literary circle of Castell-dos-Rius in early eighteenth-century Peru, one finds the premier extant effort in this direction in the poetry of Pedro de Peralta Barnuevo (Peru 1663–1743). Irving A. Leonard has outlined the biography of this polymath figure, recording Peralta's achievements in an extensive array of disciplines—mathematics and astronomy, engineering, metallurgy and architecture, law and educational administration, classical and modern languages, theology and medicine, and of greatest concern here, historiography and poetry. In short, "one of the most versatile and prodigious intellects that flourished during the vice-regal period of Peruvian history," as Leonard declares (1933, 55). Feijóo extended the praise of his distinguished American contemporary: "for in all of Europe there hardly . . . will be found any man of superior talent and learning" (qtd by Leonard 1933, 55; see also J. Williams 1998).

As a poet, Peralta's ambitions were great and his success modest. One reads in vain the more than nine thousand verses of his *Lima fundada o Conquista del Peru, poema heroico en que se decanta toda la historia del descubrimiento y sujecion de sus provincias por D. Francisco Pizarro, Marques de los Atabillos, ínclito y primer gobernador de este vasto imperio* (Lima, 1732) in search of fresh metaphors and other figurative surprises of a more brilliant imagination. One finds instead, with respect to style, merely baroque expansiveness. Nevertheless, the plan of the work merits attention.[12] The structure will return, though its ideological position will be reversed, when the authors of the nineteenth century seek to transpose the wars of independence as lyric poetry. In support of this view I will highlight two points in this vast poem: its handling of history and its expression of a self-consciously American identity in relation to the landscape. In both respects, Peralta develops in verse the foundational mechanisms detected in the prose of Salvatierra: the use of prophecy to express an incipient historical consciousness; and the use of native geography to efface indigenous culture.

From its opening verse, "Canto las armas y el varon famoso" ["I sing of arms and the famous man"] (Peralta 1863, 7) and even before, in the prologue, Peralta sets his poem in the mold of Virgil's epic: his Pizarro a new Aeneas. Hence, having determined from his study of the classics that an epic requires "amorous interludes" (vii), he provides such a passage for Pizarro, whose Dido is an Inca princess. "En la mansión de esta índica hermosura" (32) ["In the dwelling of this beauty of the Indies"], Pizarro succinctly declares his twin loyalties, on the one hand to the Spanish crown, and on the other to a God who has subdued the Inca deity—"Un Dios hay, que del Sol criador inmenso/A sus leyes sugeta su carrera" (32) ["A God there is who of the Sun, immense creator,/subjugates the course to his own laws"]. But the princess, unabashed, responds with a chronicle of Inca history to which Peralta dedicates two dozen *octavas reales* (34–41), citing such sources as Pedro de Cieza, Gómara and El Inca Garcilaso in the notes that he appends to his verses: an effort, albeit bookish, to provide the voice that Palma will efface. Nevertheless, it needs be recalled that Peralta emphasized in the prologue that love represents a distracting temptation, if not a moral calamity, that the epic hero must overcome. Inasmuch as the history that the princess enunciates reinforces her own nobility and so enhances her allure, the chronicle bears the allegorical weight of the discourse of sin. In this regard it serves as a counterpoint to the history of colonial Peru that will occupy Peralta for thousands of verses from midway through canto 4 to the close of canto 7.

The hinge between the potential moral turpitude of this chaste seduction and the state of grace under Christian domination is the episode in which Huascar and Atahualpa, sons of Guaynacapac by different mothers, came to be rivals. A further example of the dangers of love for martial leaders, Peralta stresses that Huascar was the legitimate ruler by right of primogeniture, but that Guaynacapac bequeathed the greater portion of his kingdom to Atahualpa, "impelido/De un tierno amor que le cegó lo sabio" (38) ["impelled/by a tender love that blinded his wisdom"], as the princess explains. The division of the realm is followed by betrayal, "Y el decreto despacha [Atahualpa] de su muerte [i.e. de Huascar]" (59) ["And (Atahualpa) dispatches the death sentence (of Huascar)"]. Peralta does not press the Inca princess into service when declaring the conquest of Peru a matter of divine retribution—at least in this respect psychological verisimilitude is preserved. Yet the poet himself will make this point, as though Pizarro founded Lima on Huascar's behalf:

> Por esto aquella eterna inmensurable
> Divina Geometría siempre justa
> Al hecho á proporción de lo execrable,

> Lo riguroso del castigo ajusta:
> Ceguedad de Atahualpa incomparable,
> Pues tan atroz muerte, tan injusta,
> Fué poner, al hallarse en tal mudanza,
> El agravio en poder de la venganza.
>
> (Peralta 1863, 59–60)

> Thus the eternal, immeasurable
> Divine Geometry, ever just,
> in proportion to the execrable deeds
> the rigor of punishment adjusts:
> Incomparable blindness of Atahualpa,
> for a death so horrid, so unjust,
> finding himself at such a turn of events
> was to lay grievance at the feet of revenge.

The ideology of imperial expansion is thus enunciated within the canon of the epic: the sins of the father, Guaynacapac, are visited upon the sons. According to Peralta, Pizarro does not so much extend Spanish dominion as restore the balance of divine order, specified as Geometry by this mathematician-poet. Such will be the outcome, that is, if Pizarro avoids the fatal path of his Inca precursor, foregoing the dalliance of love in favor of the progress of history.

Peralta approaches this narrative crux under the aegis of Virgil, as he explains in the prologue to *Lima fundada*:

> As for the prosopopeias and other figures, I have aspired to employ them as well as has been possible given the tenuous strength of my imagination. And . . . it should be noted that among all those [figures] that Virgil used, the most admirable is the prophecy. This prince of epic poetry wanted to combine the illustration of the homeland with that of the hero, with the recollection of the great [men] that the latter had produced from the time of the former to Augustus. . . . And since this could not be done without breaking the law of the unity of action, going beyond the catastrophe or conclusion, he decided to place those great men in a prediction, praising them in anticipation and preparing for them a song of the future. (xii)

With this model in mind, Peralta proceeded in his own composition. The colonial history founded upon Pizarro's feat of arms is presented as the prophecy of an "Hermoso . . . joven" (86) ["Handsome . . . youth"], who has spirited the hero away from the Peruvian jungle to a Virgilian "campo . . . ameno" (85) ["locus amoenus"] for that purpose: "Patriotic zeal could burn no less actively in me than in that famous poet. . . . I sought to follow him, even if from afar. . . . I determined to turn the present into the past" (xii–xiii).

To turn the present into the past and the past into the future: Peralta is clearly thinking through the relations of temporal categories so as to develop a picture of his own present-day Peru, qualified, as Oakeshott says, by its past. But his temporal structure does not reflect a modern historical consciousness. For Oakeshott, the past is that which does not survive, and thus may only be inferred from a fragmentary historical record; in this sense the present is the ruin of the past. For Peralta, the imperial glory of Spanish dominion may have been best manifest in the epic heroes of the Conquest, but it is never at an end, as attested to by the present, which is not the ruin, but the fulfilment of the past. The narration of the Inca kings is an old testament incontrovertibly cut off from the era *sub gratia* inaugurated by Spanish imperialism. The scheme, in short, is providential and owes more to the church than Aristotle.[13]

The sense of the ineluctable pastness of the pre-Columbian past remained as a problem for Spanish American historical consciousness once the providential view of Spanish dominion was rejected and independent national identities began to be forged in the nineteenth century. The generative claims of the foundational fictions of the new nations, in accordance with Sommer's cogent argument, respond to the felt illegitimacy perceived by a historical consciousness of the amputation of the pre-Columbian past from the providential scheme. The national present was then conceived of not as the fulfillment of the pre-Columbian past, but rather as the fragmentary ruins that remained after the devastation of conquest and colonization. In seeking a link to the pre-Columbian past, nineteenth-century letters practiced a similar amputation upon colonial forebears, especially the immediate antecedents of the eighteenth century. The nineteenth-century myth of *mestizaje* at the heart of those foundational fictions incorporated the indigneous past into national identity, but largely by introducing self-justifying national fantasies that erased the indigenous present. In this latter respect, nineteenth-century foundational fictions only repeated the ideological and imaginative postitions that prevailed in colonial letters. Then, in the twentieth century, Spanish American letters repeated the repudiation of the eighteenth century fundamental to early fictions of national identity, but extended that repudiation to the nineteenth-

century foundational fictions themselves. One gains further historical perspective by noting that the same problematic was already at
work in such characteristic eighteenth-century texts as *Lima fundada*. Peralta himself anticipates, albeit faintly, the matrimonial
fantasy of the foundational fictions in the love idyll of Pizarro, as
he also anticipates quite forcefully the Enlightenment strategy for
erasing the indigenous presence, namely the detour from cultural to
natural history.[14] But that observation only documents further the
same compulsion to repeat that haunts historical consciousness in
Spanish American letters. That consciousness is split, Abraham and
Torok might say, and the fiction at the foundation of the split—not
the inaugural instance, but the paradigm—is enacted by Father Salvatierra, who, finding himself exposed to the introjections of the
indigenous peoples, retreated to the entrenched position of colonial
military power *Lui, lui* or is it *Luisillo, Luisillo*. This is a poem that
remains to be read.

Peralta is not alone, therefore, in turning his attention away from
the indigenous voice that he himself evoked in the old testament of
the Inca princess, and developing instead a projectional vision. And
as I have just suggested, his prophecy proves intermittently to be
near to the writing of the late eighteenth-century Enlightenment in
the attention he devotes to land and landscape. It is a French poet
of that later moment, André Chénier (1762–94), who perhaps most
succinctly outlines such a plan in the notes he left for "L'Amérique" (in progress ca. 1784–92), an epic poem barely begun at the
time of his death. "It is necessary in this work," writes Chénier,
"either when the poet speaks, or through the mouthpiece of the
characters, or in the prophetic speeches of supernatural beings, to
describe from one end to the other absolutely the whole geography
of the known world" (Chénier 1958, 417). Peralta's purview is
more limited, but the geographical impulse is nonetheless plain.
The forty octavas reales of the prophecy that complete canto 4 are
dedicated to this task, with copious notes providing additional
information from the various branches of natural science that Peralta professed. As a sample of the peculiar mixture of a mildly
baroque periphrastic construction and the precision of a new scientific posture, I cite a description of the Paraná River as compared to
the Amazon, with Peralta's accompanying note:

> Igual, si no en grandeza, en noble fama,
> En altura mayor al mar fenece

El que del Paraguay dueño se aclama,
Líquido corazon por quien florece.*
*El río Paraná, cuyo nombre significa mar en la lengua de los Jarayes
que lo habitan: dícese que nace de una laguna de aquella region. D.
Martín del Barco Centenera, canónigo de la cuidad de la Plata, en su
poema de la Argentina, afirma tener su cauce nueve leguas. Entra en
el mar por Buenos-Aires en altura de 36 grados y tiene de boca 34
leguas con varias islas, entre las cuales son las principales las de San
Gabriel.

(Peralta 1863, 92 and note 69)

Equal, if not in grandeur, in noble fame,
Expiring, higher, to the sea it rushes
That which of Paraguay lord is proclaimed,
Liquid heart by whom it flourishes
*The Paraná River, whose name means sea in the language of the
Jarayes who live there: it is said that its source is a lagoon in that
region. Don Martín del Barco Centenera, canon of the city of the
[Río de] la Plata, in his poem about Argentina, affirms that it runs
nine leagues deep. It enters the sea at Buenos Aires at 36° latitude
and at its mouth it is 34 leagues wide with several islands, among
which the main ones are those of San Gabriel.

The composite offers a compendium of the literary values of a
belated age. Metonymic paraphrase stands in for a straightforward
designation (reference to Paraguay instead of Paraná), debouching,
ultimately, in the mild metaphor, "Líquido corazon" ("Liquid
heart"). Science is running toward high tide: the discoveries of William Harvey with respect to the circulation of the blood (first published in 1628) underwrite the figure, without, however, providing
poetic vigor. The poet's own waning confidence in the communica-
tive power of the baroque figuration is evidenced by the decision to
supply the proper name in his erudite note. There in the prose, as
Peralta follows the course of the river, his description takes on
greater specificity, but at the same time and indeed as a consequence of the increasing attention to precise observation, he
digresses ever farther from the verses he is annotating.

If Peralta concludes the note with quantitative measures in the
growing scientific spirit of the day, he finds the point of origin in
a different mode. Returning to that source, I emphasize again that
Peralta's capacious erudition included American writers, and not
only the prose of el Inca Garcilaso, but also the poetry of Martín

Barco Centenera.[15] Here, then, is an early example of internal commerce in American letters—albeit secondary to the presence of Virgil and other writers of European antiquity—which, much enhanced, will be the foundation of national literary traditions a century later. That he should turn to *La Argentina* for geographical information, moreover, alerts the reader of his own *Lima fundada* that Peralta views poetry as a source of instruction far more than a cause of delight. Like his contemporary Giambattista Vico (Italy 1668–1744), Peralta claims a priority for poetry as a cognitive discipline: "if men were constrained to political life, the constraints were the first conquests of verse"; "even ritual, before being legal, was already poetic" (Peralta 1863, vi). Hence, at the very fountainhead of the river, rumor ("dícese" ["it is said"]) preexists poetry; but more primordial still, one finds the indigenous languages of America. For Peralta, these languages form a barrier to a literate representation of historical continuity. His passing gloss points unwittingly to what will be the single most critical issue in an American literary debate a century later: is there an American poetic language? And failing that, can there be a distinctly American poetry?

   Peralta's implicit response is precisely to shift the foundation of American culture from history to geography, as Salvatierra had done before him and Bello would come to do thereafter. That is, where his Inca princess exalts her lineage by recounting her history, Peralta finds himself obliged to forego that resource at the outset of the prophecy. The only American history at the moment of Pizarro's rapture is hers. That history of indigenous peoples is effaced by the recourse to geographical description. The land itself, as though it were uninhabited, becomes the foundation of a new history and its corresponding poetry. It is here that emerges most clearly the "celo de la patria" ["patriotic zeal"] that Peralta had cited in the prolog to his *Lima fundada* as the motivation for taking up the mantle of Virgil and deploying the invention of the prophecy:

> Demás de los que cría celebrados
> Tu América animales numerosos,
> Tantos producirá nobles ganados,
> Que de lana serán golfos copiosos:
> Jamás el Bétis mantendrá en sus prados
> Zéfiros mas veloces, mas hermosos,

Ni el Jarama verá rayos mas fieros,
Dignos de ser Pegasos, ser luceros.

(Peralta 1863, 98)

Besides those beasts, numberless and justly
Famed, that your America raises,
As many will she produce, of noble flocks
Which will be abundant gulfs of wool:
Never will the meadows of Guadalquivir
Know zephyrs so swift, nor more beautiful,
Nor will Jarama see bolts more fierce,
The equals of Pegasuses and of the stars.

Already in Peralta's *Lima fundada* of 1732 it is the bountiful landscape that offers quite literally the grounds upon which an autonomous American identity may challenge Spain: American agricultural abundance against the cultural heritage of the Old World, of descriptive verse against mythological allusion.

4

Modern Spanish American historical consciousness is formed in a period in which the Conquest and its fulfillment in continuing Spanish dominion are challenged—first, from without, rather than within. The political economy of the Spanish trade monopoly comes under attack by an ascendant British navy, whose incursions raise fresh questions for an American identity in its relation to the Spanish crown. In 1741, within a decade of the printing of *Lima fundada*, the English attack Cartagena, the principle Atlantic port of the vice-royalty of Peru. The defense evokes another epic poem preserved in the Real Jardín Botánico in Madrid among the manuscripts of José Celestino Mutis (Spain 1732–1808), one of the chief explorers in a generation of scientific expeditionaries. It seems Mutis included a specimen of local poetry to complement his collections of flora and fauna.[16] The anonymous and untitled poem on the defense of Cartagena de Indias, which may be dated within the living memory of the event, is the fruit of such renewed scholarship, a text brought to light by Guillermo Hernández de Alba, and edited and annotated magisterially by Guillermo Hernández Peñalosa in 1982.

The steady march of the poem's two hundred seventy-nine octa-

vas reales, ponderous at times, gives evidence of a well-schooled
poet. The strictures of the meter and exigencies of the closing couplets to each stanza appear often to compel the poet to a baroque
accumulation of descriptive modifiers. And if late twentieth-century tastes might rue such adherence to formal pattern with its consequent verbosity, I would stress that its opposite, freedom of
expression, is a theme at the heart of the poem and its political
argument. British Parliament, held accountable here for the war, is
characterized at several reprises as the site of "furores y asperezas/
con tormentos y gritos yndecentes" (Hernández de Alba and Hernández Peñalosa 1982, 112) ["rages and bitterness/with storms and
indecent shouting"], that invert the proper political order:

> a su dictamen, a sus expedientes
> el reyno se aprisiona o se cautiva;
> cámara o parlamento es ya sublime
> que ympone leyes y aun al rey comprime.
>   (Hernández de Alba and Hernández Peñalosa 1982, 111)

> by its dictates, by its decrees
> the kingdom is imprisoned or enchained;
> chamber or parliament is so sublime
> that it imposes laws and the king himself constrains.

The English naval hero who led the invasion, Edward Vernon,
becomes a further example of the same unbridled expression when
he allows himself the liberty of a prophecy in his exhortation to his
troops in which he foresees victory, glory and a considerable booty
(168–71). Vernon's rhetorical presumption is belied by a prior
prophecy, formulated in baroque mythological trappings: Amphi-
trite is frightened and offended by the immensity of the British fleet
and complains to Neptune; the sea god then pronounces against the
English, who, like their government, "Proceden con tan libres osa-
días,/con tan boluntariosas opiniones" (163) ["Proceed with reckless boldness, / with headstrong opinions"]. Neptune's anathema
represents an interesting combination of classical poetics (i.e. the
same Virgilian figure of prophecy central to Peralta), Enlightenment philosophy and loyalist politics. The British are condemned
for their hubris, translated here as "la soberbia detestable y fiera/lo
que más abomina el alto cielo" (164) ["brute and detestable
arrogance/ that which the high heavens most abhor"]; but that sin is
glossed in the spirit of the eighteenth century as "Estraña ceguedad,

fuerte desdoro del *racional talento* peregrino" (164, emphasis added) ["Strange blindness, harsh blemish on the singular *talent of reason*"], whose antithesis is enunciated in a formula that underwrites the resistance of Cartagena in the name of the Spanish monarchy:

> saver que en la avrebiada umana ciencia
> sólo se haze feliz con la obediencia.
> (Hernández de Alba and Hernández Peñalosa 1982, 164)

> to know that in abbreviated human knowledge
> only obedience leads to happiness.

This passionate fidelity to the Spanish crown is a temporal marker. More zealous still in expression, if not in the discharge of military duties, is another anonymous poem of the same era and the same hostilities, "Dolorosa métrica esprecion del Sitio, y entrega de la Havana, dirigida a N. C. Monarca el S^r. D^n. Carlos Tercero q^e. Gue," written in ten décimas in the wake of the successful capture of Havana by the British in 1762. The latter poem assails the colonial authorities, rather than the enemy, for surrendering the city too hastily to an opposing force "tan pocos y Protextantes" (Dolorosa 1960, 38) ["so few and Protestant"], and lamenting to Carlos III "quanto en perderte perdemos" (39) ["how much in losing you we lose"], urges him—"Ay Padre! Ay Señor! Ay Rey!" (40) ["Oh Father! Oh Lord! Oh King!"] to recover Havana, "por paz ó por guerra" ["by peace or by war"], as concludes the closely related, and indeed far more vigorous prose text, "Memorial dirigida á Cárlos III por las señoras de la Habana en 25 de Agosto de 1762" (Mexico 1763 [Memorial 1982, 167]). Enrique Saínz favors the thesis that both the prose and the poetry are the work of one author, Beatriz de Jústiz y Zayas (Cuba, 1733–1803). Although Saínz inveighs against the use of biblical allusions in the "Dolorosa métrica esprecion," it would be well to underline that they move deliberately to a climactic reference to Rachel, Mary and Esther, whose purpose, all the more clear in light of Saínz's authorial attribution, can only be to distinguish the fortitude of Havana's women from the failures of the men (see Saínz 1983, 150–54).

The more ambitious poem related to the defense of Cartagena remains closer to Peralta's *Lima fundada* than to the "Dolorosa métrica esprecion," however, in its recourse to natural history. Here, too, one finds descriptions of rivers, of climate, of natural resources, accompanied by detailed prose notes. Peralta shows himself the more modern thinker with reference to the economic concomitants of his geographical interests. For where the anonymous poet concentrates exclusively on mineral wealth, Peralta's recognition of the value of agriculture participates in the shift in economic theory associated with the French physiocrats in the eighteenth century:

> Si no brillantes, útiles produce
> La tierra otros tesoros vegetables,
> En quienes especial fuerza reluce,
> Con que debela males formidables . . .
>
> (Peralta 1863, 96)

> If not brilliant, then other, useful
> Vegetable treasures the land produces,
> In which special strength shines forth,
> with which to combat formidable ills . . .

On the other hand, the anonymous poet of the siege of Cartagena introduces an autobiographical note that marks the place for an emerging self, whose development will be a leading issue for a century of literary history. A first-person voice appears in the introductory stanzas to announce the plan of the work—"Respectaré cultas discrepciones/que hazen tan bellas sus erudiciones;" "Templaré todo el brillo que contiene/la fértil mithologica profana" (Hernández de Alba and Hernández Peñalosa 1982, 110) ["I will respect cultivated descriptions/that so beautify their erudition"; "I will temper all the brilliance/to be found in fertile, profane myth"]— and to invoke King Philip V (110) only to recede quickly from view. When it returns in the midst of the geographical disquisitions of *Cantto Terzero*, however, it has shifted from the position of the place holder in that antique topos to a figure of narrative authority. At first this is only an exhortation to control an urge to digress:

> Silenciaré ¡o dulce, o patria amada!
> el ynclito valor, la docta ciencia
> con [que] ynstruies y brillas exaltada
> (Hernández de Alba and Hernández Peñalosa 1982, 139)

> I will silence, oh sweet, oh beloved homeland,
> the illustrious valor, the learned science
> with [which] you instruct and gloriously shine

But in thus apostrophizing the Navarra region of Spain, the poetic voice grants itself a geographical identity, in effect breaking silence rather than maintaining it. With this partial breach of anonymity, the poetic voice proves a moveable self, whose geographic coordinates are essential to the poem. For when the first-person speaker reenters the text, he does so as a witness to the very scenes he describes—"he logrado berle" (143) ["I have succeeded in seeing it"]—or more forcefully yet, as a unique veridical source and so a trustworthy judge:

> Del Perú y deste Reyno, yo aseguro
> con gran satisfación, con evidencias,
> que no habrá otro que tenga tan seguro
> conocimiento y claras experiencias;
> esto muebe, esto anima el cielo puro
> que bierto en estas fieles adbertencias;
> sean, para enmendar tántos herrores,
> luces mis quexas, rayos mis clamores.
> (Hernández de Alba and Hernández Peñalosa 1982, 147)

> From Peru and this Kingdom, I assure
> with great satisfaction, with proofs,
> that no one else has such sure
> knowledge and clear experience;
> this moves, this inspires the pure heavens
> that I pour into these trustworthy notes;
> in order to emend so many misconceptions,
> may my complaints be lights and my cries thunderbolts.

The stanza shows the poet as yet at a point of transition between the poetics of two different ages. He is, on the one hand, a social critic who proceeds under the aegis of the fundamental Enlightenment response to traditional dogma: "ai cosas que se esquiban a la ciencia/y sólo las percibe la esperiencia" (156) "there are things that evade knowledge/and are only perceived by experience"]. And to the witness of his personal experience, the poet adds the support of a potential network of American intertextuality: "in the far reaches of the province of Paraguay . . . they have preserved a chasuble with which [Saint Francisco Solano] used to say mass, and a notebook of the talks that he preached to the Indians, all in his own hand, that I have seen with special pleasure and veneration" (142). The anonymous poet thus diverts attention from colonial history to begin to draw the map of an independent subject, the reading and writing self, without the benefit of a central name.

Yet "mis peregrinaciones repetidas" (Hernández de Alba and Hernández Peñalosa 1982, 147) ["my repeated peregrinations"] are not sufficient in themselves to authorize his account. Instead, they are presented as a secular martyrdom which he counts upon to move the only true authority on high, whence derives the poetic power that descends through him in a closing verse still fashioned out of the cramped syntax and elliptical allusions of the baroque. The poet himself recognizes the constraint: "Ya que por largos ttiempos he tenido/comprimido el silencio en dura prensa" ["for long periods I have held/silence constrained in a strong press"] (148), though he also admits that he himself has been the agent of that repression—"Reprimeré con pluma recatada" (139) ["I will repress with pen reserved"]—at least with respect to his interest in his native Navarra. For the moment, dating the poem roughly to the mid-1740s, and for some time to come, the self may slip the *dura prensa* on condition that "no procuro mi bien, sino el de todos" (148) ["I do not seek my good, but that of all"]. Private speech is for the public good. Where the reverse holds sway, this anonymous poet directs the force of his Enlightenment critique of governmental malpractice in the colonies:

> Comúnmente es el celo al real servicio
> un fervor de la pluma y de la boca,
> que ampara el fraude, que autoriza el vicio
> y rara vez al corazón le toca.
> Hipócrita estudioso, exterior juicio
> que engaña y en lo ynterno se revoca,
> el ynterés del Rey es un boceado
> antemural a otro ynterés privado.
> (Hernández de Alba and Hernández Peñalosa 1982, 144)

> Zeal in service of the king is commonly
> a fervor of the pen and of the mouth,
> that shelters fraud and authorizes vice
> and reaches to the heart uncommonly.
> Outward judgment, studious hypocrisy
> that deceives and inwardly reneges,
> the interest of the King is oft invoked
> and yet the rampart merely of self-interest.

Maravall has drawn attention to the moral, but also political-economic judgment that condemns self-interest as a peculiar note of eighteenth-century Spain. I would offer a partial response to his open-ended questions (Maravall 1991, 262, 264), by observing here that this condemnation commits the poetic voice of this anonymous poem to the purely external language of scientific objectivity. The self has no interiority as yet, or more precisely, like the "no ymbestigada" ["uncharted"] sea, poetic language is not yet an instrument capable of sounding the depths: "la humana comprehensión tan limitada,/ . . . /sólo puede sondear la superficie" (Hernández de Alba and Hernández Peñalosa 1982, 159) ["limited human understanding/ . . . /fathoms but the surface"]. Nevertheless, the awareness of unplumbed depths, of a repressed layer ("Reprimeré") beneath the reserved pen, or more simply of the breach between expression ("exterior juicio") and meaning ("lo ynterno") opens language to just the irony that Paz signals as the keynote of modernity in *Los hijos del limo*—though he himself will not find it until modernismo in Hispanic verse—an irony that will flourish in the later eighteenth century in satiric unmaskings of the "Hipócrita estudioso" and his ilk.

The didactic stance of the poem on the defense of Cartagena ("enmendar tántos herrores") had revealed itself as a mode of racial subjugation. In a note the poet tells of a music exam in the Amazon:

Swimming from island to island across the whole Río Grande, I reached Santa Lucía the day of a festival; . . . Father Maciel celebrated mass and the Indian girls officiated, forming a chorus and singing with scores in their hands and with trained and pleasant voices. . . . I was so pleased and impressed that having had lessons at court not long ago on a musical instrument . . . when the mass was over I bid the priest call a little Indian girl whom I selected, about nine years old; having done so, I determined to examine her in solfeggio and I was obliged to admit that she was more advanced than I; in this respect, and in many other capacities the *Tapes* or *Guaraní* Indians of the missions of the reverend fathers of the Company were extremely skilled. (Hernández de Alba and Hernández Peñalosa 1982, 142–43)

Much like Peralta, this anonymous poet is more innovative in prose, and here he wears his ironies self-consciously. With respect to solfeggio, it is impossible for him to say without a note of self-deprecating humor just whose steps follow whose. The nine-year old Guaraní is surely following the course of the author's European education; but, undisturbed by geographical and cultural distances, she has already left the poet in her wake. Had she sufficient political leverage to reverse the roles, she might have forced the irony further. The poet would have been unlikely to have fared so well on an examination in the music of the Guaraní. But the poet passes over that music in silence, occluding indigenous cultural history beneath his active interest in American natural history.

Literary and political history converge here, of course. It was colonial policy that the indigenous peoples must follow in the cultural footsteps of the conquerors, with the missionaries, from Father Maciel on the Paraná to Father Salvatierra in Baja California, acting as the primary agents of the acculturation. Thus, as late as 1770 Carlos III was still issuing an edict in support of Pastoral V, "In order that the Indians learn Castilian" (Mexico 1769) of Francisco Lorenzana y Buitrón, archbishop of Mexico, wherein the king urged that "universal knowledge [of Castilian] is necessary in order to facilitate the governing and spiritual guidance of the Indians; in order that the latter might be understood by their superiors, conceive a love for the conquering nation, banish idolatry, and be civilized for purposes of business and commerce" (Edict 15, 1 April 1770, cited in appendix 1 of Heath 1972, 216). In so doing, however, Carlos III was only reiterating prior royal edicts dating back well over a century. That the same orders should be reissued to correct the "present poor knowledge of Castilian" (218) and "with the object that one day it will come to pass that the different idioms used in those same dominions [i.e. the American colonies] may be extinguished and only Castilian spoken" (220) is itself sufficient proof that the day had not come as the anonymous poet administered his music exam—nor has it yet.

It remains possible to review the exam from the indigenous perspective, if not on the Paraná, then in the Yucatan in the same period, in a poem under the heading of the Mayan couplet "Ah tzaab can/H kuukul kuul can," "Rattlesnake/And Feathered Serpent" in Munro S. Edmonson's translation (Edmonson 1982, 188), which tells of the arrival of *X ah chapaat*, The Lord Centipede in the ancient times of the giants and the hunchbacks.[17] The poem is drawn from a Mayan manuscript in Roman characters first published by Alfredo Barrera Vásquez under the title *El libro de los cantares de Dzitbalché* (Barrera Vásquez 1965).[18] Based on the orthography of the transcription, Barrera Vásquez dates the text to the eighteenth century some time after the conventions established by Fray Pedro Beltrán de Santa Rosa in his *Arte del idioma maya*, written in 1742 and published in Mexico in 1746 (Barrera Vásquez 1965, 14). Edmonson accepts the *terminus ante quem* for the manuscript, but broadens the span of composition, speculating that two of the poems (including one dated by Barrera Vásquez to the year 1742) existed in oral form in the fifteenth century, and that others may be nineteenth-century texts; however, elsewhere Edmonson and Victoria R. Bricker (Edmonson and Bricker 1985, 52) date the collection as a whole to the eighteenth century. I shall follow that dating, making *Los cantares de Dzitbalché* roughly contemporaneous with the anonymous poem of the defense of Cartagena.[19]

Edmonson and Bricker indicate that the eighteenth century is especially well-documented in the areas of Yucatec Mayan and Quiché literatures (Edmonson and Bricker 1985, 51; Edmonson 1985, 121). "Perhaps the most distinctive quality of Maya literature is that it is all poetry," they further claim (Edmonson and Bricker 1985, 59), explaining in their study of Yucatec Mayan literature: "If there is a distinction in Maya between poetry and prose, it would have to be made between formal and informal speech. . . . There is a continuum of formalization, but the basis of it is the semantic couplet, and virtually all of Mayan literature is cast in this form" (59).[20] As concerns the case in hand, both Barrera Vásquez and Edmonson stress the lyric quality of the songs of Dzitbalché. In that regard they constitute a unique specimen: "for without [this collection] we would be hard pressed to document Mayan lyric poetry," writes Edmonson (Edmonson 1982, 173; see Barrera Vásquez 1965, 13). Remembering the solfeggio exam, I also note that Barrera Vásquez further underscores the musical setting of the *cantares*, which, he states, based on the internal evidence of the texts themselves, "without a doubt were sung dancing" (Barrera Vásquez 1965, 13).

Barrera Vásquez and Edmonson diverge greatly in their translations of the conclusion of "Rattlesnake and Feathered Serpent." In Edmonson's version, "Then there was no one/Who spoke to [Lord Centipede]" (Edmonson 1982, 189), whereas for Barrera Vásquez there was in fact a reply; however, it seems that in either case Lord Centipede was enraged, "Because he was the one who was deceived" (Edmonson 1982, 189)—suggesting a cautionary note for the reading of the anonymous poet's sanguine assessment of the solfeggio exam. There is further disagreement about Lord Centipede's primary attribute: for Barrera Vásquez, he has seven heads; in Edmonson's translation they are only seven necklaces. But again, despite this discrepancy, the common element of the number seven would support Edmonson's identification of Lord Centipede with "the Spaniards of the 7-day week" (Edmonson 1982, 187), which is to say that here in Yucatan, as on the banks of the Paraná, the path of indigenous footsteps is crossed by the colonizers posing questions, which, the Mayan text specifies, are understood as a menace: "To eat you/Or to give you trouble in your life/If you did not understand." I would further conjecture that the threat of being eaten, refers the intervention of the Spaniards in the cultural life of the Maya to a fundamental cosmic conception of "the universe as a phagohierarchy," which Eva Hunt explicates: "While lower orders of animals ate one another and plants, and man ate all of them, the gods ate men to subsist" (1977, 89). In this reading the Spaniards, as the Mayan-eating Lord Centipede, have usurped the place of the divine. If so, then Barrera Vásquez's contention that the couplet "Rattlesnake/And Feathered Serpent" is so irrelevant to the text as to be a scribal error (Barrera Vásquez 1965, 63, n. 1), might be questioned. Hunt identifies the group "crawlers and swimmers" as a taxonomical category in the Mayan transformational system, including the familiar figure of the Feathered Serpent, the Mesoamerican god Quetzalcoatl (Kukulkan among the Highland Maya) (1977, 74–80). And much as Quetzalcoatl is paired with Xolotl, his dark twin, as the morning and evening star aspects of Venus, for instance, so the titular couplet links the earthbound or underworld rattlesnake with the sky serpent. Lord Centipede might then be read as a transformation of the twin deities within the taxonomic classification of "crawlers," that is, once again, usurping their rightful place on the path of the Maya.

Edmonson refers to "Rattlesnake and Feathered Serpent" as "a brief myth, rather than a prayer or lyric" (187), and Barrera Vásquez (1965, 14), too, includes this text among the few in the collection that have been transcribed in the manuscript in columns as though they were in verse without truly being so. In other cases these scholars attest to great lyric beauty and, I would add, what appears to be metatextual self-consciousness of that lyric power. I refer to the interrelated erotic poems "Let Us Go and Take the Flower" and "Flower Song," where the multivocal image of the flower is, in addition to its literal presence in the resplendent catalog of rose and first flower, dog jasmine and tangleflower, copal and cane vine (Edmonson 1982, 182), both the vulva of the maidens and their song. "Flower song," as Edmonson explains, "is the Nahuatl kenning of 'Poem' " (1982, 181). Hence, when the virgins sing their joy "Because we are going/To begin/Taking/Our flowers,/All women together,/Redeemers" (Edmonson 1982, 180), they are celebrating their immanent deflowering—in marriage, according to Barrera Vásquez (1965, 39, n. 1)—but also their own poetry in a text that Edmonson (1982, 179) signals as unique in ascribing the poetic voice to a female singer, who dedicates song and sex to the syncretistic female divinities of the moon: "The lady Christ Mary,/ Virgin Fire of the Moon,/And likewise the beautiful Corn Lady" (Edmonson 1982, 180–81). So it would appear that when Jesus came, the corn mother did not always go away (cf. R. Gutiérrez 1991), at least not immediately, at least not in song, wherein two antagonistic cultures can be wed in a couplet.

That balance remains an ideal. Transculturation, the reciprocal influence in the meeting of cultures was unequal.[21] Indigenous influence, after all, was regarded as the path of iniquity by Christian conquerors. Thus, in the face of a verbal miscue that amounted to a doctrinal error, a Franciscan friar in Mexico in 1731 could defend himself by laying the blame on the onerous effects of transculturation: "he excused himself for his blunder," Pablo González Casanova relates, "confessing that he had spent many years among the Indians to learn their languages and he had forgotten his own" (González Casanova 1958, 30). If contact can rob a Franciscan friar of his native tongue, so too on the other side of the political disequilibrium, it can make a gruesome dumb-show of indigenous peoples:

> Espectáculos horribles,
> que estaban sin voz diciendo,
> por querernos levantar
> en esta altura nos vemos
>
> (Vargas Ugarte 1951, 87)

> Horrible spectacles,
> which were mutely speaking,
> for wishing to rise up
> you see us at this height

as an anonymous poet describes the supposedly edifying spectacle of the hanged leaders of an indigenous rebellion in "Relación y verdadero romance que declara la inconsiderada y atrevida subleva-

ción que intentaron hacer los indios mal acordados y algunos
mestizos en la ciudad de Lima. 1750."

5

Political tensions, whether between throne and nobility in Peninsular Spain as described by Maravall, or between the suppressed
indigenous peoples and imperial interests, make the theme of overreaching a crucial motif in baroque literature (see Benjamin 1977).
As a concommitant, baroque poetry is replete with versions of the
fall, often worked out by allusion to the mythological figures of
crash landings. Thus José Surí (Cuba 1696–1762) writes with metatextual self-consciousness in "A San José":

> ¿No ves que á vista de tanto,
> Sublime, elevado objeto,
> Icáreas ruinas aguardan
> A faetones intentos . . . ?
>
> (Lezama Lima 1965, 1:267)

> Don't you see in plain view
> of such sublime, elevated objects,
> Icarean ruins await
> Phaetonic undertakings . . . ?

But the most brilliant explorer of the figure of the fall in and of
late baroque poetry was the Jesuit Juan Bautista Aguirre (Ecuador
1725–86). Aguirre is the best of the Spanish American poets writing in Spanish in the first three quarters of the eighteenth century
and the only rival to the Quechua poet of "Manchay Puitu" and the
Mayan flower songs of Dzitbalché.[22]

Aguirre began his poetic career around midcentury, as a flagrant
gongorista, as seen on the early elegiac occasion of "Da noticia a
un amigo suyo de la muerte de un prebendado" (1748):

> Hipocrene congelando
> su instable cristal sonoro
> llora perlas en las conchas
> de su rizo cauce undoso.
>
> (Aguirre 1984, 255)

Hippocrene congealing
its unstable sonorous crystal
cries pearls in the shells
of its deep bed and rippled.

Thus, if the waters of the Muses' well at Hippocrene are unstable, that is fleeting, the baroque poet's burden is to stay their course. Aguirre allegorizes the fundamental baroque trope of *fijeza* in his "Fábula de Atalanta e Hipomenes."[23] There the young hero, a poet too slow afoot to realize his desire finds a properly baroque artifice in Venus's golden apples, "y a la ninfa/[. . .]el curso interrumpe" ["and of the nymph/ . . . interrupts the course"] (Aguirre 1984, 236).

A more ambitious poem of 1750, "Rasgo épico a la llegada de la misión del P. Tomás Nicto Polo, de la Compañía de Jesús a la ciudad de Guayaquil por el P. J. B. A. de la misma Compañía" written, as Aguirre states in the opening octava real, at the age of twenty-four, makes emphatic claim to its baroque filiation.[24] Such staunch allegiance to Góngora makes Aguirre a throwback—polemically so. For the allusion is transumptive in Bloom's revisionary sense (Bloom 1975, 102–3), that is designed to skip over Aguirre's immediate predecessors and to found thereby a false claim to priority over them (i.e. originality), by asserting a greater kinship to the earlier and greater figure of Góngora. The intermediate poets thus suppressed are those who, like Peralta or the anonymous poet of the defense of Cartagena, have begun to temper their baroque technique with the interests and observations of Enlightenment science. The poetic procedure is especially evident, for instance, when Aguirre relates Polo's voyage to the New World not to the eighteenth-century travels of La Condamine, for instance, nor even Columbus, but rather by transumptive allusion to Jason and the Argonauts:

¡Salve, nave mejor que aquel primero
batel feliz que, en pasos del destino,
por el desierto azul abrió sendero
siendo norte a su rumbo el vellocino!

(Aguirre 1984, 274)

Hail, bark better than that first
happy ship that on its destined way
blazed a trail through the desert blue,
the polestar of its path ever the fleece.

The curious result is to cast the Jesuit mission as an expeditionary force in the conquest mode, a latter-day Pizarro of a belated baroque epic, headed to America to steal away its golden treasure.

Landfall brings calamity to this revisionary stance. As we have seen, Aguirre's contemporaries had begun, tentatively, to catalog American natural history in verse, pointing the way forward to a distinctive American thematics. I have already suggested that the naturalist idiom is an addendum to conquest, since it eliminates the presence and cultural history of the indigenous populations. Aguirre argues on a different front. An uncompromising gongorist aesthetic is his bulwark against the prosaic manner (literally, often, the prose notes) in which Enlightenment natural history made its way into verse. Thus, in contrast to precise observations of the local environment to be found in Peralta's *Lima fundada*, Aguirre limits his description of the immediate scene before Polo's eyes to the brusque notation that there was a promontory, that it was green, that it was semi-circular, before investing his poetic energies once more in classical allusion:

> de Guáyac que del sur en la tez lisa
> esmeralda se miente nadadora,
> e Icaro verde que, calzado espumas,
> al aire pena con frondosas plumas.

(Aguirre 1984, 263)

> of Gauyác which in the smooth complexion
> of the south, false an emerald bather seems,
> and Icarus green which, shod in foam,
> wounds the air with frothing, wavy plumes.

The flight of a more brilliant poetic imagination is due for a fall. Yet in alienating himself from contemporary literature, Aguirre springs farthest ahead where he looks farthest back.

A sidelong glance at English literature illuminates that course. For there we find that the breakthrough to romanticism at the turn of the nineteenth century was also accomplished by a transumptive leap: Wordsworth and company passing over the neoclassicism of Dryden and Pope and of the influential descriptive poetry of Thomson's *The Seasons* (1730) and turning back in literary history to engage the greater achievement of Milton. Thus, Byron's Cain, to choose an example dear to Unamuno, learns from Milton's Satan (the continental and secularized model is Rousseau) that the modern self is the diabolical consolation for the fall from grace. Such a self, angry and alienated, splendid in its isolation and bold in its own defense, as the villain Edmund says at the close of *Lear*—for even Milton had precursors—is its own daimon: part devil, part demiurge, a residence for an internalized genius. To round out this brief note in comparative literary history, I recall that late eighteenth-century Hispanic writers knew Milton—Jovellanos translated part of *Paradise Lost*—but led or perhaps deliberately misled by Cadalso, they read with predilection the *Night Thoughts* of Edward Young (1742–44) as did much of Europe, and imbibed from there as well as, say, the lachrymose strain in Rousseau's *Nouvelle Heloise* (1761), a melancholic sensibility without the fundamental rage that inspires much of English romantic verse, from the more tempered Wordsworth to Shelley at his wildest. Susan Kirkpatrick's suggestive remark concerning the cultural distance between Catholic Spain and the Protestant tradition in England in the later phase of romanticism is also germane here (Kirkpatrick 1988, 261). Young's Protestant consolations may seem an odd match, but Milton's direct engagement with—one might also say challenge to—the Bible make him an even more inaccessible model for poetic ambition in Spain's conservative religious culture. In this regard, Cadalso's protégé Meléndez Valdes, would be an influential source for the next generation of the Salamanca school when he wrote out his own night thoughts: "y la cítara fúnebre templemos,/ ¡Oh Young! que tú tañías . . ." ["and let us tune the funereal lyre/ Oh Young! that you were wont to play"] (Meléndez Valdés 1981, 244–45).

In the light of that literary history and its detour around the sources of romanticism, one reads with a sense of opportunity lost Aguirre's late fragment, "A la rebelión y caída de Luzbel y sus secuaces." The poem proceeds as a dialogue of styles. There is, on the one hand, a style which, if still baroque in diction and cadence, is nonetheless more subdued, allowing the lineaments of narrative to emerge more visibly. And then there is the voice of Luzbel, who continues to be the poet that Aguirre himself had been in his first youth, speaking in swirling, recondite grammar, as in this, his opening lines in the second stanza:

> ¿En lóbrego no puedo, ardiente, horrendo
> desorden, espantoso a la fortuna,

> el universo todo confundiendo,
> ahogar al sol en su dorada cuna?
>
> (Aguirre 1984, 288)

> In gloomy, can I not, burning, horrid
> disorder, awful to fortune,
> the whole universe confounding,
> drown the sun in its golden crib?

The question is not simply rhetorical. That is, even if Luzbel believes he knows the answer in advance, the rhetoric is nonetheless a staging of a complex, even unprecedented psychological situation for Spanish American poetry. For the satanic rebellion has not yet begun as he speaks those verses. Those who will be his followers are as yet among the faithful. In consequence, there is no one to whom Luzbel can address this impious thought. For want of an interlocutor, he begins, by dint of rhetorical convention, to hollow out an interiority in which he himself might answer. Luzbel succeeds in creating that space in the briefest of passages, a verse merely, though the last, in a poem of some fourteen octavas reales:

> así pagó su loco atrevimiento
> este aterrado embrión del *Aqueronte*,
> y así padece, aun más que en el abismo,
> horrible infierno dentro de sí mismo.
>
> (Aguirre 1984, 290)

> thus he paid for his mad audacity
> this frightful embryo of *Acheron*,
> and thus he suffers, more yet than the abyss,
> a hell within himself most horrible.

It is the space, however hellish, in which a first self finds a first home in Spanish American poetry.[25]

Aguirre does not tarry to chart the paths of this unexplored interiority, nor does he give his Luzbel rein to pronounce upon the dimensions of his abyss. The poem remains a fragment. Daunted by his own achievement? And if so, on poetic or religious grounds? Juan María Gutiérrez recorded a marginal note to another fragmentary text, "Poema heroico á San Ignacio de Loyola," from Aguirre's manuscripts wherein the poet declared that he did not complete that poem "for lack of time and inclination," a commentary that

Gutiérrez cited as confirmation of "the frank and easy-going character" of Aguirre's writing (J. M. Gutiérrez 1865, 237). But its import may be amplified, for regardless of Aguirre's character and inclinations, time was in fact running out for the Jesuits:

> Don Juan de Roca y seis jueces
> que manejaron la empresa,
> entre sombras de la noche
> a la Compañía llegan
> y en cuatro cuerpos partidos
> por cuatro vientos la cercan
>
> (Vargas Ugarte 1951, 106)

> Don Juan de Roca and six judges
> who managed the affair,
> amidst the shadows of the night
> came to the Company of Jesus
> and divided into four bodies
> surrounded them on all four sides

writes the student Brother Juan Abad, a Peruvian Jesuit. For Carlos III had judged the Jesuits an autonomous power and a seditious presence within the dominions of the Spanish crown and so banished them by a royal decree in 1767.

6

The impact of the expulsion on Spanish American culture was great. As Javier Alegre (Mexico 1729–88) explained in the wake of the expulsion:

> there was hardly a family in all of New Spain that did not have a personal relationship with the Company, whether through a relative or a friend, or some dependent, to which may be added the general category of [Jesuit] instruction through which the majority of all those men who held curates, parishes, magistrates, civil posts, professorships, monk's orders and positions of high rank in the Republic had been educated. (Alegre 1941, 2:211)

His list may be extended still farther. Through their missionary work, the Jesuits were also leaders in the acquisition and codification of indigenous languages—recall, for instance, that even Father Salvatierra in the first permanent mission in Baja California had the benefit of a grammar written by the Jesuit Copart. The linguistic advances, in turn, enabled the Jesuits to become scholars of pre-Columbian indigenous culture. The leading figure in this respect was Francisco Javier Clavijero (Mexico 1731–87), whose master-piece, based of course on research conducted prior to 1767, was first published in exile and in Italian: *Storia antica de Mesico* (1780–81). Thus, at one blow the expulsion of the Jesuits obstructed access to the two classical cultures of Spanish American letters, Greco-Roman and pre-Columbian, banishing many of the best educators and best educated, and with them their poetry, which, perforce, reenters Spanish American literary history as an import in an expanded transatlantic intellectual commerce.[26]

Among the first of the publications in exile was a pirated edition of nineteen cantos of *De Deo, Deoque Homine Heroica* (Cadiz 1769) of Diego José Abad (Mexico 1727–79).[27] Abad brought out his own subsequent editions, expanded to thirty-three cantos (Venice 1773), then thirty-eight (Ferrara 1775). Finally, shortly before his death, he transmitted a version of forty-three cantos to a friend, which was published posthumously in Cesena in 1780, "defini-tively complete, with nothing to add nor to polish," according to his recent editor and translator (Fernández Valenzuela 1974, 41–42 and supplementary note).

Fernández Valenzuela stresses the baroque nature of *De Deo* in his valuable introduction, most clearly manifest, he explains, in the structure of the argument: "Whereas Virgil advances in a line of ascending progression, Abad proceeds contrapuntally" (Fernández Valenzuela 1974, 22), which is to say the poem explores its central theme, the nature of God, through the repetition, from canto to canto, of contrasting elements: primarily the inconstancy of human experience as opposed to the unchanging nature of the divine. The contrapuntal development casts Abad's praise of God as a story of good and evil. But he presents neither Virgil's Aeneas nor Aguirre's Luzbel to carry the burden of epic struggle. Indeed, there is neither epic nor struggle where an omnipotent God is the term for good, only acceptance or fall from grace; and the term for the fall, for evil, is temporality. Just when a modern historical consciousness is rising in the Spanish America of his birth and the Europe of his exile, Abad undertakes a late baroque defense of fixity, of an atemporal world view.

Abad is not unaware of the past, of course. On the contrary, he repeatedly recollects the past elegiacally as the subject of loss: "Oh Babyon! Babylon! Where now the marvel of your hanging gardens and your towers and your walls reaching to heaven?" he writes in contrast to the one God, immortal and unchanging (Abad 1974, 164). Or a still more explicit allusion to the classical sepulchral inscription: "*Here lies* [*Hic Iacet*] is all that of the kings remains today"(608; Abad's italics). But for Abad that loss is absolute. The present, then, is not the vestige of a past that was, a living amputee. Rather the relation of the present to the past is that of a perfect double, destined to repeat the past by vanishing in time without a trace. To conceive the temporal world as a succession of wholesale effacements is to render the past—and the present, too—illegible. In order to restore legibility, and with it, give purpose to his or any poem, Abad posits a daring trope in the canto that closed the pirate edition (which I take as the primitive text of *De Deo*)—daring, because it constitutes a renaming of God as well as a revision of Abad's own poem in progress.

In the first canto Abad essays a definition of God, working in contrast to a deprecatory resume of the Greco-Roman pantheon—multiple, carnal, mutable. I cite here the partial verse translation of an estimable Mexican poet of the next generation, Anastasio María Ochoa (1783–1833):

> Espíritu sublime y soberano
> Es Dios, sin cuerpo alguno cual nosotros,
> Que pudiera palparse con las manos
> O verse con los ojos: á la mente
> No es dado comprenderlo, cual no es dado
> Las aguas encerrar inmensurables
> En reducida concha del mar vasto,
> O tocar con la mano las estrellas.
>
> (Ochoa 1828, 197)

> Sublime and sovereign spirit
> Is God, incorporeal, unlike us,
> Who can touch our bodies with our hands
> Or see them with our eyes: to the mind
> It is not given to comprehend him,
> As it is not ours to enclose the immeasurable
> Waters of the vast sea in a small shell,
> Or touch the stars with outstretched hand.

Poetic figuration pertains to the senses, and here, where the object of description does not admit of sensual apprehension, figuration would appear to be at a total loss. Abad, however, plays a baroque opening gambit. A poetics of excess—that is of a disproportion of figuration to literal referent—is undeterred by this most extreme mismatch. Abad makes the poetic problem itself an occasion for a metaphor, and then for another, heaping figure on figure, distant stars on immeasurable seas, like Madre Castillo's fire on fire. The procedure, as boundless as the seas themselves in principle, is only closed off by allusion—indeed, a transumptive allusion that leaps over the baroque tradition and past Virgil, the stylistic model of Abad's Latin hexameters, to the Vulgate Bible, which Abad took to be the true source of poetry, older than the pagan muses, as he argued in the verse prolog. Faced with much the same poetic problem—finding an adequate designation for God— Exodus 3:14 offers the solution of God's laconic self-naming, rendered by Abad, "He has a sublime name: *Who-Is*" [*"Qui est"*] (Abad 1974, 124; Abad's emphasis): bedrock upon which to build his poem.

At the close of the primitive text in canto 19, Abad returns to the same figures in an instance of his structure of "concentric development" (Fernández Valenzuela 1974, 22):

> Bearing as we do the heart enclosed in the middle of the chest and guarded about within the straitest frame, it is for all a closed mystery. Man opens the bowels of the earth, and with his industry he guts it of hidden gold. . . . Furthermore, he spies the immeasurable and bottomless abyss of the seas, he plumbs it and calculates its depths, voyages through its mysteries, removes precious pearls beneath the blind swirl of the waters, and he redeems vast wealth from the voracious jaws of the waves. Still more, armed with a long scope, he mixes with the stars, he follows them persistently along their courses and difficult paths. . . . But to penetrate the secrets of the heart, he has not succeeded. (Abad 1974, 365)

So science does allow mankind to read the depths of earth and sea and to make off with their secrets. And, it turns out, if not the hand, then the eye, aided by the telescope, can reach the stars. In a world, however, in which the sun itself, in an innovative trope, is but a reflection of the more familiar inconstancy of the moon—"Look how inconstant is the moon"; "Likewise is the sun inconstant" (Abad 1974, 57 and 159)—natural history is as irrelevant to the eternal story of good and evil as is human history (i.e. the history of ancient civilizations such as Gibbon was writing in this period). Abad dismisses the researches of the worldly philosophers (373), or, more severely, takes their scientific curiosity as the figure for overreaching that was the heart of Aguirre's thematics: "thus as it is impossible to contemplate at leisure the splendors of the sun, and were one brazenly to attempt it, whoever dared to scrutinize the heavenly lights [caeli scrutarier ignes/tentans], will live condemned for life in interminable night," writes Abad (149) in antithetical, baroque style.

Abad argues that while human minds are thus preoccupied—and poetry led astray along the routes of nature description and national epic—God alone reads the one true mystery of the world, present at any and every moment, in the human heart. Abad names this reading God anew, substituting Jeremiah 17:10 for Exodus 3:14: "*He who scrutinizes hearts*, is the name of God" ["*Scrutans cor* nomen divinum est"] (Abad 1974, 366–67, Abad's italics).

The heart that *Scrutans cor* must decipher is a palimpsest. A primordial text of divine law is inscribed upon the heart (Abad 1974, 368)—prior to any religious instruction, prior even to human language, thereby accounting, incidentally, for the nobility of the noble savage in the New World missions (370). The divine text is overwritten, however, by desire, *voluntas*, described by Abad as a fugitive wind that passes in and out of the heart on the figurative wings of time's traditional iconography. A modern consciousness might well conceive of voluntas as the ruins of the text of the divine commandments, a result of time. But Abad is thoroughly dualistic. Evil does not derive from good, nor time from God in *De Deo*. Time is simply alien to eternity, obscuring the divine inscription.

A merciful *Scrutans cor* reads the changeless inscription through the subterfuges of time, translated suggestively by Fernández Valenzuela as a "camino bilingue," a bilingual road (Abad 1974, 67). God is unforgiving, however, when he returns in the last canto of the posthumous edition of 1780, the final concentric ring of argument. There he is the God of Judgment Day who strips away the temporal world of voluntas altogether to determine which hearts bear his text. In this final reading, time, as a middle term between heaven and hell, is eliminated, and as in the beginning when command and creation were one, so now judgment and execution are simultaneous:

Without delay these fall, enwrapped in the flames
of the abyss, and those rise to the realm of the sublime.

(Abad 1974, 742)

The rising current for Spanish American poetry will be the ode, which will redefine the sublime in the period to come. But however much the poetry rises, all in fact will fall—and the fall from these baroque heights will be the fall into history.

2

The Road to Independence 1778–1822

I

JOAQUÍN DE SANTA CRUZ Y CÁRDENAS, CONDE DE SAN JUAN DE Jaruco y de Mopox was a late-comer to the series of Enlightenment expeditionaries to America that sailed under the Spanish flag in the eighteenth century: Hipólito Ruiz and José Pavón in Peru and Chile (1777–88), José Celestino Mutis, whom we have encountered previously as the preserver of the poem on the defense of Cartagena, in Nueva Granada (1783–1808), Martín de Sessé and José Mariano Mociño in Nueva España (1787–1803), each in their separate regions, and the most ambitious, comprehending the whole of coastal America, the mission of Alessandro Malaspina (1789–94), are the principal figures.[1] As the head of the *Real Comisión de Guantánamo* (the Royal Commission of Guantanamo) Mopox was a late-comer from the local point of view as well:

> I attempted to learn of the state of the report on roads that the *Consulado* of Havana had initiated, and that the King resolved should be one of the objects of my commission; a provision that displeased that body and that moved it to urge its own services in that regard upon his Excellency, the Prince of Peace [i.e. Manuel Godoy], complaining that the charge which they had received from the *Ministerio de Hacienda* should be taken from them; but the King declared that this pertained to the first Secretary of State as did all the roads of the kingdom, and that I should continue in my charge. Consequently, you might well imagine the little that I could count upon the help of a jealous body, resentful for the offense that it supposed to arise from such an alteration. (Barreiro 1933, 110)

Thus writes Mopox in one of the few documents of the *Real Comisión de Guantánamo* that have found their way into print (Barreiro 1933). Publications of like material abound in the same period:

117

from Fray Iñigo Abad Lasierra, *Historiografía geográfica, civil y natural de la Isla de San Juan Bautista de Puerto Rico* (Madrid 1788) to Félix de Azara's twin studies of the quadrupeds and birds of Paraguay (Madrid 1802 and 1802–5, respectively), while Antonio de Ulloa's *Noticias americanas* (Madrid 1772) came out in a second edition in Madrid in 1792. Lesser-known figures and translations of foreign travelers were also available in print (e.g. Antonio Caulin, *Historia coro-graphica, natural y evangélica de la Nueva Andalucia* [Madrid 1779] or Juan Ignacio Molina, *Compendio de historia geográfica, natural, y civil del Reyno de Chile, escrito en italiano* [1782; trans. Madrid 1788–95]) as were new editions of reports from the recent as well as the distant past (e.g. Father José Gumilla's *El Orinoco Ilustrado* [first and second eds. 1741 and 1745, reprinted Barcelona 1791] and José Acosta's *Historia natural y moral de las Indias* [1590, reprinted in 1792]). The same activity, moreover, is manifest in America, reduced in scale to the limitations of an underdeveloped printing industry. José Antonio de Alzate y Ramírez was publishing a gazette of *Observaciones sobre la Física, Historia Natural y Artes Utiles* in Mexico in 1787, and prior to Mopox's arrival in Cuba, the *Capitanía general* in Havana had already brought out Antonio de Parra's *Descripción de diferentes piezas de Historia Natural las más del ramo marítimo representadas en setenta y cinco láminas* in 1787. Nevertheless, the papers of the Mopox expedition itself—collected in the Museo Naval in Madrid, generally in well-preserved, bound notebooks and often accompanied by hand drawn maps—were left almost entirely unpublished and remained much neglected until the recent work fomented by the bicentennial of the reign of Carlos III (see Sotos Serrano 1984 and Gomis Blanco 1987).

Mopox presented himself to a society already advancing in the establishment of Enlightenment institutions dedicated to the "scientific discovery of Cuba," to adapt the phrase of José Alcina Franch (Alcina Franch 1988) to the locale. Mopox's relations in Cuba, therefore, are not to be explained away as the suspicious reactions of the ignorant. The contrast with the warm reception of Humboldt is telling. As Juan Pérez de la Riva (Pérez de la Riva 1977, 8–9) notes, for instance, the Cuban economist Antonio del Valle Hernández accompanied Humboldt on the island and provided him with statistical information for his subsequent publications, as he did habitually for Francisco Arango y Parreño, the leading figure of the *Consulado*. Nevertheless, his own "Sucinta noticia de la situación de esta colonia. 1800" (Valle Hernández 1977), though integrally related to the *Real Comisión de Guantánamo*, was withheld from Mopox's report, appearing instead in Cuba (Havana 1800). On the one side, Humboldt's posture of scientific disinterestedness proved attractive: an outsider come to observe. Mopox, on the other hand, was not an interloper in a simple sense. He was himself an American returning to his native land and land holdings. His relations with the hegemonic sacchrocracy, therefore, are an exemplary case of the negotiations between self-interest and class interest.[2] With the textual production of the Jesuit exile already a prominent feature of the new period here in question (e.g. Abad's enlarged text of *De Deo*), the papers of the *Real Comisión de Guantánamo*, too, represent an alienated American consciousness surveying the native terrain. Unlike almost all of the Jesuits, however, Mopox would see his homeland with more than the mind's eye, and further, in contrast to Humboldt, he had come not merely to observe and record, but also to engage and to build.

The initial goals of the expedition were two-fold: to explore the Bay of Guantanamo on the southeast coast of Cuba and the surrounding countryside with a view toward founding a new colony there, hence the title of the *Real Comisión de Guantánamo*; and to conduct a land survey for the purposes of constructing a canal for enhanced internal traffic with Havana. The canal was never built, although a rail line was eventually laid along the path charted by the Mopox expedition. As for the Guantanamo project, a report by Juan Nepomuceno Quintana, the governor of Santiago de Cuba, the nearest colonial settlement of any consequence at the eastern end of the island, provides a context in which to consider Mopox's relations with the Consulado. Quintana dated his report 28 May 1796, that is, once again, prior to and independent of the Mopox expedition. He sent the document to Carlos IV's all-powerful minister Manuel Godoy, through an intermediary, Eugenio de Llaguno, who forwarded the report in turn, summarizing in his cover letter of 16 October 1796, "The Governor of [Santiago de] Cuba proposes what he considers the most ready means for the development of this eastern part of his command, without greater cost to the Crown" (Llaguno 1796, 57). It is presumably Godoy himself, in a hasty marginal note to Llaguno's letter dated 19 October 1796, who links Quintana's preoccupations to the *Real Comisión de Guantánamo*, which had already set sail while the report made its way across the Atlantic (57). The same time lapse in transatlantic communications affects the Royal Order of 7 August 1796 which called upon those on the island to assist Mopox. Upon receipt, Quintana sends an acknowledgment directly to Godoy with a new copy of his own prior report. In contrast to the recalcitrant attitude Mopox detected in Havana, Quintana willingly cedes priority—against the testimony of the dates: "I acknowledge that this latest sovereign resolution proceeds from *greater forethought* and wiser meditations" (Quintana 1796, 111 verso; emphasis added). A bow to greater authority: Quintana also recognizes that through the Mopox expedition to nearby Guantanamo he found the Crown allied to his regional interests, to the exclusion, potentially, of Havana.

Quintana had opened his report by enunciating his fear of foreign invasion from Santo Domingo, now in French hands after the treaty that gained Godoy the title of Prince of Peace, and from the British in Jamaica (Quintana 1798, 59 recto). He then passes quickly to an economic review. Santiago de Cuba is poor, he declares, but the land is good. Coffee and cotton thrive, but the two to three years needed to harvest a first substantial crop exceed the holding power of the impoverished local population, which leaves the alternatives of sugar and tobacco. The workings of the tobacco monopoly, he adds, require that local production pass through Havana; but since no advance payments are made on tobacco, growers are forced to take promissory notes (una papeleta, 61 recto), which penury drives them to sell at a discount, losing 10 to 12 percent. In short, tobacco, too, is an untenable alternative. Quintana, therefore, turns to sugar and forms two corresponding petitions: "the free introduction of Blacks, and all implements of Agriculture and industry" (63 recto) and "exportation of products free of all duty" (64 recto). He would have Santiago de Cuba join the international sugar market and bypass Havana, becoming a direct beneficiary of the Free Trade Ordinance of 1778 and its sequels.

Even those two aids, Quintana further explains, depend upon a third:

> I cannot omit, and I will propose, finally, in this representation another [boon] that [Santiago de Cuba] needs with no less urgency that those others, and as the precise and indispensable base to enjoy them freely and in Peace . . . in two words, that this city and the whole region under its Governance remain forever and absolutely independent of the Ministries in Havana, without which boon I dare to assure Your Excellency that His Majesty will never be well served in this eastern part of the

Island, nor will [Santiago de] Cuba be able to enjoy fully any aid whatsoever with which the King my Lord might favor it: the material for this topic is so vast that to consider it here even with the greatest economy and taciturnity would require a thick tome for its explication. (Quintana 1798, 66 recto-verso)

On the eve of Mopox's arrival, the eastern end of the island is prepared to declare its independence of the hegemony of Havana, although under the protection of the Spanish Crown. This is indeed Quintana's basic goal. And he reads a favorable disposition in the Royal Order in support of Mopox. The Consulado in Havana, I suggest, read the Royal Order in much the same way. The threat that they perceive in Mopox is not Spanish, but Cuban—as only the inhabitants of the eastern region of the island were called (as opposed to *habaneros, villareños, camagüeyanos*) until after the drive to island-wide independence inaugurated by the *Grito de Yara* of 1868 (Pérez de la Riva 1977, 47). The self-interest founded upon a successful colony in Guantanamo appeared to isolate Mopox from the interests of his corresponding social class on the island, the Havana sacchrocracy. A new port at Guantanamo, fortified, as Mopox planned, and habilitated by the sequels to the Free Trade Ordinance to undertake commerce directly with Spain would exceed Quintana's dreams and present a serious challenge to the privileged economic and social position of Havana.

These tensions mirror the nascent revolutionary politics of the period. Adjusting once again for scale, one might well discern an analogy between the relations of Havana to Santiago de Cuba or Matanzas in Agustín de Blondo y Zavala's report to the *Real Comisión de Guantánamo* (Blondo y Zavala 1800, 3v-4r) and those of metropolitan Spain to Havana, Mexico or the newly created viceroyalty of the Río de la Plata. But Mopox was no revolutionary, and his own vested interests in Cuba come to be amalgamated to those of the hegemonic sugar planters by reference to a common enemy. Like Quintana, Mopox is aware of the depredations of English piracy: "I find the opinion of Your Excellency ever more confirmed," he writes to Godoy in an undated letter (though a marginal note bears the date of 29 April 1797), "concerning the necessity of establishing a Settlement at Guantanamo; the benefit that the English derive from its neglect is incredible" (Mopox n.d., 173v-174r). Such dangers, so palpable at Santiago de Cuba across a short stretch of water from Jamaica or across from the Cayman Islands on the Isle of Pines, as Captain Juan Tirry y Lacy reported to the *Real Comisión de Guantánamo* (1797, 50r), would not forge an immediate alliance with Havana. The successful seizure of the city, narrated, as we have seen, in scornful verse in the "Dolorosa métrica esprecion del Sitio," was still a living memory at the time of the Mopox expedition. But the brief British occupation was also something of an economic advantage to the island, if not to the Spanish crown, providing sudden access to the international market. From the Cuban point of view, traffic with England was not so much a menace as a forbidden fruit. The true threat, then, in which Quintana and the Havana sacchrocracy could find common cause and to which Mopox directed greater attention and rhetorical force, was black power.

The appointment of Francisco Saavedra as the new first secretary of state on 28 March 1798 provides Mopox with the occasion for an articulation of this danger. In a letter to Saavedra of 2 July 1798, Mopox states the following:

> The Insurrection of the Blacks on the Island of Santo Domingo and the devastation of that rich Colony, today a pile of ashes, that serves as the sepulcher of a prodigious number of unfortunate Frenchmen and as the asylum of three hundred thousand fugitive slaves, was the necessary consequence of the revolution of its Metropolis. The idea of Liberty constantly in the mouths of their Masters, their misunderstood independence and their indiscretion in sustaining these causes in plain sight of their servants, could produce no other effects. (Mopox 1798b, 44r)

> It seems that the first step has been taken that will subvert the Antilles. This Archipelago of contiguous Islands situated on the same parallel, stretching from Trinidad to Jamaica owes its production to the work of Black Slaves, without whom their cultivation would be impracticable. But how can this contagion fail to propagate itself? Nor how will those of Santo Domingo allow their fellows to suffer in slavery? (Mopox 1798b, 46r)

The rhetorical questions are not a preface to a sympathetic statement on behalf of human rights, needless to say. Rather Mopox calls for the consolidation of class interest as national interest, based on the fiction of race: "Thus it is probable that, the uprising communicated from one Island to the next, the interested Nations will lose their colonies" (Mopox 1798b, 46r). He then concludes, "limiting myself only to the Island of Cuba, by its proximity the most exposed to the contagion, it appears that the project for the Settlement and defense of Guantanamo is a remedy which in part will contain the ills that threaten" (46v), and he proposes that the Spanish troops formerly stationed in Santo Domingo be garrisoned at Guantanamo.

In Mopox's disposition one reads the possibility of the revolution that was displaced by the American wars of independence. Neither the utterly dispossessed—African and African-American slaves and conquered indigenous peoples—nor their nearest neighbors on the social scale—the castes, the gauchos—nor even the economically depressed criollos outside the hegemonic class and the administrative, mining and maritime centers—e.g. Quintana's Santiago de Cuba—succeeded in pressing their claims. The effort to give those claims a voice appears significantly, if intermittently, in the literature of the period, whose main current, nevertheless, will be the patriotic odes of the triumphant criollo aristocracy. The papers of the *Real Comisión de Guantánamo* offer an overview of the dynamics of that literary process, I will now suggest, in the debate about roads: an allegory of voice.

Writing to Saavedra on 2 July 1798, Mopox declares reconciliation with the Consulado in Havana:

> The construction of roads over the whole extension of the Island is impracticable and useless since it is unpopulated after a distance of twenty leagues from Havana. Convinced of this unassailable difficulty, I concur with the plan of this Royal Council [of Havana], which, after having reflected on the question with their customary scrupulousness and good sense, decided that the extension of the roads should be limited to a total of eighty leagues for now, divided in various branches: but since the area is not known with precision, I have disposed that a map be drawn beginning from Matanzas that comprehends the whole cultivated circumference of Havana and its environs, by the engineers the brothers Lemaur. (Mopox, 1798a, fol. 43)

Although even this most densely populated area on the island remains, surprisingly, terra incognita three centuries after Columbus, the proposal here aims at increasing internal traffic between cultivated lands, rather than extending the access into the wilderness. Opening communications between culture and nature is a project for a later day, for romanticism, which will conceive a self prior to and beyond human society—a form of hell, according to Aguirre, as we have seen. At the turn of the nineteenth century,

Mopox agrees that the end of the road is that the rich should get
richer. The sacchrocracy has defined the ambit as the area under
their own cultivation.

The Consulado had expressed its scrupulousness and sense, its
class interest and its ability to appropriate other discourses, in an
economic report signed by Nicolás Calvo O-Farrill, Joseph Ricardo
O-Farrill and Francisco Arango: *Memoria sobre los medios que
convendría adoptar para que tuviese la Havana los caminos necesarios* (Calvo y O-Farrill 1795). Available capital for road building
is of course in the hands of the plantation owners, and theirs, too,
the greatest potential return on the investment. The body of the discussion is devoted to questions of cost effectiveness and financing
and particularly to assessing self-interest as a standard for propor-
tionate capital investment. The analysis is imbued with the nascent
capitalist economic philosophy of the age, which homogenizes ine-
qualities in a vision of costs and benefits, or so the authors would
justify their proposal to universalize payments. "[A]ll inhabitants
of the towns in whose vicinity the roads would pass should contribute to their construction," they argue: "Many laborers become dis-
couraged, and do not sow foodstuffs, because they know that they
will remain at home unsold, for in order to sell them or to bring
them to market, the costs of transportation would exceed the price
of their sale" (Calvo y O-Farrill 1795, 2). The real discouragement
of the laborers, however, might be understood to arise from other
causes, especially if a demographic analysis of racial composition
were to set their lives within the rigors of the caste system.

The spirit of the times is also noticeable where the analysts pause
in their calculations and survey the landscape through which the
roads will run. "Wherever one turns ones eyes in our countryside,
one finds pastures, or *potreros* as they are called here, fenced in
with dry stone, which proves that stone for roads is to be found at
hand almost everywhere" (Calvo y O-Farrill 1795, 11–12). I would
signal the reference to direct observation, which is translated as the
rhetorical situation of the speaker in the very midst of a local landscape identified explicitly as "ours." Next, one comes upon lexical
concerns. The historical consciousness of the late eighteenth century fixes upon the diachronic evolution of language. In Spanish
America the attitude is manifest in the increasing awareness that
geographical and demographic specificity carries linguistic particu-
larity as a necessary concomitant. In Cuba, for instance, it is at this
time that Esteban Pichardo arrives from his native Santo Domingo,

and begins the investigations that will culminate in his *Diccionario provincial de voces cubanas* (Pichardo 1836). Finally, the passage in question and the report at large are circumscribed by utilitarian concerns. The land is not expressive, but productive, if only of the stones for the very road under consideration. In brief compass, then, the pillars of late eighteenth-century intellectual life emerge: science, history and progress.

The text breaks free of its analytical constraints but once and fleetingly, allowing a momentary glimpse of the political unconscious overlaid thinly by negation:

> We have not wanted to waste time in painting the very pleasant and obvious picture of what this part of the Island will be when the roads have been constructed. A most fertile and flourishing garden, lovely dwelling of the copious multitudes of our countrymen living in abundance and ease, is the happy image that offers itself at every turn, as long as we imagine the project already complete. But whoever these lovely ideas do not move, will be sparked by charity; may he realize that his poor slave who may be tormented by a malignant fever will not come to the city to be cured stretched out indecorously on the back of a mule, on a horrible road, under a burning sun, but rather he will be able to come in a comfortable carriage, and shielded from inclement weather, and to arrive quickly at the home of his master, where he will care for him with paternal affection, and the skill of the best physicians will succor him. (Calvo y O-Farrill 1795, 15–16 n. 12)

The point of road-building, and correspondingly of the text on road-building, is to save time. Digressions have been suppressed. But now the authors arrange a brief detour, though still subordinated as a footnote. The first half essays a lyrical expansion that reverses the temporal mechanism of epic prophecy as seen in Peralta's *Lima conquistada*. If the future is imagined as past, then the "copious multitudes" will be transfigured. They are not encouraged by better access to markets, however. Instead, the dream of a cultivated land—literally enabled by and metaphorically inscribed as the laying of new roads—transforms the laborers into denizens of a golden age of abundance. Real inequality is reimagined as utopian leisure. The *costumbrista* scene that closes the note is still more explicit. The Cuban sacchrocracy was at pains to defend itself against "something of a little, home-grown Black Legend" concerning the abuse of African and African-American slaves, propagated in Spain to discredit the criollos (Minguet 1988, 415). Here Calvo y O-Farrill and the Consulado rewrite the slaves' aspirations to freedom of mobility as a white legend of paternalistic benevolence, masking the simple facts of economic analysis: for the planters, new roads will mean greater facility in transporting their property—whether sugar or slaves. Twin fantasies: the landowners absorb the desires of laborers and slaves into their own self-justifying report.

Saccharine visions will not eliminate the need for labor nor the hostility that the slave economy had created. Increased profitability and the effective control of slave revolt depend upon the solidarity of the planters as a class. This is the lesson that the debate on road-building would teach. "The beauty of this countryside, and the facility of moving through it in comfort, will invite the landowners not only to go often to their haciendas, but also to visit each other on their lands, which will lead in consequence to greater sociability and union between these neighbors," write the brothers Lemaur in their "Ynforme sobre los caminos de la Ysla de Cuba of November 24, 1798 for the *Real Comisión de Guantánamo* (Lemaur 1798b, 86 recto-verso). For the first roads in Cuba had opened traffic to individual private properties, noted Agustín de Blondo y Zavala in his report to Mopox, "Proyecto para habitar el Puerto de Mariel," and so the roads remained, "with little difference after two hundred years" (Blondo y Zavala 1802, 6r): "This neglect has led to thousands of conflicts between neighbors who only look to their own private interest and never the general [good], refusing to allow passage through their lands, which obliges travelers to take infinite detours to reach the main roads, and not a few have found themselves enclosed on their own property" (6v). Internal traffic in Cuba was choked by self-interest, resulting in a baroque pattern of entanglement, of infinite, ambulatory periphrasis. For the planters, progress beyond the self-entrapment of the baroque required a rational systematization of roads, required Enlightenment. The predicament for an obstructed local commerce, I suggest, is revealing for a paralyzed local aesthetics.

The task of rationalization fell to the brothers Lemaur, Félix and Francisco, who completed their "Ynforme sobre los caminos de la Ysla de Cuba" for Mopox on November 24, 1798. Interesting in many respects, I will orient my comments around their critique of the Consulado's plans. They fault the Consulado for an idealized approach to the problem of roads, "for they treat of it without giving any indication that they conceive of the least difficulty in it" (Lemaur 1798b, 14r). The brothers Lemaur write, in contrast, as

experienced engineers: "How laborious and long it may be to represent a territory so vast with the exactitude and detail that we have
supposed, let them say who are accustomed to making maps, neither ideal nor misleading for the most part, but rather with such
precision in all parts," they conclude in orthodox Enlightenment
style, "that more than by the imagination, the design will have been
guided by measure" (12v).

The argument for greater realism—the issue is representation:
mapping, not building, as yet—based on direct observations on site,
lead the Lemaurs, as they will lead the eighteenth-century Hispanic
Enlightenment generally and well in advance of their romantic
heirs, to distinguish the American landscape from Spain:

> Whatever the difficulty in the drawing up of such plans, it is incompara-
> bly more so here than in Spain; for the territory in that peninsula is
> generally open, and unencumbered, and its very unevenness, and the
> way the towns dominate over the plains, facilitates and shortens the
> many geometric operations; here on the contrary the lofty hills are
> almost completely covered by forest and by an impenetrable under-
> growth, and the flat and cultivated plains have so many stands of trees,
> due to the multitude of natural partitions that divide them, that usually
> no greater vista presents itself than that portion in which one is walking.
> (Lemaur 1798b, 14v-15r).

In the context of their utilitarian purposes, the profusion of American flora stands as an obstacle to representation. In this, the brothers
Lemaur remain closer to the writers of the preceding period all the
way back to Salvatierra, who assessed the terrain of his Baja California landfall in terms of military defense, than to the romantics of
the period to come, who will rejoice in the circumscription of vision
to a resolutely local landscape.

The dedication of the Lemaurs to building roads appropriate to
their American setting—the task toward which literature was moving as well—leads to an early critique of the Consulado's Neoclassicism, that is their strict adherence to the modalities of European
antiquity and its avatars in Spain. The Lemaurs declare:

> In all of them [i.e. Spanish and Roman roads] it seems no more attention
> was paid to the comfort of travelers than to the magnificence and dura-
> tion of the work. But the cost of doing so here, if the models of which
> we have just spoken were imitated in construction, would make it
> impossible, not only in the present state of the population and culture of

the country, but even when these had reached their greatest perfection and growth. In addition one can generally affirm that if the resources of a rich and populous nation were sufficient for constructing the main roads with such magnificence, it would never suffice for doing the same in other places. (Lemaur 1798b, 24v-25r)

In politics the same impulse would be called democratic: the urge to broaden access to the means of social welfare. In poetry, I wish to suggest, the impulse is equally paradigmatic. The grandeur of Greco-Roman classicism remains unchallenged as the precedent upon which to establish the good taste of modern times, presented here specifically as a certain commodiousness. But the brothers Lemaur put its applicability into question. They urge a greater attention to local conditions against the universalizing spirit of neo-classicism in civil engineering, and, moreover, they do so in the name of an enlightened economics that would transform the commodious to commodity: convenient, if not roomy, commercially advantageous, if less grand in aesthetic manner.

The magnificence of neoclassicism, however, is not the only value that the brothers Lemaur are willing to sacrifice to the end of "the multiplication of those works that prove beneficial" (Lemaur 1798b, 25r). They not only admit that their cheaper roads will be less durable, but in fact they mount an argument on the grounds of their own political-economic theory that this planned obsolescence is desirable:

> In truth the greed of a people, which is more judicious than that of a single person, generally disdains to make advances from which it does not later receive the fruits; a person can redeem an encumbrance from his successors, but a people never attempts to free theirs from the daily labors to which by nature it is proper that all owe their subsistence. (26r)

Neoclassical immutability lends itself to the expression of private interest, they reason. The public good requires a continuous renewal of efforts. Though they themselves may hardly be expected to say so, in their utilitarian posture and their economic concerns, both characteristic of this period, the brothers Lemaur pave the way, so to speak, for a landscape of ready ruins such as the romantics will eagerly inhabit.

A certain preromanticism is in evidence at the turn of the nine-teenth century, even in engineering, at the cost of a diminished enlightened rationalism and a disrupted neoclassical order.[3] Thus the brothers Lemaur defend their street map for a projected city on the Bay of Jagua: "Perhaps upon seeing the irregularity of the limits in which the City is circumscribed, it will be objected that it is a defect that it is not comprehended within a regular figure" (Lemaur 1798a, 35v). The realities of a coastline found on the spot, however, cannot be made to conform to a preconceived rational ideal. And having moved to aesthetic grounds—"beauty or ugliness" (36r)—they press on, arguing for the Horatian admixture of pleasure and utility:

> Before the [future] City on the inland side one finds on the map various gardens and orchards, which, over time, it would be easy to make, and that would not only be useful to the City, but would contribute to its embellishment and to the recreation of its dwellers. The walkways that figure between the gardens and the orchards and separated from them by rows of trees, would serve more than a little to increase the amenity of [the City] . . .

And speaking of one projected garden in particular, they close with an emphatic flourish:

> and for the freshness that would always be there in that place of rest, as well as for the breeze that would be felt there perpetually, and for the shade of the trees, it would not only be the best spot in the City, but it would be difficult to find another anywhere that could be compared to it for its deliciousness. (Lemaur 1798a, 39v-40r)

The "shade of the trees," which exist as yet only in the mind's eye and the cartographic inscriptions of the brothers Lemaur, are a projected ghost: a vision from an edenic past cast as a shadow on the future. For here and elsewhere the prose of the these and other expeditionaries, of this and other expeditions, sounds the profoundly lyrical note of what is too often deemed a merely prosaic age. The constant breeze that the brothers Lemaur anticipate in their *locus amoenus* is none other than the image of voice, the trope for a poetry expressive of the prevailing winds of local circumstance (see Abrams 1984). With independence won, that breeze will be the voice of Spanish American romanticism. But it blows first, for those who would tarry to listen, in the imaginary by-ways of a neoclassical temperament.

2

It is 1778 and Spanish America is dissatisfied. The Free Trade Ordinance and other Bourbon reforms are a safety valve to release the social pressure building to autonomy, but the fundamental policy toward the colonies is containment (see Malamud and Pérez 1988). The Enlightenment itself, as Mopox would maintain two decades later, can be a useful detour in the road to independence. "[T]his city of schools of all the abstract sciences," he writes in reference to Havana and its reigning scholasticism in an "Informe sobre el modo de fomentar è instruir con utilidad del Rey, del Estado y de la juventud à aquellos naturales," addressed to Godoy on 15 November 1797,

> has not so much as one [school] in the natural and exact sciences, being perhaps the Country in which they are the most necessary in order for its agriculture and Commerce to reach that flourishing degree that the King and Your Excellency desire. It is clear that without this benefit they will remain as retarded as they are unsure in their progress, and far from expecting that the State should risk its tranquillity on their behalf, I judge that it will acquire more firmness and consistency, forming honest artisans, giving employment to the delinquents [vagos] that now abound, and distracting many from the study of the law that His Majesty has qualified as dangerous and useless on this Island, commanding that the number of *letrados* be limited. (Mopox 1797, 232v-233r)

From a revolutionary standpoint, however, the letrados are far more useless than dangerous; the *ciudad letrada*, as Rama has argued, is a conservative force in Spanish America, feasting on the beefy bureaucracy of colonial and republican administrations alike. The danger, as Mopox well understood, resided rather in the alienated social groups, the African slaves and their descendants of his immediate preoccupation, conquered and unconquered indigenous peoples on the continent, as well as *los vagos*. These groups will all be incorporated in the wars of independence, supplying soldiers to the revolutionary armies, although their political needs go largely unrepresented by the creole elite who claim the victory. The poetry of these peoples, then, manifest primarily in song (which is to say oral forms), is their voice, which speaks to and through the literary culture of the creole aristocracy. Thus a poem both exemplary and inaugural for the period is the *relación*, "Canta un guaso en estilo campestre los triunfos del Excmo. Sr. D. Pedro de Cevallos" by

José Balthasar Maziel (Argentina 1727–88), which dates to 1778, following Cevallos's successful military campaign against the Portuguese at Santa Catalina. Adopting the traditional eight-syllable ballad line, and the diction and pronunciation of a rude and rustic participant in the events, Maziel, a doctor of theology, recounts the episode from the point of view of the gaucho, the example par excellence of the vago from the social margins who is rehabilitated for the national culture by military service on the one hand and native poetry on the other, as Josefina Ludmer (Ludmer 1988) has argued.[4] Maziel structured his poem in the manner of the traditional bard of rural folk culture who sung his verses to guitar accompaniment in competition with a poet rival. But one needs register a crucial difference all the same: Maziel preserved his poetry in writing, thereby transporting the genre from the pampa to the milieu of a literate, urban circle. The awareness of the change is inscribed in his closing envoy:

> Perdone, señor Cevallos
> mi rana silvestre y guasa,
> que las germanas de Apolo,
> no habitan en las campañas
>
> (Danero 1953, 17)

> Pardon, Señor Cevallos,
> my wild and uncouth croak,
> for the sisters of Apollo
> don't live out in the fields.

The direct address to the new viceroy unmasks vernacular speech as rhetorical device: not the traditional poetry of the gauchos, but a stylized *poesía gauchesca* incorporated into the literary repertoire of the urban center.[5]

Maziel's poem celebrates a victory for colonial authority, not gaucho freedom. At most the reminder of gaucho participation in the victory at Santa Catalina that helped secure Spanish dominion in the River Plate area served to underwrite his legitimation within the colonial order, the transformation from a vago to a useful citizen. If there is revolution, it is literary. "A literary revolution," writes Ludmer apropos of Bartolomé Hidalgo (Uruguay 1788–1823) of the following generation, the acknowledged foundational figure of poesía gauchesca, "is no more than the amplification of a frontier or a leap. It consists in that what was beneath the boundary line that defined the literary . . . takes a turn and places itself, by that turn, above the boundary line" (Ludmer 1988, 43). For a more radical politics in the verse of the moment, one may read the broadsides that appeared in support of the revolt of Túpac Amaru, the vast upheaval of indigenous peoples in Upper Peru in 1780–81:

> Nuestro Gabriel Inca viva
> jurémosle ya por rey
> siendo muy de acuerdo a ley
> que lo que es justo reciba.
> Todo indiano se aperciba
> a defender su derecho
> porque Carlos con despecho
> nos aniquila y despluma,
> y viene a ser todo en suma
> robo al revés y al derecho.

> (Bedregal 1991, 44)

> Viva Gabriel, in our Inca we trust,
> let us pledge our oath to him as king
> seeing as, by rights, it's not asking
> too much, that he receive what's just.
> Each Indian is summoned and he must
> stand and defend his rights,
> because Carlos in his spite
> annihilates and plucks us clean,
> which, in sum, turns out to mean
> he robs us left and rights.

where the closing inversion, more than a strain to rhyme, aims at the *reparto* system that gives the king the right (con derecho) to pluck clean the *indiano* (not the Peninsular sojourner in America here, but rather the native American). To pluck: to take away the feather that is a European index of Indian-ness, and by extension, of American identity in the iconography of the eighteenth and nineteenth centuries. It is also to remove the quill, the pen. The depradations of the colonial regime three centuries after Columbus would leave the indigenous people destitute of goods, of identity, of voice. Túpac Amaru and the anonymous authors of these broadsides would make good the losses in the name of the Inca dynasty (see Bedregal 1991, 42–46 and Vargas Ugarte 1951, 118–35, and other related poems in the latter collection, 88–100, 136–53). Note, however, that while the rhetorical force of the texts may reach levels of overt violence—"Morirán con el soldado/alcaldes, corregidores,/ oficiales y oidores" ["With the soldier will die mayors, governors/ officials and judges"], one reads in the stanza following the verse cited above (Bedregal 1991, 44)—the diction and style borrow more frequently from baroque precedent than from indigenous languages (though see, for example, the "Décimas esparcidas en la Ciudad de la Plata contra los oidores de su Real Audiencia" in Bedregal 1991, 44). Literary and political revolution do not necessarily walk hand in hand. And indeed, in the one as in the other, the way back may be the way forward, as Túpac Amaru himself imagined when he rallied Andean peoples to struggle against the pernicious laws of the present by asserting his claim to the Inca past.

So, too, for literature. The single most important Spanish American poem from the death of Sor Juana to the birth of Heredia was written quite literally by an American in Latin, stretching its literary affiliation back to Virgil's *Georgics*. The poet was the exiled Jesuit Rafael Landívar (Guatemala, 1731–93) writing in Bolonia, Italy, where he published his *Rusticatio Mexicana* in 1782. Beyond the limits of personal experience, the exile of the Jesuits, as it inflects Landívar's poem, is both a frequently recurring historical reality for Spanish American poets and a paradigm for their poetry. On the one hand, the exile of so many writers, both central names and minor figures, meant that much poetry had to reenter Spanish America from abroad. Publication in exile and the subsequent export of poetry to the homelands led the commerce of letters into conformity with larger patterns of trade, fostering a dependency model of cultural production, manifest in the nineteenth century in the voluntary exodus of aristocratic sons whose cultivation was to be certified by extended European tours. On the other hand, exile had a specific impact on historical consciousness. Flight from home enacted the separation of present from past, disabling eternizing schemes, played out variously by Peralta and Abad, for example. But the geographical breach did not bury the past at a safe distance, as Calero's eminently modern reform of burial practices would have it, freeing the present from the deleterious influence of the dead. For life back home did not come to an end, of course, and from that perspective it was rather the poet who passed away. Exile located poets and poetry in the breach itself, and the paradigmatic result was a poet amputated of imaginative roots, obliged to recognize the past as past, but unwilling or unable to achieve detachment from it. Exile is both a cause and a model for melancholia.

In this regard Landívar's *Rusticatio* might be contrasted to Abad's *De Deo* as an extravagant and erudite expression of the paired genres of Spanish American folk poetry, *a lo jumao* and *a lo divino*; that is, secular and sacred subjects, respectively, but also Landívar's engagement with human temporality, which is to say the vicissitudes of the historical consciousness, in contradistinction to Abad's timeless view from the perspective of the scrutinizing God. The difference may be glimpsed in the poets' construction of their Muses. Landívar offers a prefatory disclaimer:

> in order that you, my gentle reader, may read this poem inoffensively, I would have you know that I am going to speak in the manner of a poet whenever mention is made of the false deities of the ancients. I solemnly realize and devoutly confess that such fictitious deities have no understanding, much less any power and might. (Landívar 1948, 165)[6]

Nevertheless, his descriptions of the geography and industry, flora and fauna of America are constantly referred to the pagan world of European classicism. Only a brief notice of a mysterious marble cross in the first book (Landívar 1948, 168–69) and more so the return of that image in the appendix as the still more mysterious Cruz de Tepic serve to inscribe the American landscape as Christian in *nature*. Yet in both of these cases, including the very renunciation of "worldly song" in the appendix (307), the verse is thoroughly infiltrated by allusions to Greco-Roman mythology: "Aonian sisters and . . . Delphian bard" (307). Abad, in contrast, opens his poem with a forceful condemnation of the "the manner of a poet" that would withdraw poetry from the domain of God's glory.

While the comparison is richly suggestive in this and other ways, historical circumstance has changed in the interim between 1769 and 1782, or more precisely, historical consciousness has evolved. Abad had already augmented the classical landscape that he inherited from Virgil with references to his native Mexico.[7] And in a note he makes these references the landmarks of an individual consciousness: "I say what I have seen" (Abad 1974, 145). Moreover, taking those historical bearings as a general orientation to reading, it would be possible to interpret the vast divine time line leading up to Judgment Day in *De Deo* as a vindication of the fallen Jesuits. But to do so, I would contend, is to incur a romantic anachronism. Abad's historical experience has given him a "sense of an ending" the better to intuit the divine scheme, but the purpose of his poetry is to transcend history and glimpse God's own eternal point of view. From that perspective, history is not an unfolding of events, but, at most, a set of exempla, palpable to human understanding, for the eternal text is already written to the very end. Hence, Abad's poem proceeds as a series of glosses of scripture, a biblical passage set at the head of each section.

Landívar writes self-consciously after a fall that admits of no redemption. There can be no return to the edenic space, for in his poetic imagination America stands in ruins and he is banished from it as from the past. This is particularly clear in the inaugural event of the poem, the devastating eruption of the volcano Jorullo in 1759, which he witnessed from Patzcuaro, only forty miles distant (see Landívar 1948, 181 and 185 n. 1). The immediate antecedent to the eruption, then, is a thriving colonial economy. Some of the lands of the valley of Jorullo, "the wealthy farmer had set apart for cane and turned over with a hundred plows; a part he devoted to the feeding of his vast herds" (177). Hence, even before catastrophe, Mexico is removed from the classical Golden Age, which may be glimpsed in its satirical reflection in the verse of Antonio José de Irisarri (Guatemala 1786–1868), who arises in the latter portion of this period as a major polemicist. Here, taking Don Quixote's famous speech (part 1, ch. 11) as his springboard, Irisarri writes:

> Mas dicen que por colmo de ventura
> Del tuyo y mío las palabras necias
> Eran de humana voz desconocidas,
> Y allí nació, para mi sayo infierno,
> La célebre doctrina proudhomiana
> De que es la propiedad patente robo,
> Aunque en verdad entonces nada había
> Que tentaciones de apropiarse diese;
> Porque el mal alimento y suelo y agua
> Bienes comunes de los hombres eran.
> Ninguna cosa por industria humana,
> Ni por trabajo, ni heredado título
> Propietario al mortal hacer podía.
>
> (Irisarri 1867, 16–17)

> But they say that for the height of fortune
> "Yours" and "mine," those foolish words,
> Were yet unknown to human voice,
> And there, I say, infernally, was born

The famous doctrine of Proudhon
That holds all property is outright theft,
Although in truth there was then nothing
tempting one to misappropriation;
Because bad food, and earth and water
Were the common lot of men.
Nothing could by human industry,
Nor by labor, nor hereditary title
Make of a mortal a proprietor.

Without labor, no property, surmises Irisarri, and he further hints, no history, whose Muse he addresses: "¡Qué siglo de Saturno, ni qué alforja!/Un disparate tan absurdo y necio,/Incapaz fuera de prestar asunto/Al canto de una Musa cual tú Clio" ["What Age of Saturn, by my saddlebags!/ A joke absurd and foolish,/Incapable of lending a theme/To the song of a Muse like you, Clio"] (Irisarri 1867, 14). In contrast, the event of Landívar's book 2 emerges out of a history of labor, of a cultivated nature, for which book 1 served as a creation myth.

Mexican history, including Landívar's natural history, begins with indigenous labor. Finding their world a void, and much as in the biblical Genesis, awash in the broad waters of Texcoco and Chalco, the native peoples create a firmament by their own industry: "Called chinampas in the native tongue" (Landívar 1948, 169). The implicit textual metaphor is spelled out in a parallel concurrence in the one episode that Landívar designates as fiction in his prolog to the *Rusticatio* (163): the gathering of Mexican poets, from his contemporaries among the Jesuits to Sor Juana, who sing in the twilight at lakeside when the Indians' labors have concluded. To weave the *chinampas* from the grasses is to sing (see Guss 1989). And having woven their land into being, the Indians begin to cultivate: "One man scatters [Hic jacit] grains of wheat over the floating fields, another finds pleasure sowing fertile vegetable seeds, and there are not wanting those for whom the flower once sacred to pagan Venus blushes" (Landívar 1948, 170). Fruitful, multiplying, the weavers experience the pleasure of their text.

To cast life upon the face of the waters is also to prepare the grounds for death ("Hic jacit," *hic jacet*). The indigenous weaving creates a surface and in consequence, a hidden depth, which is Landívar's consistent burden from the very outset. These, the opening words of book 1 of the poem:

Let another conceal his thoughts in obscure figures whose hidden meaning no one would venture to interpret or worry his mind with the thankless task. Let another bestow reason and pleasant discourse upon dumb animals, let him cover the fields with armies, the earth with death, and let him vanquish entire nations by armed force. (Landívar 1948, 166)

Yet just as he claims to forego at once baroque enigma, the verse fables so popular in the eighteenth century, and epic poetry—abandoning the models of Góngora, Iriarte and even Virgil—in order to concentrate instead on surfaces, that is on description, Landívar declares in the third stanza that in fact his poem is riddled by its own secret depths:

I ought, I confess, to have put on the garb of mourning and to have shed bitter tears, for as long as flowers grow in the meadow and stars give forth their light, my heart and soul will be filled with sorrow. But I am obliged to hide this grief in my heart though the distress force sighs from my guarded breast. (166)

A declaration of melancholia: more for the muting of the truth than for the simple endurance of sorrow. Landívar closes book 1 with a disfiguration of this riddle of surface and depth, a brief narration of the indigenous method of duck hunting. Gourds are collected and set afloat upon the waters. The ducks are frightened, but industry is so well disguised as nature, that they become inured and so deceived. A man may then introduce his head into a gourd and approach hidden beneath the surface, whence he arises to kill his prey. Hidden depths, indeed, and left unplumbed to the peril of the unwary.

The principal event of book 2, a volcanic eruption, proceeds along similar lines and from these sources: an American nature already woven as history by indigenous culture; a Spanish American literary history with its own native canon as represented by the singers at the lake; and the pain of expulsion, a poet amputated of his homeland, resisting healing, maintaining the unity of his American identity, feeling the pain in the stump, as Abraham would have it. The eruption of Jorullo is an image for a disgorging of the incorporated trauma: the depths of land and culture, literary historical ambition and personal ties all exploding to the surface of the poem.

In a procedure typical of the *Rusticatio*, Landívar attempts to cut his losses by turning abruptly from vividly depicted catastrophe to the consolations of regeneration. In a word, he attempts an elegy.

Five years of sterility in the wake of the eruption, for instance, give way to prosperity in which "production has been so great that the new advantages offset the former losses" (Landívar 1948, 184). A single verse, however, cannot counterbalance the poetic weight of Landívar's narration of destruction. Elegy fails him. And thus immediately thereafter nature and Landívar find themselves compelled to repeat themselves.[8] An earthquake strikes to reissue the horrors of the past at Jorullo in the present of Bologna:

> While I was attempting to beguile my worries with these verses near the roaming waters of the Reno which hurry across the plains, suddenly the beams of the house began to creak, its foundations resounded, the earth shook, and the house tottered (Landívar 1948, 184)

Nor does the invocation of the Virgin that concludes the passage and the whole of book 2 successfully complete the work of mourning. Despite the opening words of book 3:

> Enough attention has been given in my poem to the mountain and its fires, enough to baleful clouds and devastation. The subject of my song shall now turn to rivers, rivers whose foaming waters bound over the hard crags where modest nymphs enjoy the refreshing coolness. (Landívar 1948, 186)

Landívar is borne back immediately from the description of Guatemala's waterfalls to yet another scene of destruction, the earthquake at Antigua de Guatemala in 1773. Here the poet's pain rises to the surface of a poem dedicated, after all, to "Urbi Guatemalae," his "dear mother-city" (163), as Landívar writes in the verse preface where he declares the ambivalence of exile.

All souvenirs of Guatemala appear to be benevolent: "These things will always foster in me a love for my native land, and they will be a sweet relief in my adversities" (Landívar 1948, 163). But the celebratory affect attached to these recollections proves inconstant:

> Yet I am deceived. My tranquil mind, alas! is mocked, and idle dreams disappoint my heart. For the city which had recently stood as a citadel and the illustrious capital of a mighty kingdom is now a heap of stones. (163)

Landívar would overcome his error and give his verse a memorial efficacy—"and I shall promptly extol to heaven your illustrious tri-

umph over sudden death" (Landívar 1948, 163), but this too is
dreaming and in vain. The city of which he can say, "I relate those
things which I have seen" and not merely "those that have been
told to me by eyewitnesses" (165), is the city in ruins, not its resurrection in the new capital. Poetry descriptive of the things of Guatemala remains figurative evasion, the reminiscences themselves
dispersed fragments that cannot be made to constitute the whole,
but rather repeat his loss: "Repetam nunca flumina . . . flumina,"
an echo relived, reissued (i.e. disfigured) and not only recorded, as
the wounded Narcissus on the banks of "flumina Reni" (162).

Landívar's enormous achievement is the only Spanish American
poem of the eighteenth century to receive unflagging acclaim over
the past two hundred years, and consistent critical attention, hampered though it may be, by the increasing estrangement of Latin.
Even so, it calls for renewed and assiduous study. Landívar sets the
task before his future reader in the appendix:

> Let another, like the beasts, go with unseeing eyes through the fields
> gilded by the golden sunlight, and let him indolently waste his time in
> play. But you, on the contrary, who have great keenness of mind, aban-
> don old ideas and adopt new, and with a high resolve to uncover the
> mysteries of nature, bring into the search the full vigor of your mind,
> and with joyful work uncover your treasures. (Landívar 1948, 309)

Upending the opening verses ("et ingrato mentem torquere
labore") in his final words ("Thesauroque tuos grato reclude
labore"), Landívar proposes the uncovering of the hidden sense
(compare "arcana naturae" here at the close with "arcanis . . .
figuris" of the first verse of book 1) as labor, although fruitful. And
this reversal is suggestive of other dislocations of his opening disclaimer. If he does not give voice to the animals in the style of Iriarte and Samaniego, Landívar's book 6 nevertheless rewrites the
creation myth of the chinampas in the description of the society of
beavers, an allegory of indigenous culture disrupted by the cata-
strophic advent of the Spanish conquistadors in the role of the
human hunters: a subversive epic of "campos armis et funere ter-
ras," after all.

Attention to the text of the *Rusticatio* will also discover occulted
in its figures an American scene of writing in books 7 and 8, dedicated to mining. This extensive report on the literal extraction of
treasures ("Thesauro") from *naturae arcana* unfolds as the central

allegory of hidden depths exposed by labor ("reclude labore"): "In these ridges bountiful America conceals all her mines and from them brings forth, after much effort, the shining metal" (Landívar 1948, 217). Of particular interest here will be the story of those true *hijos del limo* whom Paz overlooked in his dismissal of the American Enlightenment:

> From the moist powder mud is formed and then sprinkled with an abundance of salt. When the following day has lighted the earth with the lamp of Phoebus, the men tread the thick mud which they have saturated with salt, and at a definite time they add more salt. Then an expert in the industry seeks to discover all the diseases of the mixture, for it often suffers grievous disorders, to find out whether the illness is causing the patient excruciating chills, or whether high fever is consuming it. (Landívar 1948, 226)

Landívar adds a note to these verses, explaining that "Metallurgists employ this same figure as belonging to their art" (232 n. 1). The figure is apropos, but misapplied. It is not the mire but its children that face the grievous maladies; for one of the metallurgical cures will be to pour mercury into the mix before recommencing the treading. Landívar seems altogether unaware of the disastrous effects of exposure to mercury, but this genuine ignorance notwithstanding, he propounds a critical attitude toward the avaricious denuding of the earth's secret depths (218) that leads to self-wounding on the part of workers (224) as well as their abject exploitation (226). Furthermore, the criticisms of mining at the center of the poem are congruent with Enlightenment economic theory and may be seen to motivate the greater concentration of description on other potential or actual natural resources. The idyll of the beavers of book 6 ends when their indigenous society is incorporated into the international commerce in pelts.[9]

As an allegory of writing, finally, the feet muddied over in the mercury and ore may be followed further along that course of commercial evolution from mines to sugar refining. The muddy prints are transfigured in the tale of black and white, of black on white, the bleaching of sugar under the tutelage of nature:

> But not yet will the sugar be clear and shine with a white luster unless you cover the cone with dark clay. . . . But who, O Muses, revealed to us these secrets? From what source have men derived the knowledge of such an art? It is said that a dove, bedaubed with mud, planted her dirty

feet on a golden cone, and then, by pecking and pecking, pilfered tiny bits of the crystallized sweets. Whereupon the bird, having finished her stolen meal, soared high into the air in flight, leaving behind dirty tracks on the yellow cone. When these had slowly dried under the fierce rays of the sun, though they had been dark before, they had assumed a snow-white color. Indeed the kindly bird repaid her theft by revealing the secret, and she showed how to bleach the molds of sugar with mud. (Landívar 1948, 241)

The purloined grains represent Landívar's canny revision of the consolatory myth of the *felix culpa*. The tale of the black imprint that whitens, played out against the background of African slavery (Landívar 1948, 208–9, 212–13, etc.), bespeaks a form of writing that is more properly effacement. And if the pyramidal form of the cones recalls volcanic Jorullo, thus representing a return of the repressed, the white sugar becomes a figure for a cultural legacy of willful amnesia in which the history of (one might also say the potential for) eruption and ruin are erased from the metaphoric blank page. It is this page, in fact, which Heredia—among Landívar's translators, I note—confronted in the "Nieve eternal" ["Eternal snow"] that crowned Iztaccihual, Orizaba and Popocatepetl in his view from Cholula (J. M. Heredia 1940, 2:151), and upon which, retracing Landívar's steps, he would rediscover the occulted meaning of American history by poetic labor in the next period. But already in the *Rusticatio*, the underside of colonial culture, whether the slaves mutilated in the sugar industry (Landívar 1948, 238) or the laboring class subject to commercial exploitation (243), presses upward, rebelliously, into literature.

3

The most widespread poetry of Spanish America's unrest in this middle period on the road to independence is satire. I have suggested that the traditional genres of folk poetry—*a lo jumao* vs. *a lo divino*—might offer a heuristic framework within which Landívar's *Rusticatio* and Abad's *De Deo* might at once be read together in a contrapuntal relationship and also integrated into a specifically Spanish American literary history. This critical fiction—for there is no textual evidence that these neo-Latin poets conceived of their massive projects in the terms of popular balladeers—may be supplemented by the upward thrust of popular culture through satire into Jesuit poetry in the self-conscious counterpoint of the *calvaristas* and *thaboristas* among the exiles in Italy. Here the poets set Latin aside and with it the twin evasions of a divine (i.e. a thoroughly ahistorical) perspective, as in Abad, and the phantasms of a melancholic imagination, verging on a historical consciousness, as in Landívar. The "Certamen Poético, que puede llamarse Comedia sobre el Calvario y Thabor," the fifth volume of Father Juan Velasco's (Ecuador, 1727–92) manuscript compilation of 1791, "Colección de Poesías Varias, hecha por un ocioso en la Ciudad de Faenza," grounds poetry in historical circumstance. The calvaristas, as Velasco explained (the note is reproduced in Carrión 1988, 79–80), were the pessimists who believed that they would die in exile, while the thaboristas took a more sanguine view, expecting to return to America someday. Francisco Xavier Lozano, a Spanish-born Jesuit active in Mexico, took up the cudgels for the former, and Manuel Iturriaga, a native of Mexico, defended the position of the latter. They met in a competition of poems and verse rejoinders, whose antecedents, on the erudite side, reach back through the *certámenes* of viceregal courts. But the poetic duel is also a staple of folk culture in Spanish America, as represented, most familiarly, in the competition of Martín Fierro, or, returning to the eighteenth century, in the palla between "Taguada el indio y Javier de la Rosa, el señor" (Dölz-Blackburn 1984, 122).

At the base of the divergent views of the future of the calvaristas and thaboristas lies a common, elegiac view of the past, that is of their former American lives, as dead and buried. Thus Lozano satirizes the temptations of melancholia in calvarista and thaborista alike:

> Son el uno y el otro un maniáco
> que sin más discreción que un *chichimeco*
> aprecian solo lo que vale un *tlaco*
>
> (Carrión 1988, 84)

> They both have gone completely wacko
> and with no more wit than a *Chichimeco*
> they value what's not worth a *tlaco*

Lozano aligns himself with the popular, rather than the scholastic strain—counterpoint rather than debate—in his move not merely from Latin to Spanish, but beyond to an emphatically Mexican vocabulary of Nahuatl loan-words, stressed as rhyme. Similarly, in satirizing both parties, he goes beyond a simple identification with America by reference to pre-Columbian culture, for the Chichimecos, as Velasco observed in his explanatory note (Carrión 1988, 84), were understood to be "barbarians," outsiders to the civilization of Mexico's central plateau. The civilized posture that Lozano would promote against the mania of melancholic attachment is the relinquishing of the past as past—to bury America, not to praise it. To set such store by the kingdom—or vice-royalty—of this world is to miss the true destination, which is heaven. Thus, Lozano admonishes in another poem:

> Si yo pidiera la vida
> para ir a comer tamales,
> beber pulque y cosas tales,
> fuera mi causa perdida.
> Mas yo la tengo pedida
> por motivo más profundo;
> pues únicamente fundo
> de mi esperanza el trofeo
> en que yo solo deseo
> las cosas del otro mundo.

(Carrión 1988, 83)

> Were I to ask for life to eat
> tamales and pulque to drink
> and such like things, I'd think
> my cause already in defeat.
> But in fact I have entreated
> for reasons more profound;
> for I lay my only claim
> to hope's trophy on these grounds:
> I have fixed my only aim
> on things of the world beyond.

The deflation of over-valuations is the stuff of satire, rendered by Lozano in just such monetary terms. The America of calvarista and thaborista nostalgia is only worth a *tlaco*, which Velasco glossed as a "Mexican coin of little value" (Carrión 1988, 84). The magnifications of both sides, in lamentations or expressions of hope, are reduced to the least and most common, but also the most local denominator. The tlaco's small monetary value is equally limited as a linguistic coinage: both word and thing circulate only in Mexico or among exiled Mexicans.

The numismatic metaphor, carried to an extreme for satiric purposes in the case of the tlaco, sets Lozano's critique in the broad cultural domain in which religious orthodoxy, focused on that *otro mundo* of God's eternity, is contested by enlightened instrumental knowledge. Rational measurement, as we saw in the cartography and engineering of the brothers Lemaur, is indeed bounded by concrete minutiae and local concerns. One finds in several of the reports to the Mopox Commission, for instance, that the expeditionaries literally can't see the forest, for they are inventorying the trees (especially to count specimens apt for shipbuilding). Thus, Fernando Alegría, taking a dim view of the "poetic vacuum" of the contemporaneous period in late colonial Chile, may ask: "What kind of societal life did these people lead that they could permit themselves the luxury of filling books without saying anything, that they never seemed to feel the urgency of thinking about transcendent questions, for whom the perspective of the time was measured strictly in terms of the most immediate reality of purely local significance?" (Alegría 1954, 107). Inasmuch as the rationalization of the world is responsible for the bounded vision of the period, then Alegría's complaint may be said to have been enunciated in period terms by Francisco de Acuña Figueroa (Uruguay 1790–1862) when he wrote:

> Ser claro no es ser fecundo,
> Si no hay otro don más raro:
> Un arroyo cuando es claro
> Indica que no es profundo.
>
> (Menéndez y Pelayo 1895, 4:408)

> To be clear is no proof of fecundity,
> If there be no other gift more dear:
> A stream, when it runs clear
> Shows that it lacks profundity.

The critique, I note in passing, underscores the importance of Landívar's alternative image of writing as a *muddy* imprint as a precursor to the romantic poetry to come.

The dissatisfaction before an Enlightenment poetry mired in "the most immediate reality" was especially acute, from the later republican point of view, when it served as an ideological screen for a significance embedded in the metropolitan masterplot of the Conquest. Salvador Sanfuentes (Chile 1817–60), a poet from Bello's conservative circle in Chile, whom Alegría takes to task on separate grounds, nevertheless may be understood to answer Alegría's own rhetorical question in advance in the first of his *Leyendas nacionales*, "El campanario," written in 1842, when he offers a satirical portrait of an epigone of the banal world that Alegría evoked:

> Cuando el siglo diez y ocho promediaba,
> cierto Marqués vivía en nuestro suelo,
> que las ideas y usos conservaba
> que le legó su castellano abuelo:
> quiero decir que la mitad pasaba
> de su vida pensando en irse al cielo:
> viejo devoto y de costumbres puras,
> aunque en su mocedad hizo diabluras.
>
> Y amaba tanto las usanzas godas,
> que él hubiera mirado cual delito
> el que se hablase de francesas modas,
> o a París se alabase de bonito.
> Sobre la filiación de casi todas
> las familias de Chile era perito,
> y de cualquier conquistador la historia
> recitaba fielmente su memoria.
>
> (Sanfuentes 1921, 3)

> In the midst of the eighteenth century
> there lived in our land a certain Marquis
> who honored customs and ideas
> bequeathed him by a grandpa from old Castile:
> by this I mean to say that he spent half
> his life thinking about reaching paradise:
> venerable elder of ways pristine,
> though in his youth a devil of a man.
>
> And he loved so his Gothic customs
> that he would have thought quite criminal
> that people may have spoken of French fashions,
> or that they praised the beauty of Paris.
> Of the genealogy of nearly all
> the families of Chile he was past master,
> and of any conquistador he could, from memory,
> recite, quite faithfully, the history.

Sanfuentes, a man of his times, like Bello himself, local literary polemics notwithstanding, responds to the myopia of the marquis along lines quite different than those proposed by Lozano. His poem becomes still more, not less local as he develops the tragic consequences of that light, satiric portrait, narrating how the prejudices of the marquis cause the love of a local upstart to founder on class distinctions. And like Quintana in Santiago de Cuba, Sanfuentes's critique aims at the replication within the colonies of the same hegemonic relation of center to periphery that is the basis of colonization itself.

This "transcendant theme," that is the investigation of class and race, politics and ethnicity, as differences that atomize the colonialist view of a Spanish American society unified by the legacy of the Conquest (as in *Lima fundada*), is more accessible from the republican point of view of contrasting national identities than in the late colonial period that Sanfuentes examines in his satire.[10] But taking quite literally Alegría's reference to "filling *books*," a route opens for the reading of tlaco poetry. For Spanish America has no substantial book industry in colonial times, and the local publications in which poetry usually appeared, in consequence, were themselves ephemeral. Periodicals could generally only accommodate shorter poetic forms, including the décimas and quintillas favored in rapid, oral composition—a material constraint mitigating against transcendent flights.

Viewing the short satiric forms as so many fragments shorn of the narrative complement (and tragic denouement) that would be the luxury of the mid-nineteenth-century book industry, criticism has in fact sought to make good the loss—when it has attended to the verse at all—often seeking to recreate the occasions that would make sense of circumstantial poetry. Alegría himself, for instance, introduces some few verses that he does admire with the tale of their setting. A certain Father López, he relates, had requested a *pie forzado* (a concluding verse upon which to base an impromptu composition, but literally, "forced foot") from a woman in a social gathering; "and the lady, giving herself airs as a great wit, said: 'Here you have it,' as she showed him the point of her own foot. The reply was not long in coming" (Alegría 1954, 114):

> Os hacéis mui poco honor,
> pues viéndoos en tal postura,
> señora, se me figura

> que yo soi el herrador
> i vos la cabalgadura.
>
> (Alegría 1954, 114)

> You hold yourself of low account,
> for seeing you in such a pose,
> your ladyship, I might suppose
> I am the smithy that you chose
> and you're to be my mount.

The unnamed woman demonstrates a certain metapoetical finesse. If one were to overhear her remark as a combative poem in its own right—as I have suggested that one overhear the contesting *lui, lui* embedded in the tale of Father Salvatierra's expeditionary force— then the woman's own satiric voice may begin to emerge. Instead, we are offered the man's response and therefore the more predominant current of the satire *of* women is merely reaffirmed.[11]

The research of Eduardo Matos Moctezuma, however, calls into question the reconstruction of Father López from the fragmentary historical record, and may serve as an admonishment to a critical history that has too easily and too often chosen to follow the main literary currents only. Matos Moctezuma (Matos Moctezuma 1980, 30) has pointed out that a variant of the same satiric invention is attributed to the late eighteenth-century *Negrito Poeta dominicano*, Meso Mónica, as well as to José Vasconcelos, alias *El Negrito Poeta mexicano*, and, in any case, he himself traces the original conceit to Quevedo.[12] But one may return to Meso Mónica for a poetics of inference and a matching thematics of the missing piece that underwrite the critical task of reconstructing a certain transcendence perceived to be lacking in the fragmentary record of eighteenth-century literary history, when he writes:

> O por fineza o por ley
> debido a vuestro decoro,
> va al monte Carmelo un toro
> que aquí en Belén fuera un buey.
>
> (Matos Moctezuma 1980, 121)

> Whether by law or punctilio
> due to your indescribable tact
> there's a bull bound for Mt. Carmelo,
> that'd be an ox 'round here, for a fact.

Matos Moctezuma provides the corresponding narrative history:

> Every year the pious nuns of the Convent of Santa Clara had the custom
> of sending their sisters of [the Convent] of Carmen a bull from amongst
> the most pure bred on the island for the lottery that they held in the
> neighborhood of their church. . . . Seeing as on one occasion they were
> unable to find a bull that met the traditional requirements, the good nuns
> resolved to make one out of sweets. Such chaste hands could not pro-
> duce the animal in its entirety, and so, when they were finished, Meso
> Mónica was called for to compose a décima to accompany the gift.
> (Matos Moctezuma 1980, 121)

The poem thus becomes a fetish in a strictly Freudian sense, a
stand-in for the missing male member, or perhaps a deconstructive
supplement to religious piety. In any case, Mónica will pursue this
course in "El robo del sombrero" and an untitled poem that might
well be called "the rape of the mortar" (Matos Moctezuma 1980,
123–24 and 125–26, respectively): a poet of absences.

One finds further signs to alternative routes along and across the
borders of popular culture in the poetry of Fray Francisco del Castillo Andraca y Tamayo (Peru, 1714–70). "His ephemeral pieces
are not preserved in print. It is negligence not to have compiled
them in an estimable collection," wrote Ignacio de Castro already
in 1791, adding: "The things done extemporaneously astonish
listeners. . . . That collection would have testified as to whether
there were sublimity and grandeur in that vein" (qtd. in Castillo
Andraca 1948, xvii). The eventual publication of Castillo Andraca's verse speaks in his favor, and of the greatest interest are the
poems in which he situates the perspective of social satire in the
marginal figures who would have had a direct knowledge of the
vices of the upper class.[13] Hence, in the "Romance 4°: Conversación de unas negras en la calle de los Borricos," the black women
debate which of Lima's alleyways is the worst in the city. They are
not yet on the road to Independence, and Castillo Andraca does not
yet attempt to reproduce the linguistic character of the class of his
speakers, black, urban and poor. On the contrary, among these
women, all of whom speak the king's Spanish, he singles out an
older figure, "sabia en idioma y oficio" ["wise in language and in
practice"] (Castillo Andraca 1948, 39), for the conclusion of the
debate. She instructs her listeners with the verbal dexterity of the
still persistent baroque, playing on the difference between *callejón*

(alley), the term that the others had been employing, and *calle* (street, but also the imperative: "shut up"):

> Calle, siendo voz que manda
> callar, toda es ironía,
> porque en la calle no hay
> quien lo que siente no diga.
> Callejón difiere de
> calle en lo que él se limita
> y la misma estrechez hace
> la diferencia cumplida.
> Por eso del callejón
> secretos se comunican
> como agua encallejonada
> que corre más reprimida.
> > (Castillo Andraca 1948, 41)

> *Calle*, taken as a command,
> "shut up," is a great irony,
> for in the street there is no one
> who does not say just what he feels.
> *Callejón*, or alley, differs
> from *calle* by cutting itself
> short and its very narrowness
> makes you feel the difference.
> That is why back alley secrets
> pass from mouth to mouth like water
> shut up in a narrow tube
> that, held in, runs all the swifter.

This brief and canny thesis in social psychology is also a telling metaphor for the literary *undercurrents* in Spanish America.

More trenchant, indeed more moving, is Castillo Andraca's "Romance 5°: "Conversación de un negro, mayordomo de chacra, con un Indio Alcalde de los Camaroneros, en la calle de los Borricos." The Indio Alcalde's tale is a variant of the picaresque adventure: he moves from one occupation to the next, ever victimized by a racist society. His suffering is all the more acute for his clear-sighted awareness of his proper birthright:

> Y siendo, gracias a Dios,
> yo natural destos Reynos

> me hubieran hecho alemán,
> por reputarme extranjero.
>
> (Castillo Andraca 1948, 52)

> And being, thank the Lord,
> a native of these realms
> they've nearly made me out a German,
> they think me so foreign.

His black friend recognizes the veracity of the account: "Bien sé que la voz primera/que pronuncia el niño tierno/es 'perro indio, perro cholo' " [" 'I well know that the first word/the tender baby speaks/is 'Indian dog, *cholo* dog' "] (Castillo Andraca 1948, 54). Elaborately arrayed in a show of wealth and well-being, he himself counsels accommodation:

> No advierte Ud. que nosotros,
> aun cuando, esclavos nos vemos,
> y nuestro color el blanco
> diametralmente es opuesto,
> no solo somos tratados
> sin rigor, mas somos dueños
> de haciendas y confianzas
> y aun de su honor tesoreros,
> en fin de todo servimos,
> toreadores y cocheros,
> sombras y tápalo todo
> y esto último es lo primero.

> Don't you see, my friend, that we,
> though we find ourselves slaves,
> and our color diametrically
> the opposite of white,
> we are not only treated
> without harshness, but are lords
> of confidences and estates,
> and treasurers even of their honor,
> in short, we serve in every way,
> cowboys and coachmen,
> shadows and cover-ups,
> and this last is first of all.
>
> (Castillo Andraca 1948, 54–55)

This being satire, the superficial message of capitulation is laden with the irony of the subordinated class, as the black majordomo deploys in closing the christological formula of the alpha and omega to point to the vices of the Christian conquistador and slave-owner as the foundation of Peruvian society.[14] The critique is especially pointed in that it brings together several of the main tenets of modernity as they will come to be conflated in the predominant view of the later nineteenth century, namely, the equation of progress with active participation in the market economy as the course of reason. The offended Indio Alcalde insists on being unreasonable, while for my part, I insist that this position is over-simplified when it is cast as merely premodern. It suggests, rather, an alternative modernity.

The figure of the rich black appears in the next generation in *Lima por dentro y fuera* (Lima 1797) by Esteban Terralla Landa (b. Spain, fl. Peru, late eighteenth century). But Terralla's extended satire, consisting of eighteen long *romances* and a closing "Testamento," written in correspondingly long sixteen-syllable lines, is a rear-guard action in every respect, including its depiction of racial stratification:

Que vas viendo por la calle	pocos blancos, muchos prietos,
siendo los prietos el blanco	de la estimación y aprecio;
que los negros son los amos	y los blancos son los negros,
y que habrá de llegar día	que sean esclavos aquéllos.
	(Terralla Landa 1978, 21)

For you go on seeing in the streets	few whites, many colored,
the colored being the white bull's-	
[eye]	of esteem and appreciation;
for the blacks are the masters	and the whites are the blacks,
for the day is sure to come	when the former are the slaves.

Baroque word-play, if still in evidence, is much attenuated in the satires of Castillo. To find the same resources deployed with unabated insistence here and throughout *Lima por dentro y fuera* some thirty years later bespeaks Terralla's determination to keep faith with a literary style that was already passing. And the reactionary literary stance serves him in the enunciation of an analogous sociopolitical posture. For Terralla to achieve his comic intentions in these lines, his reader, or at least the implicit fictional addressee of the satire, must share the view that not slavery itself, but the increasing wealth of blacks constitutes an unhealthy or even unnatural inversion of the political order. Terralla mounts his own particular political hobbyhorse a few verses later, when he adds:

que una mulata, una zamba   y otras de este corto pelo
alternan en gala y traje   a uno de título expreso
                                                   (Teralla Landa 1978, 21)

that a mulatto, a sambo   and other nappy-headed women
take their place in finery   alongside a man of ancient title

His racism, that is, extends to include all *criollos* in its deprecatory embrace, that is, anyone lacking a Peninsular pedigree. His reactionary posture is an expression of rancor for the dwindling power of a Spanish heritage to buoy the social situation of the recently arrived fortune hunters like himself.

In any case, Terralla's special animus is directed not so much at blacks and mulattoes, nor at Indians and mestizos, as at women. It is, most of all, his unrestrained misogyny that makes the poem all but unreadable today. For this very reason, however, Terralla's women evidence a small step forward for poetic expression, since, as the very lowest of the lower depths of Lima from his point of view, he allows his own poetic diction greater intercourse with popular language when the women speak. Witness the following elaborate invective:

Vaya muy en hora mala   el chapetón pezuñento,
pues para casa y corral   yo con cualquiera lo tengo,
y no me parió mi madre   sola para el muy grosero,
el hediondo, el mezquino,   el trasto, el cochino, el puerco,
el pícaro, alcahuetón   el infame, indigno, el perro . . .
                                                   (Terralla Landa 1978, 30)

Let the stumblebumb   greenhorn go to hell,
as for house and home   I can get that from anyone
and my mother who bore me   didn't make me for this oaf,
this stinking, puny, piece   of junk, this dirty pig,
this good-for-nothing pimp,   this indecent, worthless dog . . .

Or, in short, "Tú le haces los justos cargos de las finezas que has hecho/y ella te responde: '¡Gua!' " ["You ask just compensation for the gentility you've shown/and she just answers, 'Gua!' "] (Terralla Landa 1978, 30). And I recall that the exclamation, "Gua!" is the touchstone of linguistic barbarity that Santos Luzardo would still be cleansing from the language of Marisela as he seeks to domesticate a woman to household service more than a century later in Rómulo Gallegos' *Doña Bárbara* (Gallegos 1976, 623).

Terralla was dying of syphillis as he completed the "Testamento" section of *Lima por dentro y fuera*—"muero bien quemado" ["I'm burning up alive"] (Terallo Landa 1978, 74)—and one can hardly doubt that the afflictions of the man enter into the misogynist cast of the poem.[15] Nevertheless, the great strides in mid-twentieth century studies of satire by such scholars as Alvin Kernan and Maynard Mack (see Paulson 1983) are predicated on a separation of the historical personage of the poet from the satiric voice of the poem. Terralla's *Lima por dentro y fuera*, then, may be inserted into the broader panorama of eighteenth-century literature by observing the fictional frame in which he places his satire. The speaker addresses a friend who purposes to leave his native Mexico and take up residence in Lima. The satirical description of the latter city is aimed at dissuading the Mexican from that "¡Terrible absurdo! ¡Notabilísmo exceso!" ["Terrible absurdity Most notable excess!"] (Terralla Landa 1978, 5). In light of the movement toward an augmented internal commerce within the Americas and American letters that I have been proposing as a key to eighteenth- and nineteenth-century poetry—"*to remove obstacles, open communications and facilitate journeys,*" writes Arango y Parreno (Arango y Parreño 1979, 260, the emphasis is his)—this most conservative of satires is a roadblock.

Others, however, will press onward in less pedantic style and better humor. José Rodríguez Ucres, also known as Uscarrés or Uscarrel (Cuba b. prior to 1788), wrote a satiric "Viage que hizo de La Havana a Vera-Cruz y Reyno de Mexico el P. Fr. Gregorio Uscarrel (o Ucarres)," a suite of forty-seven décimas, which represent "versos de camino" ["verses on the road"] (Lezama 1965, 1:138). After the splenetic, if not to say syphilitic *Lima por dentro y fuera*, Rodríguez Ucres's serenity is especially to be admired when the fever that besets him in the eighteenth décima and remains with him to the end, leaves his jocular vein unimpaired. Even more noteworthy, and again in contrast to Terralla, is his even-handed treatment of women. The pages of conventional quintillas dedicated to the age-old topos of "Quejas que un amante despreciado envia a su dama" (1:117–28), prove to be but the pretext for the sharp satire of equal length in the "Respuesta de la dama desengañada":

Si pone triste el semblante
Cuando escuche mi rigor,
Díle que sufra y aguante,
Y espere muerte mayor
Si se me pone delante.

(Lezama 1965, 1:130)

If he should show disconsolate mien
Whene'er my stern reply he hears,
Tell him to suffer and suck it up,
and to expect a death far worse
If I ever get my hands on him.

The vigor of her reply turns upon her mocking echo of his inflated language in the first two verses, followed by the sudden shift in register to the plain-spoken denunciation. The murder of his poetry makes the closing threat to the fictional poet a matter not to be taken lightly. Satire's penchant for the deflation of an extravagance that masks, as the brothers Lemaur remarked, a felt insufficiency, combines in the good-humored Rodríguez Ucres with a traveler's longing for the simple things of home in the "Viage que hizo de la Havana a Vera-Cruz," where the satirist is out "cazando Aves" ["hunting birds"] only to supply the "falta de mi *caza-ave*" ["the lack of my *cass-ava*"] (Lezama 1965, 1:143). And this and other threads of homespun language in his décimas, along with the vituperations of Terralla's limeñas or the more feeling presence of Castillo's dispossessed Indians and trickster blacks all point to the entrance of new voices into the Spanish American lyric of the period.

Remaining within the realm of satire, a further dimension of this expanded social range may be discovered in Miguel Cabrera's "Coplas del jíbaro." Cabrera (Puerto Rico, n.d.) circulated his satiric response to the Spanish Constitution of 1812 in manuscript, and it was only printed for the first time in the periodical *El Investigador* (22 June 1820) in an article attacking the verses.[16] Cabrera's mockery, it turns out, was well founded, since Felipe VII would renege upon the liberties of the constitution as soon as he reestablished himself securely upon the throne. The greater importance for the history of literature, however, resides in the effort to reproduce the dialect of the *jíbaro*:

Que ha salio cieita
la Costitusión,
y van a jasei
una gran funsión.
   Ello debe sei
sigún lo que suena
una ciscustancia
ea diablos, mui güena.
   (Rivera de Alvarez and Alvarez Nazario 1982, 61)

It be really done,
the Cons'tushun
and they gonna make
a great cel'brashun.
   It bound to be
from what dey say
just one helluva
o-kay-shun.

Similar experiments may be found in the dialect of River Plate blacks (see Carullo 1985 and Soler Cañas 1958), such as the later "Canto patriótico de los negros celebrando la ley de la libertad de vientres y la Constitución" (1834) by Acuña de Figueroa:

¡Viva len contitusione!
¡Viva len leye patlisia!
Que ne tiela den balanco
Se cabó le dipotima.
lingo, lingo, lingo,
   linga, linga, linga,
Que ne tiela den balanco
se cabó le dipotima.
   (Carvalho Neto 1965, 263)

Long liv' de constitushun!
Long liv' de country's law!
For in de land of de whites
Despotism is no maw.
   Lingo, lingo, lingo,
   linga, linga, linga,
For in de land of de whites
Despotism is no maw.

The political impulse behind the dialect poetry may be linked to the late eighteenth-century mythology of the noble savage. In Spain, Cadalso would offer the laborer Lorenzo as the representative figure of cultural innocence, untouched by civilized ennui, in his *Noches lúgubres*: "Tediato: 'Your inocence is your excuse . . .' Lorenzo: 'I don't get it.' Tediato: 'Nor should you . . .' " (Cadalso 1987, 142). But as Tediato's condescension suggests, the broadening contours of the poetic voice do not necessarily reflect a political reality of racial and social equality. On the contrary, the literary revolution that canonizes the voice of the outsider in the most enduring of these experiments in dialect poetry, namely poesía gauchesca, developed as a parallel to cooptation through military conscription, as Ludmer has argued. I will return to Bartolomé Hidalgo and his successors, but note here that late colonial satire is the literary historical context from which the poesía gauchesca emerged—quite literally so in the case of the scant poetic production of Maziel. And in fact the poesía gauchesca served the ends of satiric poetry precisely in the measure that its distinctive voice expressed a perspective alien to its urban readers ("por reputarme extranjero," as Castillo Andraca's *Indio* said)—far more a technique of "making it strange" (Shklovsky 1990) than a utopian "jolly relativity," such as Bakhtin (Bakhtin 1984) ascribed to parody.

Mary Claire Randolph has remarked that "In any age, Satire never fails to assume the colorations of the dominant rationalistic philosophy of that period" (Randolph 1971, 175). In a highly rationalistic age like the late eighteenth century, satire itself predominates. Castillo Andraca's black majordomo is a *philosophe*, urging rational analysis of utilitarian benefits on his Indian friend and Cabrera's jíbaro a subscriber of the Rights of Man. But when the call to political action is sounded after the turn of the nineteenth century, the efficacy of satire is challenged. Camilo Henríquez (Chile 1769–1845) writes, for example:

> La sátira es el encanto
> De pueblos envilecidos
> Y esclavos, que no se atreven
> Ni aun á exhalar un suspiro.
>
> (Valderrama 1912, 256)

> Satire is the joy
> of peoples degraded

and enslaved, who dare not
so much as breathe a sigh.

and in another "Letrilla":

> Querer salvar los Estados
> Con remedios paliativos,
> Con versos y reglamentos,
> Cosa es que el diablo no ha visto . . .
>
> (Valderrama 1912, 251)

> To want to save the State
> With palliating cures,
> With verses and with rules,
> The devil himself has never seen . . .

Satire does not vanish by any means. One will find in Felipe Pardo y Aliaga (1806–68), for instance, an able heir of the satiric tradition, which, in his native Peru, reaches back two centuries to Juan del Valle Caviedes (1650–97). Moreover, the only "central name" of the this period wedged between the baroque and romanticism, José Joaquín Fernández de Lizardi (Mexico 1776–1827), publishes his great satiric prose works, as well as comic, moralizing verse fables, after the turn of the century.

Even in the midst of war, satire has a place as a weapon on the ideological front. Thus the Mexican revolutionary periodical *Sud*, for example, would undermine a certain "Oda de un ingenio poblano" that sings the royalist strain in mythological trappings, by printing the text after a brief introduction that anticipates "the bad time that the reading holds in store" (Miquel i Vergés 1941, 161), and then including a copious set of notes that lampoon both the political posture and the grandiloquent style. Still, as the wars of independence proceed throughout Spanish America, those with time enough to dedicate to poetry devote themselves increasingly to the heroic themes of a now explicit patriotism. The pompous style with its mythological mise-en-scène is neither reserved for those loyal to colonial rule, nor defeated by the skirmishes of satire. On the contrary, a staunch neoclassicism carries the day.

4

Writing against a critical tradition that has condemned neoclassical poetry in Spanish America as a paradoxically emphatic cultural dependence at the very moment when political independence was being declared, Oscar Rivera-Rodas usefully remarks: "One could hardly expect a 'daring' poetry of a 'new type' from a continent submitted to three centuries of European colonization, during which time it was precisely the 'decorum' of the West that was imposed upon it, nullifying native language and thought" (Rivera-Rodas 1988, 3). One may be bolder, for against all expectations, poesía gauchesca does in fact take hold. Furthermore, transculturation led to new amalgams between indigenous and Hispanic literatures, most familiar through the example of the poetry of Mariano Melgar (Peru 1791–1815).

Melgar found inspiration in a popular poetic form of indigenous origin, the Quechua *yaraví* (equivalent to the *Hachiruru* or *Llaquiruru* in Aimara literature [Cáceres Romero 1987, 150]), an erotic elegy with musical accompaniment, much as the melancholic protagonist of "Manchay Puitu" would have sung to the music of his skeletal quena. Infusing the yaraví with metrical forms and other poetic resources of the Hispanic tradition, Melgar produced a literary *mestizaje*. Melgar's yaravíes are swift in expression and simplified in diction, in keeping with their popular provenance. They may be compared favorably with his own elegiac pieces in traditional Castilian forms, wherein the new effort of a dawning romanticism to find a spontaneous voice for the aggrieved self is generally hampered by a ponderous rhetoricity. "¡Oh dolor! ¿Cómo, cómo tan distante/De mi querida Silvia aquí me veo?" ["Oh suffering! How, oh how do I find myself/so distant from my beloved Silvia?"] he begins the poem known as "Elegía II" (Melgar 1971, 98), where the overly emphatic initial exclamation should give the psychological grounds for the stuttering question, but in fact fails to obscure the rattle of an emotion shackled to the endecasyllable line. An analogous elegiac absence sets a yaraví in motion:

> Tengo ausente el bien que adoro,
> En tal distancia,
> Que para llegar a verla
> No hay esperanza.

> (Melgar 1971, 300)

> I have absent the treasure I adore,
> At such a distance,
> That to see her again—
> There's just no hope.

where the greater emotional—which is to say rhetorical—restraint and particularly the crisp endpoint of that laconic fourth verse borrowed directly from popular speech, give the same stylized situation renewed vigor. Melgar's success in this genre was a spur to poetry in Peru, and, in a supreme compliment to his achievement in the popular vein, his own yaravíes came to form part of popular culture, on the one hand, while on the other, numerous yaravíes of popular origin came to be attributed to him. Among the latter, Juan Guillermo Carpio Muñoz records a yaraví known as "Testamento de Melgar," (Carpio Muñoz 1976, 154), composed in the form of a sonnet. As popular poetry borrows from the resources of cultivated verse, Melgar's debt to indigenous literature is slowly resolved in a balance of trade.

Melgar's early *indianista* experimentation with the yaraví has been widely recognized by critics of Spanish American poetry, and his verses have been included in the anthologies of Menéndez y Pelayo (1895, vol. 3), Angel Flores (1966, vol 1) and Emilio Carilla (1979), to cite a few standard texts. Not so the Quechua poetry of Juan Wallparrimachi Maita (Bolivia 1793–1814). Open to the influx of his own heritage, Jesús Lara (Lara 1947, 141) points to the purity of Wallparrimachi's literary language, his facility with traditional Quechua verse forms, as well as his intertextual engagement with specific classical texts, such as the echoes of the pre-Columbian *Ollántay* in the opening lines of Wallparrimachi's "Karunchay." Yet also a strict contemporary of Melgar, Wallparrimachi conducts the same cross-cultural experiment at the interface between Hispanic and indigenous verse forms, writing from the Quechua side. In this regard Lara notes suggestively that among the few extant poems of Wallparrimachi, "in one the author attempts a fluid and elegant structure of *décimas*, as if he wished to prove that he could handle European instruments with aplomb" (141).

The analogy between the life and work of Melgar and Wallparrimachi—or, more precisely, the legend of Wallparrimachi, as Julio E. Noriega (Noriega 1991) has advocated recently in an incisive analysis—is clear. And yet the equally evident contrast between the relatively broad recognition of the former and the obscurity of the latter provides a case in point for the ideological burden—"with sacrifices and even the greatest injustices," Henríquez Ureña had said— of the winnowing process that yields the central names (Henríquez Ureña 1978, 47; see also Introduction, note 6).

An introductory note to a collection of Melgar's yaravíes published in the *Mistura para el bello sexo* in 1893 and reproduced by the distinguished committee of editors of Melgar's *Poesías completas* in 1971—a civic monument of sorts: the first title in a series of *Clásicos peruanos* under the auspices of the *Academia Peruana de la Lengua*—gives expression to the extra-literary values that contribute to the canonization of this or any poet: "We insert here several of the *yaravíes* that were composed by the illustrious and unfortunate patriotic countryman, our Don Mariano Melgar, victim of Iberian fury, for having been among the first to rally to the banner of the immortal patriots Pumaccahua, Angulo and others" (Melgar 1971, 391n). Again the legendary Wallparrimachi was no less a revolutionary patriot. Yet where Melgar's less than central name receives at least brief mention by Henríquez Ureña (Henríquez Ureña 1963, 108 and in the notes on 214 and 257), even he passes over Wallparrimachi in silence. Of "the paths of our literary history," the road of America's indigenous literatures has been the one less traveled by. It calls for increased traffic.

Returning to Rivera-Rodas's revisionary position, his argument may also be carried a step farther with respect to the Spanish-language poetry of classical diction. For the particular decorum of the period, based on the model of Horace (also an important model for satire), itself represents a new experiment in poetry. The late twentieth century is closer in its tastes to the relative liberties of eighteenth-century satire; but the tone of early nineteenth-century verse is an innovation that calls for a brief discussion of the history of an emerging poetic genre: the ode.

The ode, it is true, develops in late eighteenth-century Spain as a departure from the prevailing vogue for didactic poetry, especially the verse fable. The principal innovator was Meléndez Valdés, whose collaboration with the invading French regime continues to cost him the stature that he had once earned among his contemporaries as the restorer of Castilian poetry. Beginning his career as a protégé of Cadalso at Salamanca, Meléndez took over from the latter the exercise of the Anacreontic ode, a brief verse form in seven-syllable lines dedicated to amorous pastimes in bucolic settings—a neoclassicism of a different stripe. Meléndez's facility and, within the narrow confines of contemporary decorum, his erotic audacity made him immensely popular in this vein with the publication of his first collection of *Poesías* in 1785. Partly under the influence of Jovellanos's well-known poem, "Carta de Jovino a sus amigos salmantinos" (1776), Meléndez undertook a turn from the ephemeral to the sublime, from Anacreon to Horace—although, typical of the age, he continued to produce poetry in both strains throughout his career (see Carnero 1983). Still, the shift was perceived by the reading public, and it met resistance. Manuel José Quintana records that the second edition of Meléndez's *Poesías* of 1797 was received with great reserve (Quintana 1796–1898, 115). As for Quintana, himself a student of Meléndez at Salamanca, he would pursue the Horatian mode even more vigorously, entertaining themes in the spirit of the Enlightenment in odes "A la invención de la imprenta" (1800) or "A la expedición española para propagar la vacuna en América" (1806). If he is Meléndez's pupil, he is nonetheless the poet of a much chastened muse. Meléndez is Spain's poet for the Age of Sensibility. Yet Quintana, the stricter Horatian neoclassicist, was verging upon Romanticism from a different avenue when Napoleon invaded in 1808. Quintana then wrote his two famous patriotic odes, "A España, después de la Revolución de marzo" and "Al armamento de las Provincias españolas" (both of 1808), and thereupon turned his attention to primarily political activity and to prose (Dérozier 1978).

As the period in the history of Spanish American letters under study in this chapter was coming to a close, Quintana renounced his dedication to the lyric in two poems to his friend and fellow poet Iosef Somoza (Spain 1781–1852), "A un amigo" (1825) and "A Somoza" (1826). But in 1822, José Luis Munarriz could still attribute the "notable improvement" of Castilian poetry (Munarriz 1822, 350) above all to the leading figures of the Salamanca school: Mcléndez, Quintana and Nicolás Alvarez de Cienfuegos, schoolmate of the latter and likewise pupil of the former. Munarriz is a biased judge, forming part of Quintana's circle, but I cite his *Compendio de las lecciones sobre la retórica y bellas letras de Hugo Blair*, based on the famous English handbook that he had previously translated, precisely in order to highlight the embattled status of the ode by a critic close to its most innovative practitioners. For immediately following his praise of the odes of Meléndez, Quintana and Cienfuegos in the section dedicated to "*modern* lyric poets" (Munarriz 1822, 334, emphasis added), Munarriz interpolates a diatribe under the heading "Adición" in which he replicates the most conservative literary thinking of the period:

In recent times a novelty has been introduced into our lyric poetry, which, I believe, is destroying it. Poets of some fame, allowing them-

selves to be carried away by their impetuous talent, have written compositions in irregular stanzas that they have called *Odes*: and now
beginners believe themselves authorized by that example not to respect
the number of verses nor the corresponding rhymes in their own compositions (Munarriz 1822, 336)

Munarriz will go on to declare of this "novelty," that "reason
rejects it" (Munarriz 1822, 336). In sum, the ode was an innovation
and more; it was viewed in the period as a threat to the strictures
of eighteenth-century poetic convention. By appealing to Horace,
however, the Salamanca school circumvented the regulations of
neoclassical literary legislation without departing from the fundamental impulse to find authority among the classics.

In the period from the mid-1790s to the close of the wars of independence, the ode rises to a predominant position in Spanish
America as well. One can be even more precise. The ode was
adopted, first, in the manner of Meléndez, followed by a shift to
Quintana. The recognition is explicit, as in the advertisement for a
would-be Cuban edition of the poetry of a still adolescent Heredia:

> our contemporary Peninsular poets publish their poetry, which spreads
> rapidly to Havana; the seeds of good taste are sown, gaining more and
> more converts each day; there is no longer a youth who is not familiar
> with the manly accents of the singer of the printing press [i.e. Quintana],
> nor any who do not know by heart the best pieces of the sweet Batilo
> [i.e. Meléndez]. (Anuncio. 1823, 6)

Heredia's debt to the Salamanca school poets was real and ongoing,
and his affinity to Cienfuegos, the wildest poet of the group, has
been much chastised, if little understood. But if he was precocious
in this as in so many respects, he was by no means an isolated case.

The influence of the Salamanca school is clearest in Mexico,
where there were enough adepts of the bucolic verse of Anacreontic
inspiration to found the *Arcadia de México* in 1808. The first *ma-
yoral* of this arcadia and the best poet in the more popular vein of
Meléndez was Friar Manuel de Navarrete (Mexico 1768–1809).
Even so simple a lyric as his "Juguetillo I" gives evidence of a fine,
ear as his apostrophe to the commonplace brook expands the name
of his fictitious beloved into the echo of the refrain from Clorila to
"Corre, corre/Dila, dila" [Run, run/Tell her, tell her] (Navarrete
1939, 174).

A ripple-effect upon the surface of the stream transforms *Clorila*

(C[l]or-ila) into *corre-dila* and *la aldea* into *la adora*. Such music, however sweet, does not run deep, particularly in erotic matters. Navarrete describes the suitors wooing "la zagala que adoro,/ Muchacha de quince años" ["the shepherdess I adore/a girl of fifteen years"] in the Anacreontic "Oda XIII" (Navarrete 1939, 50) with the greatest reticence:

> Cércanla como abejas,
> Pero, vamos al caso,
> Todos huelen las flores;
> Mas nadie lleva el ramo.
>
> (Navarrete 1939, 51)

> They swarm to her like bees,
> But, let's get to the point,
> They all sniff the flowers,
> But none take the bouquet.

"Vamos al caso" ("But let's get to the point") is anything but a call to candor. Rather, Navarrete unexpectedly breaks away from the typical idealizing pastoral diction of the Anacreontic ode when the image flirts too intimately with sexuality, in stark contrast to his model Meléndez.[17]

Like Meléndez, however, Navarrete is not a poet of Anacreontic odes only. Much as Munarriz singled out the Salamanca school for special praise as descriptive poets, Navarrete is at his best in this area, though it needs be noted that the landscape that he depicts in his verse derives more from Meléndez's poetry than from direct observations of nature. Thus, when he finds in the variegated sensations of daybreak a "secreto impulso" ["secret impulse"] that raises the soul "A grandes y *sublimes* pensamientos" ["To grand and *sublime* thoughts"] in "La mañana" (Navarrete 1939, 167; emphasis added), this crucial, if commonplace term in eighteenth-century aesthetics translates in Navarrete's own poetic practice into expressions of sensibility, once again in the mode of Edward Young via Meléndez, particularly in the Navarrete's odes collected under the title of "Ratos tristes" (145–62).

With war against Napoleonic occupation on the Peninsula, the sublime takes on a different coloration for Quintana, and through his influence, on the subsequent Spanish American poetry of the wars of independence. The sublime, that is, comes to be associated with the political discourse of freedom and the civic heroism required to obtain it. To cite one of countless examples, the Mexican Andrés Quintana Roo (1787–1851) equates "el don más sublime" ["the most sublime gift"] with "la noble libertad" ["noble liberty"] in his ode "Dieciséis de septiembre" (Urbina et al. 1985, 115). The ode, then, is the typical vehicle for the sublime of patriotic virtue, which constitutes a ubiquitous body of poetry, indeed, the most widespread of all poetic expression in the decade of the wars of independence. Thoroughly neoclassical inasmuch as these patriotic odes look back through Quintana to the antique model of Horace, I repeat that the form itself, with its abrupt thematic shifts authorized by the classics, and its metrical and stanzaic irregularity—as Munarriz complained—represents an important break with the preceding poetic conventions. The poets of America's independence sought out the most revolutionary form then available in Hispanic verse in selecting the ode to exhort their fellow patriots and to commemorate their victories.

José Joaquin Olmedo (Ecuador 1780–1847), author of the most famous ode of all the patriotic poetry on the road to and in the wake of independence, "La victoria de Junín. Canto a Bolívar" (Guayaquil 1825), presents an exemplary case for the trajectory that I have been describing. As a fledgling poet he characterizes the work of his "torpe lira" ["clumsy lyre"] as the inspiration of "Mi juguetona Musa" (Olmedo 1947, 15). That is, Olmedo begins as a poet of Anacreontic odes—"A una amiga," "La palomita (Anacreóntica)" and its accompanying "Dedicatoria a J. R. O.," and even as late a composition as his "Impromptu, Versos dichos en Tacubaya en el convite que el Señor Virrey-Arzobispo dió al Diputado J. J. de Olmedo" of 1811. In another early Anacreontic ode, "Mi retrato, A mi hermana Magdalena" (1803), he marks his poetic affiliation explicitly, crowning the brief list of his personal canon of ancients and moderns (including Richardson and Pope) with a closing reference to Meléndez:

> y a ti ¡oh Valdés! ¡oh tierno
> amigo de las Musas,
> mi amor y mi embeleso!
>
> (Olmedo 1947, 22)

> and to you, oh [Meléndez] Valdés! oh tender
> friend of the Muses,
> my love and my delight!

One may compare here the roll call of Luis Vargas Tejada half a generation later in his ambitious poem, "A los poetas castellanos," in which he promotes to the ranks of the "jenios celestiales" ("celestial geniuses") such American poets as José Fernández de Madrid (Colombia 1789–1830), Bello and Olmedo himself, addressing them collectively as "cantores, que siguiendo/Las huellas de Meléndez i Quintana,/Al templo de la gloria vais corriendo" ("singers, who, following/The path of Meléndez and Quintana,/speed toward the temple of glory") (Vargas Tejada 1857, 60).

Olmedo's self-portrait in "Mi retrato" is also revealing of his conservative adherence to the aesthetic designs of neoclassicism (see Salgado 1996), the whole of the poem being an effort to situate his likeness in the middle ground between descriptive poles—e.g. "Mi cabello no es rubio,/pero tampoco es negro" ["My hair is not blond,/nor is it black"] (Olmedo 1947, 19)—a procedure that he elevates to an analogue of moral philosophy:

> Ya miras cómo en todo
> disto de los extremos;
> pues lo mismo, lo mismo
> es el alma que tengo.
>
> (Olmedo 1947, 21)

> Now you see how in everything
> I keep my distance from extremes;
> well the same, the very same
> may be said of my very soul.

There is little in such deliberate *mediocritas* to suggest the making of the "Victoria de Junín."

Explicit sign of a move toward the political concerns that animated Quintana and that would raise Olmedo's poetry in "Victoria de Junín," however, appears in "El árbol" (1808). Olmedo opens that poem within the contours of the topos of the poet in rustic seclusion, whence he sends forth his muse in the predictable images of the "fugaz y bella mariposa" ["fleeting and lovely butterfly"] and the dove; but thereafer he changes register to include a "garza atrevida/[que] traspasará los mares" ["daring crane/(that) will cross the seas"] and finally a more martial "águila veloz" ["swift eagle"] (Olmedo 1947, 49). As will be clearest at the close, the intertext, ultimately, is Genesis 8: the tree is a safe ark from which the poet may send out his exploratory muse over a world awash in the Napoleonic flood. But the specific trope refers to Spanish American history:

> ¿No ves cuán ricas tornan a sus playas
> de las Indias las naves españolas
> a pesar de los vientos y las olas?
> Pues muy más rica tornarás, mi musa,
> de imágenes, de grandes pensamientos,
> y de cuantos tesoros de belleza
> contiene en sí la gran naturaleza . . .
>
> (Olmedo 1947, 49)

> Do you not see how rich the Spanish ships
> return from the Indies to their native shores
> despite the winds and waves?
> So too will you return, my muse, the more
> enriched in images, great thoughts,
> and in as many treasured beauties
> as are found in nature's grandeur . . .

The muse, I note, reverses the course of the masterplot of Spanish conquest, flying out eastward, only to return westward with the cultural treasure of poetic imagery. The direction of indebtedness will come to be a primary issue for Spanish American poetry as this period overlaps with the next. The American muse, Bello will argue, must learn to seek the beauties of "la gran naturaleza" closer to home.

Although the attention to local treasures anticipates much poetry to come on the road to independence, Olmedo does not develop separatist claims in a poem that remains loyalist in its politics. Instead, he draws upon the propensity of the ode for sudden shifts in theme to turn from the local landscape to an excoriation of Napoleon. Moreover, he trades upon the proper tone of the ode: enthusiasm. The same poet who congratulated himself in noncommital language for his distance from extremes (see Salgado 1996, 184), suddenly discovers the political backbone to call for no less than assassination—"Bruto, ¿dónde estabas?/No es tarde aún; ven, besaré tu mano/bañada con la sangre del tirano" ["Brutus, where were you?/It is not too late; come, I will kiss your hand/bathed in the tyrant's blood"] (Olmedo 1947, 51). With that new-found will comes an invigorated poetic expression:

¡Oh musa! tú que viste
el furor de la mar estrepitosa
y los vientos horrísonos oíste
y el fracaso espantoso de las olas,
tú sola pintar puedes
el ardor de las armas españolas,
la ira y celo con que por todas partes
va y corre la nación precipitada,
¡Guerra! clamando, y a la voz de ¡Guerra!,
cómo brota la tierra
y las montañas brotan gente armada
a la guerra y venganza aparejada.

(Olmedo 1947, 53)

Oh Muse, you who saw
the fury of tumultuous seas
and heard the fearsome sounding winds
and the awful crashing of the waves
you alone can paint
the ardor of the Spanish arms,
the zealous anger which everywhere
rages as the nation runs precipitously
crying, War, and at the sound of War!
how the earth sends forth
and the mountains, too, send forth armed men
prepared for war and for revenge.

In this turbulence one hears the voice of the Biblical raven and not the dove. The myth of the original autochthon, the earth-born warriors of Cadmos's sowing, will have its resonance when political and poetic circumstance turn Olmedo to the American theme of the triumph of Bolívar.

This poem, "Victoria de Junín. Canto a Bolívar," is among the very few texts of the nineteenth century prior to modernismo that may safely be described as widely celebrated, primarily for the long central passage in which the ghost of the Inca appears to Bolívar and his troops. Readers have long noted that the device resolves a chronological quandry for Olmedo. His chosen hero is Bolívar, the triumphant general at Junín, but not at the subsequent and decisive battle of Ayacucho, fought under the command of Antonio José de Sucre. The Inca speaks a prophecy that projects the later battle as an extension of Bolívar's victory, thereby preserving the latter's ascendancy.

Olmedo's attention to the chronological problem shows a modern historical consciousness at work within the compressed time frame of current events. The present at Ayacucho is qualified by the past at Junín, and therefore only the historicizing of the later battle will allow a reconstruction of the integrity of the independence movement.[18] But in the longer view opened by his recourse to the figure of the Inca, Olmedo's poem demonstrates no greater historical consciousness than had Peralta in *Lima fundada*—and of course the prosopopeia is based on the same model in *Aeneid* 6.[19] Here, too, the pre-Columbian era is made legendary in Oakeshott's sense: a usable past that has not passed, but, following the colonial hiatus now closed by force of arms, rather is continuous with the present. Bolívar, instead of Pizarro, becomes the Incas' salvation in this version of the providential scheme, but the masterplot of the Conquest is not qualified.

Bolívar himself was the first to sound a cautionary note when Olmedo consulted with his subject on the poem in progress. The most salient of Bolívar's incisive comments is an ideological rectification in his letter of 12 July 1825:

> it doesn't seem proper that [the Inca] praises indirectly the religion that destroyed him; and it seems even less proper that he would not want to reestablish his throne and instead gives preference to foreign intruders, who, though they may have avenged his blood, remain the descendants of those who annihilated his empire. (Bolívar 1929, 38)

The critique, formulated anew in terms of postcolonial cultural studies by Mabel Moraña (Moraña 1997), opens Olmedo's poem to historical inquiry, and in particular his transformation of the *leyenda negra* of Spanish Conquest into the *narcisismo blanco* (Rotker 1997, 117) of criollo independence. One might begin to reimagine, for instance, the prophecy of the Olmedo's Inca from the point of view of the indigenous and mestizo recruits in Bolívar's army. One should like to read their poem.

Where silence prevails, one might consult the fragmentary record of the present. Witness the cultic effigy of Bolívar and the associated poetry in popular Catholicism, as documented by Yolanda Salas de Lecuna:

> Cuando Venezuela estaba
> bajo el dominio de España

aunque el yugo le estorbaba
ninguno inventaba campaña,
mas sí ese hijo caraqueño
que reclamó la nación:
como el héroe Bolívar
fue mandado por el Señor.

(Salas de Lecuna 1987, 127)

Back when Venezuela
was under the rule of Spain
though troubled by the yoke
none started a campaign,
but for this native son,
the nation he reclaimed:
our hero Bolívar
was sent us by the Lord.

Another informant's response to the question, "Do you ask Bolívar for anything?" may serve to explicate the closing verses:

on an altar the first thing you see is a picture of Bolívar among the saints. In a private home, too, the first thing you see is a picture of Bolívar. They always think of him not like someone who made history, but like something greater. And you've got to ask him for things: That's the system among us Venezuelans and even among the foreigners, because whoever isn't with Bolívar, won't be moving. (Salas de Lecuna 1987, 126)

Set within the anthropological occasion that links the poetry to the altar, these texts constitute a historical record of an alternative modernity, whose roots reach back at least as far as Bolívar's own syncretisic symbolization of the postindependence president as the sun, i.e. the very light of Enlightenment and also the very heir of the Inca pantheon (Moraña 1997, 36–37 following Pratt 1993). First, they serve to recall that alongside Olmedo's self-conscious mythologizing, in which the Inca preaches to legitimize criollo revolutionaries, stands the historical reality of Christian missionaries preaching to and converting indigenous and African peoples. The integration, albeit partial, of these peoples into the Christian community disrupted, from the very outset of cultural contact, the stable dichotomies upon which the masterplot of the Conquest was structured. Bolívar's critical question is, to my mind, more poignant than Olmedo's appropriation of the Inca; but like Olmedo, Bolívar's deliberations on the relation of the criollos to the Inca past omits the present in which many of his own soldiers were neither criollo nor Inca.

The poetic apotheosis of Bolívar as God's chosen emissary in the poem recorded by Salas de Lecuna points to a further discrepancy with customary expectations concerning modernity.[20] The sequential schema in which Enlightenment science appears as the definitive wedge that breaks knowledge loose from faith, makes secularization an inevitable aspect of modernity. Religion of any stripe is premodern, if not antimodern, from this perspective, and so, too, religious poetry. A fortiori, Spanish American syncretism, with its conservation of elements from peoples prior to their conversion to Christianity—implicitly the most nearly modern of religions in the customary understanding of a modernizing secularism—is evidence of the failure of modernity. If eighteenth-century rationalism and, belatedly for Spanish America, nineteenth-century positivism are the stages that emancipate modernity from the shackles of a religious consciousness, then modernity will surely appear to have bypassed those who *move* with Bolívar by "asking him for things" or dedicating devotional poetry to his icon. One may argue, however, that the same syncretism demonstrates, on the contrary, the dynamism of tradition, thereby complicating another standard dichotomy that divides between premodern stasis and the modern capacity for change.

Olmedo's prosopopeia is thoroughly secular; he certainly does not seek to propagate faith in the prophetic power of the Incas. But not all modernities lead to secularization. One can infer from the fragmentary record of the twentieth-century *canto a Bolívar* recorded by Salas de Lecuna a fuller body of popular poetry from the independence period itself that has not survived, and in which *worship* of Bolívar and other revolutionary heroes was distinct in spirit from Olmedo's self-consciously literary device. What the record shows, then, is at once a consciousness that the wars of independence are long past and Bolívar long gone, and yet a conviction that past is not altogether dead and buried, nor Bolívar himself lost to the possibilities of symbolic exchange in Baudrillard's sense. In a predominantly rational framework, such as Landívar's, the continuing grip of the past upon the present is manifest as poetic melancholia. The popular poem at hand recalls that in a *modern* religious setting, the same can express itself in a celebratory tone.

With the conclusion of the Inca's prophecy, "Victoria de Junín" hastens to its end. As in "El arból," Olmedo retreats from the sphere of political history to the haven of a bucolic setting, the "musa, pacífica y tranquila/cual tímida paloma" ["pacific and tranquil Muse/like a timid dove"] (Olmedo 1947, 54) restored to the end of the early poem reappears in "Victoria de Junín" as Olmedo's "humilde musa mía" ["my humble Muse"] (152). But borne by the strength of the greater lyric energy of the "Victoria de Junín," the sylvan setting, however brief, is more precise. The superfluous Greco-Roman allusion aside, it is Olmedo's finest passage of descriptive poetry:

> yo volveré a mi flauta conocida,
> libre vagando por el bosque umbrío
> de naranjos y opacos tamarindos,
> o entre el rosal pintado y oloroso
> que matiza la margen de mi río,
> o entre risueños campos, do en pomposo
> trono piramidal y alta corona,
> la piña ostenta el cetro de Pomona . . .

(Olmedo 1947, 152)

> I will return to my familiar flute,
> wandering free in the shady wood
> of orange trees and opaque tamarinds,
> or beside the painted, aromatic rose,
> that bedecks the bank of my river,
> or through the smiling fields where in great pomp
> upon a pyramidal throne and in high crown
> the pineapple displays the scepter of Pomona.

The turn to the natural—and national—environment is no more than a form of closure here, but Bello's contemporaneous enunciation of a program for a distinctive American poetry will make that move an opening.

5

Olmedo's Bolívar has come to stand for the wide panorama in which every local hero had his local bard, ranging from the anonymous madrigal, octavas and verse inscription written for the funeral service of the long-since forgotten Captain Lorenzo Buroz and published in *El Patriota de Venezuela* (1811) (*Testimonios* 1961, 343–45), to Heredia's famous ode, "La estrella de Cuba" (1823). The patriotic impulse of such poetry gave rise, moreover, to the critical efforts to delineate the contours of local literatures. Perhaps the earliest attempt was the publication of *La Lira Argentina, o colección de las piezas poéticas dadas a luz en Buenos Aires durante la guerra de su independencia* (1824), now available in the superb scholarly edition of Pedro Luis Barcia.[21]

The first impression one gleans from *La Lira Argentina* is the sheer volume of writing: well over a hundred poems were collected without venturing so far as Tucumán. And many of the leading contributors—Lafinur and Luca, Fray Cayetano Rodríguez (1761–1823) and Juan Ramón Rojas (1784–1824)—are absent from Menéndez y Pelayo's *Antología*. Whenever research finally extends investigations of the poetry of the period to the other cultural centers and their adjacent hinterlands, one may expect to discover a corresponding avalanche of material.

More than simple mass, there are poems of considerable merit and great variety in the *La Lira Argentina*. Alongside the predominant selection of celebrations of military victories, one finds *cielitos* and *unipersonales* by Bartolomé Hidalgo, as well as dramatic forms by others less well remembered, satiric verse by Fray Francisco de Paula Castañeda (1776–1832), and Lavardén's "Oda al Paraná"—an anomaly both for its strictly descriptive mode and its composition prior to the period encompassed by the collection. I would add that this enterprise in a domestic literary economy builds upon the internal commerce of the poets; "they themselves," writes Juan María Gutiérrez, "have been careful to preserve their genealogy in a cordial and gentlemanly fashion" (J. M. Gutiérrez 1865, 91), citing one another and writing poems in commemoration of each other's work.

I limit the more comprehensive study that the anthology merits to a discussion of Esteban de Luca's "Canto lírico a la libertad de Lima." Written in 1821 at the request of the new Republican government, and published that year in Buenos Aires by a special decree of Bernardino Rivadavia (J. M. Gutiérrez 1941, 69–70 and 77–78), the poem appears as number 118 in *La Lira Argentina* (Barcia 1982, 496–515). Gutiérrez is at some pains in his brief biography to reestablish Luca's credentials as a civic hero and not only a poet. For Luca had played an important role in the wars of independence as a munitions maker, Gutiérrez recalls, citing a letter of 30 April

1816 in which General Nicolás de Vedia congratulates Luca for his diligent service in terms that recall the American ingenuity of Cos: "without skilled hands to assist you neither at the anvil nor in the polishing, without lathes, without adequate tools, making up for everything with your determination, your concentration and your spirit" (J. M. Gutiérrez 1941, 37–38, n. 1). I would reiterate here the close interconnection—both as metaphor and as historical reality—between the evolution of local manufacture and internal commerce on the one hand, and the development of a native poetic voice on the other. Recalling Luca's successful experiments with local iron ore, Gutiérrez stresses that his pistols, muskets and swords "were obtained in the workshops of the nation with native materials and American hands" (39). The same might be said of Luca's verse and, more generally, of the poetry on the road to independence of which *La Lira Argentina* offers so many valuable examples.

The occasion of Luca's "Canto lírico a la libertad de Lima" was the triumphant entrance of the Argentine general José de San Martín into Lima following his victories over Spanish troops in Chile, gained by his unexpected crossing of the Andes. It is almost inevitable that discussion of the poem should turn upon a comparison with Olmedo's ode, as it does already for Gutiérrez, when he notes: "the song of Señor Luca, which embraces half the American continent as the theater of the feats that it celebrates, resounded on the plains of Chile, in the Peruvian mountains, and found a sympathetic ear everywhere. *San Martín and Luca did not yet have Bolívar and Olmedo for rivals and they enjoyed all of the advantages of their priorty, each in his own sphere*"] (J. M. Gutiérrez 1941, 79; emphasis added). Gutiérrez implies, of course, that San Martín and Luca would lose their respective competitions. I state a minority opinion by declaring a preference for Luca's "Canto lírico a la libertad de Lima." I add that the interview between San Martín and Bolívar—still a subject of literary speculation in the hands of twentieth-century Spanish American writers—which led to the withdrawal of the former and the political hegemony of the latter, figures as an extraliterary factor in the process of canonization.

I would stress that Luca's theme here is not war, but liberty. His goal is to record the impress of an abstract political value, to give it form within a concrete historical context. In the letter that he sent to Rivadavia accompanying the text of the poem upon the completion of his commission in two weeks time (again reprinted in full by Gutiérrez 1941, 71–72 and excerpted in Barcia 1982, 497 n.), and which was included in the *editio princeps*, Luca gives this task a specific impulse to engage with the future as well: "The happy future of the new world, fruit of our vigils, our privations and our blood, is what ought to delight our hearts, what ought to inflame the poets of the American Parnassus." Poetry must be prophecy. In the case of "Victoria de Junín," much as in the early eighteenth-century *Lima fundada*, prophecy was cast as a supernatural voice whose purpose was to mend the breach between chronological sequence and unity of action. In the same letter to Rivadavia, Luca registers his awareness of the classical precedent, but he demurs:

> I thought that I should use the marvelous in my composition, but I have not made use of the intervention of allegorical deities from fables when the difficulties overcome by genius suffice to evoke it [i.e. the marvelous]. That is why it seemed to me to be more proper to have San Martín see America atop the Andes and the victories of Chacabuco and Maipú, which paved our way to the liberation of Lima, which will put an end to the war of independence. (qtd in J. M. Gutiérrez 1941, 71–72)

Like the brothers Lemaur planning the roads of Cuba, Luca's is a neoclassicism in transition, altering the models of antiquity in conformity with the lay of the land. The episode of the apparition, then, proves central in distinguishing the "Canto lírico a la libertad de Lima" from the "Victoria de Junín."

The Inca's prophecy is a public event that dominates Olmedo's poem, and, much as Luca would have it too, an American destiny is enunciated in an indigenous voice.[22] For Luca, however, the vision is brief and private. His hero had already glimpsed the future before his epiphany in "el gran libro . . . de los destinos" ["the great book . . . of destinies"] (Barcia 1982, 502). A later reference to "genios ilustres, que inflamados/a la luz de la gran filosofía,/pudisteis anunciar del Nuevo Mundo/la libertad a todas las naciones" ["illustrious geniuses, inflamed/by the light of great philosophy,/you were able to announce to the New World/the freedom of all nations"]. An accompanying explicative note by Luca identifies these figures of genius as "Montesquieu, Raynal, Filangieri and other lovers of humanity" (510), thus serving to indicate that there is less divine mystery than Enlightenment authorship in San Martín's "gran libro" ["great book"]. His reading, in any case, proves a scene of poetic instruction, for the result is the emotional state of

"sagrado entusiasmo" ["sacred enthusiasm"] (503) that Luca associates with the composition of odes in his letter to Rivadavia—"I
will believe that I have earned the indulgence of the public if in this
theme, worthy of the epic trumpet of Homer, I have at least succeeded, in an abbreviated scope, in uniting the enthusiasm of the
ode to the majesty of song" (qtd. in J. M. Gutiérrez 1941, 71).

San Martín's epiphany, in consequence, is rather a poetic expression of his own imagination than a visitation. Luca's San Martín is
very nearly a poet of the romantic visionary company, bound as yet
by the diction of neoclassicism. Here, then, the brief ode-within-an-
ode:

Arrebatado
de tan alto pensar, allá en la cima
de los Andes que el sol eterno dora,
ve Colombia sentada; ella lo anima
con expresivo maternal acento
a ejecutar, como hijo denodado,
los planes que medita:
ella le muestra su fecundo seno
herido y destrozado
por el rayo y el trueno,
por la sangrienta guerra que lo agita;
ella el camino de la excelsa gloria,
la senda hermosa del honor señala
al jefe ilustre, que vengarla debe
con eterna victoria
de su tormento, a que ninguno iguala.

(Barcia 1982, 503–4)

Overwhelmed
by such lofty thoughts, there on the crest
of the Andes, eternally gilded by the sun,
he sees Columbia seated; she urges him on
with expressive maternal accent,
to execute, like a daring son,
the plans he has conceived:
she shows him her fecund breast
wounded and shattered
by lightning and thunder,
by the bloody war that stirs it;
the road to greatest glory,
the beautiful path of honor

> she shows the illustrious chief,
> who must avenge with eternal victory
> her torment beyond compare.

It is San Martín's trope—or rather Luca working through San Martín's projected imaginings—to transform the inscription of the wars of independence, figured as wounds upon the breast of Columbia, into *el camino* ["the road"] or *la senda* ["the path"] that leads to liberty. Inasmuch as the inscription upon the "fecundo seno" is the work of thunder and lightning, the allegorical Columbia must be a version of Mother Earth. Thus the turn to landscape—vivid, but still tangential in Olmedo's "Victoria de Junín"—takes a central place in Luca's ode-within-an-ode. Indeed, more than setting, the imagistic equation of America with its landscape that will subsequently be the cornerstone of Bello's poetic program in his "Alocución" is already at work in the "Canto lírico a la libertad de Lima." Luca himself will elaborate before the conclusion of this ode.

More immediately, Luca briefly reviews San Martín's course, leading up to a celebration of the freedom that a liberated Peru will now begin to enjoy, a benefit that so outweighs the sacrifice of lives, that the poet himself will address the allegorical figure, calling upon America to desist from mourning: "Cese, pues, gran Colombia,/el compasivo llanto" ["Cease, then, great Columbia/ your moving cry"] (Barcia 1982, 511). In a different literary context, Michael G. Cooke (1979) has remarked on the close kinship between satire, elegy and prophecy, and bearing his observations in mind, one may recognize more easily that having thus blocked the mourning strain of elegy, Luca but shifts along the blood lines of genre into the prophetic mode—satire is disqualified precisely because the poet has been caught by the contagion of his hero's lyric enthusiasm. Thus the poetic voice enters late in the poem, speaking in its own first person: "¡mi mente, al contemplarlos, cuál se agita/en un furor divino!" ["contemplating them, my mind is moved/by divine fury!"] (Barcia 1982, 513). That gloss on Greek *enthusiasm* carries Luca directly into prophecy:

> yo veo del alcázar del destino
> súbito abrirse las ferradas puertas,
> y allí, en letras de fuego escrita, leo
> vuestra dicha futura.

> (Barcia 1982, 513)

I see the iron gates of the stronghold
of destiny suddenly swing open,
and there, inscribed in fiery letters, I read
your future happiness.

Just as the poet repeats the scene of San Martín's reading lesson, so too he will rise to his own epiphany in which *gran Colombia* is reinvested as the allegorical figure of Liberty:

Tu prole venturosa
subirá a la alta cima
de los nevados Andes; allí el genio
inflamará su audacia hasta que imprima
gigante humana forma y asombrosa
al mayor de los montes; en la estatua
de la divina Libertad la tierra
lo verá convertido.

(Barcia 1982, 515)

Your fortunate offspring
will climb to the lofty peak
of the snowcapped Andes, and there the spirit
will enkindle their boldness until it prints
a giant and astonishing human form
on the largest mountain, transforming it
in the sight of the earth
into Freedom's sacred statue.

It is a complex, and, I will venture, a brilliant figure in which one finds condensed the very "declaration of intellectual independence" that Henríquez Ureña (Henriquez Ureña 1963, 99) associates with the first of Bello's *silvas americanas* written two years later (but see also Luca's Virgilian eclogue, "Al pueblo de Buenos Aires" of 1821). The source of inspiration is no longer the antique Muse, but rather a *genius loci*, a local deity, which, by the early nineteenth century, was all but indistinguishable from its interiorized avatar of personal genius (compare J. C. Nitzsche 1975). The artistic expression that it mandates, like the mental meanderings of enlightened road surveyors, is purely imaginary. Future Americans are not called upon to conquer the heights of the Andes, that is, but to project upon the mountain a human form, a human face; the operant verb, *imprimir* ["to print, imprint"], suggests that this is to be accomplished through writing. The mountains will almost literally echo the call to freedom: "¡Libertad! ¡Libertad! Sublime acento,/que lleva el eco desde el hondo valle/a los montes más altos y fragosos,/ y repiten los mares procelosos," Luca had exclaimed early in the ode ["Liberty! Liberty! Sublime sound,/that the echo carries from the deep valley/to the tallest and most craggy peaks"] (Barcia 1982, 501). But as the disorderly heaping of the ridge of adjectives suggests—"gigante humana forma y asombrosa" ["giant and astonishing human form"]—poetry itself will echo the mountains. It is a grand effort to found a new image of voice.

Poetry succeeds here where politics do not. The prophetic prospect of the ode is cast as a history lesson. Where Olmedo uses the voice of the Inca to turn the immediate historical antecedent, that is the decisive victory at Ayacucho, into Bolívar's future at Junín, Luca's more rational scheme sets San Martín's zeal for Independence as the paradigm for the future already opening in Lima, "que a la dulce libertad hoy naces" ["you who today are born to sweet liberty"] (Barcia 1982, 502). But to do so is to forget the pains of the present, that is the recent experience of Buenos Aires.

As has been noted in the introduction, the rapid success of insurrection in Argentina had yielded to great political turmoil by 1820. In consequence, the elegies for Belgrano in *La Lira Argentina* lament indistinguishably the passing of a founding father of the new nation and the death of that nation itself, at least inasmuch as it can be considered the embodiment of the ideals of the independence movement. Thus, Luca:

> Mi vista horrorizada allí se tiende
> en una horrenda inmensidad, buscando
> a mis conciudadanos y a mi patria;
> mis ojos ¡ay! no ven más que vestigios
> de su gloria y poder; [. . .]
> Todo desapareció de entre nosotros
> desde el fatal instante en que las tropas
> sin freno de obediencia, sin caudillo,
> sirvieron a merced de impíos genios,
> que escándalo y horror serán al orbe.

> (Barcia 1982, 377)

> My horrified view extends there
> over the horrendous immensity,
> seeking my compatriots, my country;
> my eyes, oh! see naught but vestiges

of its glory and power[. . .]
All this disappeared from our midst
from the fatal instant when the troops
without the reins of obedience, without a chief,
served at the will of impious spirits,
who will be the scandal and horror of the globe.

The impress of liberty on the rock face of the Andes is but a con-
summation devoutly to be wished, not an accomplished fact, as
Luca well knew in his elegy, a year before the optimism of the
"Canto lírico a la libertad de Lima."

Nearly a century had passed since Peralta's epic, *Lima fundada*,
and the change in historical vision could not be clearer. The history
lesson that Luca would impart to a nascent Peruvian republic is
based upon the repudiation of the colonial past in which Lima was
"la capital donde reinaba/el sangriento poder, la vil codicia,/ . . . a
ejemplo de Pizarro" ["the capital where reigned/bloodthirsty
power, vile avarice/ . . . in the image of Pizarro"] ("Canto lírico a
la libertad de Lima," Barcia 1982, 501). But historicity is as yet
temporized by Enlightenment faith. In spite of the turmoil in Buenos Aires, Luca still promotes his image of voice as a perennial
monument, as timeless as those of the Mediterranean antiquity that
underwrote his own education:

> estatua que resista al gran torrente
> de los siglos, y triunfe del olvido;
> estatua colosal, nuevo portento,
> que domine las tierras y los mares.
>
> (Barcia 1982, 515)

> statue that may resist the great torrent
> of the centuries, and defeat oblivion;
> colossal statue, new portent
> that may dominate the lands and seas.

At the antipodes of Spanish America, an adolescent Heredia,
more conscious as yet of what is lost than what may be gained with
the collapse of the colonial era, takes a different tack:

> Todo perece
> por ley universal. Aun este mundo
> tan bello y tan brillante que habitamos,

es el cadáver pálido y deforme
de otro mundo que fue.

(J. M. Heredia 1940, 2:152)

Everything perishes
by universal law. Even this world,
so beautiful, so bright, in which we live,
is the pale and deformed corpse
of another world that was.

And he will promote a different image of a different voice: the melancholic historical consciousness that threads through Spanish American modernity.

II
Constituting an American Poetics

3

Constitutional Dialogues, circa 1823

1

A CERTAIN "FILANTRÓPICO" WRITES TO *EL IMPERTÉRRITO CONSTI-tucional* of Havana in 1822 "to recount to the enlightened public having witnessed a case that I could not view with indifference" (Filantrópico 1822, 1). The case: an order had been relayed to the effect that all "colored sergeants" were to remove their hats when addressing colored officers, and furthermore, these officers, no less than the sergeants, were also to remove their hats when addressing white officers of any rank, "attending to the difference in birth, which demands that indispensable distinction" (3). El Filantrópico proceeds to review the legal precedents, compiling military statutes in Cuba in recent times, all of which authorize the same "distinction." A fine writer of courtroom drama, he reserves his own fulminating opinion until the end:

> Is it possible that the Señor Inspector General is ignorant that in this time philanthropy, impartiality, disinterestedness, etc., hold sway, refer-ring us to dispositions of the years 1782, 1806, 1811, 1816, when the pride of those in power ruled unchecked? No, Señor, beware that others are the laws that govern us now, and that all sensible men consider that distinction of birth a chimera; because, persuaded by solid principles, they know that all rational beings are equal in the order of nature; and that they are only distinguished by their virtues and actions. (Filantróp-ico 1822, 7–8)

New times have come, the Filantrópico declares, *constitutional* times, as he emphasizes in his closing reminder to the military that they have "sworn to defend general and individual liberty, religion, country, Constitution and constitutional Monarch" (8, I retain the original capitalization). But the old guard, the *insensatos*—a Zequeira, for instance, with his own related mania for hats and rank

183

(see Pérez Firmat 1985), his own racist fears—are left in place. Under these circumstances, the liberty that he invokes does not truly exist, except as a figure of speech.

The breach that opens between philosophical speculation and an as yet unrealized technological potential provides the narrative space of science fiction. Political life, too, has its juridical gaps, which in turn frame a discursive space that might well be called that of political fiction. In the case of the Filantrópico, liberty stands in the breach between eighteenth-century political philosophy and late colonial institutions. Finding that his ideal depends upon unrealized political and social conditions—an imaginary *constitución* in Jovellanos's sense—the Filantrópico turns plaintively toward a better future: "When will God be pleased to free us from partiality and give us new men who may govern us in all classes of the state!" (Filantrópico 1822, 7). What he and Cuba get instead was the old man with his old powers, Fernando VII abrogated the constitution the following year, emphatically unmasking the fictionality of liberty. This particular denouement is specific to the Spanish dominions. It is well to recall that unlike the Free Trade Ordinance of 1778, which, however limited in its practical effects, still stood as a continent-wide standard, Spanish American chronology is fractured along national lines from the beginning of the constitutional era through the end of the period under study here and beyond.[1] Nevertheless, "liberty," the ubiquitous epithet that is the legacy of the poetry on the road to independence to that of early republican times, remains in the breach throughout Spanish America. It is a predominant political fiction and its multifarious tropes want study. I might trace them well beyond the anonymous, protoabolitionist writings of the Filantrópico in Cuba (the island itself marginalized by its continuing colonial status), to a central name embarked upon the central task of the moment. Bolívar echoes the Filantrópico's call for new men when he introduces his "Proyecto de Constitución" in a message to the Congress of Bolivia in 1826. His prefatory modesty topos measures the enormity of the task he has been asked to fulfill in drafting a constitution, by asserting that even the most experienced legislator would be daunted: "what should I say, then, of the soldier, who, born amidst slaves and buried in the deserts of his homeland, has seen no more than captives in chains and comrades-in-arms to break them" (Bolívar 1976, 231). The immediate import is to give Bolivar's personal limitations an epochal extension tied to national origins. His is an American predicament. The juxtaposition of *desiertos* with the image of fettered countrymen extends the argument further through an oblique allusion to Exodus. I and all my generation are unprepared for the mission of constituting liberty, he suggests; this "divine ministry" (231) must await a generation of new men born in general and individual liberty.

Jovellanos, it may be recalled, made a similar autobiographical turn in order to promote a historical consciousness and its institutionalization in the study of law. Bolívar, on the contrary, evacuates the colonial period in the metaphor of the deserts, and condenses all of its institutions in the image of enslavement from which he cuts himself off by the sword. As Oakeshott might say, Bolívar perceives clearly the political handicap of the present, but its circumstance "is not significantly qualified" by reference to the past. The paradox is acute. Just as American letters verge upon a modern historical consciousness, the pertinence of the past is denied by Bolívar no less than the anonymous Filantrópico. And an outright denial, I recall, is tantamount to hallucination in Abraham's understanding of the aftermath of trauma. It is possible to read a more ingenuous and more fervent Olmedo at the beginnings of that same historical trajectory in that light, that is to see the Inca's prophecy as just such a massive hallucination, whose purpose is to mislead (Abraham and Torok 1994, 188), distracting the view from "a murder or primordial death" that is the originary moment of history according to Michel de Certeau (Certeau 1975, 61), such as the murder of Atawallpa and more generally of pre-Columbian culture. It was Bolívar himself, however, who offered the historical critique of Olmedo's prosopopeia. His figure of the American desert is not a denial of history, but rather a figure of America as a vast cemetery ("buried in the deserts of his homeland") from which he has removed the headstones, to defend the present from the burden of the past.[2]

Here in his "proyecto de constitución," as elsewhere, Bolívar is neither pre- nor postmodern, but rather a standard bearer of modernity in Spanish American culture. His vision participates in an intellectual tradition that conceives America as a project, always incomplete, always yet to come, ever seeking out its proper name so as to call itself into being.[3] Rafael Gutiérrez Giradot (1974, 1978 and 1982) finds the fountainhead of this utopian, projectional vision in the poetry and prose of Andrés Bello, and among Bello's immediate heirs, would be the nineteenth-century authors of foundational fictions in prose, projecting, or as Sommer explicates, generating a future to compensate for an illegitimate relation to the past. I have already suggested that this projectional vision has roots that reach back to the eighteenth century, at least in providential schemes, whether cast in orthodox Christian terms, as in Abad and even the anonymous nun who was an auxiliariy to Castell-dos-Rius's academia, or in the Virgilian mode of Peralta. And while Gutiérrez Giradot was interested in tracing the "potential routes" of the projectional vision forward from Bello to Pedro Henríquez Ureña as his late but legitimate heir, Henríquez Ureña himself characteristically elided the eighteenth century to discover the sources of that vision in the Renaissance (see Henríquez Ureña 1978 and also Fernández Herrero 1992). Indeed, one might well follow Bolívar's muted biblical allusion back along those lines to Columbus's self-figuration as a visionary captain beset by a stiff-necked crew. If Bolívar is a new Moses, he is also a new Columbus, presenting the course of liberty as an expedition—breaking of chains, an unfettering of the foot—though the liberated find themselves still hobbled by their former colonial shackles. Despite his steadfast forward gaze, Bolívar's figure recalls the wrong turn of American history from discovery to conquest, an error which he set out to repeat in reverse and so correct with his reconquest of Spain in America. And his emended text will be his projected constitution, the genre that underwrites Spanish American letters, including poetry, in the period beginning ca. 1823.[4]

In order to introduce the genre of the constitutional dialogue, I present an explicit case: a series of texts by José Joaquín Fernández de Lizardi (Mexico 1776–1827), published from May to July of 1825, and collected by Agustín Yáñez under the heading, "Constitución política de una república imaginaria" (Fernández de Lizardi 1940, 133–81). This self-conscious political fiction proceeds as a conversation between two types new to public discourse, an unnamed *Sacristán* (sexton) and *Payo* (peasant): the lower echelons of church organization and the agricultural economy.[5] The satirical mode, patent in Lizardi's better-known works, explains in part the recourse to "new men" for an estranged perspective. But beyond literary convention, Lizardi also suggests that an independent and a modern America will be constituted by social types previously suppressed by the colonial regime. To give them voice in the periodical press of the moment is to anticipate their empowerment, though, to reiterate, only as a political fiction.[6]

Lizardi fixes the time of their meeting as the time of the breach. "So the recess of the chambers has been effected?" asks the Sacristán (Fernández de Lizardi 1940, 135), to open the dialogue. The Payo's reply, answering a question with a question, marks the constitutional task as a language lesson: "What's a recess, compadre?" His simplicity punctures the Sacristán's mimicry of the high-flown rhetoric of the deputies, but his difficulties may not be strictly lexical. It may be that he knows not of "recess," for having lived a life of uninterrupted labor. One may thus read the implication that the real labors that will create and sustain the new republic do not take place in the field of politics, but in the politics of the field.[7] The Payo subsequently remarks, "Caramba, what a long vacation!" (135), bringing the implicit accusation of idleness to the fore, and provoking the Sacristán to defend the unfolding political process as a labor in its own right: "But it's necessary: those señores have worked quite a lot" (135). The Sacristán might also have pointed out that the critique is blunted—or rather that the Payo's satire cuts two ways—inasmuch as Lizardi in fact celebrates a double recess. The conversations will end, as the Sacristán recognizes sadly in the penultimate dialog, when the Payo is obliged to resume his chores: "having to head off to his land" (171). I lay emphasis on this narrative circumstance, namely that the Payo has come *to town* and engages in the dialog of folk voices during a breach in his own labors. It is the moment logically anterior to the "Diálogo patriótico interesante" in which Hidalgo inaugurated the genre of gauchesca poetry in 1821. There Contreras asks for news—"¿qué novedades se corren?" ["What news is going 'round?"] (Carilla 1979, 104)— from Chano, the gaucho who is returning *from town*—"Vea lo que me pasó/Al entrar en la ciudad" ["See what happened to me/When I got into town"] (109)—and from such conversation as passes between the Sacristán and the Payo.

Lizardi expresses an urban point of view in which the countryside is idealized as the place of work.[8] To enter the city is to leave the productive economy, to court vice, to spend one's money and one's words in idle chatter until utter bankruptcy.

Let us conclude our constitution, for even if it may not be accepted nor praised, but instead criticized and slandered, it will give testimony before the few who merit the honorific titles of wise and virtuous patriots, that we, downtrodden in the darkness and humbled by the weight of our acknowledged and confessed ignorance, have done what we could

do for the benefit of the country, with no other interest than that of serving it, exposing ourselves to the calumny of fools and the embezzlement
of our pockets. (Fernández de Lizardi 1940, 173)

Is the Payo just another cowboy riding into town with his latest pay
and staying on until the last coin is gone? His claim is that his own
diálogo patriótico interesante has carried him beyond the political
economy of buying and selling, whose motor is self-interest, to a
utopia of disinterestedness. This, too, is a rendering of the trope of
liberty.

Liberty under the name of patriotism is a freedom from human
nature, which the Sacristán delineates after a satirical preface:

> Here it is obligatory to take snuff, scratch one's head and look up at the
> ceiling, because it is necessary to consult with the character, inclina-
> tions and customs of the country to which laws are to be given, and
> above all, to know mankind, for man, full of self-regard, will not cease
> to do ill save for fear of punishment, nor do good deeds but for interest
> in the rewards. (Fernández de Lizardi 1940, 139)

The laws that the Sacristán and Payo dictate to one another over the
subsequent course of these dialogues will draw upon the premise of
self-interest and its twin corollaries, fear of punishment and zeal for
gain, to lead an imaginary Mexico to the promised land of patriotic
disinterest.

Their constitution counts upon two other sets of assumptions
enunciated in their preamble. Persuaded by the Sacristán that even
their asinine judgment will lead to no harm—"Have no fear, in
Mexico people are quite prudent, and they don't take fright at bray-
ing" (Fernández de Lizardi 1940, 138)—the Payo offers a point of
departure. "Let us begin," he says, "Will everyone who is born in
any State or territory of the Mexican Federation be a citizen?"
(138). The question presupposes a modern relation between individuals and the state in the term "citizens," indeed presupposes
precisely those individuals recognizable to the State because they
are defined by modern political economy as the self of their own
self-interest. The second assumption relates to the Mexican context
ca. 1823. Lizardi's Payo also presupposes a federation, as though
the issue could be treated thus in passing. In fact, the debate
between conservative advocates of a strongly centralized government that carried forward the essential structures of the viceregal
administration and liberals who wished to disperse the narrow colo-

nial power base over the breadth of localized government and popular representation in a federal system, undermined the constitutional process in Mexico. The constitution promulgated in 1824 was too indecisive on this point to long endure.

The Sacristán tacitly admits these points, branding him no less a liberal than the Payo. He raises an objection from an unexpected quarter, however: "Do you see? Those are old-fashioned notions; it is a plagiary of the Spanish Constitution, our own, and the Jalisco Constitution" (Fernández Lizardi 1940, 138). The cause for surprise is not so much the depth of his political culture, but the proto-romantic insistence on originality, which he had just come to pronounce as dogma: "the point is to say things that are new, even if they may be crazy" (138). The surprise is greater for the juxtaposition of this aesthetic prescription with the firmly Enlightenment principle of utility with respect to the Sacristán's politics, as represented by his substitute formula for citizenship, promulgated as the first article of their constitution: "All men are citizens who are useful to the republic in whatever respect, be they from what nation they may" (140). The call for originality seems to fly in the face of a political identity whose watchword is usefulness. And as though to confirm the topsy-turvy results, before he bothers himself to pronounce on such useful but unoriginal matters as the form of government and the division of powers, the Sacristán dictates ten articles detailing the "ribbons, bands and feathers" (140) in their colors, placement and appropriate materials, to be worn by the imaginary citizens. Public life is to be continuous public spectacle. Useless frills, it would appear, or worse than useless: for if the feathers will have an American provenance, what of the ribbons and the bands? One recalls the criollo taste for European finery behind the contraband traffic of colonial Peru in the report of Juan and Ulloa. The definition of good taste (164) has not changed, it seems, but the replacement of contraband with free trade has created a perilous situation for national industry at a time when "English manufactured goods leave nothing for the local population to do" (163; see also 156 and 164).

The Payo and Sacristán show their awareness of the aesthetic dimension of their constitutional undertaking at the outset of their second dialog. "What are they saying around here about our constitution, compadre?" asks the Sacristán, "Do they like it?" (Fernández de Lizardi 1940, 147). The Payo reports mixed reviews: "Some do and some don't. Some hail it as a witty pastime, useful and pleasing, and others slander it as the folly produced by idleness" (147). The brief foray into reader-response criticism produces a literary historical schema. A text is laudable ca. 1823 if wit, the hallmark of the baroque, is chastened by a strict neoclassical aesthetic, the Horatian maxim of the delightful and useful. But that commonplace is not sufficient in political terms—the terms of their own citizenship text. More *deleitable* than *útil*, they fall prey to their own charge of having recessed too soon; and if they are convicted of *ociosidad*, then they ought to be stripped of their plumes. The fate of writing, their own writing at least, hangs upon the verdict.

The Payo and Sacristán are driven to this humorous but self-defeating pass by an epistemological problem. The definition of citizenship (of free individuals in a liberal state) wipes away an apparently natural sign of identity, the marker of birthplace. Given that utility shows itself to be inconstant—even agricultural labors can be in recess—the Payo and Sacristán are left to wonder how will you know a citizen when you see one: "you can't tell citizens by their faces, and I want them to be recognizable above and beyond clothes" (Fernández de Lizardi 1940, 139). Discarding a racial test for citizenship ("by their faces"), as had the American delegates at Cadiz or the Filantrópico in Havana, the Sacristán's desideratum looks for a conventional sign that will be perfectly legible, perfectly superficial ("*above* and beyond"): a utopian semiotics.[9] Thus, the ribbons and feathers are not only an aesthetic caricature, but also a solution to the semiotic challenge. The joke is over, however, when the *devisa punzó* becomes the sign of loyalty to the Rosas dictatorship in the River Plate. The practice of dissembling in *Amalia* (1851), the novel of poet José Mármol (Argentina 1817–71), provides an oblique response to the Sacristán's utopian sign system from the point of view of its real political consequences. The surface hides depths, Mármol argues by midcentury: the alternative semiosis of romanticism.

But even here ca. 1823 the festive display of "so many ribbons and blue and white crests' " (Fernández de Lizardi 1940, 142) quickly reveals its darker aspect, as the Payo continues:

> and since people are so vain and superficial, it would happen that in order not to lose the use of those bagatelles, they would abstain from committing a thousand crimes, fearing, as they ought to fear, the dishonor of presenting themselves in public without them, for everyone would point the finger at them; and so here you have it, this simple van-

ity and just fear would produce salutary effects on society. But let us treat the form of government. (Fernández de Lizardi 1940, 142)

The exhortation is superfluous. This is already the form of government. The regimen of semiotic superficiality not only echoes the antidepth psychology, it provides the mechanism for creating and maintaining citizens. The pointing finger is an admonition, both a reproof in itself and a warning of punishment to come. For punishment will be the key to this liberal constitution and more generally, to the modern state project, as Foucault (1975) has demonstrated. The feathers and ribbons are the playful aspect of the panopticon, but the agents are everywhere. The parish priest "will receive scrupulous information" from the would-be bridegroom, "as to whether or not he has a profession or honest means of supporting his family; and lacking it, he will not marry them, reputing uselessness and idleness as impeding impediment" (Fernández de Lizardi 1940, 155): useless, an idler, unfit for marriage and family life as he is unfit for citizenship. After all, what is political economy but home economics writ large, as the Payo exclaims: "What do I understand of government when I hardly know how to govern my house!" (143). In addition,

In each section of four blocks the government will have a subject of confidence, adequately authorized, who will be denominated *guardian of order*. The responsibility of this individual will be to ascertain the exercise or mode of living of all the neighbors in his jurisdiction, presenting to the government a monthly report on who they are and how they occupy themselves. (Fernández de Lizardi 1940, 153–54)

Since utility is not inherent, nor permanent, and not visible when citizens are in recess from their productive labors, a sign is necessary for its recognition. Necessary, but insufficient. The sign must ever be renewed, utility ever reconfirmed.

The pointing finger of Lizardi's panopticon returns in a final section headed, comically, "Of mixed salad," but it, too, is no laughing matter. The section begins with a restatement of the Sacristán's desideratum for a utopian language: "The penal laws will be few, strong, simple and will not admit of the slightest interpretation' " (Fernández de Lizardi 1940, 173). Perfect intelligibility is useful, however, only if that language is perfectly disseminated. The Sacristán proposes, therefore, to cover the surface of the city with the text of the law: "marble tablets will be placed on all of the corners of the streets of the capitals and towns of the federation, if possible, on which will be declared in large and well-written letters the punishment that the law indicates" (179). All of the corners. All of the towns and cities.

Lizardi redeems his liberal credentials, as it were, in the penal reform that the Payo and Sacristán write into their constitution. The Sacristán can be draconian. The example he offers for the cityscape as legal textbook would be set on the corner of the calle de Tacuba in Mexico City and would read: "Penal Code.—Such and such a law.—He who robs the value of ten pesos and above will die" (Fernández de Lizardi 1940, 174). But those who make it to prison meet with an enlightened liberalism, aimed, liked the apprenticeship system of national workshops (165–68) or the army (179–80), at turning idlers into useful citizens (valga la redundancia): "for the object of the penal laws, neither being the extermination of citizens, nor the satisfaction of the vengeance of judges, but rather the correction of the wayward, after that has been verified, the punishment should be mitigated" (157). An apprenticeship system, much as proposed long since in the Enlightenment court of Carlos III in the *Discurso sobre el fomento de la industria popular* of 1774 under the direction of Campomanes (*Discurso* 1988, cxlviii–cliii), is incorporated into the prisons themselves (Fernández de Lizardi 1940, 146, compare again *Discurso* 1988, clviii–clxiii), but this will not reduce sentences. On the contrary, for those who are slow to learn, their imprisonment could be extended: "[the prisoner] will not leave prison until he has been examined by an official; and this even when he has served the term for which he entered" (Fernández de Lizardi 1940, 146). The law will be even more stern with respect to those in rags, especially women, whose "sight offends innocent chastity" (153). In this case, useful paid labor in prison will not necessarily lead to freedom, since it cannot serve as a guarantee against willful perversity. Those who leave properly dressed may return in rags, the Payo surmises, and so will be subject to— literally dressed in ("volverá a vestirse")—the same regime of paid labor (153). A third recurrence leads to life imprisonment, "for only in this manner will they be covered" (153), which givers further indication of the crucial value of the constitutional semiotics. The crime of being in rags may be understood as the revelation of a depth *aun por debajo de la ropa*, beneath the civilized surface of clothing, the psychology of depths, that is, of the legislators who project erotic choice upon unwanted poverty.

In contrast to those penal designs, then, one finds a road to freedom that runs from prison through a new colonizing project—"we must try all practicable roads," declares the Sacristán (Fernández de Lizardi 1940, 156). The proposal once again falls short of the Sacristán's aesthetic demands for an unqualified originality, since it counts upon Enlightenment precedent, notably Jovellanos's proposals for agrarian reform. It calls for the settlement of "the extensive land that this new world offers [to the government]" (156). The phrase makes the new projectional vision an echo of the old colonialism, and ominously fails to stipulate the source of "free land." Does this renewed colonization presuppose a renewed conquest?[10] In the plan of the Payo and Sacristán, the government will underwrite the enterprise of the colonists, including certain convicts: "Even prisoners will be provided with pieces of lands to be cultivated by and for themselves" (157). The article that follows indicates the means by which the correctional institution of colonization will mitigate sentences: "constancy in their work, honorable conduct and true correction of the prisoners will be an effective recommendation to the government to reduce their sentences" (157). Not any and all work, however, as the preceding examples illustrate: labor on the land is recognized as having a special rehabilitative effect.

Lizardi's faith in the land is a constant of liberal politics in republican Mexico, and elsewhere in independent America, where land reform and emancipation continued to be closely associated to the time of Lerdo de Tejeda and well beyond. Work upon the land will make useful citizens, prepared by their own labors for the responsibilities and benefits of freedom. And the land itself must be worked, must be habilitated by useful labor, so that it too may become useful. The land must earn its own freedom. When the Sacristán completes his articles of land reform, including the colonization plan with its correctional labor and the proscription limiting land holdings to four square leagues (Fernández de Lizardi 1940, 158), the Payo supports his proposal enthusiastically for several reasons, among them, his anticipation that "once your plan were in effect, there would not remain in this vast continent a single inch of uncultivated land, whereas now we have thousands of leagues of the most fertile lands that produce no more than scrub grass and weeds"

(160). The American desert of Bolívar's reckoning will be redeemed: the new world of the old promise.

The same faith provides the grounds of nineteenth-century Spanish American literature, in prose as well as poetry, and continued to do so, after the brief parenthesis of modernismo, until an incipient postmodernism began to separate letters from the land and to locate them in the virtual space of intertextuality. Lizardi is by no means the inaugurator of this tradition. On the contrary, as I have discussed in the preceding chapter, evidence abounds to argue that the road to independence was traced over a rediscovered land—the new nature invented by a new physics (Maravall 1991)—most literally, though not exclusively, in the reports of the scientific expeditions. Lizardi's heuristic value here as an introduction to the poetry of the subsequent period lies in the textual bridge he provides between that new nature and the projected institutions of an independent America, including the emerging institution of literature. For his interests in land reform may be linked to his utopian semiotics of surfaces by way of his critique of mining. Lizardi follows the main currents of Enlightenment economic theory in stating that "it is a fallacy to believe that gold and silver constitute the wealth of nations," as the Payo declares (Fernández de Lizardi 1940, 160). This late opposition to the principal tenet upon which the political economy of colonial America had been based leads the Payo to a highly condensed revisionist history, opened by an apparent paradox: "These metals in point of fact, when they are too abundant, are the cause of ruin of many families" (160). He then explains: "if this very nation had not had so much gold and so much silver, it would not have excited the greed of the Spanish, nor would the latter have come to sacrifice twenty million innocent people on the altars of Pluto, nor would the Holy Alliance currently have designs to reduce us to our former slavery to the Bourbons" (161). The *leyenda negra* undoes the colonial trope of the evangelical mission. Christianity was to have freed the indigenous population of its "superstitions" and above all of its cult of human sacrifice. But the history of mining only replaced one sacrificial altar with another. The legend of El Dorado and the classical myth of the Golden Age had been previously conflated in utopian imaginings of the Conquest: gold to be had for the picking, wealth without labor. And despite this briefest of accounts of the destruction of the Indies, the Payo himself deploys the same rhetoric: "nature, ever wise, hid the metals, from the sight of men; lazy and self-centered, they break the body of their mother in order to remove these metals and make themselves rich from one day to the next without working" (161). Much as in Luca's ode, the history of colonial oppression is imaged as a wounded earth. What this figure itself hides from view, however, is the breaking of the real bodies of the indigenous laborers in the mines recorded, for instance, in Landívar's *Rusticatio*. The *mita*, uprooting indigenous laborers from the land and sending them to a living death, if not an actual burial place in the mines, is the dark and disfiguring aspect of the metaphor of roads as intra-American lanes of communication.

In subscribing to the leyenda negra through the Payo, Lizardi poses an antithesis to oppressive, destructive mining. To reject colonial history and start afresh requires a healing of the earth by returning to its surface. For the same "wise nature" had placed before the very eyes of humanity the true source of the wealth of nations, as the physiocrats had taught: "May the sovereign and the nation never lose sight of the fact that the earth is the sole source of riches, and that it is agriculture that multiplies them," wrote François Quesnay in the *Maximes* in 1758 (Quesnay 1969, 331) translated by a young Manuel Belgrano, as noted in the introduction. Lizardi takes this rhetorical shift as the occasion for a counterfigure of liberty in the trope of the agriculture of the torrid zone, the constitution of America through the healing of the land. In keeping with the projectional semiotics, Lizardi presents the trope as a resurfacing: "Beneficent nature prepared true riches for all mortals, not in the center, but on the surface of the land, and in this sense, what land is richer than ours?" (Fernández de Lizardi 1940, 161) We are already on the verge of poetry:

everything, this America produces everything in abundance. I imagine to myself, then, all of her [i.e. America] cultivated and faithfully requiting the efforts and sweat of the laborer and then . . . Ah, what a delicious picture presents itself to my imagination! I see immense fields full of the golden grains of Ceres; others I foresee painted in the emerald green of the corn; some will be snowy with millions of boles of cotton; others reddening with the purple and pleasing grape. In some parts innumerable orchards will provide the palate with innumerable tastes, in the different fruits that season their abundant trees; the senses of sight and smell in other parts will delight in the aromas and the enchantments of a thousand brilliant and fragrant flowers; suffering humanity will find the most select pharmacy of herbs and medicinal bark; the appetite . . . go on, I can't even draw you the enticing picture that the idea of

America, completely cultivated, represents to me. Everything, I believe, would be bountiful, everything happiness, everything wealth. (Fernández de Lizardi 1940, 161–62)

This highly-wrought, thoroughly metatextual oration finished, it is the Sacristán's turn to sound the deflating, satiric note: "Caramba, compadre! I didn't think that you knew how to toss off your bits of poetry (echar sus rasgos poéticos); you can tell that you're just a novice, but your laudable intention makes amends for your lack of talent" (Fernández de Lizardi 1940, 162).

Much poetry, if less poetic talent, would be dedicated to inventorying the American cornucopia in the half-century to come: a geographical poetry, that is an earth-writing, enlisted in the utopian project of constituting America as a semiotics of surfaces. The expeditionaries had provided the tools, the method, the scientific practice of dissolving their subjective witness in the object of their research. And as one branch of poetry pursued their lead, another, alternative route to modernity would set out in search of the self that was buried in the poetic landscape.

2

Preparing the ideological grounds for independence, Bernardo Monteagudo (Argentina 1787–1825) had an interest in rewriting colonial history, and like Lizardi a decade later, he undertook the task as a fictional dialogue, a form with which he would have been familiar from any number of eighteenth-century French precedents and their Peninsular Spanish emulators. To this end, he sent Fernando VII prematurely to the grave in a text that circulated in manuscript in Chuquisaca, that is Sucre, Bolivia, as early as 1809. The king arrives in the Elysian fields complaining of Napoleon's usurpation, and he is greeted by Atawallpa, who replies: "Well, if you have considered the conquest of Spain by Bonaparte unjust and iniquitous, neither regret, nor be astonished, that I deem the domination that Spain has had over America equally usurped and furtive" (Monteagudo 1974, 57). Monteagudo needs Atawallpa, as Olmedo will need his Inca, and thus when Fernando offers his defense on various counts, there is an American perspective to refute him at every turn. "Be that as it may," remarks Fernando, for instance, in response to a brief exposition of the leyenda negra, to wit, the charge of the unprecedented cruelty of the Conquest, continuing, "what you ought to know is that Pope Alexander VI ceded and donated the Americas to my forebears and their heirs" (57). "I venerate the Pope as the universal head of the Church," replies Atawallpa, and yet, he continues:

> I cannot but say that it must have been an altogether consummate extravagance when he ceded and donated so generously that which, having its rightful owner, could under no circumstances have been his, especially when Jesus Christ, from whom the pontiffs have received all of their authority and whom they should hold as a model in all their actions, instructed that they have no power whatsoever over earthly monarchs or at least that it is not proper to exercise it. (Monteagudo 1974, 63–64)

Reference to Atawallpa is recourse to the past in name only, to a usable past that is rather a present in masquerade, as the postmortem conversion to veneration for the Pope already indicates. This line of reasoning, based upon the inaugural work in international political theory of Francisco de Vitoria and the Salamanca school of the sixteenth century (see Vitoria 1963 and Ramis 1984, 81–119), is not that of the conquered Incas, but rather the predominant argumentation in support of separation from Spain of Monteagudo's own day. In the same manner, Atawallpa's prior rhetorical question, "Do say, Fernando, is it not true that the base and unique support of a copious and well-founded sovereignty [is] the free, spontaneous will of the peoples in the cession of their rights" (Monteagudo 1974, 57) matches with precision discussions at Cadiz that grounded the legitimacy of the Cortes in just those medieval terms by which sovereignty would revert to the people in the absence of a legitimate monarch.

Paradoxically, it would seem, Monteagudo's dialogue makes that question of popular sovereignty a subject for the dialogue of kings—paradoxical, that is, with respect to the expectations that political emancipation and democratization are indissolubly linked as processes of modernity. But then Monteagudo himself was at one and the same time a militant separationist and a no less rabid monarchist, striving for the establishment of an American king and kingdom. The genre of the constitutional dialogue sets itself off from such precursors as Monteagudo's political fiction, therefore, both ideologically in its promotion of republican forms, and in literary terms in the enactment of a more popular sovereignty through the representation of a more poular voice, as in the plebeian meeting of the Payo and Sacristán. What remains a constant, however, linking the earlier separationist discourse to the constitutional dialogue is the concentration on the recuperation of popular political rights once ceded to the Spanish Crown, in terms of the right to property.

Discussion of popular sovereignty and property rights forms the specific cultural matrix out of which grew the variety of literary forms in stylized vernaculars that emerged in the constitutional period, such as Miguel Cabrera's *jíbaro* verse in the constitutional debate in the periodical press of Puerto Rico and Acuña de Figueroa's "Canto patriótico de los negros, celebrando la ley de la libertad de vientres y la Constitución," both considered in the preceding chapter. I will presently extend that assertion to the most successful of the vernacular forms, the poesía gauchesca, as it emerged ca. 1823, in this same constitutional context. But I would first remark that the same discussion is carried out in popular poetry, too, and not only in the stylizations of the erudite for the literate. In this regard, I refer to the poem "Proclama del duque infantado presidente," written in the Tzotzil language and dated 7 August 1812 in Cadiz, conjecturing as to how it might have lived in oral transmission in Guatemala in 1820, at the time of the rebellion in Totonicapán.[11]

The original purpose of the text was undoubtedly the diffusion of news about the Constitution of Cadiz among Tzotzil speakers in Central America. The verses rally support by calling attention to two articles with special interest to the indigenous population: article 18, granting equal citizenship to all people born in the empire, excepting those of African descent; and article 339, which substituted a universal, graduated tax for the colonial system of tribute in the indigenous communities.

The granting of citizenship is presented as a process of renaming. Victoria Reifler Bricker excerpts the relevant passage:

> Now there is no one
>   Who has thought to say
> That we are not Spaniards;
>   As for us,
> Indians
>   Were our names,

Those of us who were born
On the other side of the ocean;
Now Christian Spaniards
Are our names,
Beloved Sons,
Because only one is our earth,
Only one is our faith,
Only one is our nation,
Only one is our law,
Only one is Our Lord King,
Only one is our assembly seated at its head,
In the middle of our nation:
Spain
Is its name . . .

(Bricker 1981, 78)

"Indians," of course, were not their names, but rather, like the Papal donation, the erasure of a prior title. In order to avoid a misfire of the performative, therefore, which will grant a new and proper name—proper, in the sense that citizenship *is* the Cortes' gift to give—an appropriate address needs be formulated. No longer the misnomer "Indians," not yet "Christian Spaniards" constituted by the proclamation itself, the Tzotzil poet interpellates the people as "Beloved Sons," their name by birthright.

The "Proclama" explains the change of title, Beloved Sons *now* Christian Spaniards, in terms of unity. To speak for unity from Cadiz in 1812 is to pose a bulwark against imperialism, the usurpation of the "horned serpent" Napoleon (Bricker 1981, 77), and so to provide the means for national liberation. Following the logic of Monteagudo's stance, the same equation of unity and liberty for "Those of us who were born/On the other side of the ocean," may be turned against Spanish usurpation in America:

De la Patria alegres
el himno entonemos,
sus glorias cantemos
en completa unión.

(Miró 1974, 76)

Let us happily intone
the anthem of the Nation,
its glories let us sing
in indivisible union.

So writes Mariano Arosemena (Panama 1794–1868) in "A la memoria del 28 de noviembre" (1834), commemorating the declaration of independence of which he was a signatory. But this praise of an American union is made in explicit contrast to "Desunión de España" ["Disunion from Spain"] (Miró 1974, 77). Bartolomé Hidalgo took the same position in the *cielitos* that preceded his gaucho dialogues:

> Cielito, cielito, cantemos
> cielito de la unidad,
> unidos seremos libres,
> sin unión no hay libertad
>
> (Carilla 1979, 98)

> Cielito, let's sing cielito,
> cielito of unity,
> united we will be free:
> no union, no liberty.

Hidalgo, furthermore, reclaims the name of "Indian" for his criollo position, as Monteagudo had renamed his criollo speaker "Atawallpa":

> Cielito, cielo que sí,
> guárdese su chocolate,
> aquí somos indios puros
> y sólo tomamos mate
>
> (Carilla 1979, 99)

> Cielito, cielo, that's it,
> keep your old hot chocolate,
> here we're all pure Indian
> and *mate* is all we drink.

Be it noted, however, that in so saying the Gaucho de la Guardia del Monte through whom Hidalgo speaks betrays the Hispanic bias of criollo independence. He conceives of chocolate as an unwanted gift, a synechdoche for a civilization that he rejects in favor of a native barbarism. But chocolate, both the product and the word, is the native property of the "indios" in whose supposed name he resists Spanish claims. A minor aberration, perhaps, but, returning to the Tzotzil peoples from the River Plate, liberty will be understood in terms of proper titles and property rights, of native products and ill-gotten gains. The Tzotzil peoples will rebel against royal administration and criollo authority, and will find the grounds for rebellion in such poetry as the "Proclama," and a radical reading of the rights that it declares.

A first step toward that reading may be gleaned beyond the more immediate sense of the call to unity as a plea to America to aid in the war against Napoleon. Unity is, first and foremost, the natural and supernatural order of things in the Tzotzil poem: "Only one is our earth/Only one is our faith." The "Proclama" thus delineates a nature out of which spring natural rights—"The rights of citizens . . . that nature grants us," as the Payo and Sacristán asserted (Lizardi 1940, 140)—prior to modern political organization in the state and the cession of those rights, as a gift, in favor of the authority of law, king, and representative assembly, in that order, according to the poem.

The Beloved Sons are called upon to enter the secondary, national unity, assuming the responsibilities of citizens:

> Beloved Sons!
>   Open the pupils of your eyes!
> Know your tribute is gone.
>   Only equally we will pay
> A small contribution,
>   Donation is its name.
>
> (Bricker 1981, 78)

The immediate report concerns the change in political status, tribute being the forced payment of an alien and conquered people, whereas donation is the gift of the citizen to the state. The liberty which distinguishes the donation from tribute might be exercised in the decision to refuse to make such a gift. In principle, at least, one might withdraw from the national unity and, reverting to a more fundamental unity of earth and divinity, retain one's natural rights.

The right to dispose of one's own person, and on that basis, of one's own labor, and finally of those possessions that are the product or proceeds of one's labor, were written into the Constitution of Cadiz represented to the Tzotzil-speaking people through the "Proclama." Bartolomé Clavero condenses this Lockean position in the constitutional culture surrounding Cadiz: "Property, work and liberty will appear united" (Clavero 1991, 178). He then goes on to demonstrate the manner in which that culture is undermined within the self-same constitution, rights ceding precedence to laws, Locke to Bentham. The rebellion in Totonicapán in 1820 might be understood as a rejection of that turn in constitutional culture, and a reassertion of right over law.

By 1820, I recall, the constitution had been annulled and reinstated on the Peninsula. In Totonicapán, however, the spread of the constitutional culture proceeded at a slower pace. Bricker relates that on 2 April 1820 the reading of a document dated April 1812, giving thanks to Fernando VII for abolishing royal tributes, "seems to have been the first time that many Indians had heard of the Constitution of 1812" (Bricker 1981, 81). And yet the rumor of a change of name, a change of political identity—Christian Spaniards, Indians no longer, offering a donation, but no longer subject to tribute—had already filtered through the area. Earlier that same year, asserting that "a document from Guatemala City . . . had abolished the tributes" (80), the people of the Totonicapán area had begun to refuse to pay, and in some cases had returned monies already collected, before the abrogated constitution was back in force. "It is probably coincidence that their request [for the supposed document from Guatemala City vindicating their exemption from the tributes] was made only eight days after Fernando VII had reinstated the Constitution of 1812," Bricker remarks; "news of the King's change of heart could not have reached Guatemala so quickly, and official word did not reach Central America until the beginning of May" (80). One might conjecture that the oral transmission of the couplets of the "Proclama" stands behind the coincidence. Be that as it may, on 9 July 1820 in the town of San Miguel Totonicapán the reinstated Constitution of Cadiz of 1812 was proclaimed and in celebration a procession was led by Anastasio Tzul, a former *alcalde* who had previously been reluctant to collect tributes and who would soon become a leader of the tax rebellion. Bricker relates the scene:

> [Tzul was] mounted on horseback and dressed as a Spaniard in a military dress coat, velveteen trousers, tricorn hat, boots, and medallion, with a small sword in his belt and a cane in his hand. He had borrowed the dress coat from a Spaniard named Valentín Alvarado on the pretext that he needed it as a costume, for a Dance of the Conquest! (Bricker 1979, 82)

Bricker wishes to distinguish the incident from an authentic eruption of the Indian King, astutely arguing that the wearing of Spanish dress was no more than an exercise of newly proclaimed constitutional rights. "Now there is no one who has thought to say/That we are not Spaniards," Tzul might have argued in the words of the "Proclama." But Bricker's own exclamation points to a further irony, which is to say to a reading of Tzul's masquerade as a modern poem, or more precisely as a revisionary ratio between poems.

The Dance of the Conquest still extant in Central America, is itself a revision of a medieval tradition: the Americanization of the mock battle of Christian and Moors that formed part of the Peninsular carnival (see Bricker 1973, 189–91; 198–201). The *Reconquista* becomes the *Conquista* in America, and the Moors the indigenous people, or their theriomorphic stand-ins. The indigenous peoples enact their own defeat, although, the performance being carnivalesque, they take the roles of conquerors as well, dressing for the part of Christians in attire that varies according to historical referent. Valentín Alvarado is taken in by a ruse. He delivers up his velveteen breeches and dress coat, his clothing of European manufacture that is the sign of his ethnic and political distinction, in support of a farce, he believes, a Dance of the Conquest, in which Tzul's masquerade of power would underline the abiding authority circumscribing carnival liberty. To dance the Conquest, to assume power only by assuming European identity, is to reaffirm colonial relations and, symbolically, to pay royal tribute. Tzul changes that tribute into a donation. And his piracy, his contraband dress, become a poem of "libre comercio." He dances the reconquest of his rights at the head of a procession that will refuse to make a contribution to the king. The Americanization of the medieval tradition is carried here well beyond colonial authority, becoming a veritable theater of counter hegemony.[12]

I offer a further conjecture in much the same sense, to continue to suggest the transformations of poetry in the oral tradition at the advent of constitutional culture. To do so I return to another revision of the medieval legacy in America. Ramón Menéndez Pidal (1972) related that in compiling extant *romances* for the volume *Romances populares recogidos de la tradición oral* (1913), Menéndez y Pelayo confronted two opposing testimonies from America. José María Vergara (Colombia 1831–72) claimed that the Peninsular tradition was abandoned in Colombia in favor of contemporary compositions in the ballad form, while Rufino José Cuervo (Colombia 1844–1911) reported that he himself had been treated to an extensive recitation of historical *romances* in the Andes. Troubled by a doubt, Menéndez Pidal decided to contact Cuervo directly, to learn whether his informant, "a Señor named Don Manuel González," was indeed reciting from a living oral tradition, or if perhaps a literary source intervened (Menéndez Pidal 1972, 47). He lost a first letter of 1898—a synecdochical lapsus for other American losses at that date—which led to a new account, a procedure of loss and reconstruction itself paradigmatic for American literature from Fray Ramón Pané (Pané 1974; see also González Echevarría 1976) to Borges's Menard and Lezama's Oppiano Licario. Cuervo wrote again from Paris on 4 June 1906, in a letter that Menéndez Pidal reproduces at length. The testimony is rich in narrative detail, even after some forty years. Manuel González (n.d.), Cuervo recalls, recited ballads new and old for four hours, and protested against his listener's fear that he must soon be at an end by declaring, "I can go on today and tomorrow and the next day, and I will still have what to recite" (Menéndez Pidal 1972, 48).

Among the early ballads Cuervo made particular note of the recitation of *romances* from the cycles of the Infantes de Lara and Bernardo del Carpio, indicating, moreover, "He told me that the old ones he knew from his father, who did not know how to read" (Menéndez Pidal 1972, 47). I call attention to this detail which Menéndez Pidal either overlooks or negates in the further course of his investigation. For Menéndez Pidal concludes, referring now to another *romance* from the Bernardo del Carpio series collected in Bogotá by a different correspondent, a sample which he identifies with a text published by Agustín Durán in the nineteenth century and originally appearing in the *Romancero general* of 1600: "It is not, then, from oral tradition; the artisan in Bogota no doubt learned it in a book, and this assures us that 'the rude peasant' whom Cuervo heard recite numerous *romances* of Bernardo, of the Infantes de Lara and other historical ballads, was, like his father, a reader or auditor of published romances" (49).

For my own purposes, namely the difficult task of dating the presence of a given version of a *romance* to a particular milieu in America, Menéndez Pidal's question, "were the *romances* that Cuervo heard in the Colombian Andes traditional, as Menéndez Pelayo believes?" (Menéndez Pidal 1972, 48), is of little import. Rather, the supposition that the erudite version recited orally in Bogota in 1907 arrived in Colombia by way of Durán's *Romancero*, originally published in 1828–32, points to its possible presence as much as a half-century or more before Menéndez Pidal's friend

Fray Pedro Fabo came upon the performance by the unnamed artisan. That later testimony, however, does not bear upon Manuel
González in the 1860s, despite Menéndez Pidal's unsupported
inference, and even less so upon his father. Against Menéndez
Pidal's conjecture that the son and father ("who did not know how
to read") may have been familiar with or even read print versions
after all ("reader or auditor of published *romances*"), I will imagine
other versions of Bernardo del Carpio in the oral culture of the generation of Manuel's grandfather—the source from which the illiterate father would have learned to recite, like Manuel from his father,
by his own account. I am imagining, that is, ca. 1823, in the valleys
of the Andes, the soldiers of Bolívar or shortly thereafter, the veterans of his campaigns, reciting to one another and to their children
the exploits of a Bernardo, "become irreverent and bold, by force
of injustices, with the king who provoked him," according to Durán's note (A. Durán 1877, 434–35, n. 1), as the literate Bolívar
would also have known them from the *Quijote* (Cervantes 1968,
603), where, as Durán remarks (A. Durán 1877, 435, n. 2), they
appear in fragmentary form.

The cycle has many moments of high drama. The imprisonment
and betrayal of Bernardo's father by the king and indeed Bernardo's bastardy might have echoed with the fate of Atawallpa in
the mestizo bivouac at Junín for those who did not share with
Bolívar the privileged reading of Olmedo's criollo myth of the
prophecy of the Inca. But to the soldiers in rebellion against their
own king, I will suppose that the most pressing moment in the cycle
might well have been the episode in which Bernardo takes up arms
against Alfonso:

> Prendedle, gritaba el Rey,
> Pero ninguno lo intenta,
> Porque vieron que Bernardo
> El manto al brazo rodea,
> Poniendo mano á la espada . . .
>
>   (A. Durán 1877, 435)

> Capture him, cried out the King,
> But none would dare approach,
> Because they saw Bernardo
> Wrap his arm up in his cloak,
> Putting hand to sword . . .

No lone gaucho, Bernardo also calls his men to battle, which leads the crafty king to change his tactics:

> —Lo que de burlas os dije,
> ¿Tomado lo habeis de veras?
>
> (A. Durán 1877, 435)

> What I said to you in jest,
> Have you taken it as truth?

Durán records two versions of this romance with distinct denouements. In the version that I have just cited, Bernardo simply responds, "Burlando lo tomo, Rey" ["In jest I take it, King"], makes his bow and exits, leaving behind a frightened monarch, "y su injuria con enmienda" (A. Durán 1877, 435) ["and his offense corrected"]. The other version specifies a point of contention in addition to the imprisonment of Bernardo's father and the aspersion of a legacy of evil cast upon Bernardo himself; there is also a matter of property rights. "—Dite yo el Carpio en tenencia" ["I gave you Carpio as a tenancy"], the king had declared, "Tú tómaslo de heredad"["You've taken it in perpetuity"] (434). Bernardo defends his own claims by reminding Alfonso of a different episode in the cycle in which he had saved the king's life: "Allí me distes el Carpio/De juro y de heredad" ["There you gave me Carpio/By right in perpetuity"] (434). Hence, the conclusion of this version is made in reference to the disputed land:

> —Aquestas burlas, el Rey,
> No son burlas de burlar;
> Llemásteme [sic] de traidor,
> Traidor, hijo de mal padre:
> El Carpio no le quiero,
> Bien lo podeis vos guardar,
> Que cuando yo lo quisiere,
> Muy bien lo sabré ganar.
>
> (A. Durán 1877, 434)

> These jests, your highest Majesty,
> Are no jests to jest with me;
> Traitor you have vested me,
> Traitor, ill-begotten son:
> Carpio from you I'll not require,
> For yourself keep it for now,

> For whene'er I but desire,
> To win back Carpio, I'll know how.

It is here that I pause to listen for the local resonance in the reception of such medieval texts amidst their American auditors: a Manuel González and his father and his father's fathers. At Junín or Ayacucho, the soldiers of Bolívar and Sucre might well have reckoned the rebellious heroes of the romances, Bernardo or Fernán González or the young Cid, in their defiance of royal authority as prototypes for their own revolution. And in a ballad tradition less given to the superhuman than the tales of Lancelot, the auditors would have recognized that Bernardo would not have long resisted the king's men without the support of "los que comedes mi pan" ["those who eat of my bread"] (A. Durán 1877, 434). It may even be that the knife fights that will be a staple of the narrative poetry of the River Plate over the course of the nineteenth century are fortified by the memory of Bernardo, whose recitations did not omit to have him wrap his arm in his manto, like a wily gaucho, before he drew his sword. But these are conjectures. And I present my conjectural Bernardo del Carpio to a different end than to suggest distant precedents to this or that verse of *Martín Fierro*.

Rather, I would listen to the medieval poetry with an ear attuned to the constituting of America, and thereby remark that oral culture, too, offered resources for the glossing of the catch-all term or hypotext of liberty. The *romance* of Bernardo confronting his king in open and armed rebellion, links liberty to property, much as Clavero has suggested for the constitutional culture that evolved at Cadiz, and that we have seen in such American sequels as Lizardi's political fiction. The issues for the audience of Manuel González's grandparents become clear if we allow Menéndez Pidal one further conjecture—the text of the same *romance* as he reconstructs it. Here, his version of the denouement:

> —Malas mañas has, sobrino,
> no las puedes olvidar,
> lo que hombre te dice en burla,
> de veras vas a tomar.
> Yo te doy el Carpio, Bernardo,
> por juro y por heredad.
> —Aquellas burlas, el rey,
> no son burlas de burlar.
> El castillo está por mí,

nadie me lo puede dar;
quien quitármelo quisiere,
yo se lo sabré vedar.

                (Menéndez Pidal 1975, 73–74)

"How ill-tempered you are, nephew,
that these things you can't forget,
what a man jokingly tells you,
you just won't take for a jest.
Carpio I give you, Bernardo,
by right in perpetuity."
"Those jests, your Majesty,
are not jests to jest with me.
The castle stands by me,
to me no one can give it;
whosoever would take it away,
I'll know how to forbid it."

The reciters of the Bernardo cycle in ca. 1823 obviate the need for the contemporary coinage of colonial America figured as an enchained population already noted in Bolívar's message and frequent in the poetry of the period. The imprisoned father of Bernardo embodies the role. And the king's pretended seizure of Bernardo himself, visiting the sufferings of the father upon the son, along with the pretended seizure of Carpio, represent a double threat to property real enough to the veterans of the wars of independence. But where the king cannot prevail by force of arms, he attempts his ruse. He would patch up hostile relations with pleasant words and assuage rebellion by way of a donation.

To accept Carpio—or Caracas—as a royal concession is to accept the king's right. He can only alienate what is his by proper title. His American auditors will endeavor to do as Bernardo. They will see through the ruse in their own time, when its author is Fernando VII and its title, "Proclama del Rey a los habitantes de Ultramar." This royal decree of 14 April 1820 is the provocation to which Hidalgo responds in a cielito through a gaucho speaker, if not yet in gaucho speech:

El otro día un amigo
hombre de letras, por cierto,
del Rey Fernando a nosotros
me leyó un gran Manifiesto.

                (Carilla 1979, 99)

> The other day a friend,
> a man of letters, of course,
> read me a grand Manifesto
> King Ferdinand sent to us.

The Gaucho de la Guardia del Monte, as though schooled by Bernardo del Carpio, knows how to interpret the royal donation:

> Cielito, cielo que sí,
> guarde, amigo, el papelón,
> y por nuestra Independencia
> ponga una iluminación.
> Dice en él que es nuestro padre,
> y que lo reconozcamos,
> que nos mantendrá en su gracia
> siempre que nos sometamos.
>
> (Carilla 1979, 99)

> Cielito, cielo for sure,
> put away that paper, my friend,
> and set out a candle
> for our Independence.
> He says there that he's our father,
> and that we should pledge our loyalty,
> that he'll keep us in his good graces
> as long as we bend a knee.

The reaction will be as definitive in poetry, and politics too, as that of the heroes of the old *romances*. The gaucho will reject the offer, dispute the king's right to give what, a decade after the revolution in the River Plate, is not his to give, and stake his own claim to the title of Beloved Son of the fathers who died in the chains of the colonial system.

3

In the movement from this cielito in the voice of the unnamed Gaucho de la Guardia del Monte to the "Diálogo patriótico interesante entre Jacinto Chano, capataz de una estancia en las islas de Tordillo, y el gaucho de la Guardia del Monte," written in 1821, Hidalgo took the definitive step toward the formation of a genre. Poesía gauchesca found a consistent line of development throughout the century, culminating in José Hernández's *El gaucho Martín Fierro* (Buenos Aires 1872) and *La vuelta de Martín Fierro* (Buenos Aires 1879), and thereafter, the support of a substantial and continuous critical tradition: Unamuno and Lugones, Borges and Martínez Estrada, a host of research in linguistics, history and literary history, culminating in the work of Angel Rama (1982a) and Josefina Ludmer (1988). As a result the genre has effectively taken up a place as the response to the demands, otherwise contested by Rivera-Rodas, as discussed above, for a wholly new literary form for a wholly independent American poetry. The case has been overstated. As for the crucial shift from monologue to dialog practiced by Hidalgo, the preceding discussions of the political reflections of Lizardi's Payo and Sacristán, the commerce between Anastasio Tzul and Valentín Alvarado, or Bernardo del Carpio's ironic deflation of his king's donation in the recitals of Manuel González and his forebears, taken together in their diverse registers, provenances and social contexts, all point to an epochal change. The familiar Enlightenment genre of the philosophical dialogue that reaches Monteagudo is transformed in the emerging constitutional culture in which liberty, the epic theme on the road to independence, becomes a topic of popular debate. The "Diálogo patriótico interesante" forms but a part of that epochal shift, though altogether explicitly—"¡Ah tiempo aquel, ya pasó!" ["Ah those times have surely passed!"] (Carilla 1979, 105)—seeking an appropriate form of expression and an adequate means of governability in the new period of "papeletes de molde" ["printed papers"] (111).

If not a revolutionary form, then, one may look for the outstanding contribution of the gaucho poetry in its conception of liberty in terms of land and work, of personal property and the person as property. Here the reading of Ludmer is essential. The emerging constitutional culture was greatly preoccupied with labor, as we have seen in Lizardi's dialogues. The self would be constituted in political terms by a demonstration of usefulness. One needed to work for one's identity. (And since a woman's place was in the home and her work there was not considered work, she could not have a political identity nor the status of a subject in literary terms.) And yet where the Enlightenment precedent of such texts as the *Discurso sobre el fomento de la industria popular* deploy methods of a new economic science (e.g. demographic statistics) to detail types of labor, situations, rates of production, Lizardi's Payo and Sacristán leave matters considerably more abstract. Semiotic concerns lend them dress, but the laboring body beneath the clothes remains all but invisible, only reaching a marginal textual presence—not coincidentally—in the discussions devoted to incarceration and other punishments.[13] Gauchesca poetry, from its very inauguration in Hidalgo's "Diálogo patriótico" of 1821, especially in Ludmer's reading of it, develops the same central issue in the constituting of America, but lays emphasis on the body: Lizardi's distinction of *ocio-negocio* becoming a matter of the *usos del cuerpo* in Ludmer's terms.

Ludmer underlines the constitutive moment of the genre itself—

> The text constitutes its interior space with the whole word (the oral and the written voice): it divides reading and writing in the oral-written body of the poem *in order to unite them against the Spanish oppressor*. But it is not only that. Literature opens itself when music ceases. *It constitutes itself*, and above all constitutes its new internal space, upon two silences, or better, upon a single silence on the initial border and upon all silences on the final one. (1988, 80; Ludmer's emphases; my own would coincide in the italicizing of "constitutes itself")

The voice of the gaucho is constituted, she argues, by distinguishing itself from the silences beyond its borders: the positions of the *gaucho malo*, or "useless body" and that of the "used up body" (Ludmer 1988, 81),[14] specifically, Hidalgo's retired soldier "Andrés Bordón,/alias el Indio Pelao" (Borges and Bioy Casares 1955, 1:23), who lost his leg in the wars.

Ludmer localizes this constitutive moment in the passage *"Before the first word of the overseer Chano"* (Ludmer 1988, 79; her emphasis), wherein,

> the two senses of "gaucho," the legal and the illegal, the useful and the useless, the patriot and the anti-patriot, separate out and articulate the totality of the genre, that not only is a tract on written words, voices overheard and their meanings, but also on the division of the voice of the other and, besides, on good and evil. A tract on the *patria*. (Ludmer 1988, 81)[15]

Hidalgo presents that moment of silence before the articulate and articulating word, thus:

> Y con tantos aguaceros
> está el camino pesao,

> y malevos que da miedo
> anda uno no más topando
>> (Borges and Bioy Casares 1955, 1:18)

> And with so many downpours
> the road is an awful mess,
> and bandits, to scare you witless,
> you can't help but run into them.

The twin to this moment, for Ludmer, is the passage "*after Chano's last word*" (Ludmer 1988, 79; still her italics), in which the narrator arises to introduce Bordón, relate concisely the story of his wound—"y en Vilcapujio de un tiro/una pierna le troncharon" ["and in Vilcapujio he got/his leg shot off"] (Borges and Bioy Casares 1955,1:23)—and the arrival of Contreras and Chano at his ranch:

> Dieron el grito en el cerco;
> los perros se alborotaron;
> Bordón dejó la cocina,
> los hizo apiar del caballo;
> y lo que entre ellos pasó
> lo diremos, más despacio,
> en otra ocasión, qué en ésta
> ya la pluma se ha cansao.
>> (Borges and Bioy Casares 1955, 1:23)

> They gave a shout in the corral;
> the dogs began to howl;
> Bordón came out of the kitchen,
> and had them dismount;
> and what went on after that,
> we'll patiently recount,
> but at some other time
> for now the pen is tired.

Though I abbreviate the second citation, I follow Ludmer's emphasis. She will subsequently mark the boundary of this section of her *tratado* with "a final digression on silence" (Ludmer 1988, 82, cf. "the final shores," 1988, 79), in which she points to the "howling of the animals" (83), audible only when the articulate "voz (del) 'gaucho' " runs up to its limits in silence. At that point the *alboroto* introduces the *cry* of Chano y Contreras, what might be called the inarticulate voice of the gaucho that stalks the genre: neither the "voz (del) 'gaucho' " itself, nor complete silence. A prearticulate voicing, perhaps, out of which an articulate and, I add, an individuated voice might emerge. Ludmer calls it "the cry of amputation" (83). So, too, Abraham and Oakeshott. I have called it the voice of melancholia and a vexed historical consciousness.

As for the moment prior to the first enunciation of "la voz (del) 'gaucho,' " which is to say before the constitution of the genre according to Ludmer's definition, I shift her emphasis to underscore the locus of the inaugural division between good and evil, useful and useless, as the "camino pesao." This is the trammeled lane of communication of which Miranda complained, the roadblock in the development of an internal American commerce in poetry and other goods. Contrera's success in traveling that difficult passage will open the genre by establishing the traffic by which, for instance, news, if not newspapers, from a literate, urban center are transmitted to the illiterate countryside, as we have seen in Hidalgo's cielito (here the commerce brings *yerba* out to Chano). In the new generic division between silence and the "voz (del) 'gaucho,' " the *ociosos* (those who are not engaged in useful labor, therefore not upright citizens) are the enemies of such communication and so are left outside the genre. The inside term, as I have been suggesting from the beginning, is negocio. And between them, I insist again, a borderland of *alboroto*, figured as a road, in this case a *camino pesao*, an obstructed route.

The genre of gauchesca poetry narrates the passage across that route by the incorporation of the gaucho into the army. In recruiting his service against "the Spanish oppressor," the genre transforms the figure of the malevo, the vago, into a patriotic, useful body. That story marks the boundaries of the genre, which Hernández will remark by transgression, crossing the frontier in the desertion of Martín Fierro and Cruz in the *Ida*, and recrossing in the *Vuelta*, where Fierro returns after Cruz's death, accepting the limits of the national territory as his own and taking his place within it by proving that his work is his song. And that work is a peculiar agricultural labor: Fierro plants a kiss, transfiguring national geography into the space of national history, the open range into a vast, if ruined cemetery, a national burial ground of unmarked graves.[16]

The work and works of gauchesca poetry guard the borders of a national identity from a threat from without: Spanish oppression, Portuguese incursions in the Banda Oriental, the unconquered native peoples, and, in literary terms, from the imposition of European models, as will be particularly clear in the double-edged parody of *Fausto* (1866) of Estanislao del Campo (Argentina 1834–80). But gauchesca poetry and other American expressions are riven by internal divisions, too. The borders of national territories and their literatures already represent the fracture of the encompassing dream of a Pan American union, of course. Moreover, within those borders one finds outcasts, and, listening closely, one hears their voices: the marrón, disfigured symbol of the runaway slave in Zequeira, for instance; the recidivist vago in the penal system of Lizardi's Payo and Sacristán; and in the gauchesca, the Indian and malevo, on the one hand, bodies recalcitrant to use, and on the other, the disabled veteran, or body already used up. The nether world of the political economy emerges in the constitutional dialogues.

"La voz (del) 'gaucho' " speaks for unity and utility, locating liberty at their conjunction. The *grito de la amputación* is raised against this liberty, which it denounces as a political fiction. If "Todo perece" ["Everything perishes"], including nations and nature, according to Heredia at Cholula, ca. 1823 (as noted at the close of the preceding chapter), then the amputee is the antimetaphor of that vision of disintegration. He lives the figure of fragmentation literally in his own flesh and bone. Within the gauchesca the voice is plainest in the anonymous "Cielito del Blandengue retirado" (1821–23). Blandengue counts off the misfortunes of his military career and the continuing perils of civilian life: one leg, two betrayals, three patrias and now, four cows:

> Cuatro vacas hei juntado
> a juerza de trabajar
> y agora que están gordas
> ya me las quieren robar.
>
> (qtd in Ludmer 1988, 190)

> I've gotten hold of four cows
> by the sweat of my own brow,
> and now that I've fattened 'em up
> they're gonna steal 'em anyhow.

Numbers matter, as Ludmer argues throughout her tratado, and here the force of Blandengue's enumeration of loss might best be gauged against the mounting, accumulative enumerations of such prayers as the "Oración a la piedra imán" preserved over the course of colonial history in Afrocuban culture, though originating in Spain, according to Lydia Cabrera.[17] The prayer is a petition to the *piedra imán* for its intervention in the cure of certain illnesses, for good fortune and prosperity, or, most of all, for success in love (L. Cabrera 1984, 44). Blandengue, for his part, invokes a "Dios Cupido" ["God Cupid"], but as the later reference to "alcagüetes" ["pimps"] confirms, eros enters the poem only under the negating sign of irony (Ludmer 1988, 190–91). This is rather an antierotics of repulsion: of the mangled, violated body, of coercion instead of desire.

Beneath Blandengue's count, I infer a zero: no one to address. For while it is true that the genre of the cielito dictates monologue, in Hidalgo's hands the form is in search of an interlocutor. When that interlocutor is found, the cielito overflows into the new genre of gauchesca poetry. Hence, Hidalgo's cielito of "El Guardia del Monte" takes its point of departure, as I have noted, in a moment of fellowship, a reading between friends that allows for the delineation of a national unity—a *we*, inside the borders, who reject an invasive, foreign text. The same reminiscence, reported by Chano upon his return from the city, sets the "Diálogo patriótico" in motion. Blandengue, quite to the contrary, withdraws willfully from such lanes of communication:

> Bayan al Diablo, les digo
> con sus versos y gacetas,
> que no son sino mentiras
> para robar pesetas.
>
> (Ludmer 1988, 190)

> Go to hell, I tell 'em,
> with yer verses and yer papers
> that're nothin' but a pack o' lies
> to rob someone's pesetas.

He repulses the intertextual network out of which American letters are constituting themselves as national literatures by reducing literary commerce to commerce *tout court*.

Blandengue undertakes the same denunciation of political emancipation. National identities have been formed by roving armies in his dystopia, and his experience teaches that political goals merely overlay marauding as a means. The true end of the campaigns is not liberty, but theft. Blandengue revises military history by transferring it from the field of politics to that of economics, and literary history by divorcing the verse and periodical prose written in support of the military campaigns from the purported goal of political unity.

Ludmer will come to remark of del Campo's *Fausto*, that it is "the first text in the genre that neatly separates literature and politics," thereby inaugurating modernity within the gauchesca, i.e., "it introduces a typically modern sequence that can be enunciated as follows: depolitization, autonomization of the literary, problematization of the representative constructions of the genre, and opening of a new debate between writers, that is, reformulation of their specific functions" (Ludmer 1988, 242). And placing emphasis on "neatly," this is so, for the "Cielito del Blandengue retirado" is anything but neat, even if the remaining terms for modernity are equally applicable to that poem. It is instead the antimetaphor of the raw flesh at just that point of amputation that shears constitutional discourse into various modern disciplines. Del Campo's *Fausto* is a thoroughly ironic, which is to say, with Paz, a thoroughly modern reading of Blandengue's exasperated *grito*, "Bayan al Diablo" (literally "Go to the Devil"). That damnation is indeed fulfilled, though theatrically, like all else in *Fausto*, when it is received as an invitation to, if not to say a commercial advertisement for a night at the opera. But so, too, *Fausto* is read by the cielito—to invoke the modality of this two-way reading practiced by Ludmer. The cielito traces the routes of del Campo's modernity to the very voice of the devil, as in the closing words of Luzbel before Aguirre broke off his poem, amputating it of its potential modern extension. Blandengue speaks as Luzbel after the fall. The theological catastrophe contemplated by Aguirre may be greater than the fall from the heavenly city of Enlightenment political philosophy into the history of unending war and its accompanying plunder in the River Plate circa 1823. But the proportional gains for poetry are the inverse. Luzbel foregoes the perfect transparency of a paradisal language—a semiotic heaven still conceived of in the utopian plans of the Payo and Sacristán—in order to keep a secret. This is perfidy, of course, but for the poet it gives psychological depth to the baroque propensity to elaborate figuration, allowing him to hollow out a hell inside the self, to make a self of that interior hell. Blandengue, on the contrary, finds his hell all around him. Hell is personal property, including that primary property of the body, conscripted as a national resource, the body as national territory.

Blandengue's problem—political, economic and literary—is that unlike Aguirre's Luzbel, he can hold nothing back, not even his four cows. Hence, his rage, and in his rage, his bitter accusation of fraudulence leveled against the politics of emancipation:

> Dos veces me han engañado,
> como a negro de Guinea,
> ¡y por poquito . . . barajo!
> No me venden con librea.
>
> (Ludmer 1988, 190)

> They've already tricked me twice,
> like a black from Guinea, and—sh . . .
> ugar—they've almost gone and done it,
> sold me in livery into service.

Secrets, deceits, or in literary terms, figurative language, are the fabric of the political fiction of liberty from which he finds himself debarred. Blandengue claims to speak for truth, the truth of the body, as Ludmer points out, whose repertoire of expression is all but limited to antimetaphor (Ludmer 1988, 191; e.g. "miar" ["to piss"]). His is very nearly a *dégré zéro* of subjectivity: the subject of abuse, the victim. And if in his dearth he has learned aught of figuration—e.g. a wordless pointer at the wound in civil discourse and the transparent patch upon it of a rhyme ("¡ . . . barajo!" ["sh . . . /ugar"], Ludmer 1988, 190)—then it is but a poetic language in which to curse his new masters, *hijos de puta, hijos de la patria*: a Caliban.[18]

4

The "Cielito del Blandengue retirado" withdraws the support of poetry from politics. The principle tropes of constitutional culture are denounced as figures for economic injustice. The nation is no unity, nor is independence liberty. But to brand emancipation a political fiction is also to abandon those tropes, indeed to cede the power of figuration to political discourse. The result, for the cielito, is to commit poetry to a repulsive literalness. Not all poetry followed that route. The decade of the 1820s sees a continuation of the alliance of poetry and politics in the countless celebrations of liberty and commemorations of the military heroes that brought independence. Others continued to moralize and satirize in the habitual forms of the preceding era. Thus, one may recall, on the one hand, that Olmedo's "Victoria de Junín" was published in 1826, and on the other, Rafael García Goyena, probably America's greatest exponent of the genre of the verse fable in the style of Iriarte and Samaniego, died in 1823. The periodical press was also at work disseminating odes and fables by local bards throughout the period. As I have had occasion to remark elsewhere, most notably with respect to the baroque, literary styles and forms persist beyond the demarcations of literary histories. Nevertheless, the persistence of the odes to liberty and military triumph as well as the restricted wit of the fables represent the way back, a retreat from an authentic crisis for contemporary poetics of which the "Cielito del Blandengue retirado" serves as a signpost. The task for romanticism, which will emerge in a vexed relationship to constitutional culture, is the recuperation of figurative power for poetry, now as an autonomous field, amputated from politics. The principal solution, in Spanish America as in Europe, will be for Blandengue to leave off his complaining and to take a certain perverse glee in his hell, to recognize that it offers a satanic liberty without unity.

I will illustrate the dilemma and anticipate the solution at some distance from the gauchesca poetry of the River Plate. In their valuable study, *La musique des Incas et ses survivances* R. and M. D'Harcourt include "a somewhat cynical serenade," which they consider "an ancient harawi that has been a bit deformed by the Spanish words" (D'Harcourt 1925, 309). The first three stanzas lament the banishment of poetry and poet from the idyllic world of love to the reality of economics, i.e. to the world of Blandengue, after the fall from a longed-for unity:

> En la rajai de tu puerta
> Toda la noche watexiendo
> Sin abrigo y sin comido
> Siquiera pan de pedazo.
>
> La otra noche tambien tengo
> Con tu padre colerioso
> Bastante maltratacion,
> Por estarte musicando.
>
> Si yo fuera plata tengo,
> Vinieras muy humildado

Por mi casa, por mi tras,
Con merienda, chicha y trago.

(D'Harcourt 1925, 309)

At the crack of your door
On the lookout through the night
Without shelter, without food
Without so much as bread a bit.

The other night I also have
Pretty bad treatment
From your father
Furious that I music you.

If I were money have I
You'd come to me without airs
To my house, after me,
With chicha, food and drinks.

I note immediately that on the count of deformations, or as one might prefer, of transculturation, the score is even. The Spanish words also show the impact of the pressures of the Quechua language substrate, which breaks through explicitly in the mestizo verbal form, "watexiendo."[10]

The hypothesis of the third stanza glosses the first two. The father has rejected the suitor for his poverty. Money would have made the match. The equivocation, in Spanish at least, of "Si yo fuera plata tengo" ["If I were money have I"] is telling. The poet—let us call the singer of the song that—is, or would be, what he has. Thus, he is an outcast, Blandengue without so much as a "pan de pedazo" ["bread a bit"], not to mention a diminuitive herd of four cows, to his credit. This materialist definition of the self is the key to a reading of the commerce of letters in his hapless case. The poet offers his song to his beloved in hopes that she will value his expression of sentiment. His poem is his entrance fee. But once set in circulation, his tender falls—inevitably?—into the wrong hands. The father then applies the gold standard and he finds singer and song worthless in these terms.

The poet is narrating his recent past. In the present, his fourth and final stanza, he distinguishes himself from Blandengue. The amputee neither denied the loss of his leg, nor accepted symbolic compensation and with it induction into a society of, say, *beneméritos de la patria.* His is a shrill melancholia, compelled to repeat his loss in the immanent conscription of his cows, rather than find some saving grace in consigning his past to history. The Quechua singer, as we shall see, will introject the modernity of the choleric father, and so achieves a more efficacious revenge (and, not coincidentally, a better poem) than Blandengue's cursing:

> Si me quieres, no me quieres,
> Avisa mey con temprano;
> De tu laya o mas mijor
> Tambien tengo palabrado.
>
> (D'Harcourt 1925, 309)
>
> If you love me, if you don't,
> Let me know it right away;
> To your kind or much bitter
> I have also given my word.

Greater than the loss of the would-be bride, the poet has suffered the deprecation, one can almost say depreciation, of his song in the translation of poetry to economy. To recuperate the power of poetry, he turns the tables. The beloved can also be measured in economic terms, and just as the father can interpose himself as an unexpected addressee, so too, the poet has been *musicando* two (or more) well-to-do homes at once. The principles of calculation and interchangeability, moreover, alter the status of his song. What would have appeared to be a true expression of love to either of his addressees becomes, in retrospect, a figure of speech. The poet is no longer the subject of abuse. He himself disabuses his beloved—as well as the father, if he continues to eavesdrop—and gains the commanding position (the imperative "Avisa mey" ["Let me know"]) in the bargaining.

The trickster poet relates the process by which poetry is reinfused with figurative power. His frank unmasking, however, is as relentlessly literal as the cielito. In order to note something of the same process but culminating in the forging of a new figuration, I turn to a related text, "Wasil'aykita," in which an indigent singer rediscovers the riches of his song. The D'Harcourts offer no comment as to the antiquity this Quechua *harawi*:

> When I come to your house,
> Don't throw me out
> Because I'm a poor wretch.

Sun, father, moon, mother,
You well see
That I shed tears of blood.

(D'Harcourt 1925, 298)[20]

The preceding sample provides a narrative instance of the real poverty of the singer, both the momentary condition of his hungry vigil
and the enduring inferiority of his means. Such a situation would
seem to reflect upon this song as well, although one may not discard
the possibility that the singer as "poor wretch" is a literary topos.
But whether literal representation or topos, the case would be one
of the exhaustion of figuration. Having been repulsed in love, then,
this singer does not seek out a self-defense in irony, but rather
rediscovers the resources made freshly available to him by his very
exclusion. For he finds himself not in hell, but merely out-of-doors,
in the natural world ruled over, furthermore, by the deities of his
cultural (including his poetic) tradition. He changes his address to
the gods as his witness, thereby excluding in his turn, the beloved
who has cast him out. Thus, where the cielito reduces poetry to its
power to curse, this singer rediscovers its power of invocation. And
his reward: his tears are redoubled with the force of figuration, tran-
substantiated as blood.

In the absence of more accurate dating, I offer these two songs as
a paradigm, rather than a historical instance, for the route that will
carry poetry of the early constitutional culture beyond the potential
crisis of the unmasking of political fiction. For the historical case,
circa 1823, I provide the testimony of some few poems of José Fernández de Madrid (1789–1830), Colombian by birth, briefly president of the revolutionary triumvirate in 1816, well-traveled, a
sometime diplomat in Paris and London, and a poet, now much forgotten, but in his day held in high esteem. Andrés Bello may speak
for that opinion: Fernández de Madrid "is a distinguished Colombian, whose favorable disposition for poetry has been fomented by
the genius of both love and of liberty. The principal gift of his talent
is flexibility; thus it is that he is outstanding in the Anacreontic
genre, and in the sober meditations to which the important events
of his era have given rise" (Bello 1979, 308).

I situate Fernández de Madrid squarely in the constitutional culture of that era, citing, first, a poem, "A la restauración de la constitución española. Oda compuesta el mismo día que se tuvo en la
Habana la noticia, y publicada al siguiente." The occasion dates the

poem to 1820, though I refer to the 1822 text of the first collection of his *Poesías*, published in Havana, where he had sought refuge from imperial repression in Venezuela:

> Fue la Constitucion á la manera
> De un rio caudaloso,
> Que por toda la España discurriera
> Con noble marcha, curso magestuoso:
> Mas grande cada vez y poderoso
> Recibió de otros rios los tributos;
> A su paso la tierra fecundaba,
> Y los campos llenaba
> De verdura, de flores y de frutos
>
> (Fernández de Madrid 1822, 135)

> The Constitution was much the same
> As an abundant river
> That flowed though all of Spain,
> Ever stronger, ever grander,
> With noble pace, majestic course:
> Other rivers brought it tribute;
> It fertilized the earth where it flowed,
> And filled the fields
> With greenery, with flowers and with fruits.

His figure of the river as the course of constitutional liberty is nourished by other tributaries, as he says: a long cultural history that represented political power through the figuration of water courses (Schama 1995, 243–382). Here the river will provide an allegorical landscape, beginning with the traditional saturnine political fiction. The Constitution of Cadiz of 1812 introduces a new Golden Age, in which, it seems, the river itself does all the work. But bliss is short-lived. When Fernando VII returns from France he suppresses the constitution, a disruption that Fernández de Madrid represents, or rather covers over, as a kind of black magic:

> Pero desapareciendo de repente
> Del suelo castellano su onda pura,
> Los campos se marchitan nuevamente,
> Yá no hay frutos, ni flores, ni verdura.
>
> (Fernández de Madrid 1822, 135)

> But the pure waters suddenly
> Disappearing from Castilian plains,

The fields withered again;
No longer are there flowers, fruits, nor greenery.

The brief catalog of natural produce is reversed and negated. This disappearance, however, is not the end, but the beginning of the tale.

As a mythologizer of recent political history and a poet still hopeful that the reestablishment of the constitution in 1820 will yet save the union, his double project is to present constitutional culture, which is to say liberty, as arising dramatically out of inhospitable conditions, while still related to the lost paradise of Cadiz. The river provides the means in the context of a vegetal mythology, which, in and of itself, favors a conception of rebirth following a barren season. One need only figure the river, like the heroes of the *Popol Vuh*, as having spent a season in hell:

> ¡Oh! No desesperémos, que escondido
> El rico manantial, sigue corriendo,
> Subterráneo camina sin estruendo . . .
>
> (Fernández de Madrid 1822, 135)

> Oh, fear not, for hidden away
> The rich source continues running,
> Silently making its subterranean way . . .

I note that "we" enter the narrative here, that is poet and readers together, at a historical moment just prior to the writing of the poem. The exhortation, therefore, approaches prophecy, though the descriptive verbs remain in the present tense.

Poetry itself is the divining rod which allows Fernández de Madrid in a fictive 1819 to speak confidently of the river that will not be visible again until the subsequent verses:

> Ya la voz de Quiroga se ha escuchado,
> Y al golpe de su acero, que la ha herido,
> De la tierra ha brotado
> Mas brillante, mas puro, mas hermoso
> De las leyes el rio caudaloso.
>
> (Fernández de Madrid 1822, 138)

> Now the voice of Quiroga has been heard,
> And by the blow of his blade that wounded her,

> The earth brings forth
> More brilliant, purer, more beautiful by far,
> The abundant river of the law.

The river had not only disappeared, it had lost its voice ("sin estruendo" [literally, "without clamor"]). The voice is recovered by a transmutation, now as the voice of Antonio Quiroga, a leading military figure in the movement that forced Fernando VII to reestablish the Constitution of Cadiz. And Quiroga, of course, pronounces liberty. That shift of voice is made possible by another shift, this time in allusive field. The landscape has become the desert of Exodus, the river the waters of Mara, and Quiroga a latter-day Moses—as in Bolivar's self-figuration. By implication, a higher divinity than Saturn has been invoked to oversee the revivification.

Reading the poem in the light of the paradigm elucidated through the Quechua songs, I would argue that Fernández de Madrid's constitutional ode speaks to this very moment when politics and literature begin to diverge. For here the poet transforms the course of contemporary politics into a history lesson—ultimately a lesson in literary history. His allegory, that is, has more to say about poetic liberty than about political liberty, telling a tale of imagistic impoverishment overcome in the achievement of a richer figuration, "Mas brillante, mas puro, mas hermoso" ["More brilliant, purer, more beautiful by far"]. One finds an image of writing at the head of this allegory of poetic resurgence in the striking of the earth, and, remembering Luca's contemporaneous image of the wounded land, it would appear that such a scene of writing had many tributaries in the period. It is far more crucial to observe that Fernández de Madrid's allegory marks a profound departure from the semiotics of surfaces in Lizardi's burlesque utopia. The land gains depth, the capacity to hide riches ("que escondido/el rico manantial" ["for hidden away/The rich source"]) without reverting to the mainstay of the colonial imagination, which is to say of mineral wealth and mining. It is this interplay of surface and depth, I argue, that founds figuration, and that may therefore move poetry beyond the Payo's simple catalog of agricultural produce. I may add, finally, that it is the emerging historical imagination that creates those depths, hollowing out an underworld through an act of imagistic burial. The sleight-of-hand by which the river seemed to disappear, as though into thin air, is disclosed instead as a burial under the earth. Fernández de Madrid acknowledges that the heroic age of political independence as declared by the people and for the people at Cadiz is over, and accepts in compensation for that loss the renewed constitution of 1820 as a donation from the king.

The resurgence of the same river indicates something of a melancholic imagination at work at this historical juncture. I elucidate further by pairing this poem, as in the discussion of the Quechua songs, with another by Fernández de Madrid in which the break between literature and politics is explicit. *La Aguila Mexicana* published a text under the simple heading "Poesía" and signed J. F. de M. in its twenty-third issue, 7 May 1823 (91–92). I do not hesitate to attribute the poem to Fernández de Madrid, especially in light of the closing parenthetical note indicating prior publication in the *Argos* of Havana, where he was living and publishing his poetry at the time, as we have seen. The same note testifies, of course, to the development of the inter-American network of textual relations. In the case of *La Aguila Mexicana* the selection from the *Argos* represents, moreover, the formulation of an editorial program. The político predominates over the literario, in this periodical devoted primarily to the daily news of the *cortes constituyentes* then meeting in Mexico. Inasmuch as Meléndez died in 1817, inclusion of these poems was not news to the Mexican readership, but rather an embodiment of aesthetic principles.[21] To reprint J. F. de M.'s poem from the *Argos*, I infer, is to nominate him—a contemporary and an American—as Meléndez's continuator, or, as Bello will argue in his review of the London edition of Fernández de Madrid's *Poesías* (1828), his verse represents "a further step" (Bello 1979, 307). The "Poesía" in question is on the cusp in this respect. It is not yet among those poems that, in Bello's words, "clear away the fallen leaves of mythology and pastoral poetry, with which previous poets have disguised [their poetry]" (307). In fact, a sonnet published in *La Aguila Mexicana* only half a year later, "Al R. P. Fr. Manuel Navarrete, celebérrimo poeta americano," signed J. V. (J. V. 1823, 4), and apparently original to the periodical, carries that reform farther than the more accomplished Fernández de Madrid, by satirizing Meléndez's epigone, Navarrete. The emulator of Navarrete's poetry will become a "consummate Sancho Panza" (J. V. 1823, 4). Nor is the "Poesía" yet the work of an unobstructed historical imagination, which, "keeping pace with the age," has learned to "commit to its verses the memories of the vicissitudes of which we have been the spectators" (Bello 1979, 307). Nevertheless, Fernández de Madrid's "philosophy" and something of "the severity of modern taste" (Bello 1979, 307) serve to extend the Anacreontic ode, metrically no less than thematically, into an allegory of resurgence that inflects poetic melancholia for modern times.

The poem begins with a frank rejection of the historical task of poetry, "uniting itself to patriotism," in Bello's terms (Bello 1979, 307):

> Yo no apetezco el humo de la gloria
> Ni mirarme ceñido de laureles
> Sobre el carro fatal de la victoria,
> Como esos hombres bárbaros, cruëles
> De que llena sus páginas la historia.
>   Jamas viven contentos
> Los destructores del linage humano,
> Ni en sus brazos sangrientos
> Entra jamas con gusto la belleza:
> Tiembla el tímido Amor junto á un tirano
> Y triste gime la naturaleza.
>
>   (Fernández de Madrid 1823, 91)

>   I feel no yearning for the smoke of glory
> Nor to see myself with laurel crowned
> Upon the fatal chariot of victory
> Like those men, barbarous and cruel,
> Who fill the pages of history.
>   The destroyers of the human race
> Shall never live contentedly,
> Nor shall their bloody arms embrace
> A willing beauty:
> Shy Love trembles in the face
> Of a tyrant, and nature moans most ruefully.

The poet expresses his indifference to politics. It matters not who triumphs; all victories are alike barbarous and cruel; all politics a fiction disguising an insatiable destructiveness. This is a radical departure, much like the "Cielito del Blandengue retirado," from the poetry "keeping pace with the age," "an era rife with great events," according to Bello's political fiction (Bello 1979, 307). To gauge the measure of the break, it might be well to recall the verses in the same year of 1823 of the young Victor Hugo—whom Bello and virtually all Spanish American poets will learn to revere by midcentury:

Ne vouz étonnnez point que j'aime les guerriers!
Souvent, pleurant sur eux, dans ma douleur muette,
J'ai trouvé leur cyprès plus beau que nos lauriers.

("Mon enfance," Hugo 1857, 6:29)

Be not abashed that I love warriors!
Often, bewailing them, in my unspoken pain,
I've found their cypresses more lovely than our laurel wreaths.

Hugo cedes the greater glory to the soldier in his grave, but he does so knowing that the glory of the soldier is the making of the poet, who converts the grave into the occasion for sublimity. The surprise, then, is not Hugos's military strain, but rather Fernández de Madrid's claim to forego laurels altogether. In his case, however, there is also a metapoetic explanation. He relinquishes sublimity in favor of beauty, one might say in keeping with "his naturally sweet and tender vein," noted by Bello in 1827 in a review of Fernández de Madrid's play *Gautimoc* (Bello 1979, 407, n. 9). Beauty, whose themes are "el tímido Amor" ["shy Love"] and "la naturaleza" ["nature"], has been banished from patriotic verse, according to Fernández de Madrid in "Poesía": "ni . . . Entra jamas" [literally, "nor . . . /Ever enters"]. He would seek a resurgent figuration with which to restore it.

Those two opening stanzas serve the immediate purpose of introducing the Anacreontic mood—"Coróname de rosas, dulce Amira" ["Crown me with roses, sweet Amira"] (Fernández de Madrid 1823, 91)—in a context that will give otherwise typically late eighteenth-century amatory verse greater philosophical reach. The place of philosophy is an idealized bucolic retirement in the Horatian mode of the Salamanca school. Fernández de Madrid's opening stanzas motivate that retirement by a change of address. He would not withdraw from the vanity of the court, as did Meléndez, Quintana, Cienfuegos and even Zequeira in "El solitario" (Zequeira y Arango 1964, 186–90), but rather from the battlefield. He thereby maps a set of historical coordinates onto the abstract landscape of the Anacreontic ode.

The setting is specifically Fernández de Madrid's America: "Que atraviese el Océano/El estrangero siempre codicioso,/Para llevarse el oro americano" ["The ever covetous foreigner/Would cross the ocean/To carry off American gold"] (Fernández de Madrid 1823, 92). There, both the horrors of war and the bounty of love refer to his personal experience. "Habiendo padecido los horrores" ["Hav-ing suffered horrors"] (91), he writes, on the one hand, while on the other, his Arcadian Amira is explicitly his own wife, who, therefore, shares his "memories of vicissitudes" on a personal scale:

> No ignoras que la suerte
> Siempre me ha perseguido;
> Sabes que muchas veces he tenido
> Cerca de mí á la muerte
> Queriendo enfurecida
> Romper la trama débil de mi vida.
> (Fernández de Madrid 1823, 92)

> You are not unaware that fate
> Has ever persecuted me;
> You know how often I have been
> Confronted face to face
> With death, which furiously desired
> To cut the weak thread of my life.

The place is set for an adversative, an explanation, for instance, of how fortitude has triumphed over mortal danger. His Amira, after all, is also aware that he has survived each peril. That adversative does not come. Fernández de Madrid has renounced the laurels of victory that shut the door on a mendicant beauty.

To restore his muse Fernández de Madrid undertakes a sacrifice, in fact a self-sacrifice, rather than a counter-attack. Thus he capital-izes on the capacity of the ode for sudden turnings, sudden tropings, to incorporate his own death:

> La muerte ha de triunfar tarde o temprano
> Yo te suplico, pues, amiga mia,
> Que arrojes con tu mano
>   Algunas rosas en mi tumba fría:
> Siempre un rosal en élla,
> Y riègalo de llanto, Amira bella.
>   Con este dulce riego
> ¡Que abundante y hermosas
> Verás nacer las rosas!
> Cogelas en tu mano, Amira, luego
> Y al respirar su espíritu oloroso
> Respirarás el alma de tu esposo.
> (Fernández de Madrid 1823, 92)

> Sooner or later death must triumph,
> Thus I beg of you, my friend,
> That you cast some roses
> On my tomb with your own hand:
> Forever a rosebush growing there,
> And water it, fair Amira, with your tear.
>   With watering so sweet you'll see
> how beauteous and bountiful
> Are the roses it will be bear!
> By your own hand, Amira, pick them and take hold;
> And when you breathe their spirit in their scent,
> You will be breathing in your husband's soul.

A tight circuit of internal commerce: she receives into her hand the roses that are planted by her hand, but only after—only because, I venture—they pass through his grave. The roses, emblem of beauty for an allegorical *Amira bella*, are born from his tomb and he is transfigured in them. His soul becomes their spirit; his breath, his song, becomes their fragrance ("Rosas" is the collective name of the love poetry dedicated to his wife in the first edition of his *Poesías* [Fernández de Madrid 1822, 5–27]).

Elegy might have stopped here, for the projected loss of the husband is compensated by the introjection of his poetic figure. But Fernandez de Madrid tarries to spin out the allegory. His wife, he foresees, will bring their son to the grave, and the sight of the mute, allegorical *tableau vivant* that *they* form before his buried perspective suffices to raise the dead:

> Saldrá mi sombra del sepulcro helado
> A ver en su presencia
> Juntas á la hermosura y la inocencia.
>
> (Fernández de Madrid 1823, 92)

> My shade will leave the frigid grave
> To see beauty and innocence
> Joined together in its presence.

And, turning to the prosopopeia of funeral oratory, that shade will speak in his own voice (signaled typographically by small capitals). The past addresses the future, announcing his legacy: "TU MADRE, Y TU CANDOR ES TU RIQUEZA" ["YOUR MOTHER, AND YOUR CANDOR IS YOUR WEALTH"] (Fernández de Madrid 1823, 92). The dead are not quite buried; the living are not yet dead (92; "Pero en tanto que vivo" ["But as long as I live"]). And hovering between the two, a melancholic voice reinstates the power of Beauty and exchanges the poverty of Innocence (92; "Nacido entre infortunios y pobreza" ["Born amidst misfortune and poverty") for the unplumbed depths of a new poetics, dubbed the wealth of candor. Bello explicates that candor thus: "we find . . . in almost all his works, a most highly commendable gift: a tone of naturalness and truth, without effort, without emphatic affectation, without violent transports, without studied embellishments of diction. It is true that he does not refrain from placing too much trust in the facility of his talent; but nothing is rarer than to find that precise point equidistant from nakedness and pomp, from negligence and presumption; and if one must err between these two extremes, good taste will always be more indulgent toward the former" (Bello 1979, 407, n. 9).

To offer a poetic legacy of candor is to write in favor of a naturalized speech. If the goal is a conversational tone, as Wordsworth and Coleridge were seeking, Fernández de Madrid's achievements fall short; though even as late as the 1820s Bello's admonition is intended more simply as a hedge against a retrograde baroque esthetic, which Fernández de Madrid does in fact secure. Where Fernández de Madrid approaches the English romantics of whom he is the contemporary, is in an understanding that the promotion of "candor" does not entail the elimination of figuration, but rather, oddly perhaps, its resurgence. Fernández de Madrid discovers that in making the poem into the space of his own figurative internment, the biographical self can be set at the distance of history and a new self, the poet as poet, can arise in his place. The resurgence, ultimately, is a transfiguration of the self as romantic subject.

I would recall, however, that other paths remained open to the American imagination. The romantic self was not simply inevitable. The Makka of Paraguay, for instance, develop the motif of the wounding of nature in the variants of the tale of "The Woman Who Married a Tree" (Wilbert and Simoneau 1991, 196–208). With the customary cautions about dating elements of oral culture, I will suppose that some version of the story would have been contemporary with Fernández de Madrid. In the recitations of both Takaci and Kiamxe'ni, which were recorded in anthropological field work in the late 1970s and 1980s, the tale is initiated by an erotic encounter: a certain young woman habitually scratched the bark of a lignum vitae tree when out fetching water. The editors make note of a linguistic connection between a virgin girl and an unblemished tree trunk, as well as remarking the "Chaco custom of lovers scratching the face and body of their partners, similar, in a way, to our kiss" (196, n. 7 and 8). As in the poetry of Fernández de Madrid, the wounding of nature proves productive. For the tree now returns the woman's visit, coming to her at night and telling her " 'I am the one you used to scratch. . . . Here are the wounds you made when you scratched me.' Then he lay with her. They were now a couple, the woman and the lignum vitae" (1991, 201). This coupling of mankind and nature is both the narrative ground and the metaphor of a fructifying of the earth. The lignam vitae goes with his wife to her father's fields "when it is not the season for planting" (202), and the seeds he sows there grow instantly into an abundant harvest that renews itself without toil. The Makka paradise will soon be lost. A combination of marital infidelity and a willful infraction of the rules for harvest imposed by the lignum vitae—again, mirror images—causes the degradation of the mythic gift. But rather than these consequences, I would call attention to the motif of the wounding as an initial stage in a resurgence as the grounds for a comparison. For Fernández de Madrid, the planting of the rosebush is a spectral projection meant to guarantee the survival of his individual identity, his protoromantic self, in the transfiguration of his mortal body into an immortal poetic voice. For the Makka, the planting is not the symbol of a greater good, but the very substance of the tale, concerned far less with the vicissitudes of a particular woman than with the commonweal. The distinctions are not absolute, however. The lineaments of a family romance—though by no means Freudian—are visible to the Makka, who draw out the personal story of the faithless wife through the return of the father for the provision of his son. And on the other side, modern Spanish American poetry will usually situate the emerging self in a public space, retaining something of the Makka emphasis on the social whole—though not without poetic tensions that I will now explore, and which continue to affect contemporary verse, just as the Makka continue to retell their tales.

4

Hesitant Step, Counter-Sublime:
Bello and Heredia, 1823–1832

1

SIMÓN RODRÍGUEZ IS BEST KNOWN TO THE HISTORY OF SPANISH American letters as the tutor of the young Bolívar and witness of the latter's famous oath in Rome in 1805 to bring independence to the Spanish American colonies (Bolívar 1976, 3–4). His pedagogy did not end there, however, and his writings on education and other topics—radical departures in form and substance—as well as his peripatetic life earned him a place on Lezama Lima's short list of representative men for the romantic era: Miranda, Rodríguez and Friar Servando Teresa de Mier (Lezama 1977, 326–46).[1] Measuring the constitution of America late in life, Rodríguez looked back to the French Revolution as the fountainhead of "the Era of *the New Societies*" (S. Rodríguez 1954–58, 1:314) and in this light offered a brief parable of political history:

> The Monarchic Regime, after a humorless life,
> of many centuries,, took to bed in Paris, at the end of
> the last century.
>> From everywhere there came Distinguished Doctors, to . . .
> Dispute with the local practitioners, and . . .
> Disputing they have spent half a century, . . .
>> Without Reaching Any Agreement
>> (S. Rodríguez 1954, 1:337)

The passage will suffice to give some indication of his peculiar, visual style. But returning to Rodríguez's parable, he relates that "No one proffers Remedies" (S. Rodríguez 1954, 1.337), and in consequence, the debate continued. "For 12 years," writes Rodríguez in 1842, "the French are observing the appearance of their patient—taking his pulse—touching his tongue—and asking random questions, to see how he's doing" (1:338). Shifting attention, then, to the new societies of his immediate concern, the "Sociedades americanas en 1828," as his essay is titled, he declares: "The new Nations of America wish to imitate France, but they're missing the main thing, which is the Subject . . . they're missing the Patient" (1:338).

The immediate target of Rodríguez's irony is political backsliding in America, where he finds an ancien régime mentality hovering about an empty bed: would-be courtiers without kings. It is well to remember, however, that the year of 1830 to which Rodríguez recurs is also the date of the performance of Hugo's *Hernani* in Paris and the definitive inauguration of the romantic movement, intimately related, in Hugo's mind, to the history of republican politics. Rodríguez's liberal and romantic diagnosis bears upon literary no less than political history in Spanish America. In identifying the sovereign subject as *el Enfermo*, he outlines the grounds of romanticism: call it a morbid subjectivity. In proclaiming its absence in the decade following independence, he anticipates Paz's critique of the romantic movement in Spanish America with prescience and perspicacity.

Nevertheless, in the years circa 1823, José María Fernández de Madrid, whose poetry I have discussed in the last chapter, traces a different course in an exemplary tale in the prologue to the first edition of his *Poesías* (Fernández de Madrid 1822). First he posits a project for an American poem by reference to the nature poetry of the recently deceased Jacques Delille (see Delille 1859). Introducing the extensive translations of Delille that he included in the volume (63–115) a year before the publication of Bello's "Alocución a la poesía," Fernández de Madrid asserts: "The descriptive genre to which [Delille's poetry] belongs is almost unknown among us," adding, "for although some attempts have been published, they are—at least the ones that I know—greatly inferior to what may be expected of our poets" (1). He does not enumerate the disappointments, but he does refer to his own efforts in that direction, though humbly, as something of an accident in an autobiographical vignette: "Obliged to remain in the countryside for a few months as a consequence of a grave and painful illness, I attempted to distract myself with the commerce of the Muses. Were it not for that, I might well have never translated Delille" (ii).[2] The rest cure in relative rusticity is no doubt a response to disease literal enough.[3]

And yet one may also read this *enfermedad* paradigmatically as a trope for the retirement of poetry from the arena of politics and the useful labors of citizenship—a separation occasioned during the early constitutional period, as I have argued, by the predominance of the language of political philosophy in the definition of poetry's key term of liberty. Here Fernández de Madrid finds the missing subject as a patient. Removed from the political economy, Fernández de Madrid would still affirm his utility as an import agent in the commerce of letters, were it not for his infirmity:

> since these translations, which I undertook as a form of recreation, wearied me more than I imagined at the beginning, I had to suspend them, and I proposed to occupy myself by composing some light and facile poems, whence resulted my *Rosas*. It seemed to me that the pleasant images that these flowers offer could entertain my fantasy and distract me from my woes. (Fernández de Madrid 1822, ii-iii)

In sum Fernández de Madrid describes his own course from the politically engaged though loyalist poetry of the "Oda a la constitución" at the outset of Spain's liberal triennium, to his translations of Delille, to the greater distraction of facile love lyrics, this last an apparent throwback to the rage for the Anacreontic mode of Meléndez Valdés. Yet twisting and turning once more with the agility of an ode, the prolog abruptly alters that light-hearted picture in a final confession: "Nevertheless, I noticed thereafter that some of those compositions took their part in the sadness that possessed me. It is difficult to write what one does not feel and counterfeit one's own character. I have painted my *Rosas* on a black background; but perhaps this very contrast will please some readers" (iii). Recourse to a language of shadowy depths which rise up despite superficial distractions speak against Lizardi's utopian semiotics of surfaces under the impartial illumination of reason, and in favor of a new sensibility. The subject is isolated from the public sphere. His illness is literally the cause, in this case; but figuratively, it is the consequence of that separation. And from his isolation, he defends poetry as a private transaction, a candid rendering of the self (i.e. no counterfeit). The freedom of self-expression, troped here as sincerity, substitutes for the trope of liberty that had been abandoned to the public discourse; while the very isolation of the self, which is its illness, takes the place of independence.

Looking now to the England of Bello's long sojourn, I would elucidate that relation between the autonomy of the self and the development of romanticism at some remove from the epochal figure of illness. Alvin Kernan has studied the impact of the shift from an oral to a print culture in this regard, focusing on the life of Samuel Johnson (Kernan 1987; see also Kernan 1982)—an analogue to Bello in a number of ways. Kernan highlights the manner in which a private income from the trade in books, following upon the recognition of the legal rights of ownership of intellectual property in copyright laws, led to the emancipation of the writer from the pre-existing patronage system. Freed from service to the king or lesser courtiers, the writer was at liberty to become an oppositional figure, but only by competing successfully in the book market, which required the development of a clear identity for his commodity, hence, a personal style. The abiding rules of neoclassicism thus give way to an expanding creative liberty governed by the dictates of the individual imagination. The romantic self is forming: isolate and eccentric, the source of its own fictions. Kernan relates a further consequence as well: the writer becomes emancipated and even alienated from his social milieu, and in England this means particularly the society forming as a result of industrialization. The establishment of a print culture leads to the emancipation of literature itself from other forms of writing, with exegetes and editors to guard the institutional boundaries of literary discourse. The same emancipation might also be judged an exile, of course.

The situation in Spanish America remained very different at the outset of the constitutional period.[4] Simply stated, the expansion of free trade made possible by political emancipation fostered neocolonialism, rather than native industrialization, as I have noted. Nevertheless, independence brought freedom of the press—a freedom shared by the remaining Spanish possessions from 1821 to 1823—and a greatly expanded commerce in periodical publications. One witnesses the consequent, albeit slow, shift toward a print culture throughout America. More than a decade after independence, away in provincial Mexico, for example, one finds in the *Broquel de las costumbres* of 30 August 1834, a response to an anticlerical broadside in verses signed by "El amigo del filosofo rancio": "Ese ciego fanatismo/Atrevido, y lisongero,/Dice que el clero sensato/Trata de estacarle el cuero" ["That blind fanaticism/Bold, and flattering/ Says that the sensible clergy/Tries to stake his hide"] ("Amigo del filosofo rancio" 1834, 128). He concludes with the unexpected frankness of conservative militancy: "Y lo hará, porque defiende,/

De la iglesia el evangelio" ["And they will, because they defend/
the gospel of the church"] (128). Reactionary politics and also reactionary poetry, inasmuch as the thematics know only surface, *el
cuero*, and no depths. Attending to the medium rather than the message, I would underline the shift implicit when the vanguard of print
culture, the periodical press, is enlisted to gainsay a literate form of
an oral culture, i.e. the *pasquín*.[5]

2

No name is more securely linked to that cultural transformation—an instigator, a champion, almost an icon of the print culture
that emerged hand-in-hand with the constitution of America—than
Andrés Bello. And the organs that first epitomized and promoted
that change in his long career were his London-based journals, the
Biblioteca Americana (1823) and the *Repertorio Americano*
(1826). They revise the social institution of literature, replacing and
even reversing the reports of the scientific expeditions of the previous generation: they export knowledge to rather than extract it from
America, for the benefit of America rather than Europe, in printed
texts. In brief, the journals are comprised primarily of digests rather
than original works, translating—in two senses—European texts to
Spanish-speaking Americans.

Kernan's thesis would lead one to expect that Bello would be the
paradigm of the self-made man of printed letters. And this is so: his
outstanding stature in the public sphere is achieved through his service in and to the print culture as the principal contributing editor
of the London journals, as philologist and grammarian, and eventually as a codifier of laws no less than of spelling, and finally as the
rector of the university of Santiago de Chile. Yet as a poet he does
not to make a self, a subject, an *Enfermo*, committing Spanish
American poetry instead to superabundant health in the programmatic poems with which he inaugurated the *Biblioteca Americana*
and the *Repertorio Americano*, his "Alocución a la poesía" and
"La agricultura de la zona tórrida," respectively—but then, neither
is Dr. Johnson the author of "The Prelude" or the "Ode on a Gre-
cian Urn."

I do not mean to challenge the influence of Bello's *silvas americanas*, as they are usually called—though Guillermo Araya (Araya
1982, 57–66) has strengthened the case for speaking of a single,

overarching and incomplete silva under the title "América." They are probably the most praised, still more certainly the most often cited, if not necessarily the best read Spanish American poems of the nineteenth century before *Martín Fierro*. In our time, Henríquez Ureña makes the claim that "the desire for intellectual independence is first made explicit" in those texts (Henríquez Ureña 1963, 99), and Emilio Carilla takes the argument a step further by attaching Henríquez Ureña's designation for the period of 1800 to 1830 as a whole to those poems in particular in his heading "The 'Declaration' of Bello" (Carilla 1979, xv).[6] And already in the nineteenth century, Juan María Gutiérrez ratified the position of the poem as the foundation of modern Spanish American poetry, when he printed it at the head of *América poética*. As ever an excellent critic, Gutiérrez designated the anthology as an "act of patriotism" in the unsigned prologue (J. M. Gutiérrez 1846, iii), and it is in that sense that the "Alocución" stood and stands as an exemplary text, especially where patriotism is given Bolívar's Pan American breadth.

This is the manner in which Bello himself reads, or misreads, the opening two hundred verses of the "Alocución" in the remaining three-quarters of the poem. There where citation and praise and reading of the "Alocución" customarily stop, Bello abandons the development of an autonomous self in favor of the writing of a national epic, or more exactly, the compiling of his own Pan American anthology of epic moments. In this regard it is well to recall that the predominant note of the Spanish American poetry that precedes the "Alocución," the poetry on the road to independence, was the patriotic ode. Bello may be said to exceed the limits of his precursors in the inclusiveness of his vision, embracing the whole of the continent, though the gain in breadth results in a loss of depth. To take the most extreme case, one might compare the paltry verses dedicated to San Martín (Bello 1979, 39) to Luca's poem. In Bello's defense, one needs acknowledge that he did not claim for himself the epic mantle, but rather prophesies the advent of such a poetic talent and in anticipation charts possible routes for a future epic course. He proves prescient enough, for Olmedo ought to be counted among Bello's earliest readers, and the Neruda of the *Canto general* among Bello's best, as Araya recognizes (Araya 1982, 72–77).

With those mitigating factors in mind, I would still recall that Bello's poetic context, particularly living as he did in London at the time of the great English romantics, was not uniquely that of the patriotic ode. Keats and Shelley are his contemporaries, and so too is Fernández de Madrid, whose call for a descriptive poetry attentive to the American landscape foretells the poetic project of Bello's "América." Fernández de Madrid stood at that same threshold, translating Delille, before he found the task too laborious to be borne in illness. Some years later, reviewing the second edition of Fernández de Madrid's *Poesías*, Bello returned to that point of departure to trace an alternative route to Fernández de Madrid's detour from natural description into morbid confession. The translations, writes Bello,

> preserve, no doubt, the principal gifts of the style of [Delille]; but the election of the model seems imprudent to us. Delille is so purely French, and among French poets he distinguishes himself so much for his mannered style, that we believe the undertaking of translating his compositions into another language with great success to be impossible. (Bello 1979, 311)

Bello continues on at some length so as to register his respect for Delille, who "excels as much in the grand style as in the sober, and as much in the awesome as in the tender and simple. But all of these gifts," he nonetheless insists, "are peculiar to his language, to the poetic genre of his nation, to the structure of alexandrines. His works are like mosaics in which one admires the patience much more than the invention, pleasing more in the details than in the whole" (Bello 1979, 311–12). Bello's review was written after the interrelated texts that represent his frustrated attempts to fulfill his own broader vision, and in retrospect those comments highlight and affirm the goals of his "América." For it would not be enough to write a descriptive poetry dedicated to American settings, as Fernández de Madrid had suggested in 1822. Poetry must also find a native idiom, fleeing, above all, a mannered style and the ponderous elegance of European forms. Bello argues for candor, much as Fernández de Madrid had done on the reduced scale of his *Rosas*. But Bello would no more meet the mark than had Fernández de Madrid. All the same, the mark still stands and Spanish American literature continues to be measured by it. The text, therefore, requires a closer look.

The "Alocución" begins with its now familiar invocation of a mythologized poetry:

> Divina Poesía,
> tú de la soledad habitadora,
> a consultar tus cantos enseñada,

con el silencio de la selva umbría;
tú á quien la verde gruta fué morada,
y el eco de los montes compañía;
tiempo es que dejes ya la culta Europa,
que tu nativa rustiquez desama,
y dirijas el vuelo adonde te abre
del mundo de Colón su grande escena.

(Bello 1979, 20)

Divine Poetry,
You, a denizen of solitude,
Raised to consult your songs
With the silence of the shady wood:
You, who in the verdant grotto made your home,
And of the hillside echo your companion,
Time now you left cultured Europe behind,
Who loves not your native rusticity,
And turned your flight there where awaits
The great scene of the vast Columbian world.

In this beginning, poetry stood in unmediated relation to nature. This is not necessarily a paean to the mimetic mode, but the implication is strong already, and borne out in "La agricultura de la zona tórrida." Hence, Rivera-Rodas is justified, I believe, in pointing out that Bello anachronistically advocates the mirror at a time when Western poetry was taking up the lamp, to use the terms of M. H. Abrams (1953) to which he refers (Rivera-Rodas 1988, 21–27). In another respect, however, namely the very insistence on originality, the invocation is in step with the times. For poetic candor is conceived of here as freedom from instruction. The true model is the "avecilla" ["little bird"] of the closing verses of the stanza, who sings "en no aprendidos tonos" ["in uninstructed tones"] (Bello 1979, 20).

Bello's mythological machinery is presented in a greatly condensed form. Poetry, too, is winged ("el vuelo" ["the flight"]), but it is not quite the equal in purity to the *avecilla*, since it is "enseñada" (instructed). One should like to know more of the scene of instruction, including the role of Divine Poetry's erstwhile companion *eco*. Was it *el silencio,* in some primal consultation, who instructed poetry to draw its help meet echo from its own side, precisely by breaking silence with song? Does this make the relation of poetry to silence analogous to that of echo to poetry? There is a mythic drama to be construed between these three actors in which, I suspect, the role of poetry may be very nearly the role of Narcissus. In this suspicion I imply a critique that rhymes with Simón Rodríguez's parable. To say that one misses Narcissus, that one misses both narcissism and wounded narcissism (Freud 1955–74, vol. 14), is as much as to say that one looks in vain for a romantic subject, el Enfermo, in Bello's poetics.

Rather than dwell on the implications of his quite original mythopoesis, Bello steers the introduction toward the more familiar territory of a Horatian *Beatus ille*, much as it developed over the long history of Hispanic literature: *el menosprecio de la corte y alabanza de la aldea*. The invitation to rustic seclusion is offered explicitly as a compensation for poetry's lost place in the public sphere, "cuando en la infancia de la gente humana,/maestra de los pueblos y los reyes,/cantaste al mundo las primeras leyes" ["when in the infancy of humanity/mistress of peoples and of kings,/you sang the first laws to the world"] (Bello 1979, 21). These, however, are modern times. And poetry has been crowded out by a new pretender: "tu ambiciosa/rival Filosofía,/que la virtud a cálculo somete" ["your ambitious/rival Philosophy,/which submits virtue to calculation"] (21). The epithet is hardly specific, but the usurper Philosophy might be supposed to be teaching an Enlightenment political economy of self-interest. Bello still finds the self ethically tainted—a late version of rebuke for the sin of pride—and so unfit for poetry. His poetry would leave the self, the subject, behind, ceding it to the discourse of philosophy, that is the economic discourse of nascent capitalism as well as the language of republican politics. His alternative: assign poetry the task of constituting national, as opposed to personal identities, to be consolidated in the broad union delineated in the brief geographical survey of American locales as potential havens for Divine Poetry. Hence, choosing not one but all, he catalogs military exploits from across the continent in the subsequent six hundred verses of the poem. To do so, be it noted, is to reinstate poetry in a public role, a rearguard action with respect to the privatization of the self in the political economy and cultural history of print, but intended as a recuperation of antique dignity and power.

The way forward for poetry was the way back, Bello argues in the "Alocución." Nor was Bello alone. As Geoffrey Hartman has pointed out, as the gains of industrialization were coming to be questioned in the face of the diminishment of rural England, the calculating rationality of the Enlightenment was seen increasingly to be antithetical to the imagination (Hartman 1970). Poets sought an alternative, Hartman argues, in the restitution of poetry's association with prophecy, which was believed to be grounded in the east. The westward "Progress of Poesy" from Greece to Rome to England, as charted by Thomas Gray in 1757 was but a "mazy progress" after all (Gray 1966, 12), culminating in a regress or decline: from Shakespeare and Milton to "Dryden's less presumptuous car" (16). Hartman formulates the problem as a question, by no means strictly rhetorical, for Bello's time no less than Gray's: "if poetry is Oriental in spirit, and the genius of the West is on the side of the Enlightenment, how can poetry survive?" (Hartman 1970, 325). One reply would be the facile orientalism of the later nineteenth century, of which Spanish American poetry saw its share—e.g. Elena F. Lince describing Medellín in her native Colombia as "sentada cual sultana/Sobre el pérsico, expléndido cogin!" ["seated like a sultaness/Upon the splendid, Persian pillow!"].[7]

But foretelling a poet who, if lacking the "ample pinion" of poesy's eastern origins, might yet descry "Such forms as glitter in the Muses' ray/With orient hues, unborrowed of the sun" (Gray 1807, 1:18), Gray anticipates Bello's own answer. Earlier in the poem, Gray had looked so far east as to sail west to a native American poetry so primordial as to be unenlightened, uninstructed by the sun:

> In climes beyond the solar road,
> Where shaggy forms o'er ice-built mountains roam,
> The Muse has broke the twilight-gloom
> To chear the shiv'ring Native's dull abode.
> And oft, beneath the od'rous shade
> Of Chili's boundless forest laid,
> She deigns to hear the savage Youth repeat
> In loose numbers wildly sweet
> Their feather-cinctured Chiefs and dusky Loves.
>
> (Gray 1807, 1:18)

The luxuriance of agriculture in the torrid zone is wanting in this dread picture of the antipodes, but Gray already situates a poetic space of "nativa rustiquez" in America.

Gray's "Progress of Poesy" was perhaps not so well-known as his immensely popular "Elegy, written in a country churchyard"

(1751), translated already circa 1823 by Fernández de Madrid's friend Antonio Miralla (Argentina 1790–1825), but it was nevertheless the most celebrated exemplar of a European topos which enjoyed a particular vogue in eighteenth-century England, as Reginald Harvey Griffith (1920) observed. The "progress piece" included such late entries as Shelley's "Ode to Liberty" of 1821, a poem that follows the course of liberty westward from Greece to Rome to various European points until Shelley's own day when, at the outset of the liberal triennium, it made its way "From heart to heart, from tower to tower, o'er Spain" (Shelley 1951, 400). The subject of the "progress" varied greatly, but, according to Griffith, "The traveler most often sung was, not unnaturally, the Muse of Poetry" (Griffith 1920, 223; see also Hartman 1970). Thus, while no internal evidence declares an unequivocal debt to Gray or his "Chili," the "Alocución" may be set within the line of the progress piece, extending the westward trajectory of poetry from Europe, or more particularly from Spain, to America.

Bello's immediate precursor in this line was Quintana, whose "A la expedición española para propagar la vacuna en América bajo la dirección de don Francisco Balmis," written in 1806 and first published in his *Poesías patrióticas* of 1808, was an Enlightenment revision of Columbus's voyages, in Bloom's sense of antithetical completion. Sailing west from Spain, Balmis did achieve a full circumnavigation of the globe, bringing the benefits of European science to America and the Philippines, as a belated retribution for the pox once introduced by the conquistadors' "funestas naves" ["ill-fated ships"] (M. J. Quintana 1980, 302). Bello followed Balmis's course in his early "Venezuela consolada" (Bello 1979, 4–14), written prior to his departure for England. But where the young Bello portrays "celosos y dóciles vasallos" ["zealous and docil vassals"] celebrating their Enlightened monarch—"¡Viva el digno monarca que nos libra/de las viruelas! ¡Viva el cuarto Carlos!" ["Long live the noble monarch who frees us/from small pox! Long live Carlos the Fourth!"] (14)—a more daring Quintana had already made his own American discovery. In comparison with the degenerate court from which he writes, Quintana finds that America is now the refuge of liberty:

> Balmis, no tornes,
> no crece ya en Europa
> el sagrado laurel con que te adornes.

Quédate allá, donde sagrado asilo
tendrán la paz, la independencia hermosa.

(M. J. Quintana 1980, 306)

Balmis, do not return,
the sacred laurel for your crown
in Europe is no longer to be found.
Remain where peace and lovely independence
will have sacred refuge.

It is thus Quintana's "Virgen del mundo, América inocente!" ["Virgin of the world, innocent America!"] (M. J. Quintana 1980, 301) toward which Bello would have the progress of poetry tend in the "Alocución," though he in turn would revise Quintana's expansive Pan Hispanic patriotism. Bello's litany of military triumphs over Spanish colonial power completes, antithetically, the "amarga expiación" ["bitter expiation"] that Quintana prematurely believed to be accomplished "Ya en estos días" ["Already in these days"] (302).

Enthusiasm for the progress piece had long since peaked in England before the publication of the "Alocución." The same Shelley who wrote his "Ode to Liberty" in a moment of optimism, was soon leaving incomplete at death his archly antiprogress piece, "The Triumph of Life (1822, published 1824), a "waking dream" in which a gnarled Rousseau speaks of the "deep scorn" to which he had been led by "The progress of the pageant since the morn" (Shelley 1951, 344, 349). With Shelley and Keats enjoying their brief maturity as the *Biblioteca Americana* went to press, English romanticism was making good upon its claim to prophetic power against that pageant—but at a price. Shelley turns back the calculating step of progress by unleashing a "Wild Spirit/Destroyer and preserver" to blow back from west to east in his "Ode to the West Wind"; he prays to be at one with that spirit, the Aeolian lyre or "trumpet of a prophecy" played upon by the wind (393). And he achieves his faint vision of rebirth by accepting first an imagistic sacrifice of self. "I fall upon the thorns of life! I bleed!" (393), he confesses, adding a plea for the fructifying death of his own verse: "Drive my dead thoughts over the universe/Like withered leaves to quicken a new birth!" (393) Shelley's "dead thoughts," the self-inflicted irony with which he offers his poems up to the west wind, blow across the subsequent history of English poetry, blow through

Whitman and North American verse as well. And this particular image of voice (Abrams 1984) will blow across Spanish American poetry in time as well, up to the very moment when a late romanticism holds out against the challenge of modernismo in *Tabaré* (1886) by Juan Zorrilla de San Martín (Uruguay 1857–1931):

> Y sigue el ruido sordo de las hojas,
> Que en voz baja se hablan,
> En ese idioma dulce y extranjero
> En que hablan los crepúsculos al alma.
> (Zorrilla de San Martín 1980, 193)

> And on and on the muffled noise of leaves
> That speak to one another whispering
> In that sweet and foreign tongue
> In which dusk speaks to the soul.

But in London, in 1823, Bello pays no apparent heed. Later, led by the interests of younger contemporaries in Spanish America, he would find Byron and Hugo. In the "Alocución," however, he is a poet rooted in the Hispanic tradition, presided over at the time by Quintana and his patriotic odes, if haunted still by Meléndez. Bello's images of voice and self-figurations are of a milder climate than the "Spirit fierce" (Shelley 1951, 392) that gusts about him far from home.

And yet the self is not altogether absent. Much as the case of Shelley in the wind, that self appears in a moment of *aspiration*, when it seeks to confound itself with poetry within one image that might bear them both. This effort requires a new mythology, introduced almost surreptitiously in the guise of natural history. The place is marked, nevertheless, by a change of rhetorical mode. The initial mythologizing of "Divina Poesía" had yielded to the series of geographical questions concerning poetry's American abode: a guessing game rather than a sure prophetic voice. These questions, neither entirely rhetorical (unless the anticipated answer is the multiple-choice panacea: "all of the above") nor entirely sensible, are broken off when a stronger voice does intervene, the thunderous falls at Tequendama:

> mas oye do tronando se abre paso
> entre murallas de peinada roca,
> y envuelto en blanca nube de vapores,

de vacilantes iris matizada,
los valles va a buscar del Magdalena
con salto audaz el Bogotá espumoso.

                                                                (Bello 1979, 22)

but listen where the frothy Bogotá
makes its way thundering
between groomed walls of rock
and wrapped in a white cloud of mist,
with intermittent rainbow hints
it goes with daring leap to seek
the valleys of the Magdalena.

The history of criticism has preferred the opening stanzas of the
"Alocución" but this is, I believe, more truly the inaugural moment
for the Spanish American poetry to come, including even Heredia's
"Niágara." I am encouraged in this opinion by the recollection that
Gregorio Gutiérrez González (Colombia 1826–72), whose "Memoria sobre el cultivo del maiz" of 1868 represents both the closest
reading of Bello's projected "América" and one of the greatest
Spanish American poems of the nineteenth century (though again,
beyond the historical scope of this study), himself cited the last two
of those verses as the epigraph to his youthful "Al salto del Tequendama" of 1845 (Gutiérrez González and Mejía 1926, 25).

Even before one hears the falls, one hears their impact on the poet
in the shift from the interrogative to the imperative mood. Since the
command is directed to Divine Poetry and not the reader, I will further suggest that Bello reenacts the mythology of the opening
stanza, but with a difference afforded by the greater clarity of concrete geographical context. The primordial silence, it now appears,
was full of sound, though inarticulate. And if this poet is an accept-
able example, then one may say that he—or rather that his poetry—
learns to speak in a commanding voice after consulting the roar of
the waters. I will also note in passing—for Bello too, will push on
at this point—that the poet hearkening to a voice more primordial
than poetry is instructed to spy out the rainbow, his eye as quick as
his ear. The Bogotá leaps, as Bello would have poetry leap, backward to a golden age of "ocio dulce" ["sweet idleness"] (Bello
1979, 22). The vision would be classical, like the Horatian turn of
the opening stanzas, were it not that geographical specificity makes
this river flow from natural to human history: "antes que el corvo
arado/violase el suelo" ["before the curved plow/violated the soil"]

is a topos; the continuation, "ni extranjera nave/las apartadas costas visitara" ["nor foreign ship/visited the remote coasts"] (22) locates the Saturnine Golden Age in pre-Columbian America.

The stage is now set to mythologize the thundering falls. The voice in the present of the poem or the future of Divine Poetry's American residence is an echo, bearing a reminiscence of pre-Columbian myth. "La libertad sin leyes florecía" ["Liberty flour-ished without laws"] (Bello 1979, 23)—no laws, no useful labor, no citizens. Bello glimpses an unconstituted America:

> Todo era paz, contento y alegría
> cuando de dichas tantas envidiosa
> Huitaca bella, de las aguas diosa,
> hinchando el Bogotá, sumerge el valle.
> . . .
> Tu cantarás cómo indignó el funesto
> estrago de su casi extinta raza
> a Nenqueteba, hijo del Sol . . .
> Tú cantarás cómo a las nuevas gentes
> Nenqueteba piadoso leyes y artes
> y culto dio; después que la maligna
> ninfa mudó en lumbrera de la noche,
> y de la luna por la vez primera
> surcó el Olimpo el argentado coche.
>
> (Bello 1979, 23)

> All was peace, contentment and joy
> when envious of so much good fortune,
> beautiful Huitaca, goddess of the waters,
> swelling the Bogotá, submerged the valley.
> . . .
> You will sing of how the ill-fated wreck
> of his all but annihilated race
> infuriated Nenqueteba, scion of the Sun . . .
> You will sing of how pious Nenqueteba
> gave new peoples laws and arts and rites
> after the evil nymph was herself transformed
> into a beacon in the night,
> and for the first time the silver car
> of the moon furrowed Olympus.

Bello does not claim to speak for indigenous peoples, yet his initial ideal of a wholly natural, wholly uninstructed poetry notwithstanding, he acknowledges an autochthonous cultural history as prolegomena to any future American poetry and, for that matter, to the laws and arts then in the process of constitution. Still, the telltale Greco-Roman admixture, "Olimpo," alerts the reader that even in this recitation of American mythology, Bello remains a legatee of European erudition.

Bello soon returns to more familiar territory, glossing the waters of the myth with a reference to the Biblical creation at Genesis 1:2. That allusion stirs the adamic question, which, above all, I think, has made Bello a living presence in Spanish American literature in the later twentieth century: "¿quién . . . poner presumirá nombre o guarismo?" ["who . . . will presume to put name or number?"] (Bello 1979, 24). For Bello himself, the answer was Alexander von Humboldt, chiefest of all the scientific expeditionaries of the era. Bello had acknowledged as much explicitly in a preceding note where he cited the *Vues des Cordillères* as his source for the myth of Huitaca and Nenqueteba. To support that election, Bello follows the question with a set of very fine and very Humboldtian verses; that is, Bello sets the model for remaking Humboldt's prose as Spanish American verse, part natural catalog, part moral allegory:

> bejucos, vides, gramas;
> laο ramaο a laο ramaο,
> pugnando por gozar de las felices
> auras y de la luz, perpetua guerra
> hacen . . .

> (Bello 1979, 24)

> lianas, grapevines, grasses;
> branches against branches,
> struggling to enjoy felicitous
> breezes and the light, perpetual war
> embrace . . .

With respect to the conscious ambitions of the "Alocución" and "La agriculatura en la zona tórrida," Humboldt is Bello's foundation, as Pratt has demonstrated in her brilliant analyses of "The Reinvention of America" (Pratt 1992; see esp. 174–77). That influence then crosses out other unacknowledged sources to engender and delimit the poetic self as it is figured forth in the crucial lyric interlude that follows, a passage that Juan Durán Luzio (1987) has demonstrated to be, quite literally, the versification of a portion of Bello's previously published selections from Humboldt's *Voyage aux régions équinoxiales*:

> ¡Oh quién contigo, amable Poesía,
> del Cauca a las orillas me llevara,
> y el blando aliento respirar me diera
> de la siempre lozana primavera
> que allí su reino estableció y su corte!
> ¡Oh si ya de cuidados enojosos
> exento, por las márgenes amenas
> del Aragua moviese
> el tardo incierto paso;
> reclinado acaso
> bajo una fresca palma en la llanura,
> viese arder en la bóveda azulada
> tus cuatro lumbres bellas,
> oh Cruz del Sur, que las nocturnas horas
> mides al caminante
> por la espaciosa soledad errante;
> del cucuy las luminosas huellas
> viese cortar el aire tenebroso,
> y del lejano tambo a mis oídos
> viniera el son del yaraví amoroso!

(Bello 1979, 24)

> Oh, who might carry me with you,
> sweet Poetry, to the Cauca's banks
> and give me the soft breath
> of the ever verdant spring to breathe,
> that founded there its realm and court!
> Oh, if already freed of troubling cares,
> along the lovely banks
> of the Aragua I might move
> with languid, hesitating step;
> reclining, perhaps,
> beneath a fresh palm on the plains,
> I might see burning in the azure vault
> your four lovely lights,
> oh Southern Cross, that measure
> the nocturnal hours for the wanderer
> who walks the spacious solitude;
> I might see the luminous trail
> of the fire beetle cut the darkened sky,
> and from the distant inn the sound
> of the amorous *yaraví* might reach my ears!

Bello's attentive critic Guillermo Araya considers the stanza an "element of rupture of the plan": "These twenty verses are splendid. . . . But they are floating like a strange island in the 834 [verses] of the whole poem" (Araya 1982, 60). I think not. The explicit appearance of a *yo* is striking, I grant, but it has been implicit throughout in the very fiction of an allocution. Moreover, that personified abstraction Poetry has been directed from the beginning to endeavor upon a lyric career, that is to surrender pretensions to a public position, since a significant public role was lost long ago, and to undertake a return to nature which will also be a return to "memorias de tempranos días" ["memories of early days"] (Bello, 1979, 22) so as to speak with recuperated candor. Deciding in this interlude no longer to tell the dancer from the dance, the poetic self embodies the journey prescribed for Poetry.

More arresting to my mind than the first-person pronoun, therefore, I would point to the modal dissonance between the interlude and the rest of the poem. Bello the grammarian may justify the series of imperfect subjunctive forms as the expression of a purely imaginary flight. But elsewhere, Bello the critic draws special attention to the abuse of the imperfect subjunctive as a characteristic mark of Meléndez Valdés, whose contagion, Bello complained, had tainted the verses of the young Heredia (Bello 1979, 276–77). Following Bello's similar criticism of Meléndez's nearer disciple, Nicasio Alvarez de Cienfuegos (1764–1809), one might argue contra Araya, that in the lyric interlude of the "Alocución," "the dominant taste is not that of noble simplicity; the style is not natural" (251). My point, however, is not to denigrate the stanza, but rather to suggest that in addition to the acknowledged source in Humboldt, the verb forms hint at an unacknowledged and perhaps unconscious source in Meléndez. When Bello descends from the abstraction Poetry to the concrete case of Spanish American poets—himself, for example—the lyric model that forces itself upon him, no less than on Heredia, is Meléndez.

What Meléndez had learned from Jovellanos, and taught to two generations of poets, I recall, was that poetry must place itself under the tutelage of philosophy to move beyond the vain pursuits of light amatory verse. Bello would follow that course beyond Meléndez himself. He is hampered, however, by the "tardo incierto paso" ["languid, hesitating step"] that marks a caesura of sorts near the center of the lyric interlude.[8] This is the hesitating cadence—and I invoke both the common meaning of rhythmic beat

and the etymological echo of a fall—of the "descendental" trajectory of the era (Hartman 1975, 152), which found itself perplexed
at the crossroads between east and west, prophecy and progress,
and certain only that poetry was in decline. Hartman (1975) has
shown how the "evening song," dedicated to the gathering darkness at dusk and the sun's decline, was the most acute expression
of that descent in English poetry. In Spanish, Meléndez was the
poet of that moment:

> mientra su ardiente faz el sol inclina,
> solitario filósofo el umbroso
> bosque, en la mano un libro discurriendo . . .
>
> (Meléndez Valdés 1981, 259)

> whilst the sun inclines its burning face,
> the solitary philosopher, taking,
> book in hand, the course through shady wood . . .

he writes in "Mi vuelta al campo," where he plays upon the metapoetic resonance of "discurrir" to present the progress of Poetry as
the bodily course of the errant poet. And the poet, both here in "Mi
vuelta al campo," where Meléndez, like Bello in his interlude,
changes a Horatian topos into an autobiographical geography ("los
campos que labraron mis abuelos" ["the fields that my grandparents tilled"], (Meléndez Valdés 1981, 259), and in the closely
related poem, "La tarde," the cadence of that discourse reflects the
retiring course of the twilight, "que retrae/indeciso el sol los pasos"
["the sun withdrawing/in indecisive steps"] (132).

Meléndez's indecision, his vacillating step, becomes the figure of
poetic melancholia. He cannot let the dead rest in peace, for he has
found his own poetic self-in-progress, his own voice, when it was
still among the dead—or as Bello mythologizes, consulting with
silence. So Meléndez exhumes that self and in the closing prosopopeia of the funereal oration, he gives it voice in the poem-within-a-
poem, or poem-to-end-a-poem of "Mi vuelta al campo." The errant
voice of the self he did not become, of the self he left behind in his
youth, haunts the poem and his poetry at large, as a ghost. And that
ghost, detached from the body of the poem by its quotation marks,
repeats the moment of severance, figured as the separation of the
young poet from his source, his speaking brook. In so doing, he
reminds the mature poet that he is not whole, that he remains for-

ever an amputee. "Aquí moran la dicha y el contento" ["Here reside my joy and contentment"], Meléndez begins that final passage, wherein the *here* of the projected voice of his lost youth is the *there* of his imaginary return. And from the later perspective of the poem, what youth pronounces as "Aquí moran," age knows to be more properly *hic jacet*. The intimation of mortality permeates youth's blessing of *morar,* the staying, that in life became a leave-taking:

> ¡Afortunado el que en humilde choza
> mora en los campos, en seguir se goza
> los rústicos trabajos, compañero
> de virtud e inocencia,
> y salvar logra con feliz prudencia
> del mar su barca y huracanes fieros!
>
> (Meléndez Valdés 1981, 261)

> Fortunate is he who in humble hut
> resides in the fields, enjoying the pursuit
> of rustic labors, in comradery
> with virtue and with innocence,
> and succeeding with blissful prudence
> in saving his bark from fierce hurricanes and the sea.

And in this relay between prospect and retrospect, between youth and age, between staying and pursuing (*morar* vs. *seguir*), the poem ends and the poet breaks off.

Bello follows the "indecisos pasos" of Meléndez in the "tardo incierto paso" of his lyric interlude, and incorporates the pervasive atmosphere of poetic decline under the "pardo estandarte" ["dark banner"] of Meléndez's Hesperus (Meléndez Valdés 1981, 132) in his recumbent position beneath the palm tree of his own imaginary return to his native campo. He traces the descendental path of late eighteenth-century lyric poetry still farther in his metamorphosis of the stars in the figure of the "cucuy," whose miniature and desublimated lightning cutting the darkness inverts quite precisely the raising up of Huitaca as the nocturnal luminary who first plowed the night sky. If poetry has come down in the world, however, the lesser lights, like the greater, are still a sign that the storm has passed and the threat of flood has ended. Thus, poetry's image of voice rebounds. The thunder of the falls on the Bogotá that filled the silence of the American landscape, Divine Poetry's mythologized tutor in Bello's beginning, is also transmuted in the interlude as the echo of a "yaraví amoroso."

Bello is no Melgar. He will not fashion Spanish-language versions of Quechua songs, not under the palm in his mind's eye, nor from the nostalgic vantage point of London. Indeed, the effect of Bello's discovery of the yaraví in his lyric interlude is much the opposite. Instead of a living presence in oral culture and as such a source for contemporary poetry, Bello's mythologized framework casts the yaraví backward in time. An echo of the falls, and therefore a voice nearly as primordial as nature's own, i.e. of the silence that precedes poetic articulation, the yaraví is the song of the American place before the arrival of poetry from Europe. This telescoping of time is accomplished by transumption. The more proximate source passed over by explicit reference to the "yaraví amoroso" is the amatory verse of Meléndez—his voice as it was in youth and not as memory fabled it when as a mature and melancholic poet, philosophical verse took over the place of his more popular poetry. The allusion thus sets both the yaraví and Meléndez in the past, creates a literary *history*, from which Bello, no melancholic, now departs with a decisive step into the "zona/de Febo amada" ["zone/ beloved of Phoebus"] (Bello 1979, 24–25)—at once a daytime to reverse the descent of and into night, and eventually, the *zona tórrida* of American agriculture. Predicting a Georgics, much as Fernández de Madrid had done, in the coming of "algún Marón americano" ["some American Virgil"] (24), whom he foretells immediately following the lyric interlude, Bello then misreads that reference as a call for a Virgilian epic for the next six hundred verses. The step beyond melancholia is a decisively modern step into history, or still more precisely, it is the step beyond the mythological prehistory of the yaraví into the modern history of America.

The overarching structure of the "Alocución" is thus framed by an exchange of "la culta Europa" ["cultured Europe"] in the opening stanza for the "culta historia" ["cultured history"] of the final verse (Bello 1979, 40): hence, its modernity. But in terms of *literary* history, the revision is in fact a step backward. In the following six hundred verses, Bello by-passes Meléndez only to return to the course already outlined by Quintana, the poet of Bello's own youth; the "Alocución" evolves from the Enlightenment progress piece only as far as the patriotic ode. Doing so, Bello repeats Quintana's own detour around Meléndez, whether in shunning the erotic in Quintana's *vuelta al campo*, "A don Nicasio Cienfuegos, convidándole a gozar del campo" (1797) or in balking at his brush with the sublime in "Al mar" (1798). To put the matter most broadly, Bello, following Quintana and reacting against the greatest possibilities in Meléndez, speaks for the nascent independent state, which he constitutes, poetically, in a series of elegies that set recent events at the distance of history. And for this history in the making Bello offers a still more distant prehistory of the buried nation through his allusion to the yaraví. But the yaraví is a transumptive allusion in this sense as well. For the reference to an anonymous, popular poetry in oral culture at the very moment when an identifiable, personal voice is breaking through in print in the lyric interlude, bypasses, if not to say excludes the self from modern national history and from modern literary history.

3

Bello might well have had his way. In large measure the widespread dismissal of Spanish American romanticism is evidence that he did. But then there was Heredia. He had begun writing poetry at least as early as 1817, close to the time of his fourteenth birthday, and compiled the first manuscript collections of his verse in 1819, while in Mexico, where his family settled briefly after sojourns throughout the Hispanic Caribbean (Santiago de Cuba, Havana, Pensacola in Florida, Santo Domingo, various points in revolutionary Venezuela). And it was in Mexico in late 1820, shortly after the death of his father, a prominent member of the colonial justice system, set the family on the road back to Cuba, that Heredia wrote the first version of his first major lyric, "Fragmentos descriptivos de un poema mexicano," better-known in an augmented version under the title, "En el teocalli de Cholula." I take the original title that Heredia chose for the Cholula poem in the New York edition of his *Poesías* (1825), along with the note he appended there to the text— "Este poema se hallará entero en las *poesías americanas*" (J. M. Heredia 1940, 2:153)—to be a direct response to Bello's aspirations as set down in the final parenthesis of the full title of the "Alocución": "(Fragmentos de un poema intitulado 'América')" (Bello 1979, 166). A dialogue was forged between the poetry of Bello and Heredia in the middle years of the decade—the "Alocución" in the *Biblioteca Americana* of 1823, the first edition of Heredia's *Poesías* (New York 1825), "La agricultura de la zona tórrida" in the *Reper-*

torio Americano of 1826—and continued in the Mexican edition of Heredia's *Poesías* (Toluca 1832) and Bello's later poetry after his return to America. It is a dialogue that confirms that an internal commerce of American letters was underway. It is the dialogue that constituted Spanish American poetry for modern times, marking divergent routes, one forward and the other back.

The one explicit moment of interchange between Bello and Heredia took place—emblematically, I would say—as a prose response to poetry: Bello's review of the New York edition of Heredia's *Poesías,* which appeared in the *Repertorio Americano* in January 1827 (Bello 1979, 270–80). Bello's remarks are encouraging in their appreciation and perspicacious in their criticisms. Referring to "A mi padre, en sus días" and "Carácter de mi padre," Bello declares, "we wish . . . that there were a greater number of compositions dedicated to domestic and innocent emotions, and less in the erotic genre, of which we already have a pernicious overabundance in our language" (276). No one, I believe, has expressed a wish for more adolescent eroticism in Heredia's verse (see Lezama's definitive critique, 1977, 950–51). But twentieth-century criticism has been less interested in this domestic strain than in Heredia's stance as a patriotic poet of frustrated independence, of *lo cubano* recalled in exile (Vitier 1970, 73–89).

The effort has largely sought to reconstrue Heredia in the image of Martí, as Martí himself had already done in his famous address at Hardman Hall in New York in 1889; but the result has been an Heredia resembling Bello, which is to say, in the terms of my present discussion, that the dialogue between the two has been reduced to a monologue. A note of dissent on the part of Jorge Mañach helps to restore some balance. Against those who view Heredia primarily as "the first public spokesman of our patriotic vocation," Mañach argues: "Let's not fool ourselves, however: that is not Heredia's great poetry. . . . Heredia is more a true poet when he sings, not what triumphs, but what dies" (Mañach 1957, 211). This position, then, affords Mañach an insight into the biographical context of Heredia's "Fragmentos descriptivos," namely, that he wrote "[s]ensitized by the recent death of his father, which has given him a personal reference in his soul for the stoic Spanish sense of the fleetingness of human things" (Mañach 1957, 211). Bello himself had already made the connection explicit. His notice of Heredia's "domestic" poems gave occasion for "a digression" on the exemplary service of his father as magistrate in Venezuela attempting to rein in the oppressive regime of Monteverde. Bello's words form a prose elegy, explicitly calling for a Pan American burial society in the sense that I have outlined in the introduction, "to pay tribute to the memory of the late Sr. Heredia with the respect and gratitude that all Americans owe him for his conduct in extraordinarily difficult circumstances" (Bello 1979, 275).

Heredia the son would appear to have shirked that duty incumbent upon "all Americans" in his Cholula poem, whose composition he dated to December 1820, less than two months after his father's death. The funeral atmosphere is patent, embodied in the "Fantasma colosal" ["Colossal phantom"] (J. M. Heredia 1940, 2:151) that is the figure for the advancing shadow of dusk. Nevertheless, the father is not mentioned, not introjected in a name; the poet does not mourn, does not accept a place as a member in that imagined community of "all Americans" at the remove of a critical distance from their past.

The poems cited by Bello stand against any implication of hardheartedness on the part of the son. And even the rudiments of Heredia's biography deepen the impression of loss, for the elder Heredia personally supervised his son's education, including his initiation into poetry.[9] The silence concerning the father at a moment when the son is engaged in a funereal contemplation, and especially in the form of an ode, which might otherwise have enabled a sudden shift to personal material and back again is, I contend, an anomaly that calls for interpretation.[10] The need is all the more urgent, I add, when "Niágara," roundly recognized as Heredia's other signal achievement in lyric poetry, is understood, as Lezama saw, as a replay of the precocious Cholula poem (Lezama Lima 1977, 2:954).

The historical and psychological complexities touch upon the whole of the younger Heredia's generation, which grew into poetry in the incipient constitutional culture. The elder Heredia stands forth in Bello's brief portrait as a figure of unimpeachable virtue, but, nevertheless as a man of the ancien régime. He was "more attentive to justice than to liberty," to cite the words with which Mañach (Mañach 1957, 200) described the political career of the son in the late years of his life. The father, in a word, remained a royalist. Soon after his death, on the other hand, Heredia the son became engaged in the abortive emancipation movement in Cuba through the Masonic lodges (see Garrigó 1929), and narrowly avoided prison by escaping the island for exile in the United States. In the shift from the politics of the father to those of the son, the history of Spanish American independence is condensed as a thwarted family romance. Bello, both in his digression in the review and in his verse, urges commemoration—that is elegy—that would bury the heroic dead at a distance, in the preserve of history, while separating the present as new and modern times. But Heredia would neither mourn his father, nor fully historicize the past at Cholula, in Oakeshott's terms. Instead, he takes Abraham and Torok's middle route in the face of his loss. He incorporates his father's death, acting it out in the abrupt truncation of the poem in the 1820 version (as published in 1825)—rather than introjecting it, turning it into words. He falls asleep, falls into silence, into the death of poetic language. And in this reenactment, Heredia arrests and reverses the westward progress of poetry that aligns Spanish American historical consciousness with the masterplot of the Conquest from Peralta to Bello (or indeed before and since). Heredia is not travelling the route of Cortés to the massacre at Cholula, but the diametrical opposite, the eastward route of Quetzalcoatl from Cholula to the sea and to his own embarcation with his family and his return to Cuba. The demise of the expiring Quetzalcoatl is invoked, and his own muting foretold, at the outset of the poem in the form of the dying breeze—"ligera brisa/Las alas en silencio ya plegaba" ["light breeze/was folding its wings in silence"] (J. M. Heredia 1940, 2:150), that is of Quetzalcoatl as Ehecatl, the wind god. Heredia atop the pyramid is cast in the role of the Enfermo in its specifically pre-Columbian form: the human sacrifice—a death not his own, I reiterate, but of another that he has incorporated: the death of his father, the death, too, of Queztalcoatl, priest or god, culture hero, giver of arts and of agriculture. In this American version of the interstitial moment between death and life, dying breeze and rising star, human sacrifice atop the pyramid is a cosmic necessity, rather than a tragedy, a rebirth for which there is no mourning.[11]

Heredia eventually awakens from his poetic sleep, his death-in-life of poetry, and retells his dream vision of twilight from the enlightened perspective of the day. In the Mexican edition of his *Poesías* of 1832 he publishes an augmented version of the Cholula poem in which the scene of human sacrifice is made explicit as the Joycean nightmare of history. The pre-Columbian past is now truly past, and if exhumed, then only so as to apply the modern critical judgment that condemns the sacrifice as superstition. The critical distance opens, I would suggest, in "Niágara"—recalling that the latter dates to 1824, that is between the original composition at Cholula in 1820 and the augmented second edition of the poem in 1832. Here, following his own death sentence in absentia as a separatist—i.e. on his own terms and in his own right, not his father's—what was incorporated, that is buried but not mourned, at Cholula is at last introjected as elegy, a proleptic elegy for himself (for what was buried alive in himself). Like Fernández de Madrid, who is, I believe, Heredia's most immediate precursor in the poetry of the mid-1820s, Heredia pronounces his elegy as though he could constitute his own burial society from beyond the grave, and thus learns how to end his poem. When Martí leads the representatives of the various Spanish American republics in a chorus of commemorative naming at Niagara—" 'Heredia!' said the son of Montevideo, getting to his feet; 'Heredia!' uncovering his head, the son of Nicaragua; 'Heredia!' said the son of Venezuela, remembering his glorious childhood; 'Heredia!' the Cubans of that company were saying, unworthy of him and of themselves; 'Heredia! said the whole of America" (J. M. Heredia 1940, 457)—he fulfils the prolepsis by making an imagined comunity of "all Americans" joined as mourners at Heredia's figurative gravesite.[12]

The dialogue between the detached historical consciousness of Bello, a member of the *New Societies* (recalling Simón Rodríguez) of American mourners, and the melancholic attachment of Heredia, is constitutive for modern Spanish American poetry. The former will provide the foundation for a national literary identity wedded to progress. The latter will offer the grounds for a modern subjectivity, split between its acknowledgment of the pastness of the past, that is its recognition of its own modernity, and its compulsion to repeat the past in the present, to experience the past as eternal return. In poetic practice, the dialogue between Bello and Heredia was conducted and needs be read as a counterpoint of conflicting and independent responses to Meléndez and Quintana. But those responses proved definitive, and thereafter Bello and Heredia themselves took the place of Meléndez and Quintana as the necessary interlocutors of Spanish American poets. Their dialogue was both a debate about the course of modernity and the foundation of the future network of communication in the commerce of Spanish American letters, at least within the print culture.

By 1823, when the "Alocución" was appearing in London, Heredia was already moving beyond his initial engagement with the Anacreontic mode to a deeper reading of Meléndez's philosophical poetry. In "El desamor" and "A D. D. D., desde el campo," both published in Havana's *Revisor Político y Literario* that year (see Anuncio 1823 and J. M. Heredia 1823, respectively), which is to say before he would have been familiar with the *Biblioteca Americana* (whose prospectus was dated 16 April 1823 [García del Río 1972]), Heredia worked through the tribulations of adolescent love toward an adequate image of voice. The adolescent poet, rather too literal minded, inscribes his love on the palms and sugar cane, so as to make the landscape his testament. Needless to say, it is an ineffectual ploy. When love turns to deception—if nothing else, then in order to escape a tired trope—the hapless poet finds the tables turned, as his erstwhile beloved fills his ear with the rival's name, figuratively inscribing a wound in his own breast. Finally, he pleads:

> . . . jamás el eco dulce
> De tu divina voz, que un tiempo al pecho
> Más grato fuera que al marchito prado
> El sonante correr del fresco arroyo,
> Torne a rasgar la ensangrentada herida
> De aqueste corazón . . .
>
> (J. M. Heredia 1940, 1:217)

> . . . may the sweet echo
> Of your divine voice, that once was more pleasing
> To the breast than the resonant rush
> Of the cool brook to the withered plains,
> Never return to scratch the blood-soaked wound
> Of this heart . . .

But Heredia's effort to overwhelm the tranquillity of the Horatian topos by dint of his adolescent anguish bears no such fruit. The genre is not significantly reformed, for the degree of the emotion is unpersuasive. Youth serves as a defense of the lover, but not of the poet. And so the poems might be forgotten as relatively original, but ultimately unsuccessful revisions of Meléndez.

Reading those poems in the shadow of Cholula, however, the wound may be seen as a return from oblivion of the latent figure of the sacrifice of a human heart atop the *teocalli*. The wound is a first effort to return to find a voice for all that he had silenced: the loss of his father and through him of an idealized system of justice; the repudiation of that system as an obstacle to liberty, and through it of his father. In the figure of the *Herido* (and I would conjecture that the onomastic relay of *herida-Heredia* was intentional on the part of the poet), Heredia was moving toward the discovery of that sovereign subject that Rodríguez knew as the Enfermo, renouncing the "feliz prudencia" ["joyous prudence"] of Meléndez's poem-to-end-a-poem in "Mi vuelta" in order to embrace the "feliz melancolía" ["joyous melancholy"] articulated in his own "El desamor" (Anuncio 1823, 7).

Bello would yoke verse to "el rico suelo al hombre avasallado" ["the rich soil indentured to mankind"] (Bello 1979, 24), a subservient earth that is the faithful parallel of the domesticated heavens in which the once rebellious Huitaca was metamorphosed as a luminous plowhand. Heredia, on the contrary, is unfettered in Cuba, circa 1823, where, buoyed by the echo of Cienfuegos, he steps deliberately into the "huracanes fieros" that Meléndez would avoid, lifting up and empowering the quiet *brisa* that had died down at Cholula:[13]

> Huracán, huracán, venir te siento
> Y en tu soplo abrasado
> Respiro entusiasmado
> Del señor de los aires el aliento.
>
> (J. M. Heredia 1940, 2:209)

> Hurricane, hurricane, I hear you come
> And in your scorched blast
> I breathe, exalted, the breath
> Of the lord of the winds.

"En una tempestad," composed, astonishingly, alongside of such immature verse as "A D. D. D.," reverses the many vueltas al campo of his precursors and his own. This is decidedly the way out of the Horatian topos of native rusticity and a rising above poetry's felt decline under the aegis of the Enlightenment.

As though in answer avant la lettre to Bello's challenge to find proper names, Heredia begins the poem of his climate by calling the storm by its American name (*huracán*, of Carib origin). As at Cholula, he invokes the corresponding native mythology as both José Juan Arrom (1971) and, more comprehensively, Fernando de Ortiz (1947) have discussed. The mythic substratum, however, is not a bookish citation of Humboldt, as in the case of Bello an ocean away from home. Instead, there is citation in the deeply Hispanic sense of *citar*, the inciting of the bull. "En una tempestad" presents, ultimately neither Carib nor Taino myth, but rather Heredia's own myth of poetic origins staged as a cosmic bullfight in which a self is borne upward and into sublimity: the self as heroic subject of its own poem. Recalling the preamble to the "Alocución," the incitement of "En una tempestad" constitutes not mythography, but mythopoesis, and hence adequate grounds upon which to contrast Heredia and Bello and their alternative routes to modernity in Spanish American poetry after independence.

The storm begins as an ominous calm: the silence which, for Bello, preceded the arrival of Poetry. No vacillating, declining sun, instead the wind approaches "En su curso veloz" ["In its rapid course"] (J. M. Heredia 1940, 2:209). In the face of the onslaught, the earth is overawed and reduced to passivity: "La tierra . . . / contempla con pavor" ["The earth . . . /contemplates in fear"] (2:209). Thus Heredia casts the earth in the role that Bello will assign to the self, when he makes the self the eavesdropper of the yaraví and the observer of agricultural abundance. Bello elaborates upon that role under the heading of "the contemplative naturalist" (Bello 1972, 90) in his communication, "Consideraciones sobre la naturaleza, por Virey" from the *Biblioteca Americana* of 1823. The *yo* idealized as the contemplative naturalist asserts itself as a discoverer ("yo te encuentro" ["I find you"], 90), and what it finds is a universal harmony, even in decline and death, a harmony that Bello invokes in the words, "Oh love, source of life!" (90). Such love carries him well beyond Meléndez's coy eroticism, of course. But inasmuch as in this conception creation precedes the self, contemplation suffices for a mimetic poetry barely distinguishable from natural philosophy—which is to say that Bello surrenders Poetry to her rival.

The distinctive note in the earth's contemplation before the coming of Heredia's hurricane is the *pavor,* the fear. For Heredia, it is destruction rather than creation that precedes both self and poetry: the "primordial death" (de Certeau) of indigenous culture, of the father, of law; the wounding of the son and the lover. If there is to be creation at all, then it must proceed as self-defense. The passive subjectivity of his poems in rustic retreat had foundered. The figure of the bull in "En una tempestad" is wounded still, but no longer infirm, and plays out the trope of the inscription once again, though to vastly different effect, in the scratching the earth:

¿Al toro no miráis? El suelo escarban,
De insoportable ardor sus pies heridos:
La frente poderosa levantando,
Y en la hinchada nariz fuego aspirando,
Llama la tempestad con sus bramidos.

(J. M. Heredia 1940, 2:209)

Do you not look upon the bull? His feet,
Wounded by the unbearable heat,
Paw the ground: lifting his powerful head,
And breathing fire through his dilated nose,
He calls the storm with his bellows.

The bull plays this pivotal role by presenting a voice that responds actively to the incitement of the storm's initial, one might say primordial, silence. The position is underlined through an imagistic transfiguration of the yo from the opening stanza. The earlier "soplo abrasado" reappears as the "insoportable ardor" and the poet's respiration breathes out again in an incipient image of voice as fiery aspiration. Having thus secured the identification between poet and bull, Heredia then identifies the bull with the storm, the "bramidos" ["bellows"] of the one returning in the third stanza as "el huracán *bramando*" ["the hurricane *bellowing*"] (J. M. Heredia 1940, 2:209, emphasis added). The initial poetic aspirations may be fulfilled thereafter by eliminating the middle term.

The subsequent unmediated conjunction of self and storm finds its beginnings, its scene, in the torrential downpour unleashed only in the penultimate stanza, and by which the world reverts to the chaos before creation, where "todo es confusión, horror profundo" ["all is confusion, profound horror"] (2:210). It is the world of Huitaca before her domesticated metamorphosis. The universal catastrophe drives Heredia toward elegy:

Cielo, nubes, colinas, caro bosque,
¿Dó estáis . . . ?

(J. M. Heredia 1940, 2:210)

Sky, clouds, hills, forest dear,
Where are you all . . . ?

He will claim that the world's familiar signs of life and perhaps the very possibility of signification ("caro bosque" ["forest dear"] had been his rustic topos of inscription), have passed away.

But the hurricane has turned the world topsy-turvy. What was below appears to be above—"La tormenta umbría/En los aires revuelve un oceano" ["The shadowy tempest/Overturns an ocean in the air"] (J. M. Heredia 1940, 2:210)—a visual turmoil, or even a blinding ("oscurece el mundo" ["the world darkens"], 2:210) that buries the poet's perspective beneath this upended sea "Que todo lo sepulta" ["That buries all"] (2:210). In a word, the self speaks from within the grave. But this is to say that the speaking subject of elegy (*ubi sunt*?, "Dó estáis . . . ?") and its commemorative object are one and the same.

It will be recalled that Meléndez had traced such a path as the course by which to foreclose his vacillating step. But the self Meléndez sacrificed in order to lead his poem on to a close was the former self of his youth. Meléndez relinquished continuity with that youth, and in compensation, the mature self gained a history. For Heredia the situation is more fraught. Still under twenty years old when he first composed the poem in 1822, he has so precious little personal history upon which to trade, no time in which to distance himself from his own past. At most—and in Heredia's case the most is very much—he has a prehistory of the self, half glimpsed, still dormant, at Cholula, which he would awaken, a Jonas in the storm. For in "En una tempestad" he writes not as a survivor redeemed by some Nenqueteba, but as a contemporary of the flood. The self that speaks, hesitant (note the four ellipses in the stanza just quoted), is in the very process of being buried. The position proves untenable and the elegy-to-end-a-poem that could not even begin at Cholula now breaks off. But the poem itself continues and will not truly end until "Niágara." Between Cholula and Niagara, between the poles of incorporation and introjection, a cleaving to the past and a progressive historical consciousness, Heredia invents a self beyond that figured in the indecisive step of Bello and Meléndez:

> Al fin, mundo fatal, nos separamos:
> El huracán y yo solos estamos.
>
> (J. M. Heredia 1940, 2:210)

> At last, fatal world, we separate:
> The hurricane and I, we are alone.

Heredia reaches this extreme point by conducting a Cartesian reduction—that of the rational mind, conscious of its own fictions, nullifying the world by its own intellectual power so as to affirm its own existence—but with a difference. And the difference is romantic. For Heredia, power will not reduce to the interiority of mind, nor to the mind's fictions of self-aggrandizement, as in Aguirre's baroque hell. Instead, power remains firmly outside the self in the chaotic storm. The self, therefore, may only aspire to power as "solemne inspiración" ["solemn inspiration"] (J. M. Heredia 1940, 2:210). The self is constituted for poetry as an in-spiriting, typically as the influence of a *genius loci* that remakes the poet as local genius, a process frequently figured as a penetrating aura (breath, wind, spirit), which the poet then expresses as a poem.

Heredia will sacrifice his world for such poetic power. He repeats his elegiac question in the final stanza with a self-wounding frankness: "¿Dó está el alma cobarde/Que teme tu rugir?" ["Where is the cowardly soul/That fears your roar?"] (J. M. Heredia 1940, 2.210), where the soul he repudiates is his own, himself but moments ago in the preceding stanzas. That soul in its fear of the *rugir,* the bull-like voice of the storm was earth-bound, earth being the site of *pavor*: a passive self, merely contemplative, merely enlightened. The imagination, on the contrary, turns upward—"Y alzo la frente" ["And I raise my head"] (2:210), like the bull, "La frente poderosa levantando" ["Lifting its powerful head"]—toward the "¡Oscuridad universal!" ["Universal darkness"] (2:210). And with the eyes closed by the darkness, bull-poet in a bull-storm, locked, the two, in reciprocal incitement, the self opens its ears. Not I think (a baroque hell within), but I hear (a romantic hell without), therefore I am. And listening, the yo triumphs over the storm.

That yo at last enters the poem in an apotheosis of the self that lasts only as long as a half a verse, no longer:

. . . Yo en ti me elevo

(J. M. Heredia 1940, 2:210)

. . . I raise myself in you

It is imagistically, if not perhaps also qualitatively, the highest point in Spanish American poetry from Sor Juana to Darío—high above Luca's Andean statue of Colombia, for instance, and even above Heredia's own perch atop the pyramid in Cholula. Leaving the cowardly soul and its unheroic elegy behind, the self would leave the very storm behind as well, rewriting the sublime aspirations of

"El huracán y yo solos estamos" as the still greater ambition of being alone above the wind and rain. The pronoun, implicit throughout, rises to the surface of the poem unaccompanied in that hemistich; indeed it reflexively raises itself, its own agent, its own source.

At this height, the self has reached its limits. The eye perhaps is deceived by the line break, but this is a poetry of the ear, and there is no audible pause in which to savor the triumph of the yo in its self-proclaimed sublimity. The grammar rules against:

> . . . yo en ti me elevo
> Al trono del Señor: oigo en las nubes
> El eco de su voz, siento a la tierra
> Escucharle y temblar. Ferviente lloro
> Desciende por mis pálidas mejillas,
> Y su alta majestad trémulo adoro.
>
> (J. M. Heredia 1940, 2:210)

> . . . I raise myself in you
> To the throne of the Lord: I hear in the clouds
> The echo of his voice, I feel how the earth
> Listens to him and trembles. Fervent tears
> Descend across my pallid cheeks,
> And tremulous, his great majesty, I revere.

The trembling earth is far below, and even the storm is at sufficient distance to recognize that its power is derivative, its voice no more than echo. The poet may take the place of the storm, his tears themselves the rains, but only by acknowledging a new subservience, accepting himself to be but a lesser god. The confessional attachment of state to church that circumscribes even the most liberal constitutions of the period, delimits the constitution of Spanish American poetry as well.

Heredia, a demiurge in the chaos of universal darkness, can also be a poet by day. The vaguely Christianized deity of "En una tempestad" who reigns supreme above both self and storm, both poet and *Divina Poesía,* appears elsewhere in his verse as the sun, most famously in "Al sol" (1821) and "Himno al sol" (1825). When this sun shines for Heredia it puts to flight "La confusión de las nubes" ["The confusion of the clouds"] (J. M. Heredia 1940, 2.217) of the "huracán inclemente" ["inclement hurricane"] (2:231), and reveals a resurgent landscape to a recuperated eye. This is the daylight of a potential harmony such as Bello philosophized in "Sobre la naturaleza," and the landscape of patriotic emotion such as Bello filled with the abundant produce of American agriculture. But under the cover of darkness, Heredia asserts and explores an alternative poetics: of self-expression rather than national identity, of hidden depths that force their way to view by figuration, rather than a utopian semiotics of the surface. The course of Spanish American poetry thereafter, at least to the time of Darío, if not, perhaps to the present, is constituted by the mapping of those distinct but interrelated routes of modernity.

4

Although the voices of this dialogue emerge independently, circa 1823, as Bello works on the "Alocución" in England and Heredia begins the lifelong project of rewriting his vision at Cholula in "A D. D. D., desde el campo" and "En una tempestad," they will come to be as conjoined as those of Lizardi's Payo and Sacristán or Hidalgo's gauchos by the end of the period in question, beginning in Heredia's own poetry. This was most notably the case at Niagara. Heredia remembers himself there as a poet of the darkness, specifically, the poet of "En una tempestad," and so asserts his own counterbalancing sublimity:

> Yo digno soy de contemplarte: siempre
> Lo común y mezquino desdeñando,
> Ansié por lo terrífico y sublime.
> Al despeñarse el huracán furioso,
> Al retumbar sobre mi frente el rayo,
> Palpitando gocé . . .
>
> (J. M. Heredia 1940, 2:221)

> Worthy am I to contemplate you: ever
> The common and the base disdaining,
> Did I yearn for the terrific and sublime.
> When the furious hurricane let loose,
> When thunderbolts resounded o'er my head,
> Palpitating, I took joy . . .

Alternatively, he introduces the *agricultura de la zona tórrida* into the scene through the famous phantasmagoria of Cuban palms above the falls.

The dialog with Bello is clearer, however, in two poems that Heredia writes shortly after his return from the United States to Spanish America in 1825. Shifting the scene from "la famosa/Cholulteca pirámide" ["the famous/Cholultec pyramid"] (J. M. Heredia 1940, 2:151) Heredia sets "Las sombras" (1825) at Chapultepec in Mexico City, "Cuando una tarde, al acabar el día,/Silencioso vagaba tristemente/En el monte sagrado en que reposan/De los reyes aztecas las cenizas" ["When one evening, at day's end,/Silent and sadly wandering/On the sacred mount where the ashes/Of the Aztec kings repose"] (2:81). Much like Monteagudo and his Atawallpa, though more expressly as a revindication of the "indígenas menguados" ["diminished natives"] (2:81), Heredia makes this ancient site of prophecy the setting in which to exhume Moctezuma, who will converse with a series of famous shades, both Aztec and Inca, retelling "la ensangrentada historia/De la infeliz América" ["The bloody history/Of unhappy America"] (2:87). The immediate model for the poem is Quintana's "El panteón del Escorial" (first published in the *Poesías patrióticas* of 1808). But Quintana's model, of course, was *Aeneid* 6, to which Heredia alludes directly in his epigraph to "Las sombras." In this new *poema mexicano*, therefore, Heredia openly heeds Bello's call for an American Virgil, though the dialogue between them is conducted here, as elsewhere, through their common engagement with the poetry of the Salamanca school. Moreover, in keeping with Bello's programmatic "Alocución," Heredia would severely curtail the role of the self in "Las sombras" to that of a mere eavesdropper, overhearing the words addressed to Mexico and to heaven by Moctezuma and his peers, much as Bello overheard the yaraví—in contrast to Heredia's active participation in the hurricane.

The result is public poetry. Heredia restores the role Bello thought poetry had lost to philosophy in Enlightenment Europe, and by the very means Bello himself projected in the "Alocución" following the lyric interlude. Heredia assigns to poetry the task of proclaiming national history. Only reaching back beyond Bello's references to the wars of independence, Heredia founds the epic of America in the Conquest, which is then repeated and reversed by the defeat of the Spanish in his own time. His contemporaries recognized the relevance to the emancipated republic: "we insert with the greatest pleasure," declares the editorial preface to "Las sombras" in the *Gaceta Diaria de México* in October 1825, "the sentimental poem of those august shades that ceaselessly disturb the insomnia of Ferdinand the Cruel. Thus, Heredia will be recognized as the poet of the liberty of the New World. Young, like America, he makes one feel the vigor of his age and the tremendous voice of vengeance (reproduced in J. M. Heredia 1940, 2:88).

Heredia himself furthers that reading in his own verse prolog to the poem, added sometime after that original publication, when he identifies the common enemy—that is common to both ends of the colonial period—as a personified "despotismo" ["despotism"] whose "voz terrible" ["terrifying voice"] opens this new version of the poem. Despotism calls for chains and continuing human misery and concludes: "yo lo quiero,/Yo lo mando, y será" ["I want it,/I command it, and it will be so"] (J. M. Heredia 1940, 2:79). The malignant fiat will be overturned by providential design—"El Ser Supremo/A ser feliz te destinó" ["The Supreme Being/Destined you to be happy"]—manifest in the catalog of American natural history with which Heredia closes his belated prolog, in strict accordance with Bello's plan:

> tus campos,
> De frutas mil salubres, deliciosas,
> Cubiertos siempre están: de tus montañas
> La plata y oro en manatial perenne
> Corren por siempre a enriquecer al mundo.
> Tus bosques hermosísimos, soberbios.
>
> (J. M. Heredia 1940, 2:80)

> your fields
> Are forever full of myriad fruits,
> Nutritious and delectable: from your mountains
> Silver and gold in perennial abundance
> Spring forth forever to enrich the world:
> Your proud forests, most beautiful.

But thus to cast himself in Bello's mold is to forget that at Cholula it was not the fruits but the "arco oscuro" ["dark arch"] (J. M. Heredia 1940, 2:151) that covered the poet and the land, and moreover, that a different view of liberty had freed the yo from association with despotism or simple material self-interest in "En una tempestad."

There is, however, dialogue with Bello and not mere dictation by the latter in "Las sombras." Heredia had attempted a compromise by illuminating the darkness of the scene under the moon, Bello's domesticated Huitaca, who here "bañaba el suelo/con su plateada luz" ["bathed the ground/with her silvery light"] (J. M. Heredia 1940, 2:82). "Mas de repente el cielo oscurecióse; A la luna ocultó" ["But suddenly the sky turned dark, and hid the moon"] (2.88), at the poem's close, and Heredia's own preferred trope supervenes:

> Allá a lo lejos el furioso trueno
> Estalló, resonando en mis oídos;
> Relámpagos sin fin brillar se vieron,
> Por el aire las sombras se esparcieron,
> Y el monte resonó con sus gemidos.
>
> (J. M. Heredia 1940, 2:88)

> There in the distance furious thunder
> Exploded, booming in my ears;
> Endless lightning was seen to soar,
> The shadows scattered through the air,
> And the hills resounded with their moans.

The storm brings patriotic poetry to an end, reinstituting the darkness of hidden depths.

The same dialogue, that is the same attempt at compromise with the same resulting reassertion is still more evident in the poem first known in public recitation in 1826 on the occasion commemorated by its title, "En la apertura del Instituto Mexicano." Heredia speaks on behalf of the Enlightenment, embodied as Minerva, whose efforts, he anticipates, "Levantarán el velo" ["Will lift the veil"] covering nature, the "Virgen, robusta" ["Virgin, robust"]:[14]

> Y en la alta majestad de su belleza
> Brillará, cual saliendo de las nubes
> La blanca luna en el profundo cielo.
>
> (J. M. Heredia 1940, 2.89)

> And she will shine in the great majesty
> Of her beauty, like the white moon
> Issuing from the clouds in the depths of heaven.

If pride of place in the newly opened institute belongs to Enlightenment natural philosophy, Heredia nonetheless foresees a role for poetry in a passage that begins as an echo of the opening of the "Alocución":

Y las Musas también su trono de oro
En Anáhuac pondrán: Naturaleza
A nuestra juventud doquiera brinda
Fuentes de inspiración. El panorama
Del Universo todo nos circunda.

(J. M. Heredia 1940, 2:89–90)

And the Muses too their golden throne
Shall set up in Anahuac: Nature
Everywhere offers founts of inspiration
To our youth. The panorama
Of the whole Universe girds us around.

A first review of the scene, however, reverts to the language of his
own panoramic vista from atop the *teocalli* in Cholula. "En él se
juntan bajo el mismo cielo" ["In it are joined beneath the same
sky"], he continues in "En la apertura":

Eterna nieve y perennal verdura,
Y en un estrecho círculo se abrazan
Los polos y los trópicos.

(J. M. Heredia 1940, 2:90)

Eternal snow and perennial greenery,
And in a tight circle
The tropics and the poles embrace.

The verses would have reminded his Mexican audience of the introduction to what was still known at that time as his "Fragmentos
descriptivos de un poema mexicano":

¡Cuánto es bella la tierra que habitaban,
Los aztecas valientes! En su seno
En una estrecha zona concentrados,
Con asombro se ven todos los climas
Que hay desde el Polo al Ecuador.

(J. M. Heredia 1940, 2:150)

How beautiful is the land inhabited
By the valiant Aztecs. In its breast
Concentrated in a tight zone
Are seen, astonishingly, all climes
There are from the Pole to the Equator.

and still more the subsequent verse, "En yelo eterno y perennal verdura" ["In eternal ice and perennial greenery"] (2:150).

The interchange of voices proceeds, as Heredia takes over Bello's question from the "Alocución" ("¿quién . . . /poner presumirá nombre o guarismo?"), giving it a new accent:

> ¿Quién puede contemplar sin entusiasmo
> Los magníficos cuadros que Natura
> Nos prodiga en América?
>
> (J. M. Heredia 1940, 2:90)

> Who can contemplate unmoved
> The prodigious scenes that Nature
> Lavishes on us in America?

The query might well introduce such brief sketches of American locales as found in the "Alocución," or the more extensive panegyrics of the "Agricultura." Instead, Heredia's prime example of American magnificence is the scene of his own sublimity, displaced to the south, under the aegis not of Bello, but rather of Bello's acknowledged source, Humboldt at Chimborazo:

> ¿Quién puede
> Indiferente ver las tempestades
> Vestir de oscuridad las anchas bases
> De los Andes altísimos, en torno
> Hervir el rayo, retumbar el trueno,
> A torrentes bajar la gruesa lluvia,
> Y encima descollar nevadas cumbres,
> Y dibujarse en el desierto cielo
> Inundadas en luz . . .
>
> (J. M. Heredia 1940, 2:90)

> Who can
> Watch indifferently the storms
> Dressing in darkness
> The broad bases of the highest Andes,
> The bolts roiling 'round them, the thunder roar,
> The heavy rain in torrents fall,
> And standing out above the snowy peaks,
> Engraved upon the empty sky
> And flooded in the light . . . ?

The zone of "Nieve eternal" ["Eternal snow"] of Mexico's volca-
nos (J. M. Heredia 1940, 2:151) as seen from Cholula, later divi-
nized as the overarching "trono del Señor" ["throne of the Lord"]
above his Cuban hurricane, becomes a *vue des cordillères.*

The dialogue with Bello allows Heredia to *cultivate* the darkness
that he had experienced at Cholula and acknowledged as a threat to
poetry at Niagara Falls-like Nenqueteba after the flood, cultivating
the night sky by the plowing of the moon, a displaced and disarmed
Huitaca. This *astrocultura,* finally, provides a compromise figure
for "¡Sagrada libertad!" ["Sacred liberty!"] (J. M. Heredia 1940,
2:91), the ever-present concern for Heredia and Bello, as for the
constitutional period at large. For in the Enlightenment outlook of
"En la apertura del Instituto Mexicano," "los climas del norte"
["the northern climes"] (2:91) are tempered and the power of the
storm brought under control by reference to Ben Franklin:

> Allí sereno
> Con impávida frente mira Franklin
> Venir tronando por el aire oscuro
> La negra tempestad. Su mano fuerte
> Arranca el rayo a la cargada nube,
> Y le arroja a morir lejos del hombre.
>
> (J. M. Heredia 1940, 2:91)

> There serene,
> Franklin watches with impassive brow
> The black storm come thundering
> Toward him through the darkened sky.
> His strong hand tears the bolt from heavy cloud
> And casts it out to die far from mankind.

To acknowledge Franklin triumphant over lightning and Fulton
master of "el contrario furor del Oceano" ["the contrary furor of
the Ocean"] (J. M. Heredia 1940, 2:91) is to place before the stu-
dents of the Instituto the hope that the cultivation of modern science
and technology will make it possible that the new nation "alza flotantes fortalezas/De su patria en los mares, do segura/Lidie la Libertad, e invulnerable/Sobre siervos y déspotas fulmine" ["raise the
country's floating fortresses/On the seas, where, secure,/Liberty
fights, and invulnerable/Fulminates against lackeys and despots"]
(2:91). But for the poet, this admission cedes too much to progress,
that is to a modernity with no alternatives. The victory of Franklin

and Fulton, and behind them of Bello and Humboldt, is the defeat of Heredia, of his melancholic resistance to a mourning that would cut him off from the past. A fine reader of his own work, Heredia excluded "En la apertura del Instituto Mexicano" from the final edition of his *Poesías*. But in spite of that omission, his poetry was already on the wane as early as these poems of 1825 and 1826. The balance in the dialogue of darkness and light, of self and nation, of unfulfilled depths and optimistic prospects, of ambivalent attachment to the past and determined separation from it under the guise of historical consciousness, tilts toward Bello.[15]

5

Taking Root: Echeverría and Gómez de Avellaneda, Midcentury

1

LIKE THE POLITICAL CONSTITUTIONS OF THE 1820S AND THE CONVER-
sations that they spawned in verse and prose, the constitution of
Spanish American poetry in the dialogue of Bello and Heredia was
not all-inclusive. Old romances were still recited and new ones
composed and disseminated, as Juan Alfonso Carrizo's vast compi-
lations from the Argentine hinterlands attest. The childhood recollections of ballad transmission of one of his informants, Don
Apolinar Barber, aged ninety-one at the time of Carrizo's research,
serve to date with certainty some of the oral texts to the close of the
period under study here, "in his childhood, back between 1850 and
1855" (Carrizo 1937, 1.313). The indigenous populations, too,
maintained their traditions. The Quiché dance-drama *Rabinal Achí*,
for example, was transcribed by Bartolo Zis in 1850, and performed
in 1856 after a silence of three decades, according to the testimony
of Brasseur de Bourbourg (*Rabinal Achí* 1944, 7–9). Bello and Heredia speak to and for the emerging print culture. Despite the continued vitality of oral traditions and, morever, in the face of massive
illiteracy, print culture was already in the ascendancy. Indeed, the
distinction that arrogates the term of "literature" to the poetry of
Heredia and Bello and even Fernández de Madrid, while assigning
Quechua songs and Don Apolinar's recitals to the category of folklore and the domain of anthropology is the result of that ascendancy. My purpose here, however, is not to trace the general
outlines of the institutionalization of literature in Spanish America.
I will focus, rather, on a constitutive moment within the print culture
in which the network of Spanish American intertextuality begins
to fulfil Miranda's implicit desideratum of intercommunication and

273

internal traffic. For if the dialogue of Bello and Heredia of the mid-1820s developed largely through their independent responses to the Salamanca school, as I have been arguing, they themselves succeed in displacing their Spanish models for the American poets to come. Quintana's "Al mar" is still necessary reading for Heredia at Niagara Falls, but it is Heredia's own "Niágara" in its commerce with Bello's Tequendama and the lyric interlude of the "Alocución" that becomes the inescapable source for Spanish American poetry in the print culture.

I would begin to indicate the impact of that legacy by considering Esteban Echeverría, who, though less than two years younger than Heredia, may be counted as the chief representative of the first generation of modern Spanish American poets for whom this is so. Echeverría may appear an unlikely choice. Credited in his day and often since as the fountainhead of Spanish American romanticism, Echeverría himself referred his innovations primarily to European sources. Witness, for instance, the selection of epigraphs from his early poetry: Wordsworth in *Elvira*, Byron, Chateaubriand, Hugo, Lamartine, Schiller and Goethe, among others, for the poems of *Los consuelos*, the volume that established his reputation and popularity in the River Plate upon its publication in *Buenos Aires* in 1834. Twentieth-century critics generally concurred that his attributions are all too revealing, and that Echeverría the poet is but a pale reflection of the European romantics, with critical interest turning, in consequence, to his short story, "El matadero." I would draw attention, however, to the verses of Heredia, cited from the 1825 edition of "Niágara," that head Echeverría's poem "Contestación" in *Los consuelos*, an epigraph that hints at a more substantial inter-American traffic. I will proceed to make my case, then, not against the preponderance of European sources, but rather admitting them within the context of the overarching parallel between literary and economic history. In this respect, Echeverría's career reads as an exemplary case for the commerce of American letters in the postindependence era.

Juan María Gutiérrez offers himself as a guide to the prehistory, as it were, of that career. Citing a letter written by Echeverría in 1836 in his "Noticias biográficas sobre don Esteban Echeverría," which he wrote for the fifth volume of the *Obras completas de Estebán Echeverría* (Buenos Aires 1874), one reads: "I continued my student life . . . until the end of 1823, at which time I was separated from the classroom, for reasons beyond my control, to devote

myself to commerce" (J. M. Gutiérrez 1940b, 7). Gutiérrez specifies that Echeverría went to work as a customs clerk in the commercial firm of Sebastián Lezica y hermanos, until the time that he set
sail for France in October of 1825. The portrait Gutiérrez offers of
Echeverría at that time, a servant of two discourses, is suggestive
for the formation of the new generation of Spanish American letters:

> The humble and prosaic occupations of the job that he undertook
> against his inclinations could not extinguish those that predominated in
> him, and the clerk in the Lezica firm did not cease to be the same student
> and the same ardent and imaginative youth that he had been before
> occupying himself with policies and bills. In his free time, and on top
> of the bundles of merchandise of the wholesale warehouses of his
> employers' firm, he studied his French lessons and immersed himself in
> books written in that [language], which he soon acquired to perfection,
> in the reflective reading of subjects of "history and poetry." (J. M.
> Gutiérrez 1940b, 7)

The final, telling words are taken once again from Echeverría himself, cited by Gutiérrez from an autobiographical fragment which
he possessed in manuscript. They point to the conjunction of
modernity: a present that sacrifices its continuity with the past in
the name of history in order to assert its continuity with the future
in the name of progress.

One may say more of Echeverría's thoroughly modern situation
so succinctly expressed by Gutiérrez. First, we find Echeverría far
from the old system of literary patronage, obliged to earn his
moments of dedication to French, to history and to literature, in the
very place of commercial trade. His literary proclivities, therefore,
arise as a rebellion of the will against the impositions of the commercial world and in its interstices of *ocio*. Literary activity is
defined in opposition to useful labor. For utility is understood in the
River Plate of the 1820s as the export of agricultural products, the
all but exclusive source of national revenue.

The youthful Echeverría finds himself torn from his studies—as
Jovellanos had been—to take his small place in the heart of that
trade, poised between the vast land tracts of the interior and the
overseas markets, which are as well the sources of manufactured
consumer goods. Just as in the time of Juan and Ulloa, a protection-
ist economic policy that might have fomented homespun industry
was passed over as Argentina and all of Spanish America rushed
headlong from colonialism to neocolonialism. Echeverría's impor-

tation of European poetry not only coincides with economic development in the River Plate, but moreover, may be seen as an expression of cultural values implicit in and furthered by transatlantic trade. His personal course has the force of allegory. He leaves Buenos Aires, himself a native product, carrying with him, among a few other volumes—an algebra text, Blair's *Rhetoric*—his copy of the *Lira Argentina*, that early compilation of a self-consciously local expression (though manufactured, that is printed, in Paris) "in which at the same time that he found the enthusiasm of patriotism, he received his first lessons in Castilian versification, which, from that time on, became one of his most persistent inclinations" according to Gutiérrez (J. M. Gutiérrez 1940b, 11). Coincidentally, but emblematically, he strikes up a friendship on shipboard with Drs. Johann Rudolph Rengger and Marcelin Longchamp, the Swiss scientific expeditionaries who were joint authors of *Essai historique sur la révolution du Paraguay*" (1827): the ocean crossing of poetry and history. He will than settle in Paris, whence he will return in 1830, and by the time of the letter cited by Gutiérrez, he will have become the chief purveyor of European poetic fashions in the River Plate, and as such, the center for the local commerce of letters that is formalized in the *Asociación de Mayo* of 1837.[1]

Echeverría no more forgot the lessons of the *Lira Argentina* while in Europe than the lessons of European poetry upon his return. Of the three poems published in Buenos Aires before *Elvira*, and later included in *Los consuelos*, the one whose perspective is set explicitly in France ("desde el suelo,/Que el tosco Galo hollaba" ["from the soil/that the rude Gaul trod"], Echeverría 1951, 740), "En celebridad de mayo" is patriotic poetry in a style, and under an epigraph, learned from the *Lira*: enthusiastic, declamatory and out-of-date, it being rather late, in 1830, when the poem first appeared in the *Gaceta Mercantil*, to write in the future tense, "Cantaré las cadenas" ["I shall sing the chains"] (740).

The temporal dilemma is transcribed, however, as a geographic matter in the moment that Echeverría would pose as the critical point in the poem from which his imagination must recover:

> ¿Mas do la Musa mía,
> Por entusiasmo patrio enajenada
> Vuela con osadía,
> Y no oye la algarada,

Que en el foro se enciende;
Cual corre la turba apresurada?

(Echeverría 1951, 740)

But where my Muse,
Transported by patriotic fervor,
Flies with audacity,
And hears not the uproar
Unleashed in the public place,
As the throng runs on in haste?

The elegiac opening to the stanza allows one to fear—the fear in fact is borne out in this unimpressive ode—that the Muse has died, slain by the patriotic spirit it has been called upon to celebrate, revolutionary liberty giving way to wanton riot. But the facile rhetorical question has a ready answer, an answer made ready by Bello. The Muse, like "Libertad sacrosancta" ["Sacrosanct liberty"] (Echeverría 1951, 740) itself, has flown the old, decrepit world of European despotism, where poetry was muted—"¿Cómo cantar podría/En medio de los tronos degradados . . . ?" ["How could I sing/In the midst of degraded thrones . . . ?"] (740)—and made its way to America, in the wake of Bello's "Divina Poesía." The erstwhile estrangement of poetry is then displaced to the landscape, where figuration may be recuperated as a natural inscription. In times of war, Luca had taught—and so Echeverría learned in the *Lira*—a resurgence of the poetic imagination wherein inscription was figured through the wounding of the earth. Echeverría's "trazadas letras inmortales" ["undying letters traced"] (740) remains close to that argument in his patriotic ode. But with political independence already a reality and liberty apparently secured, Echeverría warms his poem in the sun of Bello's poetics—"Salud ¡oh sol fecundo/En portentosos frutos!" ["Hail, oh sun ripe/With portentous fruits!"] (740)—presenting America as a bountiful landscape auspicious to poetry.

As the perspective moves closer to home in "El regreso," also published in the *Gaceta Mercantil* in the summer following his return to Buenos Aires, Echeverría produces a progress piece still closer to Bello's "Alocución." He charts the path of liberty to its triumph in America, pausing to insert a note that will be new to the River Plate. He introduces a reference to the freedom of Switzerland, a topos of the period among European authors (Schama 1995,

478–86), so as to set up the counter-rhyme (*Helvecia, Grecia*) of the extinction of liberty in contemporary Europe by the Ottomans. The latter, as European readers of poetry at that time would have known, recalls the figure of Lord Byron, invoked explicitly at the outset of the poem in its epigraph. Yet far from the Byronic posture of pride willfully going before a fall, Echeverría demonstrates a sudden loss of nerve in a closing supplication to the River Plate— "Modera un tanto" [Moderate a bit] (Echeverría 1951, 737):

> Que con giro suave
> Fluyan [esas ondas] y den camino silenciosas
> A los flancos estrechos de mi nave,
> Que juega con tus crines espumosas.
> (Echeverría 1951, 737)

> May [your waves] flow with soft
> Turn and silent may they make their way,
> For the narrow flanks of my craft,
> That plays with your frothy mane.

The triumph of liberty he had set out to celebrate ends in this moment of arrest—of his own biographical journey and of his verse—quite precisely analogous to the roadblock in Peninsular letters of the previous generation manifest in Quintana's stammering supplication to a rough sea in "Al mar" ("Calma un momento tus soberbias ondas,/Océano inmortal" ["Calm a moment your proud waves/Immortal ocean"], M. J. Quintana 1980, 229).

I would highlight the impasse by reference to Echeverría's acknowledged European models. Echeverría's engagement with Byron develops primarily as an identification with the latter's Lara, who "left in youth his father-land" and has returned, "nor yet is past his manhood's prime,/Though sear'd by toil" (Byron 1855, 118–19), rather than with that same character in his more popular guise as Conrad in "The Corsair" (Espronceda's choice). Echeverría would be the seafarer at home, and a recluse on land (though not all his adventures are done), rather than the swashbuckler. But to select a strictly contemporaneous standard against which to gauge Echeverría's particular assimilation of his European reading, I turn to Hugo's "A M. de Lamartine," published in *Les feuilles d'automne* of 1831, but dated to June 1830, like "El regreso," shortly after of the reception of Alphonse de Larmartine (1790–1869) into the Académie Française. Hugo begins the poem with the image of himself and Lamartine as ocean travelers who have braved the open seas—"Naguère une même tourmente,/Ami, battait nos deux esquifs" ["But lately, Friend, a single storm/ beat our two little skiffs"] (Hugo 1857, 7.53). As the metaphor extends into allegory, he celebrates Lamartine's public accolade as a Columbus of the poetic imagination returned safely to port—"Tu reviens de ton Amérique!/Ton monde est trouvé!" ["You return from your America!/Your world is already discovered!"] (7:60)—while consigning himself to a continuing life upon the metaphorical sea:

> C'est mon tourbillon, c'est ma voile!
> C'est l'ouragan qui, furieux,
> A mesure éteint chaque étoile
> Qui se hasarde dans mes cieux!
> C'est la tourmente qui m'emporte!
>
> (1857, 7.63)

> This is my storm, this is my sail!
> This is the hurricane which, wroth,
> Extinguishes by turns each star
> That chances through my skies!
> This is the storm that bears me off!

Hugo admits to envying Lamartine the haven of his success in the final verses ("Pleure, mon ami, mon ombre jalouse!" ["Weep, friend, my jealous shade"], Hugo 1857, 7:64), but the predominant note is rather that of pride in the *isolement* of the poet, unswerving in his purpose and his chosen path. Indeed, Hugo has written the poem against the possibility of his own triumph, against, that is, the temptation that had whispered "Abritons mon navire./Ne livrons plus ma voile au vent qui la déchire" ["Let us give haven to my ship/Let us no more deliver my sail to the wind that rends it"] (5:159) in a previous poem dedicated to Lamartine, "A M. Alphonse de L."—a possibility that he had rejected in an outburst of prophetic fury.[2]

Echeverría, too, presented himself as a reader of Lamartine in "El infortunio, en el mar," composed on 11 June 1830, two days before "El regreso," according to the dates adduced by Gutiérrez (see Echeverría 1951, 713; 1940, 23). The explicit reference to "L'isolement," which headed Lamartine's *Les méditations poétiques* (Paris 1820 and already in its twelfth edition as Echeverría arrived in France) is suggestive of Echeverría's ambitions: would he inaugurate a new series of poetic meditations on his return? The adaptation itself, however, is truncated and unpretentious, hardly more than an exercise, transposing the mountain scene of the original to the seascape surrounding him as his transatlantic voyage neared its end, but before land was sighted. Lamartine's prototypical *méditation* was written in the wake of the death of his lover, unnamed here but always his "Elvire," irregardless of the changing real-life referents. Echeverría assimilates Lamartine's initial note of indifference, while restricting its explication to the unelaborated remark, "temprano/Se voló su esperanza" ["early/The hope flew off"] (Echeverría 1951, 737). This limiting reference to "esperanza" foreshortens Lamartine's "l'espoir et l'amour" ["hope and love"] (Lamartine 1968, 4), which not only obfuscates the poetic occasion, but also eliminates the possibility of redemption. Thus one finds neither the expression of despair that leads Lamartine to identify his perspective with the dead—"Je contemple la terre, ainsi qu'une ombre errante:/Le soleil des vivants n'échauffe plus les morts" ["I contemplate the earth like a wandering shade:/The sun of the living no longer warms the dead"] (3)—nor, at the other extreme, the sudden outbreak of a nearly mystical hope of erotic reunion in an afterlife—"Là, je m'eniverais à la source où j'aspire" ["There I would drink 'til I were drunk at the source to which I aspire" (4). Like Hugo, therefore, Echeverría has before him a model of poetic melancholia in which continuing attachment to the dead becomes a form of severance from the living. Hugo would follow Lamartine as a model of extremity for a self formed of its own solitude, eschewing the consolations of a mourning society. Echeverría, author of the consolations, would moderate Lamartine in "El infortunio," as he would moderate the Río de la Plata in "El regreso."

Viewed teleologically with Hugo's poetry as the endpoint, Echeverría's offshore topos, the most crucial and characteristic moment in the formation of his verse, is very likely the greatest disappointment in a century of Spanish American letters. A well-supplied Echeverría proves unable to dock the goods of European romanticism to a new and eager overseas market. Such disappointment has long since been registered. Yet market conditions, to continue the commercial metaphor, were already determined by the preceding and ongoing dialogue on liberty. And political conditions in the River Plate in 1830—and nearly everywhere else in Spanish America as well at that date—were such as to place that dialogue in peril, both as a foundation of government and as a fundamental trope for poetry. Speaking confidently from offshore, Echeverría enjoins the "Patria querida," "Muestra un ejemplo más a las naciones" ["Show yet another example to the nations"] (Echeverría 1951, 737); this is a language lesson: "Que no son nombres vanos/ La libertad, sus fueros soberanos,/Sino para las *almas degradadas*. [That liberty, their sovereign rights,/Are not mere empty names/ Except to *souls corrupt*] (Echeverría 1951, 737; emphasis added). This faith in the authenticity of the name of liberty—that is, once again, in liberty as a trope—may serve as a reminder that Echeverría had set off for France from the liberal Argentina of Rivadavia, that he was a reader of the *Lira* on board, and that Bello, rather than experience taught that despotism now lay not before, but behind him in "Europa degradada" (736). Thus, in the wake of Bello's "Alocución," Echeverría was writing that "La libertad de Europa fugitiva,/Un asilo buscando/Ha pasado el Océano" ["Liberty a fugitive from Europe/Seeking asylum/Has crossed the ocean"] (736).

But the reality ashore is the Buenos Aires of Rosas's government. A more open-eyed and more experienced Heredia could make the offshore topos a platform for the denunciation of despotism in his "Himno del desterrado," composed in 1825, but not collected in book form until the 1832 edition of his *Poesías*, and so unavailable to Echeverría upon his return. In 1830 Echeverría is less forthright. All the same, his closing call for moderation is a political statement, and not merely a faint-hearted imitation of Byron; and his fear of the waves figures forth an authentic poetic crisis in the face of the undermining of the name of liberty in a degraded America. The immediate response of "El regreso" follows the lead of Bello, seeking refuge for poetry in the American landscape. The closing metaphor of the mane transforms his boat riding the waves into a horseman of the Argentina pampa. This figurative route will lead to "La cautiva," originally included by Echeverría in his *Rimas* (Buenos Aires 1837), whose much heralded landscape is first presented as an extended simile, "Como el mar" ["Like the sea"] (Echeverría 1951, 454). But the fuller meditation on the crisis of liberty and poetry is carried out primarily by expanding the threat of the waves in "El regreso" into a full-blown storm, in which Echeverría presents himself as a diminished survivor or ruin of his own past: "ya agostada/Siento mi juventud" ["I feel my youth/Already withered"] in the words he borrows from Heredia's "Niágara" at the head of his "Contestación" (Echeverría 1951, 723), which he rewrites in the body of the poem by reference to "En una tempestad":

> Mas cual roble soberbio que derriba
> El feroz huracán de cumbre altiva,
>   Al impulso violento
> De fogosas pasiones, abatida
> Cayó mi juventud que sólo vida
>   Tiene para el tormento.
>   (Echeverría 1951, 724, see also 719 and 735)

> But like the proud oak struck down
> By the fierce hurricane from haughty heights,
>   So fell my youth, defeated,
> To the violent impulse
> Of passions, unabated,
>   Leaving torment and aught else.

Echeverría returns to the same image to open "La ida," the last poem of what will be *Los consuelos*. It is his revision of "El regreso" from the perspective of his experience of Argentine despotism and disarray, at once the most vigorous in the collection and the most deeply indebted to Heredia: an Argentine rewriting of "Niágara."

Gutiérrez remarked that in *Los consuelos*,

> beneath the lyric forms of a personal poetry . . . the situation of the country was reflected. . . . What was this [situation] at that time, but a martyred victim, discontent and complaining about the past, resigned to the fatality of the present, and hopeful in the secrets of the future? What were the *Consuelos* but the likeness and the personification of these same pains and hopes? (J. M. Gutiérrez 1940b, 33)

Both lines of the parallel are legible in "La ida." A *yo* introduces himself and the poem, reflecting on his loss of poetic vitality until he is startled by fresh inspiration, not by a present spectacle as at Heredia's falls, but by the memory of Layda. The homophonic overlap with the title (*Layda/La-yda/La ida*) makes the fate of the heroine a stand-in for the fate of the poem and of poetry. On the one hand she is loved and abandoned with child by a man who is almost certainly the young Esteban of the customs house, subject of "love affairs, ravings, passions of the blood, and occasionally of reflection," by Echeverría's own account (qtd by J. M. Gutiérrez

1940b, 8). The child dies and, fleeing the scene of her double loss of love, Layda sets sail across the River Plate. She is overtaken by a storm modeled closely on "En una tempestad," with this difference, that where Heredia rose above the winds in apotheosis, Layda sinks to her death, a grim realization of the threat in "El regreso." This history of Layda explicates Echeverría's reticence before the unbridled exultation of the romantic self, whether Heredia's or Hugo's. The separation of the poetic subject from all human society in their figures of a man committing himself to the storm may be viewed, from the perspective of the woman left behind, as mere egotism and simple self-interest. And insofar as egotism and self-interest are the roots of despotism, according to Echeverría's repeated assertion in the "Dogma socialista," "La ida" offers itself equally as political allegory. Layda is a personification of liberty abandoned, whose child, the Argentina of the Revolution of Mayo, has died as a consequence of that neglect, driving her to the brink of madness, to exile across the River Plate in Montevideo, to death.

"La ida" is dated to September 1832, the month in which *Elvira, o la novia del Plata* was printed anonymously, receiving scant and superficial comment. "The times were by no means literary," Gutiérrez observes, in a passage that merits extended quotation:

> For Buenos Aires, the year of 1832 began with the official celebration of the victories of General Quiroga, with the suppression of the freedom of the press, and ended with the famous abdication of Governor Rosas, which was no more than a hypocritical truce before the aims that he later achieved. The public mood had the tone of resignation and weariness, and the society of Buenos Aires, increasingly materialistic, surrendered itself without regrets to the fate presented by an irresistible despotism which it already felt upon its shoulders, so spirited in other times. If one adds to this political situation in the country the oddity of the literary structure of *Elvira*, without precedent in Spanish poetry and allied to the romantic poetry of England and Germany, according to the express declaration of its author, it will be easy to understand the indifference with which the public greeted the appearance of that little book, despite its beauties and what these promised for the benefit of national letters. The great devotees of verse had fled with the altar of their muses to the other side of the River Plate, and one or another amateurish pen arose to celebrate and criticize *Elvira* in timid articles in the newspapers, without penetrating its epidermis, and debating energetically whether or not the frequent change of meters practiced by the author was well-conceived. (J. M. Gutiérrez 1940b, 29–30)

Gutiérrez provides an admirable and concise contextualization, which itself calls for an ideological frame. Gutiérrez wrote his "Noticias biográficas" as a commemorative act, and in this monument to Echeverría he portrays his subject as the apostle of Mayo. In this argument, the poetic revolution that Echeverría would inaugurate with *Elvira* in the time of despotism parallels the political revolution of May 1810 in the face of colonial power, They both fail initially for the inexpert response of an unprepared populace; they both await renewal and redemption in the *Asociación de mayo* of 1837 and its principal texts in verse and prose, "La cautiva" and the "Dogma socialista," first published under the heading, "Código, ó declaración de los principios que constituyen la creencia social de la República Argentina" in the *Iniciador* of Montevideo on 1 January 1839.

Echeverría calls into question that commonplace parallel of historical analysis in his "Discurso de introducción" to the *Salón literario* in 1837, at least with respect to the revolution. "Shall we repeat, gentlemen," he asks, "as many reputable men in our country do, that our society, still swaddled in the diapers of infancy, was not in a condition to take advantage of those ideas, those lights that the press or the congress disseminated [that is the liberal ideology emanating from Europe at the foundation of the revolution]?" (Echeverría 1940, 265). Echeverría himself will subscribe to such a view in the "Dogma socialista," but in the "Discurso de introducción" he answers with a firm negative, first, because, as he declares, societies are ever in the process of renewal and so are neither old nor young. "But there is more," he argues: "We were an integral part of Spanish society and . . . we ought to count the centuries of existence that the latter had when the revolution broke out" (266). I would return to *Elvira* in the light of these conflicting historical perspectives.

In addition to epidermic questions concerning metric innovation, Echeverría affiliates *Elvira* with his European models from the very title of the poem, which, in conjunction with its erotic theme, points directly to Lamartine. With regard to "literary structure," moreover, the extension and continuous narrative design are drawn primarily from Byron—the *Lira Argentina* included long poems, of course, but they are odes of triumph, whereas *Elvira*, is modeled upon the Byronic tale of collosal defeat. Thus Echeverría's hero is felled, following the example of Byron's Lara after his fantasmagoric combat; though the more throughgoing Byron will wake Lara

from his swoon, continuing the poem to his literal death, a burden
that Echeverría will not undertake until "La cautiva." The intention
to hold fast to the same mentors who preside over his offshore
poems is therefore patent in structure, theme and scansion. Nevertheless, *Elvira* opens with an altogether unexceptional return to the
Hispanic tradition of the later eighteenth century, evoking the
vague landscape of the Anacreontic world ("cual céfiro apacible
con su arrullo/Halagando a la rosa en su capullo" ["like a peaceful
zephyr with its lullaby/Fawning on the rose in bud"], Echeverría
1951, 445), with no more seasoning than minor moments of titilla-
tion.

Echeverría plants the seeds of dramatic tension in this garden of
delights, leading to the peripeteia in Elvira's song:

> Creció acaso arbusto tierno
> A orillas de un manso río,
> Y su ramaje sombrío
> Muy ufano se extendió;
> Mas en el sañudo invierno
> Subió el río cual torrente,
> Y en su túmida corriente
> El tierno arbusto llevó.—
>
> Reflejando nieve y grana
> Nació garrida y pomposa
> En el desierto una rosa,
> Gala del prado y amor;
> Mas lanzó con furia insana
> Su soplo inflamado el viento,
> Y se llevó en un momento
> Su vana pompa y frescor.
>
> (Echeverría 1951, 446)

> There may have grown a tender bush
> On a gentle river's side,
> And there its shady branch stretched out
> In the fullness of its pride;
> But in the winter's raging rout,
> The river rose up like a torrent,
> And in the river's swollen current
> It bore off the tender bush.—
>
> There was born in desert expanse
> An elegant and pompous rose,

> Reflecting cochineal on snow,
> The pride of love and of the plains;
> But with destructive fury,
> Its fiery breath the wind sent,
> And bore off in an instant
> Its freshness and pompous vanity.

A flood and a storm are the figures by which he expressed the threat to figurative power in his seascapes. Only here, unlike the offshore poems, he steers by a different star than that of his European masters. Counting on those centuries of experience that preceded any Americanist intent, he has recourse to the Hispanic tradition. Not Meléndez and Quintana, but reaching back to the Siglo de Oro, he circumscribes the power of wind and waves within a baroque homily that deflates the ecstasy of Lamartine's "l'espoir et l'amour" ["hope and love"] as illusion:

> Así dura todo bien;
> Así los dulces amores
> Como las lozanas flores
> Se marchitan en su albor;
> Y en el incierto vaivén
> De la fortuna inconstante,
> Nace y muere en un instante
> La esperanza y el amor.
>
> (Echeverría 1951, 446)

> Thus endures all good;
> Thus sweet loves,
> Like pretty buds,
> Wither in their morn;
> And in the uncertain moves
> Of fortune inconstant,
> Love and hope are born
> And die within the instant.

Or, as he will declare in still more familiar language: "El amor y la esperanza/No son sino un vano sueño" ["Love and hope/Are no more than a vain dream" (Echeverría 1951, 449). *Y los sueños, sueños son.* (Calderón, I point out, supplied the epigraph to "La ida.") Needless to say, Echeverría is not usually classed as a forerunner of the neobaroque, and yet, unexpectedly in this author who has claimed his place in literary history as a champion of native themes and imported styles—American raw material and European manufacture—the baroque persists.

Echeverría takes the road back to the Siglo de Oro, I believe, because he finds that the routes forward to Spanish American modernity are obstructed. The Argentina of his return is neither the natural world nor the heroic past of the independence movements to which Bello had directed poetry, but rather a disspoiled nation at war with itself. In this Argentina, liberty is drowning. And there is as yet no safe haven after the flood from which to write an elegiac history—as Bello would have American poets do in the wake of the wars of independence—in which liberty might prove resurgent, speaking a new language, under a new name. Nevertheless, Echeverría is as loathe to relinquish his attachment to Mayo as Lisardo his love for Elvira. The result is a political and poetic melancholia without, however, the counterbalancing strength of the egotistical sublime, which Heredia experienced in the hurricane, but which Echeverría rejects for its destructive consequences: death in love and political dictatorship. The Anacreontic mood of the opening sections of the poem is insufficient to carry Echeverría beyond this impasse. But the minor baroque lyric of Elvira's prophetic song proves a spur to the stalled imagination, drawing, as it does, on deeper sources.

Structurally, Elvira's song-within-the-poem takes the role of Bello's yaraví. Lisandro overhears her conceit: "escuchaba/Con asombro y encanto/De Elvira el triste canto" ["he listened/With surprise and delight/To Elvira's sad song"] (Echeverría 1951, 446).[3] He is aroused into a countersong, and more than song, of erotic passion in excess, I believe, of anything written in Spanish America in the period—with the exception of occasional extensions of the baroque tradition of flagrant burlesques.[4] In Echeverría's case, it is as though the recollection of the bolder poetry of the Siglo de Oro propels him to lift the veil from the coy sensuality of the late eighteenth-century poets in the Anacreontic mode. Echeverría respects decorum just enough for a minimal ambiguity. Nevertheless, the situation, as pregnant Layda knew, is clear enough. "Mientras que de su sien por las orillas/En madejas ondeantes/Sus cabellos airosos se extendían" ["While at her temple on the banks/In wavy locks/Her respendent hair spilled forth"] (Echeverría 1951, 446): she lies upon the bank, the flood untamed but transformed into a wave of sexual abandon. Elvira will pay, like Layda, with her death.

I do not wish to overstate the case. Elvira's song beside the river has neither the scope nor generative power of, say, the "New Water" in the *Watunna* of the Marikitare, which accomplishes a thoroughgoing mythic transformation: "You couldn't recognize the Earth anymore from the beginning. Now there were buds everywhere. The Earth became green. The forest bloomed, our *conucos* blossomed. The forest filled with trees. Our *conucos* filled with yuca" (Civreux 1980, 135).[5] But her invocation and enactment of the flood of passion, "nadando en delicias" ["swimming in voluptuousness"] (Echeverría 1951, 447), generate a new poetry for Echeverría. Recalling that his seascape, and especially its definitive extension in the stormy crossing in "La ida," drew upon Heredia for the delineation of a poetic crisis—the point at which the imagination falls inarticulate—the effort of *Elvira* returns to Heredia's own source, when "En tal contemplación embebecido/Sorprendióme el sopor" ["Absorbed in such contemplation/I was surprised by sleep"] (J. M. Heredia 1940, 2:152), cutting short revelation in the 1825 version of the Cholula poem. Moving beyond his own offshore poems, he would move beyond the young Heredia as well by opening that sleep to a dialogue of dreams. Unfortunately, the verse is unequal to the attempt. He would promote Elvira's song to the level of prophecy by congealing the baroque constellation of *vanitas* elements in a dream vision of Hell. But thus seeking to outflank Heredia he stumbles upon Bello and introduces his netherworld with a catalog of demons that reads, perhaps intentionally, as a parody of the "Agricultura de la zona tórrida."

Echeverría finds a surer path when baroque echo effects, embodied first in the "infernales alaridos" ["hellish shrieks"] of the wind—"Y el eco de los vientos penetraba/Resonando con hórrida armonía" ["And the echo of the winds penetrated/Resounding in horrid harmony"] (Echeverría 1951, 448)—assert an insurmountable obstacle to poetry. Lisardo, the quest figure of his dreamscape, finds himself mocked and defeated by echolalia:

> "Elvira, Elvira," Lisardo
> Agitándose en su lecho
> Exclamó entonces, y "Elvira"
> Repitió lánguido un eco.
> "Dadme a mi esposa y mi vida,
> Horrorosos esqueletos,
> Dadme a mi Elvira" y "Elvira"

Por los aires repitieron.
Calló Lisardo . . .

(Echeverría 1951, 449)

"Elvira, Elvira," Lisardo
Then exclaimed, twisting
In his bed, and "Elvira,"
A languid echo repeated.
"Give me my wife and my life,
Horrific skeletons,
Give me my Elvira," and "Elvira"
They repeated through the air.
Lisardo fell silent . . .

Struggling for an insight that Freud would later formulate, Echeverría glimpses that beyond the pleasure principle, beyond passion on the river bank, there is an experience of attachment and loss and continuing attachment that constitutes a compulsion to repeat—in poetry—and that this echo covers over a silence. Thus his Lisardo sleeps and wakes and sleeps and wakes again only to find his dreams realized and his beloved Elvira dead: baroque fulfillment, but also an inkling of the uncanny that will become melancholia's characteristic note in the literature of the later nineteenth century. Faced with the reality of the funeral cortege, Lisardo can no more than echo the echo of his dream:

                . . . tendió su vista
        Sobre aquel ataúd, y repitiendo
        Con grito de dolor "Elvira, Elvira,"
        Exánime cayó en el duro suelo

(Echeverría 1951, 450)

                . . . he stretched his gaze
        over that coffin, and repeating
        "Elvira, Elvira," with a cry of pain,
        He fell senseless to the hard ground

His loss of consciousness suggests that for Echeverría in *Elvira*, as for Heredia surprised by *el sopor* at Cholula in 1820, subjectivity has reached its expressive limits.

2

I do not find in the scholarship devoted to Echeverría, generally more attuned to European dependency than to the possibilities of the internal commerce of Spanish American letters, an indication of if and when he would have known the Toluca edition of Heredia's *Poesías*. Nonetheless, I interject here, from the same year of 1832, a consideration of Heredia's return to the scene of the swoon. The new version of the Cholula poem, now under the more familiar title of "En el teocalli de Cholula," takes a step beyond the expressive limits of the original "Fragmentos descriptivos" and also provides a background for, if not perhaps the formative influence, upon Echeverría's own step beyond.[6]

Taking up the original text at the point of its final hemistich, Heredia completes the verse and goes on to produce the nightmare vision of human sacrifice that haunted his poetic sleep. I have already noted that in the lyric interlude in the "Alocución," Bello was saved from sleep and its consequent curtailment of poetic possibility by the sound of a distant *yaraví*. He did not reproduce that indigenous poem, but drew upon its inspiration when he proceeded to his elegiac history of American independence. In a final response to Bello, Heredia gives that indigenous poem voice, as it were, a wounding voice, which, unlike the perfidy of his beloved in his erotic complaints or the thunder of the storm, he draws from within himself, making the self the site of all American history, the burial ground of its victims. It is an antiprogress piece. "La vasta procesión" ["The vast procession"] of mankind is leading not to perfection, but rather to "Sacerdotes horribles, salpicados/Con sangre humana rostros y vestidos" ["Horrible priests, their faces and their vestments/Splattered with human blood"] (J. M. Heredia 1940, 2:152). Nor can a historical consciousness safely consign to the past the endless repetition of violence done to "el pueblo esclavo" ["the enslaved people"] (2:152), since, as he had already declared in the earlier version of the poem, addressing himself to Popocatepetl, "Pueblos y reyes/Viste hervir a tus pies, que combatían/*Cual hora combatimos*" ["You saw peoples and kings/Seething at your feet, they fought/*As we now fight*"] (2:152, emphasis added).[7]

From this perspective, the work of art as cultural monument splits into a dialog, obfuscated by superimposition:

> Esta inmensa estructura
> Vió a la superstición más inhumana
> En ella entronizarse. Oyó los gritos
> De agonizantes víctimas, en tanto
> Que el sacerdote, sin piedad ni espanto,

Les arrancaba el corazón sangriento;
Miró el vapor espeso de la sangre
Subir caliente al ofendido cielo,
Y tender en el sol fúnebre velo,
Y escuchó los horrendos alaridos
Con que los sacerdotes sofocaban
El grito del dolor.

                                        (J. M. Heredia 1940, 2:153)

This immense structure
Was throne and witness to the most
Inhuman superstition. It heard
The cries of victims in their death throes,
While the priest, unmoved and unafraid,
Tore out their bloody hearts;
It watched the thick vapor of blood
Rise up still warm to the offended skies,
Covering the sun with funereal veil,
And it listened to the horrendous shrieks
With which the priests drowned out
The cry of pain.

Heredia had fallen in the first version of his poem—fallen into sleep
as a figure for the silence and unconsciousness of death. And then
he had risen in the apotheosis of the self, cut loose from all earthly
ties, in "En una tempestad." And now he closes his career with
another fall. For in this rising of the thick haze of blood, in which
the human heart is quite literally the source of the clouds ("vapor
espeso") that hide the sun, he reproduces that apotheosis as a
ghastly ritual that secures nonetheless a gruesome power for poetry.
He rediscovers an origin far from Bello's idealized progress of
Divine Poetry. Stripping away all utopian sentimentality, he
grounds the poetic imagination in American culture, rather than
American nature. It is an alternative foundational fiction in which
that culture is presented as a manifestation of inerradicable violence, before, during and after the Conquest. Independence, in this
antiprogressive history, brings neither a resolution of colonial violence nor a vindication of indigenous peoples, but only another episode in an endless repetition. This is a critical, and so in that respect
a modern discourse, but not in the mode of the tradition of rupture.
It is the discourse of melancholia.

   With culture rather than nature at its source, Heredia presents the origin of poetry as a dialogue of voices, as opposed to Bello's consultation with silence. The aboriginal dialogue of poetry is an overlay: the sacerdotal "alaridos" echo, rather than memorialize, the still more primordial "grito del dolor" of the sacrificial victims. What rupture there is, then, is internalized as wound. And in that internalization Heredia's melancholic poetry sacrifices the future—cedes the projectional stature that will give Bello institutional force in the delineation of Spanish American identity—but incorporates the power of past. Elegy fails at Cholula, but symbolic exchange prevails in the sacrifice of the red and steaming heart to the sun, its mirror image, and in the rising haze of blood over the *teocalli* mirroring the volcano Popocatepetl. The poetic self, an incurable *Enfermo*, fuses with the wounded landscape.

Heredia was at his endpoint as a poet. He wrote little verse after 1832, devoting himself instead to political life, to public instruction through his various journals, and to the law. But in 1832, after the pusillanimous reception of *Elvira*, Echeverría was only getting started. Gutiérrez reports that in a letter just prior to the publication of *Los consuelos* in 1834, Echeverría had written:

> In poetry, for me, short compositions have always been of little importance, whatever their merits. In order for poetry to be able to fulfill its prophetic mission properly, in order for it to work upon the masses and to be a powerful social element, and not as up until now amongst ourselves and our forebears, a futile pastime, and at most, agreeable, it is necessary that poetry be beautiful, grand, sublime and that it manifest itself in colossal forms. (qtd. J. M. Gutiérrez 1940b, 64)

The step beyond *Elvira*, then, would not be the short poems of *Los consuelos*, but "La cautiva," a long and ambitious text with which Echeverría seeks to restore poetry to full citizenship, a useful laborer in the public sphere. *Los consuelos* won Echeverría his first popular success, but it was in fact "La cautiva" that first secured his place in literary history.[8]

Gutiérrez notes in his biographical study of 1874 the critical success of "La cautiva" among Argentine and foreign readers, while underlining, for his own part, "its social reach and its revolutionary tendency" (J. M. Gutiérrez 1940b, 37). It has long since been reappraised. Alberto Zum Felde may speak for the virtually unanimous opinion: "only its Americanist *intention* remains for posterity, frustrated in the weakness of its poetic language, in the lack of epic authenticity" (Zum Felde 1954, 91). The final observation concerning "epic authenticity" begs a question, the standards of Byron being distinct from those of Homer and Virgil. Nevertheless, there are times when it is enough to bury Caesar. Echeverría cannot be saved from himself and his own phrasing, capable, for instance, of assassinating the post-Miltonic tradition of negative sublimity as the "trasunto estupendo/de la infernal terriblez" ["the stupendous likeness/of infernal terribility"], to cite but one example of the awkward gait of "La cautiva" (Echeverría 1951, 467). But setting aside the infelicities of his ear and moreover, his intentions as both an importer of new fashions and as a champion of native themes, I would underline once more that the poem is *americanista* above all because it develops within a preexisting dialogue of American poetry. In the epilogue to *Los consuelos* Echeverría may regret his reliance in some of the poems in that volume on Spanish models, "whose lyres have rarely sung the strains of liberty" (Echeverría 1967, 81); hence he charts a different future for himself: "If, my country recuperating its splendor, I had the joy of celebrating its glories once again, I would follow a different route; for only by untrodden paths are unknown worlds discovered" (Echeverría 1967, 81)—though in so saying he relies once again on the frankly Peninsular trope of Columbus the discoverer. The political situation in the Buenos Aires is still bleaker by 1837, and the hope of celebrating the glories of Mayo more faint. To proceed, Echeverría takes the route of indirection, tracing the massive irony to which the legacy of Mayo has been submitted through the fate of one of its heroes, his Brián, who "dies in a delirium of glorious battles," as Gutiérrez remarks (J. M. Gutiérrez 1940b, 37). And if he finds the paths of such an American poetry trodden by Bello and Heredia, he submits them to the same critical irony, which is to say, in Paz's terms, he is their modern reader.

Taking his lead from his own offshore poems, where the ship at sea became a rider on horseback in the final verse of "El regreso," as I have noted, Echeverría moves the locus of his poetry of broad social ambitions to the Argentine landscape. It is the trajectory of Bello's "Alocución." But the America he encounters is no longer the robust virgin of Quintana, Bello and even Heredia. The shift to the interior situates his tale at the source of the despotic power that defeated liberty in the River Plate. Read as political allegory in which the marauding Indians substitute for *gauchos malos* (Facundo, Rosas), the plight of María, the captive, is the fate of lib-

erty in the toils of barbarism—in advance of, and as a model for
Sarmiento. Yet read alternatively as political realism, Brián and
María are among the invaders and subsequent settlers of such lands
as those conquered by Rosas in the campaign against the indigenous inhabitants of the pampas that initiated his rise to power. If
these military exploits are the heritage of Mayo, then Rosas's patriotic lineage is ratified by the poem; if the incursion is related to the
beginning of Rosas's career of violent usurpation, then Brián, as a
soldier on the frontier, is tainted. María and Brián must flee to their
death, one might surmise, because to await rescue by the army
might be to admit Rosas as their liberator, which is more irony than
Echeverría can stand.[9]

In any case, Echeverría does not specify the locale, but the effects
of this contemporary political geography are none the less visible
in the workings of the poetic imagination. His bleak landscape
empties out the cornucopia of Bello's agriculture. As a result,
observation turns from "reflecting the colors of the physical nature
that surrounds us," that he anticipated in the epilogue to *Los consuelos* (Echeverría 1967, 81), but which are largely lacking in the
impoverished setting of "La cautiva," to "the vivid picture of our
customs" (81). He rediscovers the human element wanting in Bello's natural history, though this locates his imagination in the
dream world of Heredia's nightmare history: the world of the
wounded, whose groans are covered over by the *alaridos* of the
festín.

The rhetorical question, the omnipresent strategy that mars so
much of the poetry of the age by forcing so many poems into the
strait jacket of the allocutionary form, introduces the din:

> ¿Quién es? ¿Qué insensata turba
> Con su alarido perturba,
> Las calladas soledades
> De Dios, do las tempestades
> Sólo se oyen resonar?
>
> (Echeverría 1951, 456)

> Who is it? What mad mob
> Perturbs God's hushed and barren
> Landscapes with its shrieks,
> There where only storms
> Are ever heard to sound?

Stumbling past the opening rhyme of the stanza, Echeverría's juxtaposition of the *alarido* and the *tempestades* conflates two of Heredia's principal topoi: the dreamscape of the teocalli and the
hurricane. The *bando salvaje* is, metaphorically, the storm—
"atronando/Todo el campo convecino . . . Como torbellino/Hiende
el espacio veloz" ["deafening/All the surrounding countryside . . .
like a whirlwind/Swiftly rending space"] (Echeverría 1951, 456).
Heredia, I reiterate, was at pains to keep them separate, so that the
experience of sublimity above the storm might be isolated from the
engulfing sense of defeat, sacrifice, pain and death in the two versions of the poem at Cholula. ("Niágara" consolidates the whole
cycle within a single poem: fall, then rise or sublimation of the self,
and finally fall into a premonitory death.) Echeverría's condensa-
tion, therefore, raises pointed and not merely rhetorical questions.
The contemporaneous presence of the indigenous people of the
pampa and of the war against them that is but the continuation of
the Conquest supports and extends Heredia's argument about violence in America, updated for the constitutional period. But that
very updating, with its greater realism, highlights that Heredia had
mythologized the violence for the sake of founding a poetic voice.
In Echeverría's scheme, moreover, the alarido appears to precede
the "gritos/De agonizantes víctimas" ["cries/Of victims in their
death throes"] heard in "En el teocalli de Cholula" (J. M. Heredia
1940, 2:153). There is some sleight of hand here crucial to the plot,
for Echeverría begins his poem after the raid, the capture and slay-
ing of settlers, that is after the "grito del dolor" ["cry of pain"] had
died into silence. But as a matter of poetics, the priority given to
the alarido leads Heredia's mythology of origins back into the fold
of Bello's mimeticism. The alaridos of the tribe are not a ceremo-
nial repetition of a human voice, but rather an echo, however lugubrious, of nature.

A new question supervenes to extend the trajectory of Echeverría's critical irony:

> ¿Qué humana planta orgullosa
> Se atreve a hollar el desierto
> Cuando todo en él reposa?
>
> (Echeverría 1951, 456)

> What proud human foot
> Dares tread the desert
> When all there is in repose?

The simple answer to the first question is "el bando/De salvajes" ["the band/Of savages"] (Echeverría 1951, 456). Literary history complicates matters, however. From the time of the myth of Pegasus opening the Muses' well at Hippocrene with his stamping hoof, the figure of the footprint—human or equine—has been variously a trace of the scene of writing or an *imago vocis*, but in any case a figure for poetry itself. Hence, the simple answer deflates the rhetorical question, which anticipated that only poetry—the arrival of Bello's Divine Poetry, for example—may stamp its imprint on the virgin soil of America.

That virginity is impugned by the rude intervention of the horde. María, quite concretely, must answer to the charge leveled at her by Brián, who, though himself defeated in battle and dying of his wounds, still takes the high ground and the time to reject his beloved and his savior, because he suspects her of having been dishonored, that is raped, by her captors. "María, soy infelice" ["María, I am unhappy"], he tells her, "Ya no eres digna de mí" ["You are no longer worthy of me"] (Echeverría 1951, 461). But María has defended her honor, whose sign is now her "puñal sangriento" ["bloody knife"] (461); her virginity, like that of the land, is intact, though it is the virginity that follows an immaculate conception in both cases: María a mother, and the pampa a landscape of "maravillas,/Sublimes, y al par sencillas" ["marvels,/Sublime and yet simple"] which "Sembró la fecunda mano/De Dios allí!" ["The fecund hand of God/Sowed there!"] (455). America's virginity, then, remains undefiled by the irruption of the Indian raiders in the place of poetry. Rather it is poetry itself that is reconceived by the dashing of the rhetorical question. Poetry, one might say in the terms of Echeverría's story, has failed to defend the integrity of its projectional vision.

That critique touches upon Bello and the unfulfilled optimism of his "Alocución" as read in 1837. But Heredia is set upon as well, more subtly, perhaps, but to greater effect. The metonym extending the descriptive eye along the path of advancing feet, and its embedded metaphor for writing are crucial to Heredia's poetry. The blank page of snow-capped peaks is his preferred figure for moral integrity and its loss—his father's grey hair, on the one hand, that he compares to the "nieve pura" ["pure snow"] of Popocatepetl in "A mi padre, encanecido en la fuerza de su edad" (J. M. Heredia 1940, 2.249); and on the other, his condensed retelling of the Conquest as the humbling of the mountain in "Al Popocatepetl" (see esp.

2:147–48), written at much the same time. Heredia suggests that the mountain remains undefiled in the "Fragmentos descriptivos": "¿cómo el vuelo/De las edades rápidas no imprime/Alguna huella en tu nevada frente?" ["How is it that the flight/Of the rapid ages does not imprint/Some trace upon your snowy brow?'] he asks Popocatepetl (2:152). But he knows this is not so. The ideal had been pulled down by Spanish conquest, by loyalty to Spain, by death. The text of that defeat is written in the landscape, and— Echeverría implies what Heredia would deny—that text is American poetry. If so, Echeverría's own poetry is not proof against the critique. The set of rhetorical questions closes with a return to the language of his own offshore topos: "¿Quién viene seguro puerto/ En sus yermos a buscar?" ["Who comes to its wastelands/To seek sure haven?"] (Echeverría 1951, 456). Seen now from the perspective of the barren pampa, the image of the safe haven of the port appears an egregious misconception. But the simple answer to the question is nonetheless me, I Esteban Echeverría thought it so.

The self-wounding irony of "La cautiva" is, finally, the leading characteristic of a poem as bleak as anything in Byron, from whom Echeverría surely learned much. All of María's heroism is misspent. She flees with Brián just before the nick of time in which the cavalry arrives to annihilate the captors, and her efforts are as pointless as they are fruitless. In this ironized quest, even the death of Brián does not suffice to end her misery. She must struggle on to learn at the end what she has known from the beginning, that her child, as José Hernández would reflect in the *Vuelta de Martín Fierro*, "Los indios lo degollaron" ["The Indians slit his throat"] (Echeverría 1951, 474). The prosaic announcement of the soldier halts her illusory progress. It is too late for her to produce that *grito del dolor* whose ritual repetition would be poetry. And she dies without a word.

Echeverría goes on to bury María. He marks the place with "una solitaria cruz" ["a solitary cross"] (Echeverría 1951, 476), and then he achieves her apotheosis, along with Brián, raising them as "Dos 'luces' " ["Two 'lights' "] (476). Two stars, not three, I emphasize, for Echeverría thus subjects their child to the same hallucinatory denial in the epilogue as María herself had practiced in the course of her wanderings. The result is a final celestial panorama more barren than the opening desert landscape and far more so than the beating of Bello's Huitaca into the plowshares of the moon. One might recall, by way of contrast, that Heredia's melancholic attachment to the past, however blemished by the injustices of conquest and colony, maintains the possibility of symbolic exchange as a source of poetic inspiration in the "Fragmentos descriptivos" of 1825:

> Yo os saludo,
> Fuentes de luz
> Iluminais el velo,
> Y sois del firmamento poesía!"
>
> (J. M. Heredia 1940, 2:151)

> I salute you,
> Fountains of light,
> You illuminate the veil
> And are poetry of the firmament!

Those stars were the vigilant eyes of the ancestors (his father's included, if unacknowledged) since pre-Columbian times and they invite the poet to dialogue. But in Echeverría's poem, heroine and hero are sublimated to the night sky as the "mudos habitantes . . . del páramo aerio" ["mute inhabitants . . . of the airy plain"] (Echeverría 1951, 476) foreclosing further poetry. María and Brián leave no living heir to recite commemorative verse: no elegist-historian. And yet their apparent dead end institutionalizes poetic melancholia in the River Plate. It becomes the point of all returns, especially Hernández's *Vuelta*, when Fierro reinters Cruz, but leaves the *cautiva's* child unburied.[10]

One nation's dead end may be another nation's path to poetry. Echeverría's poetic silence becomes the antimetaphor of Fierro kissing the ground beneath the *ombú*, while in contemporaneous Puerto Rico, the same return is told explicitly as the genesis of literature by José G. Padilla (1829–96). He introduces his lyric of national identity, "A Puerto-Rico" with a prefatory autobiography in a verse "Dedicatoria" under the title of "Las dos madres." There he tells the tale of the formation of the poet, though at the distance of a third-person narration. As a child the "dos apuestas matronas" ["two elegant matrons"] (Monge, Sama, Quiñones 1879, 223) led him by the hand to his point of departure:

> De aquella loma en la cumbre,
> Bajo un ceibo secular,
> Álzase rústico altar,
> Do brilla perpetua lumbre
>
> (Monge, Sama, Quiñones 1879, 223)

From the crest of that hill,
Beneath a ceiba ages old,
Is raised an altar rude,
Where an eternal flame burns still

Tropical botany substitutes *ceiba* for *ombú*, but the scene is the
same: a border marked off as a sacred space. There the twin tutelary
figures bear witness to an oath:

> Luego, sobre un Crucifijo
> Puso la mano el garzon,
> y con sentida emocion
> Así á las ancianas dijo:
> "La vida debo á las dos,
> TODO á entrambas pertenezco,
> Y TODO á entrambas me ofrezco
> Aquí, delante de Dios:
> Amaros es mi deber,
> Pues en ambas la fortuna
> Me dió Madre de la cuna
> Y Madre me dió del sér,
> Y haya goces ó dolores
> En mis destinos futuros,
> Yo siempre guardaré puros
> Vuestros dos grandes amores.
> Con ellos y con mi fé
> Ilustre, quizá, mi nombre,
> Y entonces, ¡Madres!, ya hombre,
> A vosotros volveré.
> (Monge, Sama, Quiñones 1879, 224)

> The youth then placed his hand
> Upon a Crucifix, and
> Feeling deeply moved,
> He told the aged dames:
> I owe life to you both,
> I am yours ALL in ALL,
> And ALL I offer both of you,
> Here, standing before God:
> My duty is to love you both,
> For fortune in both of you
> Gave me a Mother from the cradle
> And Mother of my being, gave me, too.
> And be there pains or pleasures

> In my future destinies,
> I will always preserve pure
> Your two great loves.
>   With them and with my faith,
> My name, perhaps, well-known,
> And then, Mothers! become a man,
> To you I'll come back home.

With that final future tense the youth announces his departure in the present. Like the young Bolívar before Simón Rodríguez in Rome, therefore, the oath will initiate an independence movement.

Before the youth leaves his mothers, he gives a token that he will repay the larger debt of life by first repaying the smaller debt of a kiss, or two:

> Así el niño se expresó
> Y con amoroso exceso,
> Pagó á las Madres su beso
> Con otro, que á entrambas dió
>
> (Monge, Sama, Quiñones 1879, 224)

> Thus the boy expressed himself
> And with amorous excess,
> He repaid the Mothers' kiss
> With another he gave them both.

The multiplication and division make for hard arithmetic here, to be resolved by simplifying the redoubling of the mothers as a substitution for an absent father. Had he too run away from native rusticity to seek his fortune? Or, as I suspect, is the crucifix upon which the oath is sworn a cross to mark a grave site in which the father lies buried?

The text breaks off, the years go by and a second section of the "Dedicatoria" narrates the appearance on the spot of a "viajero/ Un libro en la mano" ["a traveler/Book in hand"] (Monge, Sama, Quiñones 1879, 224):

> Delante el altar se pára
> Y descubriendo la frente,
> Con ademan reverente
> El libro puso en el ara
>
> (Monge, Sama, Quiñones 1879, 225)

> Before the altar he stands
> And uncovering his head,
> With reverent gesture
> He placed the book on the altar.

What he reveals, of course, is that he is the same boy become a man, that he has returned from his expedition, and that he is prepared to draw up accounts:

> "¡Oh Madres! . . . ¡Miradme aquí!
> Ante vuestro altar estoy,
> Que vengo á cumpliros HOY
> Lo que AYER os prometí:
>   Entre azares y dolores,
> Por caminos inseguros,
> IIe guardado SIEMPRE puros
> Vuestros dos grandes amores:
>   Con ellos traigo un cantar,
> Fruto de tiempo y trabajo . . . ,
> Deuda que el niño contrajo
> Y el hombre viene á pagar
>
> (Monge, Sama, Quiñones 1879, 225)

> Oh Mothers! . . . See me here!
> I am before your altar,
> For I come to fulfill TODAY
> What I promised YESTERDAY:
>   Amidst chance and pain,
> Along uncertain roads,
> I've ALWAYS preserved pure
> Your two great loves.
>   With these I bring a song,
> Fruit of time and labor . . . ,
> The debt that the boy contracted
> And the man comes to repay.

He has not gone to town like Lizardi's Payo or the gauchos of Hidalgo and del Campo, that is for the sake of *ocio*, which was rather his lot as a rustic youth. Instead, reversing Bello's course, he cast off his native rusticity to undertake the work of literature. His poetic labors have taught him to analyze his juvenile "TODO . . . TODO" as a historical sequence, embodied, furthermore, by the mothers, one of whom still lives ("HOY") while the other has died in his absence ("AYER")—though they remain bound together ("SIEMPRE") by his book: "Es página que en concierto/A las dos, Madres, escribe" ["It is a page that in concert/With the two of you, Mothers, he writes"] (Monge, Sama, Quiñones 1879, 225).

For Padilla, then, the internal circulation of literature in the print culture has led to a resurgent figuration: the silent kiss of his first youth finds a voice by becoming a book, as the narrator indicates when he joins his poet-hero by repeating verses—but with an eye and an ear toward the differences interposed by historical experience:

> Tomádlo, ¡oh Madres! las dos:
> Es mi canto á Puerto-Rico,
> Y yo á entrambas lo dedico
> AQUÍ, delante de Dios."
>   Así el hombre se expresó
> Bajo el ceibo secular,
> Y sobre el rústico altar
> Ved el libro que dejó
>   (Monge, Sama, Quiñones 1879, 225)

> Take it, oh Mothers, you two:
> It is my song to Puerto Rico,
> And I dedicate it to both of you,
> HERE, standing before God.
>   Thus the man expressed himself,
> Beneath the ceiba ages old
> And on the altar rude,
> See the book he left behind.

And having constituted the self as the author of the book, the book itself, thus dedicated, may now speak of and for the nation as its embodiment in verse.

3

The triumph of poetry as the archive of national history is short-lived. Echeverría once again presents an exemplary case. He went on to write a substantial body of verse during the years of his subsequent exile in Montevideo, but he finds his way around the closing silence of "La cautiva" in a turn to prose, a modal shift that bespeaks a major alteration in the literature of the nineteenth-century print culture. For if "La cautiva" may be read as a social program, civilization versus barbarism before *Facundo*, then Echeverría's social program, the "Dogma socialista," may be read conversely as a formal constitution for an American poetics. The chapter dedicated to the "Emancipación del espíritu americano" ["Emancipation of the American spirit"] (Echeverría 1940, 193–97) has long been considered in just that regard. Zum Felde may once again be cited for a characteristic assessment, when he declares the "Dogma" "a form of definition of American consciousness . . . since prior [to the 'Dogma'] it exists only empirically as a spontaneous impulse" (Zum Felde 1954, 92). "In the social emancipation of the homeland is bound its liberty," declares Echeverrería (Echeverría 1940, 194), an Enlightenment position reminiscent of Kant, but also of Lizardi who claimed, it will be recalled, that originality was the sign of liberty. But I would venture that Echeverría's originality with regard to an American poetics resides elsewhere in the "Dogma" than in his emancipation proclamation. I look rather to his formulation of the "law of progress" (159). Given priority over the old revolutionary language of "Fraternity. Equality. Liberty," the *palabras simbólicas* of chapter three of the "Dogma socialista," Echeverría interposes "Progress" in chapter two. Only "Association" is more primordial in this exposition, and even so, progress appears there as human association's final cause.[11]

In a retrospective consideration of the "Dogma" written to introduce the edition of 1846, Echeverría lucidly elaborates the context in which "Progreso" is to be read as a *palabra símbolica*:

> It is quite some time that we, like everyone, are out in search of an illuminating socialist criterion, and as long as no one else offers that revelation, we must be permitted to take for a guide that which we have glimpsed, and to state our thought out loud.
>
> From the beginning of the revolution, all of the parties have shouted, and they have made war in the name of liberty; Rosas, Oribe, and many of their antagonists, all cry out liberty; but, what is liberty? *I* am liberty, they will answer. Each one calls liberty, said Montesquieu, the government most in keeping with his own inclinations.
>
> We are saying since the year of '37—*May, Progress, Democracy*, and we explain that formula. (Echeverría 1940, 146)

In the years separating the revolution of May of 1810 from the Asociación de mayo of 1837, the trope of liberty had been so adulterated as to lose imaginative power. The "Dogma socialista" rings the death knell of liberty as the constitutional trope of American poetry and reconstitutes the poetic dialogue around the trope of progress. Old tropes, like old styles may persist, but a new course is thus charted. It will carry through the positivism of the later nineteenth century (i.e. that which ushers in modernity according to Paz) and into twentieth-century discussion of development and underdevelopment in the American corner of the Third World.

Facundo is the great text of the trope of progress in the River Plate and all of Spanish America near midcentury. It has been studied often and well, and continues to attract valuable critical attention.[12] I will simply note, then, that Facundo also marks the definitive ascendancy of prose over poetry in Spanish America in the nineteenth century and ever since. In the context of that changing balance, though setting Facundo aside, I would pause for another moment over Echeverría's circle in the River Plate to consider the enunciation of the new trope. For it was the Asociación de mayo, of which Echeverría was the guiding light, that gives the trope of progress and the vehicle of prose an institutionalized setting. Concretely, the setting was the private library of a bookseller, Marcos Sastre (Uruguay 1808–87), who hoped to foment intellectual life (and increase sales?) among the young dissidents of the Rosas regime in Buenos Aires by making a suitable collection of books available for internal circulation among members and a space available for their meetings (see Echeverría 1940). Literature as a social institution presents itself here as a private enterprise whose business it was to establish a network of internal traffic between River Plate writers themselves, as well as to maintain the lanes of communication with an international commerce of letters.

Sastre addressed the inaugural session of the Salón literario to situate his project in relation to a broader vision of progress. "The great South American Society must hasten to proclaim the great principle of the peaceful progress of civilization, which is the soul of perfectibility," he declared (Sastre 1940, 235), and "the good road, the direct route" (236) to that end, he proposes, leads through a literary association that will educate its members to avoid three cardinal sins:

Error of political plagiarism:
Error of scientific plagiarism:
Error of literary plagiarism.

(Sastre 1940, 232)

The typography represents what the Sacristán might have called his "rasgos poéticos." Sastre's thoroughly Enlightenment position, moreover, recalls the will to originality expressed at the outset of the constitutional period by Lizardi. It is echoed in the accompanying speeches of Juan Bautista Alberdi (Argentina 1810–84) and Gutiérrez on the same occasion.

Alberdi specifies that the notion of universal progress that Sastre inherits from Saint Simon is subject to local variation: "This individual mode of progress constitutes the civilization of every people; every people, then, has and must have its own civilization; it ought to find it in the combination of the universal law of human development and its conditions in time and space" (Alberdi 1940, 246). The combination, he then argues, is the basis for distinct routes to progress. What is universal may be learned from Europe "which does not cease to progress": "[Europe] today has new ideas that our predecessors could not have known, and that we today are called upon to import into our country" (249). Elements related to national and natural history, on the contrary, "need not be consulted with anyone, except with our reason and our own observation" (248–49). Alberdi sums up the forking paths of letters, then, as follows: "Thus our spirits want a double direction, foreign and national, for the study of the two elements of every civilization: the human, philosophical, absolute element; and the national, positive, relative element" (249). The closing words of that passage anticipate the expansion of the trope of progress in the later nineteenth century.

For Gutiérrez, speaking self-consciously as "a new man" (J. M. Gutiérrez 1940a, 251), as though in fulfillment of the *Filantrópico*'s wish, Alberdi's divergence between universe and nation in the course of progress leads to a dichotomy between science and literature. Gutiérrez divides Sastre's conception of the role of letters into constituent disciplines. "Science," he states, "is a cosmopolitan matron, who acclimates herself in all zones, and nourishes herself with the fruits of every clime. Literature is a tree that degenerates when it is transplanted; it is like an inhabitant of the mountains, who goes off and is nullified far from his native land" (252). The matron is respectable, and in that sense mitigates against the image of a despotic and decrepit Europe presented in Bello's "Alocución." With regard to science, that is, "cultured Europe" (258) is a valuable and necessary resource, much as Alberdi saw it with regard to philosophy (including natural philosophy, one may suppose) and all that refers to the universal and "absolute." Yet in Gutiérrez's matron there is also a faint echo of Bello's traveling or transplanted virgin, and thus a hint that Divine Poetry of the "Alocución" was actually a figure for science and not poetry all along. If so, I share Gutiérrez's view. In any case, the self-designation of "new man" is a generational distinction for Gutiérrez, and from the perspective of youth, the "matrona" appears unenticing, already spoken for, by no means a correspondingly "new woman." His preference is for literature, understood narrowly, along the lines of the modern institution (see Godzich and Spadaccini 1987). And still more narrowly, his literary preference is romantic. I would underline that literature is "a tree," singular and isolated like Echeverría's ombú, or, say, Wordsworth's figure in "The Thorn." This depiction of literature as rooted to its locale would appear to link it to the past, as the ombú (or the thorn, "erect, and like a stone," Wordsworth 1904, 75) attests: a grave marker in dialogue with the Indians, that is with the most traditional society of the River Plate, the most resistant to the opening of lanes of communication. But in this crucial sense, literature rejoins science for Gutiérrez, for the value of poetry in his account is its function as the motor of progress:

> Above the reality of things, in the purest atmosphere of the social region, a genius that never leaves peoples unsheltered moves its wings; showing to man the nothingness of his works, it impels him always onward, and indicating to him in the distance beautiful utopias, imaginary republics, joy and happiness to come, it infuses in his breast the valor necessary to set out on the road toward them, and the hope of reaching them. This genius is *poetry*. (J. M. Gutiérrez 1940a, 259)

Poetry, in sum, enunciates a utopian vision, and thereby recaptures its public stature. But not just any poetry.

Gutiérrez offers his own selection of commendable authors: Chateaubriand, Byron, Lamartine, Schiller, Manzoni (J. M. Gutiérrez 1940a, 256, 259). All modern, all foreign. Their richness highlights a dearth in the local literary economy. Gutiérrez illustrates with a brief parable of reading: "Have you not experienced, gentlemen, on your solitary walks—in those hours in which the soul, remembering its destiny, wishes to rise up from the earth, and to breathe the air of a better world—have you not experienced the need of a book written in the language that you have spoken since the cradle?" (256). The impasse in the progress of local letters thus posed, the solution would appear to lie in the development of the isolated self in the experience of sublimity. The echo of Rousseau's solitary *promeneur* provides the literary historical base. In the absence of books that can speak to Spanish American writers with the needed intimacy to awaken the imagination, the yo might read nature, or more properly, might read itself into nature. That path leads to Heredia's experience of the hurricane, "to rise up from the earth, and to breathe the air of a better world." Even with that American model at hand, however, Gutiérrez answers his own question otherwise: "Yes, without doubt you have experienced such a need, without being able to satisfy it with a single production from ancient or modern Spanish literature" (256).

A frontal assault on the Peninsular literary tradition follows, and a call for the emancipation of American arts and letters, "as we knew how to do in politics, when we proclaimed ourselves free" (J. M. Gutiérrez 1940a, 257), redirecting the progress of poetry away from the experience of the self to that of the nation. The beloved sons of Mayo move the field of battle to Sastre's bookshop, whence they take aim at "the Spanish classics" (257), while Rosas patrols the streets outside their door. The project of intellectual emancipation from Spain gains legitimacy by its claim to the heritage of Mayo. Viewed in the most favorable light, that same legitimacy would raise an indirect challenge to the authority of Rosas, who would appear in contrast as an illegitimate son of Mayo. Nevertheless, one might also say that the dissidents encircled in the bookstore are so many deluded Quixotes.

The murder of the constitutional project by Rosas preceded the sally against the windmill of Peninsular letters. The writers of the Salón literario would be obliged to confront that reality in the end, when they found themselves imprisoned and exiled. But for the moment, convened by Marcos Sastre in 1836, they could still speak hopefully of their battle on two fronts. Against Spain and the attachment to the language of the cradle, Gutiérrez recommends instruction in foreign languages and letters. "We remain as yet bound by the strong and close link of the language. But this will weaken day by day insofar as we may go on entering into the intel-

lectual movement of the advanced nations of Europe" (J. M. Gutiérrez 1940a, 257). Balanced against this European orientation,
Gutiérrez also propounds a local solution. "Let us try to give ourselves an education analogous to and in harmony with our people
and our things"; Gutiérrez declares, "and if we are to have a literature, let us make it *national*; that it may represent our customs and
our nature, just as our lakes and wide rivers reflect only the stars of
our hemisphere in their waters" (258). As a political position, the
emphasis on us and ours, on union, partakes of the effort to circum-
scribe the yo, whose unlimited growth had eviscerated the trope of
liberty.[13] The rights of the individual were not abjured, but the role
of the individual was to be delimited by the needs of *association*:
"It is necessary to work to the end that all individual energies, far
from isolating themselves and concentrating themselves in their
own egotism, concur simultaneously and collectively in a single
purpose—the progress and betterment of the nation" (Echeverría
1940, 157, see also 148, 149, 162 et al.). Echeverría writes from the
political experience of an Argentine reign of terror—"The predominance of individuality has ruined us," he added to the preceding
remark (Echeverría 1940, 157). As regards poetics, the principal
impact touches upon the self of the solitary promenade and all the
more so on the reconcentrated imagination that declares "el huracán y yo solos estamos" ["the hurricane and I, we are alone"]. In
this light one may read the geographical criteria (rivers and lakes
and stars above) and the implicit poetics of mimetic reflection in
Gutiérrez's educational imperative as a vote for Bello over Heredia.
The progress of poetry, ultimately Bello's trope, has therefore led
the reconstituted project for an American literary identity back to
its roots in the early constitutional period. All national poetry will
be a progress piece, but that would mean, as in Bello's own case, a
poetry moored in a form and committed to an outlook that modern
European poetry had left behind.

4

Progress as a trope for liberty led the River Plate poetry of
Echeverría's circle toward national expression at the expense of the
self. The task of reincorporating the trope of progress into a problematics of the self fell particularly to one poet in a decidedly different milieu, beginning in the same year of 1836: Gertrudis Gómez

de Avellaneda (1814–73). Echeverría was already a modern poet in
Paz's sense. "La cautiva" is an ironic poem, providing a critical
response to the constituting of America in both politics and poetry
from the disenchanted point of view of Buenos Aires under Rosas.
Gómez de Avellaneda is not primarily an ironic poet, and she is
more appreciative than critical of Hispanic poetry on both sides of
the ocean; but she is modern, the first great, unequivocally modern
poet in Spanish American letters in the terms that have formed the
basis of my own argument. Born in Cuba to a criolla mother and
Spanish father, she migrated with her family to Spain as a youth,
and hence it was her personal lot to experience America itself as
the object of loss, to maintain a melancholic attachment to the ghost
of her past and the language of her cradle, and finally to consign
America to history through the elegiac work of mourning. Gómez
de Avellaneda's poetry is a compendium of American tropes from
a century and a half of literary history, a rewriting of the routes of
modernity as she works her way, fitfully, tragically, to a historical
consciousness of her American identity as a woman and as a poet.

Gómez de Avellaneda earned an outstanding critical reputation in
her own lifetime in the Spain of the aged Quintana and of the repa-
triated poets of the Spanish romantic movement. Her reputation
seems to have remained intact thereafter, although her lyric poetry
as well as her work in drama was relegated to the stack of honorably
mentioned but unread texts through much of the twentieth century.
As was the case for Echeverría, whose short story, "El matadero,"
was virtually the only survivor on the reading list of his extensive
oeuvre, critical attention to Gómez de Avellaneda shifted toward
her novel *Sab* (1841).[14] The mid-nineteenth-century triumph of
prose in the emerging print culture of Spanish America receives
further confirmation in the subsequent lapse of their poetry. Feminist criticism is largely responsible for the rescue of Gómez de
Avellaneda's lyric, and it is in that vein that a brilliant poet met with
a brilliant critic in Susan Kirkpatrick's *Las Románticas, Women
Writers and Subjectivity in Spain, 1835–1850* (1989).[15] In general,
I have framed my discussions of eighteenth- and nineteenth-century
poetry by reference to contemporaneous prose contexts, due to the
relatively limited attention of later criticism. But as my argument
reaches its endpoint, here the exception: at present, and no doubt
for some time to come, discussion of Gómez de Avellaneda's
poetry must begin with Kirkpatrick.

I will not rehearse the whole of Kirkpatrick's penetrating explication of romantic subjectivity in general and its expression in Spain, but rather turn to her chapter devoted to Gómez de Avellaneda's poetry. Concentrating on Gómez de Avellaneda's reaction to the social and literary historical delimitation of gender, Kirkpatrick demonstrates a tension, visible already in Gómez de Avellaneda's earliest extant poem,

> and restaged in some form or another in succeeding poems: on the one hand, the poet adheres to the social and literary codes of gender differ-ence; on the other, she attempts to break free of the constraints inherent in these codes. The effect of the contradictory impulses embodied in the process of producing these texts frequently shows up as a division of the speaking subject, a splitting of the self into heterogeneous parts. (Kirkpatrick 1989, 177)

The split is especially evident in what is probably Gómez de Avel-laneda's most familiar poem, "Amor y orgullo," where it is mani-fest structurally as a division between a first-person narrative voice and the embedded lyric of another woman, María, herself split, as the title indicates, between love and pride.

"Pride" is Gómez de Avellaneda's figure for the abuse of liberty that Echeverría called "egoismo." [16] When she reflects on her period of pride, María presents herself as tyrannical, much as Echeverría might have imagined ("Egotism incarnate are all tyrants." Echeverría 1940, 162):

> "Mas yo, altanera, con orgullo vano,
> Cual águila real al vil gusano,
>   Contemplaba a los hombres."
>   (Gómez de Avellaneda 1974, 267)

> "But I, arrogant, with vain pride,
> Like the golden eagle the vile worm,
>   I contemplated men."

Yet the experience of liberty and of love is distinct for women, as Echeverría himself explored through his female characters in "La ida," *Elvira* and "La cautiva." Where personal liberty is annulled by social restrictions, "love" becomes a figure of self-destruction, which, as Kirkpatrick points out, is represented in Gómez de Avel-laneda's poem as captivity (Kirkpatrick 1989, 193).

With respect to "Amor y orgullo," Kirkpatrick concludes, "The poem that presents María's plight, then, turns the romantic construction of the sovereign self inside out, representing desire, as experienced by the female subject, not as the driving power of imperious consciousness but as an internally divisive, destabilizing force" (Kirkpatrick 1989, 194). That force may be generalized. The split between love and pride is tantamount to the difference between submission and independence for the woman in the poem; but for the writer in the woman, the split is that between the self-destruction and self-defense of her voice. When "su antigua arrogancia/ Perdió el corazón" ["her former arrogance/Lost heart"], as Gómez de Avellaneda laments in the late poem, "El último acento de mi arpa" (Gómez de Avellaneda 1974, 320), her voice falls silent within the poem, and the book closes on her second collection of poetry. The anxieties of sustaining her own voice that form a constant and complex theme in Gómez de Avellaneda's verse link her poetry to a pervasive issue in women's writing in the nineteenth century (see the fundamental study of Gilbert and Gubar 1979).

Kirkpatrick proceeds to a closely allied demonstration in the context of Peninsular Spanish romanticism when she contrasts the characteristic split in the female speaking subject in Gómez de Avellaneda's "A él" to the predominant male paradigm manifest in Espronceda's "Canto a Teresa" from El diablo mundo (1840–41). "Again in this poem," Kirkpatrick writes, "a feminized desire leads not, as in Espronceda, to disappointment or frustration but to annihilation" (Kirkpatrick 1989, 200). She goes on to an insightful elucidation in which she demonstrates the process in which the poetic self is constituted for Gómez de Avellaneda: "in 'A él,' the subject initially creates a mental image of the object of desire and then invests it with an autonomous power capable of turning against the self that generated it" (200). She then notes a "final step" in "A él," namely, "to equate the self with objects that represent lack of control" (200). Kirkpatrick concludes her discussion of the poem by observing that "The wind-blown leaf," one such object in the poem, "is a predominant metaphor for the self in Gómez de Avellaneda's poetry" (201), which carries her back to the poet's starting point and her own: the analogous image of the ship driven by the wind from the poet's native land in the sonnet "Al partir," where the split was first manifest as the distance between Cuba and Spain.

Kirkpatrick is aware of that political geography, of course. "One fault line [of the split self] concerns national identity," she writes; "In an era when Cuba was still part of the Spanish empire, Gómez

de Avellaneda could—and did—consider herself both Cuban and
Spanish . . . but strong political tensions between metropolis and
colony troubled the issue of national identity" (Kirkpatrick 1989,
177–78). She sets the problems of national identity aside, however,
in order to dedicate her analysis to that other, crucial fault line of
gender identity, which she pursues, as she indicates from the very
title of her book, in the context of Spain. As a result, when Kirkpatrick delineates the split in "Al partir" between "an irretrievable
past, a childhood concretely and materially associated with the
unspoiled nature of the New World, and the present, lonely exile in
the European centers of civilization" (178), she invokes a trope for
America no less conventional and distorted than the tropes for feminine identity and desire against which both she and Gómez de
Avellaneda struggle.

The image of "unspoiled nature" in a peripheral America as
opposed to "European centers" is qualified, for instance, by the
debate over railroads that occupied the Cuba of Avellaneda's childhood (i. e. beginning in 1830). A royal order opened the way to the
British financial interests in 1834, while Avellaneda was still on the
island; and the first trains would depart only shortly after her boat
for the metropolis. The first line was inaugurated on 19 November
1837, over the route once surveyed by the Mopox expedition for
the proposed canal de Guines, which is to say prior to the building
of the first railroads in Spain. Nor is it industrialization and the concomitant exploitation of the Cuban landscape alone that urge a reas-
sessment of the figure of America as the virgin land. As Gómez de
Avellaneda's contemporaries did not fail to note in regard to the
same commonplace, "the beauties that nature has so prodigally lav-
ished on this Eden of the Gulf" were in fact spoiled by "the social
and political aspects of life," in the words of Maturin M. Ballou
(Ballou 1854, 215), though he was troubled more by the despotism
of the colonial regime than by its continuance of slavery: "In the
clime of sun and endless summer we are in the land of starless political darkness" (216).

It is Gómez de Avellaneda of course and not Kirkpatrick who
names Cuba "edén querido" ["beloved Eden"] (Gómez de Avellaneda 1974, 237). Indeed the poet repeats the trope (as well as the
opening verse of "Al partir") upon her return some two decades
later, when she characterizes Cuba as the "Tranquilo edén de mi
infancia" ["Tranquil Eden of my childhood"] (340). But in shifting
the focus from the Spanish to the Cuban context of Gómez de Ave-

llaneda's formation, the concrete and material distance between trope and reality illuminates the landscape of her imagination and the split in her subjectivity. Thus, recalling the reality of Cuba in the years of Gómez de Avellaneda's childhood, one may educe a different parable of the paradisal garden from the autobiographical memoir of Juan Francisco Manzano (1797–1854), the slave whose poetry won the attention of the critic Domingo Delmonte (1804–53), who collected money within his literary circle to purchase Manzano's manumission in 1834. Manzano recounts:

> one afternoon we went out to the garden for a long time helping my Mistress pick flowers or transplant a few plants to pass the time while the gardener went about the whole garden doing his duties when we were retiring without paying attention to what I was doing I picked a little petal, that's all a little petal of a donatus geranium this extremely sweet-smelling malva was there in my hand but I didn't know what I was carrying distracted with my verses in my head I was following my Señora at a distance of two or three steps and I was so unaware of myself that I went on tearing the petal to bits which ended up making a greater fragrance when we entered the hall she stepped back I don't know for what reason, I stepped aside but as she passed in front of me the odor caught her attention furious instantly with a loud and angry voice she asked me what have you got in your hands: I was dead my body froze suddenly and with barely the strength to hold myself up from the trembling in both my legs, I let the portion of little pieces fall to the ground. (Manzano 1970, 51)[17]

In a paradise without pencils Manzano engages in poetic invention as a bodily transaction. The picking of the flower and the transfer of its aroma to his hands in a rubbing that is a metaphor for writing run parallel to his preoccupation with his verses. But in this Eden, the poet is a slave, and so this and all flowers are as the forbidden fruit. His fear of punishment is by no means hyperbolic. The scent of unspoiled nature may be the essence of poetry, but the result for the slave is corporeal punishment: "they busted my nose" (Manzano 1970, 52). Read against the backdrop of this Cuban parable for the process and the price of poetic incarnation, I would then note that Gómez de Avellaneda, too, consistently presents her allegories of writing as the bodily transaction of erotic relations, and that in Cuba, the "autonomous power" that threatens her annihilation as a woman and a poet, was, as Manzano knew, more than a metaphor.

Gómez de Avellaneda, the author of the abolitionist novel *Sab*, was aware of this context, as is Kirkpatrick in the chapter that she dedicates to "Feminizing the Romantic Subject in Narrative" (Kirkpatrick 1989, 133–73). There, Kirkpatrick observes the conflation of "slavery and racism" with "marriage and the subjection of women" (151) in Gómez de Avellaneda's adoption of the "perspective of a marginalized subject" (147). The process is not unambiguous, she notes, since "Gómez de Avellaneda also colonized the mulatto slave's subjectivity to suit her own purpose" (158), but she concludes that the obliquity with which a feminist argument presents itself as an antislavery novel "reveals the power of the social injunction against any female subjectivity that remained unsubordinated to love" (158). It is, once again, a thoroughly convincing argument. But I would add to the superimposed subjects of the woman and the slave in *Sab*, the situation of Cuba itself, subjugated, marginalized and exploited in the reduced colonial empire that survived the wars of independence elsewhere in Spanish America. This situation, concretely and materially, politically and economically, represents the extreme form of the American identity problematized by Echeverría's circle in the contemporaneous River Plate in the call for emancipation from the cultural hegemony of Peninsular Spain. And I would read Gómez de Avellaneda's poetry as a participant in that *era americana*, in Lezama's terms, her "Al partir," for instance, a counterpoint to Echeverría's offshore topos. There is less certainty that Gómez de Avellaneda knew *Los consuelos* or "La cautiva" in her adolescence in Cuba than that she avidly read and staunchly resisted the attractions of Espronceda's poetry during her maturity in Spain. I do not debate here the question of access—Manzano's autobiography also remained unpublished during Gómez de Avellaneda's lifetime—but rather underline her engagement in the dialogue that constituted American poetry as it entered modernity.

In this light, I would return to "A él" as a myth of poetic origins, masked as erotic fantasy and projected backward as a moment logically anterior to "Al partir." It is the time of Gómez de Avellaneda's "juventud florida" ["blossoming youth"] (Gómez de Avellaneda 1974, 253), and a place, in contrast to the idealizations of her poem "En el album de una señorita cubana" ("Allá . . . No se albergan crudas fieras,/Ni viles sierpes se arrastran" ["There . . . neither rude beasts find a home/Nor vile serpents crawl"] 289), in which the garden had its serpent:

Mas ¡ay!, yo en mi patria conozco serpiente
Que ejerce en las aves terrible poder . . .
Las mira, les lanza su soplo atrayente
 Y al punto en sus fauces las hace caer.
(Gómez de Avellaneda 1974, 254)

But, oh! In my homeland I know a snake
That holds such a fatal power over the birds . . .
It looks at them, breathes its seductive breath
 And instantly they tumble down its throat.

Listening to the echo of the trope of Eden, it is possible to surmise that the onset of poetry was also the sin of Eve, eating from the tree of knowledge, and that "Al partir" is the course of Gómez de Avellaneda's consequent fall.

This echo is all the more evident when it is transcribed into the Greco-Latin mythology of Gómez de Avellaneda's late fragment, "El deposorio en sueño." There she presents the rapture of the maiden by the "ser ideal" ["ideal being"] ("A él," Gómez de Avellaneda 1974, 253) through the story of Cupid and Psyche. It is an important poem in which Gómez de Avellaneda recuperates and revises much of her own most successful work. She adopts a structure reminiscent of "Amor y orgullo," and attempts to gain control of her theme of insomnia, a frequent trope for her anxious struggle to sustain a poetic consciousness, by transforming it into the more propitious state of *duermivela*—"*Amla* aún no duerme; más tampoco vela,/Que en éxtasis dulcísimo cayó" ["*Amla* is not yet asleep; nor is she quite awake/But she has fallen into sweetest ecstasy"] (313). The god appears to her in that state and speaks in an embedded lyric in which he declares his union to the lyric self—"¡Ya tuyo soy!" ["I am already yours"]—while guarding his mystery: "Mas nunca ¡oh Amla!, con mortales ojos/Quieras mirarme" ["But never, oh Amla! with mortal eyes/Attempt to look upon me"] (314). The fragment breaks off before Avellaneda is obliged to acknowledge Alma-Psyche's irrepressible curiosity. But reading back to Cupid's earlier apparition as the "ignoto señor" ["unknown lord"] of "A él," the central enigma that will drive Amla finds a clear expression:[18]

¡Oh, alma! Di: ¿quién era aquel
Fantasma amado y sin nombre? . . .
¿Un genio? ¿Un ángel? ¿Un hombre?

¡Ah! Lo sabes! Era *él*;
Que su poder no te asombre.

(Gómez de Avellaneda 1974, 253)

Oh soul! Say, who was that
Phantom, beloved and unnamed?
A spirit? An angel? A man?
Ah! You know! It was *he*;
Be not astonished by his power.

Kirkpatrick's Espronceda is a pertinent response to those questions, but only in the present tense of Gómez de Avellaneda's Spanish milieu—"*es* él" (Gómez de Avellaneda 1974, 253; emphasis added)—real, influential and illuminating by contrast; but derivative, recognizable only as the embodiment of a prior phantasm, himself a second él in Gómez de Avellaneda's literary formation. The first él appeared in the Cuban landscape. And it was in that mythologized space that Gómez de Avellaneda rediscovered her subject, the subject of "Al partir," from her present vantage point in Spain—a subject split and split again, like the structure of "Amor y orgullo". On the one hand, I refer to the subject that is the self, her split subjectivity. On the other, I mean the subject that is her *suzjet*, her abiding story, itself split between her love for her abandoned homeland and her erotic relations with love objects that are always a reincarnation. It is to the Cuban context that I would repair, therefore, to rediscover, as well, the identity of Gómez de Avellaneda's inspiration at its source.

The poem ends in despair, its questions transformed into the defeat of questioning and the consequent metapoetic disarray of Gómez de Avellaneda's loose leaves:

A la hoja que el viento potente arrebata,
¿De qué le sirviera su rumbo inquirir? . . .
Ya la alce a las nubes, ya al cieno la abata,
Volando, volando, le habrá de seguir.

(Gómez de Avellaneda 1974, 254)

For the leaf driven by the potent wind,
What would it serve to question the direction? . . .
Now raised up to the clouds, now sunk into the mud,
Flying, flying, it cannot choose but to go on.

Nevertheless, Kirkpatrick's meticulous research provides the means
to an answer, a name. She quotes the analogous passage from the
1841 edition of Gómez de Avellaneda's *Poesías*:

> ¿Dónde van, dónde, esas nubes
> Por el viento compelidas?
> ¿Dónde esas hojas perdidas
> Que del árbol arrancó?
>
> ¡Vuelan, vuelan resignadas,
> Y no saben donde van,
> Pero siguen el camino
> Que les traza el huracán!
>
> (Kirkpatrick 1989, 200)
>
> Where do they go, oh where, those clouds
> Compelled on by the wind?
> Where those lost leaves
> That it tore from the tree?
>
> They fly, they fly resigned,
> And know not where they go,
> But follow still the road
> Traced for them by the hurricane!

Verging on elegy for the lyric self born *en route* in "Al partir," she
has voice enough to trace that route back to the hurricane, to trace
her roots to Heredia.

Contra Kirkpatrick, then, I would assert that there is no "exact
correspondence" (Kirkpatrick 1989, 199) between the two figures
of the beloved in "A él." Kirkpatrick suggests that the attractions
of Espronceda's poetics for Gómez de Avellaneda, struggling with
the split in her subjectivity, was the integrity of his lyric self,
defined by its undeviating desire for transcendence. Gómez de
Avellaneda's experience as a woman led her to resist that attraction,
Kirkpatrick demonstrates. But the path of her resistance was the
split itself, and her model was the poetry of Heredia. For Heredia's
lyric subjectivity was itself already split—the scene of the split
being Cholula—first obliterated in sleep, and then repeated in the
dream of the antimetaphor of human sacrifice. This scene, with all
of its conflict and ambivalence concerning Heredia's identity as an
American-born son of a colonial magistrate, is ultimately the American ground of Gómez de Avellaneda's poetry.

In "A él" Gómez de Avellaneda engages the less complex version of self-sacrifice presented by Heredia in his "Himno del desterrado." Heredia is in fact closer to the surface of "A él" in the geography of the split than anywhere else in her poetry. Passing onboard ship within sight of a local landmark—" '¡Tierra!' claman . . . /Le conozco . . . /Es el Pan" ["Land! They cry out . . . /I know it . . . /It is Pan"] (Heredia 1940, 2:74)—between his exile in New York and his exile in Mexico, Heredia foresees the island's liberation from colonial oppression:

> Aunque viles traidores le sirvan,
> Del tirano es inútil la saña,
> Que no en vano entre Cuba y España
> Tiende inmenso sus olas el mar.
>
> (J. M. Heredia 1940, 2:76)

> Although vile traitors may do his bidding,
> The tyrant's cruelty is in vain,
> For not for nought between Cuba and Spain
> Extend the immense waves of the sea.

Gómez de Avellaneda would heal the split—Heredia's and therefore hers—by claiming that her voyage has allowed her to realize the projectional vision, though transposed to the erotic register, through the overlap between the first and second él:

> Por ti fue mi dulce suspiro primero;
> Por ti mi constante, secreto anhelar . . .
> Y en balde el destino—mostrándose fiero—
> Tendió entre nosotros las olas del mar.
>
> (Gómez de Avellaneda 1974, 253)

> For you I gave my first sweet sigh,
> For you my constant, secret desire . . .
> And in vain destiny—showing its ire—
> Extended 'twixt us the waves of the sea.

The split in subjectivity cannot be mended by the simple defense of ironic reversal. For even were it possible to reconcile Cuba and Cubans to their subjugation to Spain through the example of her own acceptance of subjugation in her love (or her mother's) for a Spaniard, she would only be redressing the disappointments of the American projectional vision, relieving the failures of the independence movement in Cuba and elsewhere, by forging anew the links of a Pan Hispanic identity. There would remain the voice from the other side of the split, opposite Heredia's patriotic poetry, that is the poetry of his melancholia, itself divided, once again, between the abject tone of his wounding, as in Cholula, and its reversal in the sublime tone of "En una tempestad."

Gómez de Avellaneda would grapple with Heredia's melancholia throughout her poetry. The constant figure of her insomnia responds to the nightmare of the Cholula poem. She would outlast the menace to the poetic voice, so that where he succumbed to the figurative death of sleep and the attendant horror of his dream, she discovers the revitalitizing power of the morning sun. For Gómez de Avellaneda it is always a Cuban sun, whose "rayos a mi cuna lanzaste abrasador" ["burning rays you cast on my cradle"] (Gómez de Avellaneda 1974, 288); though there, too, she is anticipated by Heredia: "¿Quién cantará tus brisas y tus palmas,/Tu sol de fuego, tu brillante cielo?" ["Who will sing your breezes and your palms,/Your sun of fire, your brilliant sky?"] she asks in her elegy in his memory (256). On the other side, though greatly buffeted by the winds that blow from his hurricane in the images noted by Kirkpatrick, she would nonetheless contest their force by directing a pointed question to the storm in "Al mar," "¿Al mundo acaso anuncias algún eterno arcano,/Que oculta en los abismos altísimo poder" ["Do you announce perhaps some eternal secret to the world,/That almighty power hides in the abyss"]—as Heredia himself would have it—"O luchas blasfcmando con la potente mano/ Que enfrenta tu soberbia, segundo Lucifer?" ["Or do you fight, blaspheming, with the potent hand/That, oh second Lucifer, your pride reprimands?"] (243), as she suspects, revealing the satanic substrate of the romantic ambitions underlying ascension in "En una tempestad." Unlike the "noble Quintana" (331), another, Peninsular él behind her "Al mar," she closes the poem asking that the sea carry on its endless, reckless motion. And elsewhere she can give the destructive, Luciferian element full range, in the "Del huracán espíritu potente" ["Potent spirit of the hurricane"] of "Venganza" (266), for instance, though she call it the wrath of God in the grand display of "El día final." Her antidote for Heredia's sublime, like his, but more convincing, is her celebration of the Christian mysteries—"¡Alzad la cruz!" ["Raise the cross!"] (310)—that counters his rising through the storm. Her modernity, like his, and generally that of Spanish American poetry, continues to present an alternative to rational secularism.[19]

Evidence of Gómez de Avellaneda's engagement with the poetry of Heredia may be multiplied, but my aims here are not limited to demonstrating a particular affiliation. In the wake of Kirkpatrick's successful critical effort to reinstate the reading of her poetry as the cornerstone of an understanding of romanticism in the Peninsula, I would take the firm foundation of Gómez de Avellaneda's intertextual relation to Heredia as the point of departure for a parallel reclamation of her place in American letters. I would read her poems, in short, as American poems. And I now offer two demonstrations. In the first I will examine the way in which Gómez de Avellaneda's contribution to the American dialogue provides a modern critical point of view on her American heritage. In the second I will consider the endpoint of modernity as she commits the living tradition she receives to the cemetery of the past.

My first prooftext will be "A mi jilguero," a poem set in motion by the silence of the goldfinch in resistance to his mistress's cajoling. The text is linked to Gómez de Avellaneda's dialogic poems, such as "Amor y orgullo," by its tripartite structure divided between two first-person addresses. The yo of the opening and closing narration empathizes with the bird in its cage, while in the middle section the goldfinch appears to rebuke the lyric self:

> ¿No es igual mi cruda pena
> A la que te agobia impía?
> ¿No nos une la cadena
> De una tierna simpatía?
> —"No, porque en extraña tierra
> Tus cariños te han seguido,
> Y allí la patria se encierra
> Do está el objeto querido."
>
> (Gómez de Avellaneda 1974, 239)

> Is not mine the same raw pain
> As that which cruelly weighs you down?
> Are we not joined by the same chain
> Of tender sympathy?
> "No, because in a foreign land
> Your affections have followed you,
> And there the homeland remains bound
> Where the beloved object may be found."

The poet will subsequently specify that the voice set off in quotation marks is a projection of her own: "Esto me dicen tus ojos,/Esto tu silencio triste" ["This your eyes tell me,/This your sad silence" (Gómez de Avellaneda 1974, 240). The dialogue is the work of ventriloquism. Here and in a virtually all of Gómez de Avellaneda's greatest poetry, the reality of the interlocutor is incidental. True dialogue is internal, taking place within the split self; and as Abraham and Torok teach in such cases, the incorporated voices may replay a cryptic conversation, typically a scene of accusation and defense and impugned testimony.

It is not my purpose to decode the enigma for Gómez de Avellaneda's personal history. But for literary history, an account may begin by noting that generically "A mi jilguero" is a captive's tale—that American genre manifest in Echeverría, and grounded in Heredia's sleep and dream at Cholula, in which the self is the heir of a tarnished independence, and a witness of the death of liberty. In Gómez de Avellaneda's treatment, captivity represents the loss of poetic voice. The silence of the goldfinch is a threat to her mistress's own lyric self, hence the emotional charge of the poem. So it is in defense of poetry, her own fledgling poetry, as it were, that Gómez de Avellaneda seeks a remedy in prosopopeia.

The trope, it will be recalled, has a distinguished American pedigree that links Olmedo to Peralta and both to the *Aeneid*, to which Heredia also turned, as we have seen, in "Las sombras." And in fact, the more expansive dimensions notwithstanding, the insertion of the prospopopeia within the narrative frame of *Lima conquistada* or the "Victoria de Junín" provides those poems with much the same structure as "A mi jilguero." In the light of that tradition it is possible to think of the birdcage in "A mi jilguero" as a version of Virgil's hell. But more importantly, from the point of view of Gómez de Avellaneda's poem, it is possible to rethink the tradition of the prosopopeia as the trope for projectional vision. Gómez de Avellaneda does not share Peralta's faith in the Enlightenment nor Olmedo's faith in liberty, neither as a woman nor a Cuban. From the position of her own marginality, she can see the goldfinch as a mirror of her own subjectivity, rather than as a simple object of colonial exploitation. Hence, the explicit recognition of the fiction of her prosopopeia within the text of the poem functions as an unmasking of a ploy and a rejection of the exclusivity of the American "utopian" project, wherein Olmedo's subjugated Inca, it will be recalled, is made to speak in favor of a criollo victory.

And yet Gómez de Avellaneda, too, would lend the goldfinch a voice. In contrast to the prosopopeia in the service of the trope of liberty, however, when the language of the mistress passes through the goldfinch—another Caliban—it turns upon her, as Kirkpatrick anticipates, with curses: "Y tu cariño maldigo" ["And I curse your affection"] (Gómez de Avellaneda 1974, 240). This ventriloquism, I reiterate, transcribes the accusations and defense of a cryptic scene that touch intimately upon the split subjectivity of the yo. Where is "allí"? Which "patria"? Whose "objeto querido"? And what "se encierra"? In sum, who speaks through the yo in the poem as the yo speaks through the goldfinch?

Through it all the bird maintains its steadfast silence. Prosopopeia fails as dialogue. The only hope the yo may hold for restoring the true voice to the goldfinch is to set the bird free. She implores the bird to return—"Qué yo te escuche,/Sólo un momento" ["May I hear you/If only for a moment"] (Gómez de Avellaneda 1974, 240)—but the pleading tone suffices to indicate that this will not be. The tension of this captive's tale, finally, arises from a double bind for poetry: if the *jilguero* remains, he is condemned to silence; if he goes, his song will be lost. "Al partir," I suggest, is likewise just such a captive's tale, in which Edenic Cuba is Gómez de Avellaneda's "jaula preciosa" ["precious cage"] ("A mi jilguero," 238), and her voice in Cuban poetry is at stake in the question of her confinement and departure. The tension of Gómez de Avellaneda's poetic trajectory, both initiated and summed up in that first poem, may be charted as a flight from silence into silence. And for the poet of "Al partir" or "A mi jilguero," the model of Heredia is particularly pertinent: the exile lost to the island who yet returned as voice, a voice, or rather *the* voice of Cuban poetry.

The Heredia of "Niágara" is especially poignant for Gómez de Avellaneda, hemmed in by threats to her voice. For it was at Niagara Falls that Heredia himself claims to recover from silence:

> Dadme la lira, dádmela, que siento
> En mi alma estremecida y agitada
> Arder la inspiración. ¡Oh! ¡cuánto tiempo
> En tinieblas pasó, sin que mi frente
> Brillase con su luz . . . ! Niágara undoso,
> Sola tu faz sublime ya podría
> Tornarme el don divino, que ensañada
> Me robó del dolor la mano impía.
>
> (J. M. Heredia 1940, 2:221)

> Give me the lyre, give it to me, for I feel
> In my stirred and trembling soul
> The inspiration burn. Oh! How much time
> Passed in darkness, in which my brow
> Shone not with its light . . . ! Undulent Niagara,
> Your sublime face alone had power enough
> To return to me the god-like gift, that, furious,
> The pitiless hand of pain had robbed from me.

And it is to these verses that Gómez de Avellaneda returns at the close of her poetic trajectory in "A vista de Niágara," recollecting Heredia, "gran vate de Cuba" ["great bard of Cuba"]:

> Si cual él a tu voz inspiradora
> Sentir pudiera, ¡Niágara!, mi mente
>   De súbito agitada
> Por aquel *don divino, que ensañada*
> *Me robó del dolor la mano impía,*
> ¡Cómo también mi poderoso canto
> —Rival del suyo—ufana elevaría! . . .
> (Gómez de Avellaneda 1974, 352)[20]

> If like him I could but feel,
> Niagara! your inspiring voice, my mind
>   Suddenly stirred up
> By that *god-like gift, that, furious,*
> *The pitiless hand of pain had robbed from me,*
> How powerful my song, too,
> Rival to his—would lift itself with pride.

It is a peculiar poem and a peculiar moment for American poetry. The citation is itself a witness that the intertextual network of American poets formed by their reading of other American poets is now firmly in place. But Gómez de Avellaneda practices a reversal in this repetition. Heredia speaks as a political victim of colonial injustice, verging on an imaginary return route to Cuba—or so he declares. In point of fact, the phantasmagoria of the Cuban palms is initiated by his sudden recognition that he has found himself, imagistically, back at the *teocalli*: the turbulent mist from the falls "sube,/Gira en torno, y al cielo/*Cual pirámide inmensa* se levanta" ["rises,/Spins about, and to the sky,/*Like a giant pyramid* it rises"] (J. M. Heredia 1940, 2:222, emphasis added). His attachment to his homeland covers over a more profound attachment to the scene in

Cholula where he buried his father alive in his poem, rather than releasing him to death in an elegy. "Niágara" is split between the public and political language of its surface and the private, cryptic language of its depths. Gómez de Avellaneda, on the contrary, sets her poem on the outward bound route of her return to Spain after a sojourn in Cuba. Still rewriting "Al partir," she turns the surface of the text to the language of personal loss. The *mano impía* is no longer a figure for colonial despotism but rather for death itself, which had just robbed her of her second husband. What remains from Heredia is the crypt, the split, embodied in Gómez de Avellaneda's poem as the division between her superimposed lament for her husband and her lament for her beloved poet.

Gómez de Avellaneda attempts to overcome personal loss by generalizing to "la extraña condición del hombre/ . . . bajo ley continua de mudanza" ["the strange human condition/ . . . under continuous law of change"] (Gómez de Avellaneda 1974, 352). In a final, illuminating insight concerning that gesture of abstraction, Kirkpatrick speaks of Gómez de Avellaneda's poems "belonging to the genre then called 'philosophical' " in terms of an "anxiety to find stability in a transcendent guarantor [that] explains the increasing frequency with which she wrote religious poetry, particularly in periods of turmoil" (Kirkpatrick 1989, 206). She closes this observation with a further remark a propos of Gómez de Avellaneda's address to the Virgin: "the lyrical subject seems to be regressing to a fantasy associated with a time before the construction of the individualized, autonomous romantic ego—a time of infantile dependency in her own personal history and a time of premodern religious tradition in Spanish cultural history" (206). In sum, a retreat from the modernity of her own split subjectivity. I have reservations about the particular psychoanalytic model implicit in that position and about the exclusion of religious sensibility as an alternative modernity, but my more immediate response would be to contrast Gómez de Avellaneda's echo of the Siglo de Oro to Echeverría's overt allusion to Calderón when stymied in *Elvira*. Gómez de Avellaneda's "philosophical" mode expands on the baroque *vanitas* motif as a reflection on individual death and the fate of the soul in the manner of the Enlightenment and its secular concern for the fate of nations, which must perish if there is to be progress. But the transcendent, if imperfect guarantor, for her, has always been Heredia. The philosophical turn of "A vista de Niágara" repeats his strategy at Cholula and in much the same terms: her "ley continua de mudanza" ["continuous law of change"] is a felicitous variant on his declaration "Todo perece/Por ley universal" ["All perishes/By universal law"] (Heredia 1940, 2:152). She had been less felicitous in the earlier "philosophical" poem, "El genio poético" in which she had mined his source in Volney, only to bring forth Heredia's own verse: "Por ley universal todo perece" ["By universal law all perishes"] (Gómez de Avellaneda 1974, 260).

For Heredia the philosophical mode was an attempted resolution of the fundamental split in his poetry between the patriotic ode of the independence period and the discovery of a self amidst the ruins of liberty. At the level of abstraction of universal laws, the injustice that so troubled him is negated, but so is independence. Self and nation, more precisely an American self and an American nation, disappear from the final verses when the "¡Gigante del Anáhuac!" ["Giant of Anahuac!"] (J. M. Heredia 1940, 2:152) and the sacrificial victim's "grito del dolor" are glossed over as a neoclassical "Titán" ["Titan"] (2:153) and an Enlightenment "lección saludable" ["healthy lesson"] or at most an "ejemplo ignominioso" ["ignominious example"] (2:153). The greater daring of the 1832 version of the Cholula poem is thus stifled by the greater loss of nerve, augmenting that of the 1825 text, where "tal contemplación" ["such contemplation"] (Heredia 1940, 2.152), i.e. the Enlightenment abstraction of universal law, brought the poem to its false ending. And when Heredia recovered his voice in "En una tempestad," he still found his imagination bounded at the close of the poem, I recall, by the acknowledgment of the superiority of the throne of God.

Submission to God's majesty was a defeat of the lyric self for Heredia. Gómez de Avellaneda's religious poems make that same submission into a triumph. Her lyric voice is never more sure of its self, so to speak, that is more completely healed of its split, than when the erstwhile insomniac makes her normally anxious wakefulness the joyous condition of witnessing God's glory: "¡Canto la cruz! ¡Que se despierte el mundo!" ["I sing the cross! May the world awake!"] (Gómez de Avellaneda 1974, 310). Nor is Heredia's cataclysmic wind ever so completely her own as when she elevates his mere hurricane into the cosmic apocalypse of her poem "El día final," reversing the satanic power that she discerned in his storm into further proof of a majesty beyond Heredia's own verse.

Rather than reading Gómez de Avellaneda's religiosity as a regression to a premodern sensibility, therefore, I would argue that it represents an attempt to progress beyond the Cholula poem and beyond "En una tempestad." Heredia had made the same attempt in his own "Niágara." And even Gómez de Avellaneda's religious turn is contained in the transformation of the Enlightenment crepuscular meditation into the anticipated resurrection of his lyric self at the close of that poem:

> Y yo, al hundirse el sol en occidente,
> Vuele gozoso do el Criador me llama,
> Y al escuchar los ecos de mi fama
> Alce en las nubes la radiosa frente.
>
> (J. M. Heredia 1940, 2:224)

> And when the sun sinks in the west,
> May I fly joyously where the Creator calls,
> And when I hear the echoes of my fame,
> May I lift up to the clouds my radiant brow.

Here at the "point of no return" (Kirkpatrick 1989, 207) in *Heredia's* poetry, Gómez de Avellaneda finds what will be her ubiquitous trope of flight, including its first appearance in the departing ship of "Al partir" ("y silencioso vuela!" ["and silently flies!"] Gómez de Avellaneda 1974, 237), that is the complement of Heredia's wind in her verse.

From Gómez de Avellaneda's very beginnings as a *Cuban* poet in "Al partir," regress and progess were confounded along the route between colonial homeland and metropolitan capital, the language of her cradle and the cradle of her language. Now, having received her poet's laurels in both Spain and Cuba, having left a dead husband behind in both places as well, she relives "Al partir" alongside Niagara Falls and finds, as ever, that for her the way out and the way back are the same way. As a lyric poet she appears to be on a verge whose alternatives are silence and Heredia:

> Del voraz tiempo en rápidos turbiones,
> Cual tus fugaces ondas, desaparecen
> —En sucesión sin fin—generaciones . . .
> Sólo se libran, sólo permanecen
> Sobre el abismo donde todo se hunde,
> Las nobles obras en que el genio humano
> —Forma feliz prestando a las ideas—

Graba su sello y poderoso infunde
De la belleza el soplo soberano.

(Gómez de Avellaneda 1974, 352)

In rapid sweeps of voracious time,
Generations, like your fleeting waves
—in endless succession—disappear . . .
Alone remain, alone are spared
Above the abyss wherein all sink
The noble works in which human genius
—Lending to ideas felicitous form—
Engraves its stamp, infusing powerfully
Beauty's sovereign breath.

The abyss is that nature subject to the law of mutability; the saving grace would be the figure of eternity that bridges time, and so recuperates loss, God's Niagara and Heredia's:

Así, ¡Niágara!, así eterno seas
—Como en la tierra te hizo el Sumo Artista—
Hará en su canto el trovador cubano . . .
Mientras yo humilde—

(Gómez de Avellaneda 1974, 352)

Thus, Niagara! may you be thus eternally
—As the Great Artist made you on this earth—
The Cuban bard will make you in his song—
While I, in all humility—

The dash might have cut short the poem, but Gómez de Avellaneda proceeds farther. I interrupt her next verse so as to underline that faced with the twin examples of divine majesty, the presence of the falls and the recollection of "Niágara," Gómez de Avellaneda adopts the modesty topos. This is truly a point of no return, for if in the beginning were God's creation and Heredia's word, then to turn back can only lead to self-effacement: the elimination of the split, of the self, of the voice at liberty to sing them. Niagara, too, is a cage in which the poet, like the goldfinch, appears condemned to a willful silence as the only measure of her independence.

But Gómez de Avellaneda, an altogether remarkable poet, does not end her poem at this brink, but rather fashions one last time a route across the abyss of her silence. She finds she has no more self-defense than her own modernity and she commits herself to it:

Mientras yo humilde—al apartar la vista
De tu hermosura—admiro otro portento
De humano poder gran monumento.
 ¡Salve, oh aéreo, indescriptible puente,
Obra del hombre, que emular procuras
La obra de Dios, junto a la cual te ostentas!

(Gómez de Avellaneda 1974, 352)

While I, in all humility—averting my gaze
From your beauty—admire another portent,
Great monument of human power.
 Hail, oh suspended, indescribable bridge!
Work of man, that succeeds in emulating
The work of God, next to which you are on display!

Al partir, al apartar: she splits off from her own poem ("la vista") in a final trope for the sublimity of flight. She sees at last what Heredia literally could not: John Augustus Roebling's suspension bridge across the Niagara River.[21] Heredia in exile looked back from this site and imagined an idealized past in the phantasm of Cuban palms above the falls; Avellaneda looks down and finds that she already inhabits the future, whose poetry is the "signo valiente/ Del progreso industrial" ["valiant sign/Of industrial progress"] (Gómez de Avellaneda 1974, 352).

Gómez de Avellaneda crosses that bridge when she comes to it. In her vision of industrial progress she leaves the past definitively behind—Cuba, Heredia, melancholia, her own split subjectivity— and so flies into the silence she was fleeing. Her parting words are an ominous prophecy:

¡Feliz aquel que debe a la fortuna
Tener en la región privilegiada,
Que tan tarde conozco, alegre cuna!
¡Feliz quien de la vida en la alborada
—Cuando el cansancio al corazón no oprime,
Y se le siente palpitar ufano
Al contemplar lo bello y lo sublime—
Tu ambiente aspira, ¡oh pueblo americano!,
Que si tienes—cantando tu grandeza—
Prodigios como el Niágara en el suelo,
Para ostentarte en superior alteza
Cimentarte supiste instituciones

Que el genio liberal como modelo
Presente con orgullo a las naciones!

(Gómez de Avellaneda 1974, 352)

    Happy is he who owes to fortune
Happy birth in this privileged realm
That I come to know so late!
Happy he who in the dawning of his days
—When the heart is not borne down by weariness,
And it beats cheerfully when it contemplates
The beautiful and the sublime—
If you have—singing your grandeur—
Prodigies like Niagara in your land,
You also knew to found institutions
That liberal genius may present
With pride as a model to the nations.

Odd lines to write in the course of the American Civil War, but the poet has confessed, after all, that she has averted her eyes from the split. And confessing as well that the lyric self is tired of its poetic burden, Avellaneda finds her poetry rerouted to questions of national identity. She writes a poem-within-a-poem, a poem to end her poem, an independence ode—so progress and regress remain confounded!—where liberty in the present and the bridge to the future seem to lie in North America. The routes of Spanish American modernity lead to neocolonialism.

Conclusion: *América Poética*

1

In exile from his native Argentina, Juan María Gutiérrez published *América poética, coleccion escojida de composiciones en verso, escritas por americanos en el presente siglo* in thirteen installments from February 1846 to June 1847 in Valparaiso, Chile (J. M. Gutiérrez 1846, 823).[1] It is an all but obligatory reference in Spanish American literary histories, where it usually receives mention as the first attempt to collect the poetry of the whole of Spanish-speaking America as a concerted enterprise under the aegis of Bello's "Alocución," which is printed as the initial entry in the compilation. It would be as well to say that the whole of *América poética* constitutes Gutiérrez's multivocal effort to complete Bello's larger project, of which the "Alocución" was but a sampler. The anthology, in short, is more than the sum of its parts. *América poética* is, by self-conscious intention, a "foundational text" that constitutes America for poetry by embodying in print a network of intertextual routes for the internal commerce of American letters.[2] As such the anthology invites a reading as a single vast poem: *Fragmentos de un poema . . . titulado "América—Poética."* And the reading of that poem will be my task in this closing chapter.

The position of the "Alocución" reflects a privileged thematics, but not a prescriptive poetics. In addition to Bello's argument for poetry as a progress piece and the related projectional vision of Olmedo and Luca, one finds the Anacreontic mode of Navarrete, the dialogic, if not to say polyphonic form of Hidalgo's poesía gauchesca, and the fractured poetics of Heredia, Echeverría and Gómez de Avellaneda among the most ample selections in the anthology. I may add that reference to Fernández de Madrid in Gutiérrez's unsigned prologue, first by name and then obliquely (J. M. Gutiérrez 1846, vii–viii), present him as the model of a transition from national to self-expression. In contrast to this breadth, however, there are also gaps. Most notably, Gutiérrez makes reference to the pre-Columbian poetic heritage in his preface, but he does not include any indigenous-language poetry extant in the oral culture of the nineteenth century, nor for that matter does he collect material from the living Spanish-language oral tradition, whether of Peninsular or local origin. *América poética* is very much a product of the print culture, and in fact a signal of the triumph of print in the definition of literature and its canon.[3] Some of the poetry reaches Gutiérrez in manuscript, but more frequently the poems in the anthology are gleaned from printed sources. Uneven access to those sources for a native of the River Plate living in exile in Chile at the time of the compilation accounts for further geographical gaps. In addition to Florencio Varela's *Comercio del Plata*, to which he himself had contributed as a poet during his exile in Montevideo, and the *Museo de Ambas Américas*, published in Valparaiso in 1842, the place of his continuing exile, Gutiérrez demonstrates a broad and diligent reading of the periodical literature of America. A copy of the Mexican *Apuntador* of 1841, reaches him, for instance, and he makes it the source for his selections of two poets, Alejandro Arango (n.d.) and José María Lafragua (1813–75), neither of whom had then or since a solid literary reputation, though Lafragua was a significant participant in Mexican political debate.[4] On the other hand, he seems not to have had any periodicals from Central America. Thus, the vivid exchanges in the local press between two very substantial Guatemalan poets, García Granados and Juan Diéguez (1813–66), escape him, and so from that region as a whole, Rafael García Goyena (Guatemala 1766–1823) alone appears in the anthology, his fables known to Gutiérrez from the Parisian edition of his poetry (1836). And despite the fact that the first anthology of poetry in Puerto Rico, the *Aguinaldo puertorriqueño* (1843), was published in time for consultation, it appears that this volume was unavailable to Gutiérrez. Puerto Rico is entirely unrepresented.

Bearing in mind the obstacles to Gutiérrez's research at a time when the lanes of communication were still largely undeveloped in America, even within the exclusive domain of print culture, the signal achievement of the anthology lies in the effort to venture beyond the relatively central names of early nineteenth-century verse mentioned above. Gutiérrez publishes selections from Andrés Mármol's "Canto del Peregrino," while noting that fragments of the incomplete poem continue to appear in the *Comercio del Plata* (J. M. Gutiérrez 1846, 541, n. 1). He presents Eusebio Lillo (1826–1910), though "his biography," Gutiérrez declares of the twenty-year old law student, "is in the future". He selects verse by Guillermo Prieto (Mexico 1818–97) from the *Museo Mexicano* and the *Recreo de las Familias* and the satirical poetry of Pardo y Aliaga from "various periodicals in whose collections there remain many [compositions] that we have been unable to obtain" (664)—to cite some of the poets who will only thereafter gain national or Pan American recognition. The choices speak to Gutiérrez's editorial skill, but also to a certain literary program made more evident in his omission of Irisarri *père*, while including his son, Hermógenes, even when the principal selection, "El poeta" (373), is merely an unoriginal imitation of Zorrilla. Among his various tasks, that is, Gutiérrez makes a generational argument:

> It would be very easy to say why we have reached a point at which we are attempting to take account of those deeds by virtue of which we have been born into political existence, forming independent States: why we now note that we have behind us a time already past; why, finally, a hidden impulse leads us to researches in our history. But leaving this explanation for a more opportune place and for clearer minds than ours, we will take for ourselves the liberty of warning that we lack a compilation of data sufficiently well organized to reach the truth, walking the road to which those impulses that we have just indicated are leading us. (J. M. Gutiérrez 1846, v–vi)

Gutiérrez stands as the founding figure of modern Spanish American literary criticism; there have been no clearer minds. But this may be a more opportune place—largely because *América poética* supplies the organized materials—to clarify his argument, *andando el camino* to which he refers. It is the road of a modern historical consciousness, the consciousness of his own generation that a certain dream of liberty had ended in nightmare, that the poetry of progress was the death of true independence.

2

Both the secret impulse and the vexed historical moment might be outlined by reference to a representative poet of the generation that came to consciousness when the constitutional dialogue of

America had broken down and a certain dream of liberty had given way to the nightmare of civil discord. To this end I choose the Uruguayan Adolfo Berro. Thereafter I will make a brief anthology of the anthology, deliberately avoiding poets better-known or already considered in favor of the byways opened by Gutiérrez, in order to read *América poética,* as I have suggested, as a single, albeit fragmentary and unfinished poem, written in response to the political and literary vicissitudes that are exemplified in Berro's verse.

Born in Montevideo in 1819, Berro died shortly after his twenty-second birthday in September 1841.[5] Thus among the *novísimos* recorded and promoted by Gutiérrez, his case recommends itself as representative for being neatly circumscribed by the moment in question. He may also be taken as an exemplum of the transition to a print culture in that period, which, I reiterate, is definitively achieved for Spanish American poetry in *América poética.* The transmission of Berro's poems begins as a domestic incident:

> Adolfo kept them with special care: these inspirations were his secret. A happenstance undid his precautions, and a sister of his who caught him by surprise, told his brother-in-law, Don Jacobo Varela, that Adolfo wrote verse. Berro's esteem and affection for Varela were extreme, and yet [the latter] was unable to persuade him, without great effort, to show him his poetry. (J. M. Gutiérrez 1846, 96)

The fortunate circumstance is in fact two-fold: that his sister should happen upon his secret manuscripts, and that she should also happen to be connected, through her husband, to the dean of print culture in the River Plate. "[Adolfo] consented at last and allowed the verse to be shown to don Florencio [Varela]. To this we owe the publication, undertaken by [Don Florencio], and the praises that determined Berro's vocation to this genre of literature" (96). After Berro's death, the poetry passed from the periodical press of Florencio Varela to book form, published in Montevideo in 1842, "in a vol. in quarto of 200 pages with a portrait of the author and a prefatory discourse written by Sr. D. Andrés Lamas," as Gutiérrez specifies in a characteristic bibliographic note (95, n. 1). Gutiérrez then adds: "We extract the present biographical notice from that discourse, which we have not wished to expand with our own memories" (95, n. 1); that is, Gutiérrez himself was also a member of Varela's circle, but he foregoes his own personal testimony to offer the reader of *América poética* a portrait of Berro as he is known in print. Finally, the Berro thus reduced for reprinting is also representative with respect to Gutiérrez's editorial task. For there were poets of whom it appears Gutiérrez includes those few isolated poems that he found in periodicals, and other, more central names, who are represented not by selections but rather by complete works. "We are publishing all that we have found written by Heredia," writes Gutiérez, for example, "without daring to exclude even those compositions which, it appears, he had removed from the Toluca edition, which we have not seen. Readers may well thank us for this decision, born of the love that we profess for the Cuban poet" (286). But in Berro's case, true to the promise of his prospectus to avoid any personal prejudices (vi) Gutiérrez exercises the critical judgment of the anthologizer and presents but two dozen poems from those two hundred quarto pages.

One finds a brief compendium of the history of Spanish American poetry of the preceding century and a half in Berro's verse. The selection spans the range from a reminiscence of the baroque in the opening poem, "El azahar," with its allegorizing of nature for the purposes of the *desengaño* theme,[6] to Berro's positioning of his poetry as a response to the contemporary writing of the River Plate in "A D. Estevan Echeverría" (J. M. Gutiérrez 1846, 98–99) and "El ombú," the final section of his "Mañanas de estío," with its engagement of the figure of the gaucho (119).

Between the two and at the crux of this anthological selection, and of *América poética* as a whole, Berro heeds the call of Bello's "Alocución." The first section of "Mañanas de estío" narrates an episode of erotic and poetic awakening. The setting is a riverbank and a girl who contemplates a "ramo . . . /De marchitos azahares" ["branch . . . /Of withered orange blossoms"] (J. M. Gutiérrez 1846, 116). An echo of *Elvira*, as well as of his own "El azahar," the topos sets the scene for a song of experience, whether modulated as the bitterness of baroque *desengaño* or as the melancholy of a later age. Paradoxically, the withered branch "la pone así festiva" ["makes her festive"] (116). The paradox is to be explained as a secular immaculate conception. Her experience has been strictly literary. The branch is accompanied by "Unas décimas sentidas" ["Some heart-felt verses"] (116), and whose anonymity represents an ostensible puzzle. However, the query, "¿Mas por quién fueron escritas?" ["But by whom were they written?"] (116)— proves to be a rhetorical question.

The author of the double gift is he who had of late taught her to read the text of nature as the poetry of a discreet eroticism:

> Y se cuenta que él la hizo,
> No habia mucho, compañía,
> Al volver de unas carreras
> Hasta el rancho donde habita.
>   La plateada luna, entonces,
> Derramando luces vivas
> Se mostraba, con la madre
> Del amor, toda encendida.
>   ¡Cuán hermosa está esa estrella!
> Prorrumpió la dulce niña,
> Que entregada a ideas vagas
> Contemplándola venia
>
> (J. M. Gutiérrez 1846, 116–17)

> And he, it is told,
> But lately kept her company,
> Returning from some races
> To the ranch that is her home.
>   Then the silvery moon above,
> Pouring forth its vivid lights,
> Showed itself all aglow
> Alongside the mother of love.
>   How beautiful that star is!
> The delicate girl broke out,
> Given over to vague thoughts
> As she walked on contemplating.

It is a belated evening star poem, since in terms of astronomy, the moon has already risen and in terms of literary history the topos of the interstitial moment was old in the poetry of Meléndez before Berro was young, and already incorporated by Bello as the time of his lyric interlude in the "Alocución." A generation or two later, Berro's young woman, playing the role of an innocent and untutored Divine Poetry, consults the mystery of Venus not with silence, as in Bello's poem, but with a poet, her unnamed companion.

This poet companion proves an excellent teacher, for he directs her attention without imposing an answer:

> Y él la dijo, luego al punto,
> "Es verdad. . . . siempre divina"

Y clavó sus tiernos ojos
En los de ella distraida.
    El misterio que esas voces
Y miradas envolvian,
No sé yo si desde luego
La inocente entenderia,
    Pero sí que desde entonces
Siempre está imajinativa,
Cuando vé cómo esa estrella
En el puro cielo brilla.

(J. M. Gutiérrez 1846, 117)

    And he told her, without hesitation,
"It is true . . . always divine,"
And he stared with tender eyes
Into hers in her distraction.
    I cannot say for sure
If she, in her innocence,
Could possibly comprehend
The mystery in those looks and words.
    But surely ever since that time
She is lost in flights of fancy
Whenever she sees that star
Shining in the limpid sky.

Not only the rhetorical question, but in fact the present scene on the riverbank is forgotten. The décimas have been replaced by her admirer's greater poem from the prior scene of instruction. But his mystery, too, is replaced in the end as far as concerns the yo, who suddenly intervenes in that penultimate stanza. The question for this yo is just how innocent is the young woman who has been touched by poetry.

The lyric interlude is central to the "Alocución," but it is not all. And just as Bello turns from self to nation, so, too, Berro's question has a broader scope. In the middle section of "Mañanas de estío" he poses the matter in Bello's own terms:

    De Europa altiva sorprende
    La desmayada natura,
    Que el arte en vano procura
    Lozana y fértil tornar

(J. M. Gutiérrez 1846, 117)

> The faint nature of haughty Europe
> Is taken by surprise,
> That art procures in vain
> To turn it fertile and lush again.

He follows with an enumeration of social ills, which serve as a contrast "Al virjinal Continente/Que vió Cristóbal Colón" ["To the virginal Continent/That Christopher Columbus saw"] (J. M. Gutiérrez 1846, 118) and the counterbalancing enumeration of American natural bounty—"Montañas tiene soberbias," "rios sin cuento," "abundantísimos frutos" ["Fecund mountains it has"; "countless rivers"; "most abundant fruits"] (Gutiérrez 1846, 118)—as Bello had instructed by example in both the "Alocución" and "La agricultura de la zona tórrida."

But the fable of liberty and poetry progressing hand-in-hand from a decadent Europe to an innocent America was implausible in Montevideo in 1839. Berro read his Bello through the intermediary of Echeverría:

> El vuelo arrebatado de tu mente
> 　Mi espíritu seguia,
> 　Y absorto te veia
> Luchai con espantosa iealidad
> 　　(Berro, "A D. Estevan Echeverria,"
> 　　　　　　　(J. M. Gutiérrez 1846, 98)

> The precipitous flight of your mind
> 　My spirit pursued,
> 　And, absorbed, I saw you
> Fighting with frightful reality.

That is he read "La cautiva" as we now read Echeverría's prose tale "El matadero." And while he enjoins Echeverría himself, recently arrived in Montevideo, to continue in his "Poética mision" ["Poetic mission"] (J. M. Gutiérrez 1846, 98), Berro takes up the same burden, struggling with the same "espantosa realidad" ["frightful reality"] that he finds from his position, at the age of twenty, as the public defender of slaves (96, following Lamas). Thus Berro's most notable contribution to *América poética* is his parallel defense motions in civic poetry: "La espósita," "El mendigo," and above all, "El esclavo." Unlike the Heredia of "En una tempestad," therefore, he contains the yo within its social dimensions, and channels its potential for sublimity into social reform:

> La voz del que concierta el Universo,
> Con mano fulgurante,
> Al mundo zozobrante
> Habló en medio a la rauda tempestad.
> Sus écos a mis labios han pasado
> En pura santa llama
> El pecho ya se inflama. . . .
> ¡Mortales descarriados, escuchad!
>
> (J. M. Gutiérrcz 1846, 102)

> The voice of he who conducts the cosmos
> With hand ablaze,
> Spoke to the dazed
> World from the middle of the whirlwind.
> Its echoes have passed to my lips
> In pure, holy flame,
> My breast is now inflamed. . . .
> Wayward mortals, hear!

A passionate poet in this prophetic role, Berro remains nonetheless clear-minded about the limitations of his excoriations. In "A mi lira" he laments:

> Tú sola sabes, solitaria lira,
> Herir las auras con doliente son,
> Mas no apagar del vencedor la ira
> Huellas dejando de piedad y amor.
> ¿Qué importa, dime, que del pecho mio
> Templen tus ecos el cruel dolor,
> Si eternos viven en el mundo impío
> Los fieros males que lloró mi voz?
>
> (J. M. Gutiérrez 1846, 106)

> You only know, my solitary lyre,
> How to wound the breeze with mournful sound,
> But not how to snuff out the victor's ire,
> Leaving behind traces of pity and of love.
> What does it matter, tell me, that your song
> Calms the cruel pain in my breast,
> If in this impious world the furious wrongs
> My voice has wept live on eternally?

America's liberty, Berro admonishes, is plagued by slavery, economic inequality and the double standard of gender bias. Independence itself is undermined by civil strife. For the realist, then, the question of innocence is decided against the defendant:

> Tiene América rasgadas
> Por lides fraternales
> Los ropajes virjinales
> Con que el cielo la vistió.
>   Y su seno mal velado
> A ese viejo mundo incita,
> Que una virjen necesita
> Para alivio a su pasion.
> ("A don Andrés Lamas," J. M. Gutiérrez 1846, 123)

> America wears torn
> In fraternal strife
> The virginal attire
> That heaven has bestowed.
>   And its poorly clad breast
> Arouses that old world
> That needs a virgin
> To assuage its passion.

In "La espósita," and its reverse, "El ruego de la madre," in which the mother of an *espósito* confesses herself "indigna de perdon" ["unworthy of forgiveness"] (J. M. Gutiérez 1846, 104), and most of all in the uncharacteristically merciless attack of "La ramera," Berro demonstrates little sympathy for the virgin left unprotected to salacious men. The America whose garment of natural innocence is rent by internal wars—the break up of Gran Colombia, the siege in Berro's Montevideo, the conflict between Chile and the alliance of Bolivia and Peru—will be held guilty in the scales of Berro's prophetic justice, should she fall victim to the rape of external powers. And he is clairvoyant with regard to the threat, though he mistakes the source. Though he himself does not live to see the day, in the months that Gutiérrez would have been compiling his *América poética*, the United States declares its "Manifest Destiny" and war on Mexico. General Winfield Scott entered Mexico City two months after the final installment was in print.

Against the realistic strain that perceives both present evils and imminent menace, the projectional vision that is Berro's inheritance from Bello as well as such River Plate poets as the brothers Florencio (1807–1848) and Juan Cruz Varela (1794–1839), appears as a most slender hope:

> ¿Y callar podrán los labios,
> En la lira no habrá acentos
> Que mitigan los tormentos
> De la América infeliz?
> Sí, que el vate es para el pueblo
> Un fanal que en la tormenta,
> El pavor del alma ahuyenta,
> Con la luz del porvenir.
>
> (J. M. Gutiérrez 1846, 123)

> And will the lips be able to be still
> And will the lyre's accent be heard again
> That would suffice to mitigate the pain
> Of America in its sorrow?
> Yes, for the bard is for the people
> A lighthouse in heavy weather,
> Driving from the soul its terror
> With the light of their tomorrows.

The bard whose realistic vision is the scourge is blessed with a second sight in which the American utopia remains visible:

> Vendrán, amigo, los serenos dias,
> Si fé tenemos y confianza en Dios,
> Si al pueblo abrimos anchurosas vías
> Por donde corra de la dicha en pos.
>
> (J. M. Gutiérrez 1846, 123)

> The peaceful days will come, oh friend,
> If we have faith and trust in God,
> If the people seek their happiness
> On the broad ways that we have opened.

It is equally a measure of Gutiérrez's faith that he makes this projectional vision Berro's last word in the selections of *América poética*.

Reflecting back upon the Conquest in his romances históricos, Berro had explored the question of America's utopian innocence through the suspense plot of a murder mystery. In the romance of

"Yandubayu y Liropeya" the young warrior Yandubayu throttles his Spanish adversary in equal combat, but spares his life at the request of Liropeya. She does not speak for Christian charity, I note, but rather reminds him that his pledge to her requires combat with American rivals:

> "¿Así te olvidas, cacique,
> De tus promesas? Ingrato!
> ¿Así en combates sin premio
> Digno de tu heroico brazo
> 　La vida espones . . . ?"
>
> 　　　　　　　　(J. M. Gutiérrez 1846, 113)

> 　So, cacique, you forget
> Your promises? You ingrate!
> You thus expose yourself to harm
> In combat without a prize
> Worthy of your arm . . . ?

The battle plan reflects the internecine struggles of pre-Columbian America. Plácido, that is the mulatto poet Gabriel de la Concepción Valdés (Cuba 1809–44), provides the more famous example for both military and literary history in his own *romance*, "Gicontecal," drawn from the warfare of the Tlascalans against Moctezuma's empire at the time of the invasion of Cortés.[7] In Plácido's case the poem gains in poigancy when read in the context of the poet's own times and personal fate. The triumphant chieftain Gicontecal cuts short his victory procession—his progress—to intervene on behalf of the slaves, that is the captives taken in battle. He spares them from human sacrifice and sends them back to Moctezuma with this message:

> "Que el jóven Gicotencal
> Crueldades como él no usa,
> Ni con sangre de cautivos
> Asesino el suelo inunda."
>
> 　　　　　　　　(J. M. Gutiérrez 1846, 778)

> "For the young Gicotencal
> Turns not to cruelties like his,
> Nor does he murderously flood the ground
> With the blood of his captives."

Arrested for alleged involvement in a plot to foment a slave rebellion, Plácido and his confederates receive no such clemency.

Similarly, Berro's *romance* may be read with one eye toward the political history of his day, especially in the light of his poem "A don Andrés Lamas." The downfall of Yandubayu and Liropeya enacts the fears Berro expresses for America at war with itself, namely that internal strife will distract Americans from their real enemy from abroad. Recalled to his native rivalry, Yandubayu releases his Spanish adversary from his choke hold, "De paz la diestra tendiole/Sin rastro alguno de enfado" ["In peace he offered his right hand/Without a trace of anger"] (J. M. Gutiérrez 1846, 113), and turns his ingenuous back. "Fresca y hermosa es la india" ["Fresh and beautiful is the Indian"] (113) or perhaps, *la India*, virgin America, inciting the covetousness of the Old World:

> Bien lo notó el Castellano,
> Que por salaces deseos
> Y torpe saña llevado,
>   Hunde la espada traidora
> En el cacique preclaro.
>
> (J. M. Gutiérrez 1846, 113)

> The Castilian marked it well,
> For borne by misbegotten
> Urges and a brutish will,
>   He plunged his treacherous sword
> Into the noble chieftain.

The Spaniard, a certain Carvallo, would carry off Liropeya as his booty. She conceives a plan. She plays the *ramera*:

> "Seguirte quiero," le dice,
> "Si con tus ajiles brazos,
>   Abres la fosa que encierre
> Este cadáver helado . . ."
>
> (J. M. Gutiérrez 1846, 113)

> "I want to go with you," she said,
> "If, with your dexterous arms
>   You open up a tomb to hold
> The cold body of the dead . . ."

The killer in this is plain to see, but the burial plot must still unfold: does Liropeya ask for a grave so as to put her American past behind her, embrace European civilization, and break faith with the dead? Carvallo seems to think so and sets to work. While he is occupied, Liropeya, unnoticed, prepares to acquit herself by picking up the sword of her revenge. She does not bury her tormentor alongside Yandubayu, however. Instead, sword in hand, she orders him, "Oh maldecido cristiano!" ["Oh cursed Christian!"] to open another grave, "Y con la espada sangrienta/Se pasa el seno angustiado" ["And with the bloody sword/She smites her anguished breast"] (J. M. Gutiérrez 1846, 113). For Berro, then, the safe-guarding of America's innocence, in both the colonial era and the later times of a debased liberty in which he writes, lies in the grave.

At the outset of the present study I proposed that the roots of modernity lay quite literally in a burial plot. Berro extends the argument of the *Mercurio Peruano*. His sympathies lie very clearly with Yandubayu and Liropeya, but their rural cemetery nonetheless sets the past aside so that the present, which belongs to Carvallo, can make way for progress. And in the course of progress, Liropeya's innocence, like that of the indigenous peoples on the coast of Baja California, is by no means secure. The narrative voice concludes abruptly, without a lyric turn to sing her elegy within the world of this *romance histórico* or foundational fiction, in Sommer's sense. In that world it is Carvallo alone who will remain to translate Liropeya's final words to his own purposes, like Father Salvatierra a century and a half before Berro. A second *romance* does follow in *América poética*, but it only obviates the point, for it is set before the murder and the suicide, before the tale and Carvallo's retelling, at the very founding of Montevideo. But that foundational fiction already shows the retroactive effects of Carvallo's deceit. Caravallo has buried the tragic couple, but left no monument to mark the spot. What remains, therefore, is the unencumbered prospect of a welcoming landscape, a present with a long future and no past: "Desierta estaba la tierra" ["Deserted was the land"] (J. M. Gutiérrez 1846, 114), the Spanish assert while imagining that the Charrúa, "Como flotante fantasma" ["Like a floating phantom"] (114)— *fantasma*, as though he were dead; *flotante*, as though the land were already a Spanish dominion and indigenous peoples, rather, came from the sea—would offer no resistance, "Miedo llevando en el rostro" ["Fear showing in their faces"] (114). As I have pursued that burial plot across this century and a half of poetry, I will pursue

it now through the pages of *América poética* in my own brief
anthology of the anthology, on the lookout for signs of Liropeya's,
that is America's, contested innocence, and in search of the grave
site of the past along the course of America's progress toward neocolonialism. For these, I believe, are the cryptic impulses that drive
the anthology and Gutiérrez's researches into the history of modern
American poetry.

3

Liropeya's elegy is lacking, but an elegy for Berro himself is supplied by his fellow Uruguayan Juan Carlos Gómez (1820–84), one
year younger and living in Valparaiso at the time Gutiérrez was at
work on *América poética*. Gómez is a throwback in various ways,
among them, that he enters the anthology without passing through
an intermediary in the print culture: "we offer our most express
gratitude for the sacrifice imposed upon his modesty," writes
Gutiérrez in his introductory note, "providing the poems that we
include hereafter, the majority unpublished" (J. M. Gutiérrez 1846,
269). The poem "A Adolfo Berro" is a cry-baby elegy, whose sim-
ple-minded logic—Adolfo cried a lot, he made us cry with his
poetry, now he's dead so it's time to cry again—admits an extreme
that can only be read as self-parody: Adolfo's poetry even made his
miserable subjects (the slave, the orphan, the prostitute, the beggar)
cry. Hence, in Berro's memory, Gómez offers this blessing: "Feliz
quien ha conseguido/El llanto del desgraciado! . . . " ["Happy he
who has obtained/The tears of the unfortunate!"] (276). The exclamation point is his, as is the ellipsis in which, by this argument, the
blessing extends to the slave owner and other sociopaths who likewise made their unhappy victims cry. In other words, it is well to
recall that not all of Gutiérrez's choices make for great poetry. But
I open my own selection with Gómez, because, as a derivative poet,
at least in these, his early years, he demonstrates the persistence,
now not of the baroque, but of the predominant tropes of American
poetry from the road to independence through the constitutive dialogue of the 1820s.

Gómez's most ambitious poem in *América poética*, "La libertad," is dated to Montevideo, 25 May 1842, and determined by its
civic occasion as a rallying cry for the spirit of independence as the
expression of a national identity. The commemorative purpose

places the poem, like the anthology as a whole, under the auspices of Bello, and so it begins, like the "Alocución," as a progress piece. The failures of liberty in Europe enumerated in the first section bring Gómez to America in section two:

> América desploma sus rios como mares,
> Las cumbres de sus montes se ocultan al mortal,
> Sus bosques están llenos de místicos cantares
> Que acaso son el eco del coro celestial.

> América es sin duda la tierra prometida,
> América la virjen del universo es,
> ¡Oh Libertad quién sabe si para darte vida
> La mano de Dios mismo no la formó despues!
>
> (J. M. Gutiérrez 1846, 271)

> America unravels its rivers like unto the seas,
> Its mountain peaks are hidden from the eye of mortal man,
> Its forests are full of such song as heard in mystic lore,
> Which may well be the echo of the celestial choir.

> America is, without a doubt, the Promised Land,
> America is the virgin of the universe,
> Oh Liberty who can say if it was not the hand
> Of God that, to give you life, gave shape to hers.

The first verse gives a specifically River Plate view of the American landscape, but thereafter Gómez repeats the continent-wide argument of Bello and of Gutiérrez the anthologizer. *América* is *poética*. And it is so because of its virginal purity.

This purity is asserted as late as the mid-nineteenth century not in terms of the geography of ocean crossing, but rather in topographic terms: there remain undefiled mountaintops that bear as yet no footprint, no imprint of civilization. "¿Quién es el que ha estampado/En las eternas nieves que las cubren/El rastro de su planta?" ["Who is he who has stamped/In the eternal snows that cover them/The trace of his foot?"] (J. M. Gutiérrez 1846, 261), asks Juan Godoy, a resident of the Valparaiso of Gutiérrez and Gómez and himself a member of the generation of Mayo commemorated in "La libertad." The answer in Godoy's "Canto a la cordillera de los Andes," is of course that no one has done so. Even the condor "Jamas fijó la garra ensangrentada/En tus crestas altísimas" ["Never fixed its bloody claw/On your highest crests"] (261), where the emphasis must be laid on the blood as a sign of the hordes of Spanish despotism, which "desde la Plata a Catamarca/Y del pié"—but not above—"de los Andes a Corrientes,/Con sangre señalaron su camino" ["From La Plata to Catamarca/And from the foot of the Andes to Corrientes/Blazed their trail with blood"] (263). The *cordillera* above the tree line, therefore, constitutes a final redoubt beyond the expansion of a barbarous civilization.

The climactic historical exception to its impregnability proves the rule. San Martín did cross the Andes—"Ví yo escalar tu cima" ["I saw your peak scaled"] (J. M. Gutiérrez 1846, 263)—but his passage spelled liberty for America, and so left the mountain unprofaned. The mountaintops will remain immaculate in this world, and will only become legible as text in the next, after the flood foretold at the end of the poem:

> Y en vasto horizonte
> El punto enseñarán donde algun dia
> La Libertad tuviera sus altares.
>
> Cual cruz solitaria en el desierto
> Anuncia al caminante
> Que en aquel punto ha muerto
> Y sepultado está su semejante
>
> (J. M. Gutiérrez 1846, 264)
>
> And on the vast horizon
> They will point out some day the spot
> Where Liberty would have its altars.
>
> As the solitary cross on the deserted plains
> Announces to the traveler
> That his counterpart has died and his remains
> Lie buried at that spot.

Godoy remains close in style and poetic argument to Luca, and the tone of the prophetic voice is fundamentally optimistic. The projectional vision forecasts that liberty will outlive the ages. But the cataclysmic storm that occupies the closing section of the poem is nonetheless an expression of fury. The explicit motif is the revelation of God's judgment at the end of days, but the emotional force, if less fierce than Gómez de Avellaneda's apocalypse, has strength enough to suggest that the object of the admonition is near at hand.

Godoy is speaking for the generation of Mayo, and from that point of view, the world already seems the burial ground of the liberty they had fought to secure.

A more clear-sighted and more necessary poem, Godoy's *alocución a los Andes* severely qualifies Gómez's poetic America with his greater animosity toward the colonial times of his own youth. He recalls that the virgin forests were subjugated by "el brazo nefario /[que] La cortante segur al tronco aplica" ["the nefarious arm/ (that) the cutting blade to the trunk applies"] and moreover, that this anti-Genesis was conducted for the benefit of despotism:

> De allí a la húmeda playa
> El esfuerzo del hombre hace que vaya:
> En bajel se transforma y ¡quién creyera
> Que este árbol tan gallardo, tan lozano,
> Que en la remota selva había nacido,
> Exento no estuviera
> Del poder formidable de un tirano!
> Él ordenó que nave se volviera,
> Y nave se volvió, do ahora truena
> El cañon matador cuando él lo ordena.
>
> (J. M. Gutiérrez 1846, 263)

> From there to the damp shore,
> The efforts of man cause it to go:
> Into a ship it is transformed, and who
> Would believe this tree, so spirited, so
> Beautiful, born in the distant jungle,
> Was not exempt
> From the tyrant's awful power!
> He orders that it should become a ship,
> And a ship it became, where the murderous
> Cannon now thunders when he orders.

Godoy circumscribes America's "místicos cantares" ["mystic songs"] though without foreclosing on the possibility of poetry altogether.

Thus, in "La palma del desierto" (dated Lima, 25 May 1843), Godoy turns the occasion of Mayo commemoration to the private meditation of love elegy, as though "sparing as much as possible," in the words of Gutiérrez's prospectus, "the exaggerations of enthusiasm in the hymns of national triumph" (J. M. Gutiérrez 1846, vi). The palm provides an image of voice from the American forest—"De tus abanicos verdes,/Por el céfiro movidos,/Los misteriosos sonidos/Creo que palabras son" ["Of your green fans,/Moved by zephyrs,/The mysterious sounds/Seem words to me"] (265). But in light of the "Canto a la cordillera de los Andes," it is clear that the palm may serve the needs of poetry precisely because "Jamas una tabla has dado [a las naves]/Ni a una lanza duro astil" ["You have never given a plank (to ships)/Nor hard shaft to a spear"] (265). This pacific retirement situates the poem in the space of Bello's lyric interlude, before he continued his progress on to his own elegies of national triumph in the last three quarters of the "Alocución." And Godoy's palm may be seen not only as a resting place, like Bello's, along the road of progress, but rather as a sign-post that marks an alternative, regressive path.

It is along that path that M[anuel] M[aría] Madiedo (1815–88) self-consciously disengages himself from the ocean and "su horizonte lejano/Que inspira la libertad" ["its distant horizon/That inspires liberty"] (J. M. Gutiérrez 1846, 450). He pauses "Sobre el escombro de un puente" ["Upon the ruin of a bridge"] (450), which is to say at the antipodes of Gómez de Avellaneda's symbol of progress, the "puente aereo." Speaking from a more full-bodied subject than that available to Godoy's neoclassical witness, his yo literally immerses itself in the state of American innocence:

> Al fin, desnudo, a la sombra
> De algun cancho centenario,
> Al blando concierto vario
> Del viento y del agua azul;
>   Oyendo sobre mi frente
> El tierno canto de un ave,
> Quisiera a su voz suave
> Mezclar mi triste laud.
>   En un recodo apacible,
> Bajo un dosel de verdura,
> Vigor, placer, y frescura
> Hallo alegre al zabullir;
> Y mientras hundido vago,
> en las olas jugueteo,
> Acariciado me creo
> En un regazo jentil.
>   Aquí la planta del hombre
> Apenas tiene una huella:

El agua duerme o se estrella
Con belleza natural.

(J. M. Gutiérrez 1846, 450)

    At last, naked, in the shade
Of some aged boulder,
In the soft and varied concert
Of blue water and the wind;
Listening to the tender song
Of a bird above my head,
I wish to mix my sad
Lute with its gentle voice.
    In a peaceful corner,
Under a headboard of green,
Happily, I find delight, vigor
And coolness when I dive in;
And while submerged, I wander
Playing about under the waves,
I imagine myself in a fair lap
Caressed in fair embrace.
    Here the foot of man
Has barely left its print:
The water sleeps or shatters
With natural loveliness.

Barely, and yet a little: the concession to realism reinvigorates the Edenic commonplace with concrete experience; the poet himself has been here before. He is transported to his childhood ("jugueteo"), where the caress, if not unambiguous, expresses more maternal security than erotic excitement. But paradise regained is not paradise, nor is innocence recaptured a successful trope for liberty lost. Hence, Madiedo's very fine poem leads nonetheless to an impoverished poetics in the concluding allocution to nature:

    El hombre, pobre copista
De tu elegante belleza,
Busca en vano en su cabeza
Algo mas bello que tú

(J. M. Gutiérrez 1846, 451)

    Man, poor imitator
Of your elegant beauty,
Searches vainly in his head
For aught more beautiful than you.

Sublimity, presented by Gómez in more orthodox Christian terms as the "eco del coro celestial" ["echo of the celestial chorus"], is thus located outside the self, and as such must be experienced as surprise, as in the walking tour of Illimani undertaken by Mariano Ramallo (Bolivia, b. 1817), "Cuando al volver una peña/Por un torrente cortada/Se presentó ante mis ojos/Esa gigante montaña" ["When on rounding an outcrop/Cut off by a torrent/That gigantic mountain/Appeared before my eyes"] (J. M. Gutiérrez 1846, 712).

Ramallo, too, transposes his encounter with sublimity in Christian terms as a mystical blinding on the model of Paul on the road to Damascus:

> Como al salir de un letargo
> Si el sol la pupila hiere,
> Palpita, vacila y muere
> Velada en negro capuz.
> Y los ojos deslumbrados
> Y en las tinieblas sumidos,
> Quedan de pronto perdidos
> En un torrente de luz
>
> (J. M. Gutiérrez 1846, 712)

> Like the pupil of one rising from
> A drowse, if wounded by the sun,
> It blinks, it vacillates, and veiled
> In a black hood, it dies.
> And his dazzled eyes
> In darkness sunk
> Are of a sudden lost
> In a torrent of light.

The poet recovers his sight, but remains in an ecstasy, "sin movimiento y sin voz" ["without movement, without voice"] (J. M. Gutiérrez 1846, 712), as he contemplates ". . . su nieve virjinal" [". . . its virginal snow"] where "Jamas ha sido posada/Del hombre la planta osada/Ni del águila real" ["Never has there been posed/The bold footstep of man/Nor of the golden eagle"] (712). Poet and poem descend thereafter into a *locus amoenus* more beautiful than sublime. Then, as in Godoy's final cataclysm, the world is obliterated, if only by the darkness of dusk, leaving just the very crest of Illimani visible in the final rays of the sun. The peak appears "desprendida/De su eterno pedestal" ["detached/From its eternal pedestal"] (713) enabling its metaphoric transformation into an evening star, "una infinita perla/Colgada en la inmensidad" ["an infinite pearl/Hung in the immensity"] (713).

Godoy, I recall, thought the mountain peak separated from its base by the flood would form a cross in the universal graveyard. In the only other poem by Ramallo that Gutiérrez prints, a voice speaks from that graveyard at the base of Illimani, the real and ruined world of the American interior isolated from the sea and the trope of liberty at "su horizonte lejano" ["its distant horizon"], for lack of lanes of communication. The opening situation of "Inspiración" is as bitter as the orange grove and its garden of balsamic flowers in the "Canto a la cordillera de los Andes" were sweet:

> En un árido desierto,
> Bajo un cielo nebuloso,
> Del huracán proceloso
> Combatido sin cesar;
> Al pié de incultas montañas
> Celebradas por sus minas,
> Alienta entre viejas ruinas
> El pueblo do está mi hogar.
>   Parece que el cielo quiso
> Condenar en él mi vida . . .

(J. M. Gutiérrez 1846, 714)

> In an arid desert,
> Beneath a cloudy sky,
> Combated ceaselessly
> By tempestuous hurricanes;
> At the foot of uncivilized mountains
> Celebrated for their mines,
> Respires the town where I reside
> Amidst ruined remains.
>
> It seems as if the heavens wished
> To condemn me here for life . . .

Whatever the experience of rustic life may be for shepherd or farmer, Ramallo declares that for the poet obliged to live in Horatian retirement, the ideal of innocence is in reality stultification. This is the world that he will flee, a world outside the commerce of letters, and Ramallo's critique, therefore, might be no more than a foreshadowing of modernista irony, were it not for the conscious-

ness of history in the reference to the mines. This is not the uncultivated land that the Spanish liked to believe that they had found, a
belief perpetuated by their American heirs in such foundational fictions as Berro's tale of Montevideo, but rather the uncultured land
of their own creation, the America of the outposts of the colonial
mining industry. In Ramallo's "espantosa realidad" ["frightful
reality"], that colonial heritage persists, giving the lie to the trope
of liberty and Bello's related mythography of the progress of
poetry.

The metaphors of the virgin landscape collapse into their oppo-
sites under the weight of the drudgery. The undefiled snowcaps that
are sublimated as the shining pearl in Ramallo's twilight vision of
Illimani, descend here, leaving nature "en las nieves del invierno/
Envuelta, como un sudario" ["Wrapped in the snows of winter/As
in a shroud"] (J. M. Gutiérrez 1846, 714). And this "naturaleza
muerta" ["still life," literally "dead nature"] (714) offers no inspiration, no breath of air for an American poetry:

> Jamas escucho el susurro
> Del céfiro entre las hojas,
> Ni la angustia y las congojas
> Llegan a mi soledad
> De la tórtola amorosa . . .
>
> (J. M. Gutiérrez 1846, 714)

> I never hear the whisper
> Of the zephyr in the leaves,
> Nor do the anguish and the grief
> Of loving turtle-doves
> Reach my solitude . . .

This is a dead end for the poetics of mimesis and the utopian semiotics of legible surfaces, for Gómez, Lizardi's Payo or Bello. The
"tierra prometida" ["promised land"] of "La libertad" has become
"el dominio de la muerte" ["the dominion of death"] in Ramallo's
poem (J. M. Gutiérrez 1846, 714).

If there is poetry at all in this dismal netherworld, it is associated
with mining, as it was in Aguirre's hell and still so in Landívar's
Rusticatio. Hence, the path to a resurgent figuration for Ramallo is
the commercial route that silver continues to travel in his own time
from Bolivia to the sea, where, he imagines, "flotantes fortalezas/
Que dominando el elemento audaz,/Conducen en su seno las rique-

zas/Siempre con vivo infatigable afan" ['floating fortresses/Which, commanding the bold element,/Bear riches on its breast/Forever with lively indefatigable zeal"] (J. M. Gutiérrez 1846, 714). In this view, poetry is an extractive industry, delving beneath barren surfaces to uncover hidden meaning. Thus, when Ramallo recoils from his cursing, he concludes:

> Oiré en la voz del desierto
> Tu omnipotente entereza;
> Y el himno de tu grandeza
> En la ronca tempestad
>
> (J. M. Gutiérrez 1846, 715)

> In the voice in the desert
> I will hear your omnipotent integrity;
> And the hymn of your majesty
> In the roiling tempest's roar.

Ramallo means this "respeto relijioso" ["religious respect"] as he calls it in "Canto a la cordillera de los Andes" (J. M. Gutiérrez 1846, 712), as a humbling of the poet, as was the case for Madre Castillo, Heredia and Gómez de Avellaneda. Following the order of composition, according to the dates appended to the texts, this reining in of the poet's power to curse and his humility in "Inspiracion" would lead to his rise at Illimani to the confrontation with the sublime and a final meditation in "Canto a la cordillera de los Andes" on the "¡Obra jigante de Dios!" ["Gigantic work of God!"] (713). In their chronological order Ramallo's poems can be conjoined as a single progress piece—whether the pilgrim's progress from despond to grace or more strictly Bello's poetic progress from images of decadence to the purity of a virgin land.

By reversing that order in *América poética*, Gutiérrez highlights the moment in the midst of progress toward renewed purity when the American poet abandons the posture of innocence and admits his guilt—"Perdon, no escuches, Dios mio/Mi terrena queja impia" ["Forgive me, do not listen, my God/To my impious, earth-bound complaint"] (J. M. Gutiérrez 1846, 715). Ramallo is awed to silence by the resurgence of the wind from his heretofore breathless mining town in the voice of the storm in the midst of the "soledad inmensa" ["immense solitude"] (715). Cut off from the commerce of letters, Ramallo may not have known that Heredia had already found inspiration in that isolation from the phenomenal world of the "pobre copista" ["poor imitator"] and that in response to the poetics of Bello, he had taken the storm as the occasion to discover not beauty, but grandeur, and not without, but within. Ramallo, I repeat, very well may not have known the counter-sublime of Heredia (his debt to Bello is patent), but Gutiérrez did. And his editorial hand in the simple reversal of chronological order in the presentation of Ramallo's poems brings to the fore the virtual dialogue constituting modern American poetry in the verse of an unfamiliar poet in the otherwise unread pages of the Bolivian periodical press. As Gutiérrez also knew, modernity traveled all the routes.

4

Before one comes to the "Alocución" in the pages of *América poética*, before one reads even Gutiérrez's prospectus, reprinted in the expanded prolog to the anthology, one finds his epigraph on the title page: "Ningún lazo de union y afecto entre los pueblos será jamas tan fuerte como el del cultivo de las mismas artes y del mismo idioma." Gutiérrez takes this first, fragmentary entry from the *Resumen de la historia de Venezuela* by Rafael María Baralt (Venezuela 1810–60) in its original edition of Paris, 1841 (see Baralt 1939). The selection is doubly significant. The choice of a prose text to introduce poetry is symptomatic of the shifting balance in the commerce of letters. In the year before the first fascicle of *América poética* appeared in print, I recall, Sarmiento was publishing *Facundo*. Furthermore, the choice of a work of historiography is a prognosis. The emergence of a historical consciousness had defined the modern task of poetry. Baralt's *Resumen* is representative of a challenge that constituted the "hidden impulse" that led Gutiérrez to his "researches in our history" through the printed text of poetry. Gutiérrez would foment the progress of poetry through his forward-looking attention to the youngest poets of his day. But poetry would lose out to its rival in the second half of the nineteenth century. Baralt and Sarmiento and later Mitre, Restrepo, Alamán and many others including, in their different ways Palma, the *costumbrista* writers throughout the continent and eventually the novelists, and indeed Gutiérrez, who abandoned a promising career as a prize-winning poet to devote himself to literary history, are the composite authors of an *América histórica*, which is also an

América prosaica. In this sense, Gutiérrez's great compendium now reads as a cemetery of the lyric.

I have sampled the anthology as a source for the rediscovery of individual authors and as an integrated text whose ambivalent argument is that America is poetic, an argument that turns upon the question of America's innocence. In a final pass through the cemetery, I will read *América poética* as a literary history, that is as a sourcebook for the reconstruction of modern national literary histories very much in progress but already discernible at midcentury. I will concern myself with a single case, the literary history of Venezuela, as a direct response to the challenge of Baralt's prose history of the nation. I will concentrate on the poetry of two Venezuelans, José Antonio Maitín (1804–74) and Abigaíl Lozano (1821–66), and among those selections, the poems that they dedicate to the memory of Bolívar.

Restricting biographical information to the introductory notes provided by Gutiérrez, as Gutiérrez himself had limited his portrait of Berro to the printed source of Lamas, an epochal distinction is already visible. Maitín, a member of the generation of Heredia and Echeverría, is presented as a man coeval with the whole period of poetry encompassed by *América poética*. He was born in the colonial Venezuela of Monteverde's despotic regime on the brink of Bolívar's insurrection; and his family left for Cuba, like the Heredias, when José Antonio was still a boy. There, again like the younger Heredia, Maitín made the acquaintance of Fernández de Madrid, who, in Gutiérrez's words, "infused in him a love for literature and named him his secretary in the Colombian diplomatic mission to London" (J. M. Gutiérrez 1846, 503). Thus, Gutiérrez's brief biography conjoins Maitín's initiation into poetry and political life. He goes on to note that after a second London sojourn in the legation of Colombian economist Santos Michelena (1797–1848), Maitín reestablished himself definitively in Venezuela, where he found a place in the print culture of Caracas, while choosing for himself a rustic retirement in Choroni, "a most lovely spot, not far from Caracas, where the poet sweetly lives his life" (503).[8] Gutiérrez further fills out the literary background of Maitín's verse by relating that "it is believed that the reading of the early poetry of Zorrilla greatly impressed him" (503). In sum, a witness of colonial oppression, a participant in the constitutional dialogue, a patriot attached to his American locale, but also a reader active in the international commerce of letters. In contrast, the few biographical lines dedicated to Lozano present him through the words of the local press as a noble savage: "the young Lozano had neither studies nor even the books necessary to undertake them" (425). Gutiérrez then adds his editorial judgment: "If this is true, the beautiful compositions of this poet will have even greater merit for our readers" (425).

The merit would be the confirmation of the mythology of poetic originality. Lozano would be the very model of romantic genius, whose personal gift it is to transmute experience directly into art without the aid of books. This view supplies a certain nostalgia in the print culture, suspicious from the outset of the implications of its own bookishness, for the forms of learning and modes of communication that it had superseded. Traditional and popular poetry are absent from *América poética* in Gutiérrez's commitment to print, as I have noted, but the absence is countered by this mythology of the new-found poet as an individualized version of the folk. Finally, Lozano without books is the embodiment of Bello's Divine Poetry after its arrival. He sings, like the American *avecilla*, in "uninstructed tones," or so the press in Caracas likes to paint him, and so, too, Gutiérrez would like his readers to believe.

The literate prehistory of Maitín's elegies for Bolívar may be condensed by reference to the elegies of his mentor Fernández de Madrid, whose "Canción al padre de Colombia y Libertador del Perú" heads the selection of the latter's poems in *América poética*. Gutiérrez presented a Fernández de Madrid who differs significantly from the poet circa 1823 of my prior discussion. There are two further occasional poems dedicated to Bolívar and two elegies for Atahualpa, which might well be read in connection with the more effective, satiric vindication of "los descendientes/Del grande Huayna-Cápac" ["the descendants/Of the great Huayna-Cápac"] in Fernández de Madrid's "La hamaca":

> Hace mui bien el indio
> Que, en su choza de paja,
> De sus ávidos amos
> Engaña la esperanza:
> Para que estos no cojan
> El fruto de sus ansias,
> En su hamaca tendido,
> Se ocupa en no hacer nada.

> (J. M. Gutiérrez 1846, 490)

  The Indian does very well,
Who, in his hut of straw,
Deceives the expectations
Of his avaricious lord:
To keep them from enjoying
The fruits of his travails,
He busies himself lying
In his hammock, doing nothing

Fernández de Madrid's *indio* appears as a subtle revolutionary, deliberately undermining the constitution of modern political identity in terms of useful labor, for he knows that the corresponding equation of liberty and property continues to exclude him from the fruits of independence.[9]

  As regards Maitín's "Canto a Bolívar," it will suffice here to observe that the Bolívar of Fernández de Madrid's poetry was a living contemporary, the "Tremendo guerrero" ["Tremendous warrior"] (J. M. Gutiérrez 1846, 453) of the wars of independence. The two birthday odes of October 1825 are dated less than a year after Ayacucho. Yet as another contemporary, José María de Pando (Peru 1787–1840) wrote in his verse letter to Bolívar of the following year, "Epístola a Próspero" (dated Lima 1826), military success alone would not secure his posterity:

  El duro casco y la coraza arroja;
  Y la cándida toga revistiendo,
  Dócil a inspiraciones de Minerva,
  Sabias, justas, estables, dános LEYES.
         (J. M. Gutiérrez 1846, 661)

  Cast aside the breast plate and hard helm;
  And donning anew the candid toga,
  Obedient to the inspirations of Minerva,
  Wise and just and stable, give us LAWS.

Fernández de Madrid also presents a Bolívar for these constitutional times, "sumiso al freno de las leyes,/Mas que guerrero, digno ciudadano" ["submitting to the bit of the law,/More than a soldier, a worthy citizen"] (J. M. Gutiérrez 1846, 469) in stark contrast to Iturbide's claim to imperial power in his "Fragmento de una oda a Iturbide en 1823." Yet even Pando is aware of murmurings: "Deja ladrar a la calumnia infame/Que en todos tiempos vierte su ponzoña" ["Leave infamous calumny to bark/For it spills its venom in every age"] (661). And Heredia, still the son of Bolívar's erstwhile adversary, Heredia senior the judge, clarified the accusation in his "A Bolívar," a poem that Gutiérrez did not include in *América poética*:[10]

> . . . Letal sospecha
> En torno de tu frente revolando
> Empaña su esplendor: yacen las leyes
> Indignamente holladas,
> Sin ser por ti vengadas.
>
> (J. M. Heredia 1940, 2:107)

> . . . Lethal suspicion
> Hovering at your brow
> Dampens your splendor; the laws
> Are trodden infamously underfoot,
> And you have not avenged them.

Writing as a Venezuelan native and after Bolívar's death, Maitín's elegy would acquit his hero of all charges, restoring his innocence and his glory. Greater than Alexander, "Ni sangre inútil derramó al pasar" ["Nor did he spill blood in vain"] (J. M. Gutiérrez 1846, 504); greater than Caesar, "Jamás holló frenético las leyes" ["Never did he tread upon the law in frenzy"] (504); greater than Napoleon:

> . . . Cual colosal estátua
> No alza hasta el cielo la cabeza altiva,
> En tanto que a sus piés jime cautiva
> Y entre dorados hierros la Nación.
>
> (J. M. Gutiérrez 1846, 504)

> . . . As a colossal statue
> Does not raise its proud head to the skies
> While at its feet the Nation cries,
> A captive in its golden chains.

The statue is an oddly static answer to the riddle of the poem, which begins as a processional, and whose first movement, almost in a musical sense, is the translation of the question from the cause of celebration ("¿Qué gritos de victoria . . . ?" ["What cries of victory . . . ?"] J. M. Gutiérrez 1846, 503) to the name of the champion:

> ¿Quién es, ¡oh Musa! indómito el guerrero
> Que como el rayo entre la nube espesa,
> De triunfo en triunfo intrépido atraviesa
> La selva, el llano, el risco aterrador?
>
> (J. M. Gutiérrez 1846, 504)

> Who, oh Muses! is the invincible warrior
> Who, intrepid, crosses like lightning
> Through thick clouds, the jungle, terrifying
> Peaks and plains from victory to victory?

The unnamed hero of the progress piece then continues past those failing antecedents to the triumph of liberty in ancient and modern times, leaving European history behind, and "El resplandor celeste de su espada/Como un rayo benéfico del dia/Rasga la nube lóbrega y sombría/Que a la virjen América eclipsó" ["The celestial brilliance of his sword/Like a beneficent ray of daylight/Tears the dark and gloomy cloud/That eclipsed virgin America"] (J. M. Gutiérrez 1846, 504).

The second movement comes to an end with the expansion of the metaphor of the "¡Jenio feliz, meteoro deslumbrante/Que rápido surcó la vasta esfera!" ["Happy genius, blinding meteor/That swiftly blazed the vast sphere"] (J. M. Gutiérrez 1846, 505):

> Así el ambiente está cargado
> De impuros, de mefíticos vapores,
> Recoje el sol sus bellos resplandores
> y su broche jentil cierra la flor;
> Dobla la espiga el vástago marchito,
> Enmudecen las auras fujitivas,
> y sus notas brillantes y festivas
> Interrumpe asustado el ruiseñor.
> El cielo se oscurece lentamente,
> El mundo calla de terrores lleno,
> Solo el acento lúgubre del trueno
> Se oye en la negra esfera retumbar.
> Revienta el rayo al fin, rasga la nube,
> Ronco turbion en remolino crece,
> Y la celeste bóveda parece
> De lava y sangre un espantoso mar.
>
> (J. M. Gutiérrez 1846, 505)

Thus the atmosphere is charged
With impure, sulfurous odor,
The sun gathers its beauteous splendor
And the flower clasps its lovely brooch;
The grain bends down its withered stalk,
The fleeting breeze is stilled,
The frightened nightingale leaves off
Its brilliant notes and cheer.
    The heavens slowly darken,
The fearful world goes mute,
And only thunder's doleful note
Is heard in the black sphere.
Bursting, at last, the bolt rips the cloud,
The hoarse whirlwind twists and grows
And the celestial vault shows
Itself a frightful sea of lava and of blood.

It is not the least of Maitín's accomplishments to have condensed the whole history of Spanish American poetry of the period into this passage: from the detailed observations of Enlightenment science through the undoing of the representative images of the Arcadian world to a fully romantic trope for cataclysmic eruption.

But Maitín is constrained by his rhetorical form. The allocutionary frame requires him to return to his riddle—"¿Quién es *entonces*?" ["Who is it, *then*?"] (J. M. Gutiérrez 1846, 504); I add emphasis so as to ask whether the poet himself is not growing tired of his own ploy. Where Heredia achieves the sublimation of the self in the face of universal disaster, Maitín reins in the storm and restores the world of innocence:

Mas el Iris benéfico aparece,
Y la niebla que flota al horizonte,
Prende en las faldas del lejano monte
Su gasa trasparente y virjinal.
Levanta el tallo la marchita espiga,
Abren sus tiernos cálices las flores,
Canta de nuevo el ave sus amores
y alza la tierra su himno universal.

(J. M. Gutiérrez 1846, 505)

But Iris, bountiful, appears,
And the mist that floats on the far horizon
Drapes the skirts of the distant mountain

With virginal, transparent lace.
The withered grain lifts up its stalk,
The flowers open their saintly, tender cups,
The bird once more its song of love takes up,
And the earth raises its universal hymn.

The Enlightenment ideal of liberty triumphs over darkness, and the world is safe for the agriculture of the torrid zone once more. The poet is not yet finished, however. The triumph of liberty was the task of the unnamed hero. His naming is the task of poetry, and the enigma has not yet been resolved. The same triumph of liberty must be repeated, therefore, as the progress of poetry.

The poet himself is the new hero of the new quest, for which he takes his muse as his guide. But her arrival poses a new riddle as well:

¿Mas qué estraño pesar cubre tu frente?
Tu labio puro y virjinal suspira,
Y de fúnebre gasa trasparente
Velas la dulce, la sonante lira.

(J. M. Gutiérrez 1846, 505)

But what strange grief covers your brow?
Your lip, pure and virginal, sighs,
And with funereal, transparent lace
You veil the sweet, the sounding lyre.

The reappearance of the virginal figure dressed in her black weeds allows the *transparent* identification of the Muse with America in eclipse. The questing poet is puzzled by her melancholic aspect, as well he might be after the celebratory tone that introduced the relentlessly triumphant progress of liberty.

The explanation to this and all the pretended riddles of the "Canto a Bolívar" are broadcast in his more forthright, but less interesting, "Homenaje a Bolívar. Desahogo patriótico." There, for instance, Maitín pronounces the ineffable name at several reprises, though not without an awe and supplication ("perdona si te nombra/Quien a cantar tus glorias no se atreve" ["excuse me if I name you/He who does not dare to sing your glories"] J. M. Gutiérrez 1846, 520 and 521) that will ultimately silence him ("La débil voz en la garganta espira" ["The weak voice expires in the throat"] Gutiérrez 1846, 521). And he names the cataclysmic darkness as

well by reference to the political landscape of the 1820s: for
America, "la noche fatal de la anarquia" ["the fatal night of anar-
chy"] (521), and for Bolívar personally, the "maliciosa insidia"
["malicious plot"] of those accusations, such as Heredia's, that
stained his glory:

> Así el disco del sol es mas divino
> Despues de oscura y tempestuosa noche,
> Cuando a su rayo rojo y matutino
> La flor despliega su encendido broche.
>
> (J. M. Gutiérrez 1846, 520)

> Thus the disk of the sun is more divine
> After a dark, tempestuous night,
> When in the red ray of the dawn, the brooch
> Of the flower unfurled is bathed in light.

The American Muse of the poet's quest through the darkened
landscape of "A Bolívar" is Bello's *Divina Poesía* after her arrival,
not to the bucolic paradise Bello himself dreamed of from London,
but to the *espantosa realidad* of a militant liberty unable to sustain
itself after the success of independence. And as I have had occasion
to discuss, the Virgil most active in Spanish American letters was
not so much the Virgil of the *Georgics*, of Landívar's *Rusticatio*
and "La agricultura de la zona tórrida," as the Virgil of *Aeneid*
book 6, the Virgil of the greater part of the "Alocución," of
Olmedo, of Zequeira, of Peralta.

Maitín's funerary Muse leads him through that literary history
until he is unsure where life ends and literature begins:

> Si es ilusion no sé: pero yo ignoro
> Si estas sombras fantásticas que miro,
> Si este que escucho lamentable lloro
> Es pura realidad, o si delirio.
>
> (J. M. Gutiérrez 1846, 506)

> If it is illusion, I cannot say: nor do I know
> If these fantastic shadows that I see,
> If this I hear, this cry of sorrow,
> Is mere delirium or pure reality.

The poet only assures himself that he is faced with reality when,
"En medio de esta noche tenebrosa/Descubro un monumento fun-

erario" ["In the midst of this dark night/I discover a funerary monument"] (J. M. Gutiérrez 1846, 506). In short he has passed through
a hallucinatory underworld only to find himself, in fact, in a cemetery. Now he begs his Muse to reveal the name on that monument,
hidden, once again, by "la gasa trasparente/Que la lápida vela mis-
teriosa" ["the transparent crepe/That veils the headstone mysteri-
ously"] (506), unawares, it would seem, that the end of this quest
would also be the resolution of the prior riddle. "Por mi no temas"
["Do not fear for me"], he tells the Muse:

> . . . la inscripción descubre
> Que yo la copa apuraré de acibar:
> El velo caiga que la losa encubre.
> Aliento corazon! . . . Leeré . . . ¡¡BOLIVAR!!!
>
> (J. M. Gutiérrez 1846, 506)

> . . . uncover the inscription
> For I shall drain the cup of sorrow:
> Let fall the veil that covers up the stone.
> Bear up, heart! . . . I shall read . . . BOLIVAR!

The future tense is the poet's last trick. Are we reading the inscription on the stone along with him after the veil falls? Or, a prophet
at the last, does he write out the inscription that he has not yet read?
He is, I venture, both surprised and sure all at once. His task has
not been discovery, but uncovering, not to learn the name, but to
restore it as a national monument after the dark night of calumny.
What appeared throughout to be an expedition is rather a compulsion, indeed a national necessity to repeat. A statue after all: he has
been on a visit to the museum of American history.

I might look along the trajectory of that future tense to a more
fully-fledged Spanish American romanticism beyond the pages of
América poética in Maitín's own "Canto fúnebre" in memory of
his wife, one of the most ambitious elegies of the nineteenth century, and one of the best. The poem interiorizes what is rather a
national epic in the "Canto a Bolívar" through its amplification of
the traditional terms of the sepulchral inscription, Requiescat in
pace, in which the poet's deceased wife is named, "Mi descanso,
mi paz, *mi independencia*" [My rest, my peace, *my independence*"]
(Barnola 1935, 45, emphasis added). The poem builds to a domestic
sublimity without abandoning the delicate intensity of its conversa-

tional diction, whose key is the recollection of the traditional posture of the melancholic, elbow bent, head propped in hand:[11]

> Sin objeto, sin plan y sin camino,
> Alrededor de mi desierta casa,
> Vago de senda en senda y sin destino.
> Recorro los lugares
> Que ella en sus horas de ocio frecuentaba
> El codo en la rodilla,
> Y en la entreabierta mano
> Apoyada la pálida mejilla.
>
> (Barnola 1935, 48)

> With no goal, no plan, no road,
> I wander aimlessly
> From path to path about my empty home.
> Returning to those places
> Where she in idle hours would be,
> Her elbow on her knee,
> And resting her pale cheek
> Upon her open hand.

His beloved has bequeathed her melancholia to him. Unable to deny his loss, unwilling to complete the work of mourning, his independence has become his utter dependence upon her memory to direct his steps. Internal traffic has imploded and as a result all routes to commerce with the outside world are dead ends. From this poetic stance, the regressive, demetaphorizing pressures of melancholia manifest themselves in the poet's veneration of the household dust, dust which his wife has literally become by a barely displaced metonymy. The poem staggers through a certain moralizing that weakens this and much romantic poetry in Spanish America, where, as in Ramallo's "Inspiración," the poetic potential of despair is often accounted too close to blasphemy. Maitín recaptures the vigor of his melancholia only in the final verse. "Descansa en paz" ["Rest in peace"], the line begins; but once again the poet amplifies. An ellipsis supervenes and the words beyond the caesura transform the future tense of the "Canto a Bolívar" into the compulsive voice of the death drive: "Yo volveré mañana" ["I will return tomorrow"] (Barnola 1935, 62). The poet thus translates Liropeya's final words: "I will soon join you in the grave," he predicts, and at the same time he promises to keep faith with the dead through his own death in life. He will be her revenant—"Cual máquina ambulante,/Sin senda, sin camino conocido,/las manos extendidas, delirante" ["Like a walking automaton,/Without a path, nor familiar road,/Hands extended, delirious"] (62)—shuttling between the grave itself and the house in which he entombs himself with the settled dust of the dead.[12]

Gutiérrez was attempting to document that trajectory in the earliest stages of its formation in *América poética*, at a moment in which the routes of modernity, previously traced across the breadth of national life, were turning steadily inward. Lozano's "A Bolívar" stands at a turning point in that road between Maitín's "Canto a Bolívar" and his "Canto fúnebre." For Lozano was neither a participant in the emancipation of America, nor in the formation of the republics in the early constitutional period, like Fernández de Madrid and Maitín. His Bolívar, therefore, is already not quite his own, but rather the subject of history as his mother fashioned it for domestic consumption:

> Ayer cuando era niño mi madre me contaba
> La historia de tres siglos que América escribió:
> Contábame que un hombre (que al recordar lloraba)
> Sobre un caduco cetro la independencia alzó.
> Contábame que ese hombre do quiera con su espada
> Sepulcros dió al tirano y a América un altar;
> Que cuál Jehová los orbes sacara de la nada,
> Él supo un mundo libre del caos levantar.
>
> (J. M. Gutiérrez 1846, 429)

> Yesterday, when I was a child, my mother used to tell
> The history of three centuries that America had written:
> She used to tell me that a man (whose memory brought her tears)
> Raised up independence over an outmoded throne.
> She used to tell me that where're he went with sword in hand,
> He brought altars to America, and to the tyrant, tombs;
> That he succeeded in lifting a free world from the abyss,
> Just as Jehovah a cosmos out of nothing drew.

Lozano's repetition of "contaba" ["used to tell"] obviates further emphasis on my part. Here is Lozano's own version of the myth of poetic origins. He has no books nor need of them, since he learns American history by word of mouth. Yet by this account of his own poetic prehistory, his source proves not to be experience after all, but popular culture.

Lozano's own history of Bolívar begins immediately thereafter as his encounter with high culture:

> Pasó mi edad de niño, mas luego me hice hombre
> Ví en un salon suntuoso la forma de un varon:
> Avida la pupila buscó a sus piés el nombre,
> Y sorprendida el alma deletreó "Simon!!!"
>
> (J. M. Gutiérrez 1846, 429)

> The age of childhood passed, but once I reached a man's estate,
> In a sumptuous hall I came upon the shape of a man:
> Avidly my pupil sought the name written at its feet,
> And much surprised my soul deciphered, "Simón"!

The painting stands in for print, the *salon suntuoso* for a *salon luctuoso*. The portrait is Lozano's version of Maitín's funerary statue, and the reading lesson not only repeats and resolves the riddle of the "Canto a Bolívar," but also the ambiguities of its final, future tense. The reading eye is avid because it knows the name even before it is fully revealed—as in Maitín's case—but it is surprised nevertheless because the soul is unprepared for the impact. The unpreparedness is characteristic, as we have seen in Ramallo's excursion to Illimani, of the encounter with sublimity in the aesthetic world of the *pobre copista*—Bolívar's portraitist, for instance. But in Lozano's poem the surprise is distinct. He is in fact prepared by his maturity and the stately circumstances to witness for the first time with his own eyes the grandeur of the national hero, "mas sublime que el sol" ["more sublime than the sun"] (J. M. Gutiérrez 1846, 430). What startles him is the uncanny familiarity. National history, including Maitín's elegy, has written "Bolívar," but the young Lozano finds "Simon"—unlike Maitín, his title has not given away his riddle in advance.

Lozano knows and repeats the imagery of Bolívar's triumphs familiar from the elegies of Fernández de Madrid, Maitín and many others, but from his later vantage point he also goes on to report:

> Mas tarde abrieron tu historia
> Por baldon arrinconada,
> Y arrepentida y turbada
> Lloró una jeneracion.
>
> (J. M. Gutiérrez 1846, 430)

> Later they opened your history,
> Closeted away, for shame,
> And troubled and ashamed,
> A generation wept.

These are the tears that accompanied his mother's recitation of Bolívar's story during the period when his personal, political ambitions were held suspect for overriding the constitutional process he had set in motion with his victories on the battlefield. Lozano's poem is dedicated not so much to the glorious figure in the portrait, as to the icon of the domestic altar bewailed by his mother, which is the same portrait defaced by calumny: "Que el malo tu retrato rabioso conducia,/Y le arrastró en el suelo con torpe frenesí" ["For raging, evil men brought your portrait/And they dragged it in the dirt with gruesome ecstasy"] (J. M. Gutiérrez 1846, 431). Maitín had obscured Bolívar's fall from grace in the account of national history as a metaphorical veil cast over his name. He claimed that the veil was lifted in the end, predicting that the name would be cleared, the blemish expunged in a restored national monument.

Lozano proceeds otherwise. His is a tale from beyond the crypt. His Bolívar will not rest in peace—"rompe la losa yerta tu sombra" ["your shade breaks the rigid sepulchre"] (J. M. Gutiérrez 1846, 429)—until the history of *his defacement* is also acknowledged. The accusers who disfigured Bolívar are themselves blemished by their own accusations: "En tu funeral congoja/Te vió riéndose, espirar" ["In your fatal troubles/They watched laughing as you expired"] (430), where the immediate antecedent is "el malo," but could as well be "Venezuela." The tearful recollections of Lozano's mother may disfigure her own features in her retelling of Bolívar's career, but they also provide an alternative image of voice to the sardonic laughter of a self-interested national elite—an image of popular voices that were to have participated in the constitutional dialogue, but instead were marginalized in the new national discourse and its poetry.

And yet, unfortunately, Lozano too retreats from the greater possibilities at which he hints. Like Ramallo after emptying the American landscape of its idealizing topoi, Lozano recoils from the upending of the standard elegiac tropes for Bolívar as the "Libertador de un mundo" ["Liberator of a world"] (J. M. Gutiérrez 1846, 429) or, in Fernández de Madrid's still more rotund epithet, "Libertador de un mundo entero" ["Liberator of a whole world"] (460).

One might have wished otherwise, but, no Heredia, he cannot make a self-wounding into a trope for a counter-sublimity, and instead closes beseechingly:

> Perdona, o patria mia, si en mi cantar te ofendo
> Si recordé insensato lo que olvidar debí;
> Perdona . . . en tu semblante yo tímido comprendo,
> Que acaso al son del harpa tu corazon herí.
>
> (J. M. Gutiérrez 1846, 431)

> Forgive me, oh my homeland, if with my song I give offense,
> If I remembered foolishly, what it is better to forget;
> For from your face, abashedly, at last I start
> To see that I may have wounded your heart with my harp.

He sacrifices his melancholic attachments to the designs of national history.

5

Even anthologies have a history, whose fragmentary historical record may be no more than a title or an epigraph. When the Cuban poets José Fornaris (1827–90) and Joaquín Lorenzo Luaces (1826–67) sought to promote a cultural emancipation that might support, in time, political independence for the island, they compiled an anthology that would define a national poetic identity. Anticipating the insufficiency of their efforts, they aver the lack of proper models in their own defense: "To form a true Parnassus, it is necessary that there have previously existed works of the same genre, to construct, with their materials, a book worthy of posterity" (Fornaris and Luaces 1858, v). This form of the modesty topos, with its fine understanding of intertextuality, would constitute an unexpected reaction against the romantic trope of originality, were it not that they were thereby presenting themselves as true originals. The implicit claim holds no further, however, than the echo of Gutiérrez in their title: *Cuba poética: Coleccion escogida de las composiciones en verso de los poetas cubanos desde Zequeira hasta nuestros días* (Havana 1858). If not the first anthology, they might still hope to have compiled the first national collection, but this patriotic design is also disappointed, since they conclude, despite themselves, that it is premature to declare the existence of a "truly

Cuban literature": "But if we do not achieve such satisfactory results, it may at least serve as a stimulus to those who may finally publish a classic book, thus raising a true 'Parnaso cubano' [Cuban Parnassus], a monument to the glories of our poetry" (v). The drive to emancipation leaves the cultural field a decade later in the *Grito de Yara*, with much greater disappointment for Cuban patriots. In the aftermath of the failed uprising Antonio López Prieto answered Fornaris and Luaces's call explicitly with his *Parnaso cubano* (Havana 1881), working from a loyalist position, convinced that their goal of a national literature was an impossibility (see López Prieto 1881, lxix–lxxxi). Thus, when López Prieto links his anthology back to their forebear by reciting the self-same epigraph from Baralt—"Ningún lazo de union y afecto entre los pueblos será jamas tan fuerte como el del cultivo de las mismas artes y del mismo idioma" ["No bond of union and affection between peoples will ever be as strong as that of the cultivation of the same arts and the same language"]—he reverses the sign of *América poética*. For López Prieto on the eve of modernismo, the language of Cuban poetry marks its ineradicable dependency on Spain. For Gutiérrez, on the other hand, publishing his anthology during the North American war on Mexico, *América poética* is already a delineation of "Nuestra América."

I have been suggesting in this concluding chapter that *América poética* provides a foundation for the aesthetics, no less than the anticolonial ideology of modernismo, as delineated by Zavala (1992). I had begun this study as a whole by contesting Paz's view of the absence of "criticism" and thus of modernity prior to the modernistas. Recalling the opening discussion of philology in which I extended Aníbal González's thesis back to the eighteenth century, I would point out that López Prieto seeks to bolster his colonialist reading of the epigraph from Baralt, by citing the philological argument of Enrique Piñeyro, the great Cuban literary critic working from Rénan's Paris: "Language is the clear and ineffable reflection of the character of a people . . . for that reason I have always considered it an axiom to say that those peoples who have not created their own language . . . can never come to have a truly original literature" (qtd by López Prieto 1881, lxxii).[13] Otherwise stated, the museum against which the modernistas will develop an aesthetic of the workshop, in dialectical opposition, is already present in Maitín's statuary and Lozano's portrait of Bolívar in a rather strict sense. More broadly and more telling, Luis L. Domínguez

(Argentina 1819–98), whose poetry Gutiérrez includes in *América poética*, completes Berro's unfinished "El ombú," as it were, by enumerating the flora and fauna that make the shade of the tree their habitat, "Cual museo de la Pampa" ["Like a museum of the Pampa"] (J. M. Gutiérrez 1846, 154).

The museum of philology, or as I have preferred throughout, of natural and national history, is well established as a discursive form by the time of *América poética*. In fact, *América poética* itself is just such a philological museum, as is made explicit in the title of its own precursor, the *Museo de Ambas Américas*, whence Gutiérrez reprinted the poetry of Domínguez, and is exemplified as well by the latter's "El ombú":

> Desde esa turba salvaje
> Que en las llanuras se oculta
> Hasta la porcion mas culta
> De la humana sociedad,
> Como un linde está la Pampa
> Sus dominios dividiendo
> Que vá el bárbaro cediendo
> Palmo a palmo a la Ciudad.
>   Y el rasgo mas prominente
> De esa tierra donde mora
> El salvaje que no adora
> Otro Dios que el *Valichú*,
> Que en *chamal* y poncho envuelto,
> Con los *laques* en la mano
> Va sembrando por el llano
> Mudo horror, es el ombú.
>
> (J. M. Gutiérrez 1846, 154)

>   From those barbarian marauders
> Undiscovered on the plains,
> To the most cultivated portion
> Of human society,
> The Pampa is like a border
> Dividing their domains,
> That the barbarian relinquishes
> To the City, inch by inch.
>   And the trait that most impresses
> In that barbarian land,
> Where the savage adores
> No deity but *Valichú*,

Where in *chamal* and poncho he dresses
And with his *laques* in his hand,
He goes spreading speechless horrors
Through the plains, is the *ombú*.

In the face of progress, in the double sense of a triumphant processional and the disengagement from traditional American social
structures in favor of European civilization, Domínguez takes up
the curatorial task of preserving a vanishing present as it disappears
into the past. He does so as a philologist, underlining lexical specimens and explaining them in a note (e.g. "chamal" = "chiripá";
"laques" = "bolas"): "I believe that poetic language should prefer
the words 'chamal' and 'laques' as well as the accentuation that I
have used in the word commonly pronounced 'gaulichu' or 'vali-
chu' " (J. M. Gutiérrez 1846, 154, n. 1). Poetry should serve as a
philological museum. The same justification, I may add, would hold
for the word "ombú," which serves as a linguistic boundary line
that will perpetually mark off a barbarous (i.e. other-tongued)
Pampa against the progress of the cities. The modernista reaction
to philology, I am arguing on the one hand, develops a discursive
formation that had already been integrated into American poetry—
and *América poética*. Domínguez's enumerative technique may be
situated neatly between Bello's agricultural catalogs and the late
modernista geography of Luis Palés Matos (Puerto Rico 1898–
1959, see, e.g. Palés 1974, 70).

On the other hand, the museum, especially as a collection of
specimens for a natural history, relates the trope to the eighteenth-
century scientific expeditionaries: Captain Tirry y Lacy cataloging
trees on the Isle of Pines for the Mopox Commission; Mutis, including the anonymous poem on the defense of Cartagena among the
native species of Venezuela; and above all Humboldt, brother of the
pioneering philologist Wilhelm, the indefatigable collector—and
publisher—of all things American from its smallest flowers to
Chimborazo; as well as their antecedents in American savants like
Peralta.

And in the beginning of the end, the road was transfigured as
progress, only to be demetaphorized as the railway and the canal,
the sale of America to modernity, paid for by neocolonial investment. Modernismo reacts critically to that positivistic interpretation
of the road, Paz argues. But that reaction, too, is already in evidence
in the preceding century. For when the Enlightened reformers of

the *Mercurio Peruano* had their way, and the grave was removed from the church, a paradigmatic expedition was set in motion between the town and its cemetery. I refer less to the moment of interment, wherein the bereaved still accompany and are accompanied by the deceased, than to the return, when the mourner visits the grave, as we say. The reformers anticipated that the communion of symbolic exchange would still be possible, and that the living, liberated from the vicinity of the dead, would nonetheless be able to consort with the past. The cemetery, after all, would be the natural setting of the dead—a modern irony to please even Paz.

But Domínguez, completing Berro once again with just such an ironic twist, tells the story of that paradigmatic expedition in "El cementerio viejo. Montevideo," as the calamitous triumph of progress over death, what Shelley called with even greater irony, "The Triumph of Life." A certain Carlos interrupts an epithalamion, by undertaking a military expedition on his very wedding day:

> Mas él, de amor, la corona
> Mezclar con palma ha querido,
> Por eso al campo ha salido
> Con su valiente escuadron.
>
> (J. M. Gutiérrez 1846, 155)

> But he, wishing to add
> Laurels to the crown of love,
> Has gone to the battlefield
> With his valiant squad.

He is killed, predictably, but his Dolores accompanies him to the grave without Liropeya's suicidal rigor. Her graveside speech sanctifies the rural cemetery and invokes a premonitory curse to preserve his memory as it is figured metonymically in the dust: "Cubre esta tumba con tu excelsa mano" ["Cover this tomb with your lofty hand"], she implores, "Y si a este polvo toca algun profano,/Tu ira, Señor, castigue su impiedad!" ["And if someone profane should touch this dust,/May your wrath, Lord, punish his irreverence!"] (J. M. Gutiérrez 1846, 156).

A moral interlude reinforces Dolores's anathema, and then a twilight scene is depicted for her expedition to the grave:

> De la mar sobre la espalda
> Se dibuja el negro manto

De una mujer que se acerca
Al cementerio arruinado.

(J. M. Gutiérrez 1846, 156)

A black shawl is etched
Above the broad back of the sea;
It is a woman who draws near
An abandoned cemetery.

The topos of the cemetery in ruins, almost a rhetorical redundancy, is refreshed with unaccustomed horror, as is the traditional epitaph, *Sta viator*:

De repente se detiene;
Lleva a los ojos las manos;
Mira atenta;—observa todo;
Parece fria de pasmo!
En otro tiempo, severo
Estaba aquí el *Campo-santo*;
Hoi todo es ruinas, escombros;
Y entre ellos huesos y cráneos.
Ni una cruz se vé que diga:
"Aquí reposan cristianos."
Dolores, pobre Dolores!
Por qué no vuelves el paso?
Pero ella sigue adelante
Que la fuerza su cuidado;
Y entra al recinto que alumbra
De la noche el astro pálido.

(J. M. Gutiérrez 1846, 156–57)

Suddenly she halts;
She raises her hands to her face;
She looks about attentively—
She sees all; frozen, she is seized!
In other times, severe,
Here lay a *Burial place*;
Now all in ruins, only debris
Amidst which, bones and skulls,
Not so much as a cross to say,
"Here lie Christian souls."
Dolores, poor Dolores!
Why don't you turn away?
But she continues her advance,

> Driven by her cares;
> Entering the place
> Lit by the night's pale star.

Her expedition has become a compulsion to progress. She cannot turn back, one might say, because the cemetery in ruins is the very symbol that there is no past behind her to which she might return. If the road to independence leads to the ongoing siege of Montevideo, then no *lazo de unión y afecto,* neither common language nor common arts may be trusted to secure American innocence. The past is rifled by the present and the modern expedition ends with a curse upon the future. The text of history has been erased by progress, the tales of personal attachment and national heroism are left untold by the gaping mouths of the empty graves.

6

I might allegorize Domínguez's gruesome expedition as an admonishment to literary historiography, which, having buried the eighteenth and nineteenth centuries at a considerable distance from the living tradition of modernismo, has allowed them to be emptied of poetry, severing both modernismo and its heirs from their past. This need not be so. Looking beyond the boundaries of *América poética*—for no anthology or literary history succeeds in including all the heroes—José Eusebio Caro (Colombia 1817–53), a poet of the generation of Gutiérrez's *novisimos*, addressed the past in an elegy for his father. "El huérfano sobre el cadáver" is the poem that Heredia never wrote—a missing word that determined, in large measure, the course of Spanish American literary history thereafter, riddled by his silence, through Domínguez's graveyard and beyond. Questioning whether the cadaver and his father are one and the same, whether the present—and the future—are significantly qualified by the past, Caro answers:

> ¡Oh, no! ¡que hablabas, y este cuerpo calla!
> Calla y nunca hablará: tu lengua muerta
> Fija, trabada al paladar se halla . . .
>
> (Caro 1951, 48)

> Oh, no! You spoke and this corpse here is mute!
> Mute, never to speak again: your dead tongue
> is tied to your palate, fixed . . .

Death is figured synecdochically as a hobbled tongue. And this death, painful as it is to the son, is understood by the poet as a special problem, for it leaves the past, his literary history, bereft of voice, and himself, in consequence, orphaned of a native language. But a persistent poet, Caro makes a new expedition to the grave in his poem "Despúes de veinte años," where he unfetters his father's tongue. The dead, he rediscovers, are not inexorably past; the past not irremediably amputated from the present, but rather may return as voice, to haunt, to instruct, to inspire modern poetry. Caro transcribes "la postrera y mejor de tus promesas" ["the last and best of your promises"] a promise that Heredia kept to Martí, that his age kept to modernismo, and that the poetry of the years from 1700 to 1850 might keep to us, were we but to visit the graves where the texts lie buried. I give the poet, ghostwriter for his father, the final word:

> "José no llores más.—Aunque yo muera,
> Morir no es perecer. ¡Tu padre he sido,
> Imposible que siempre no lo sea!"
>
> (Caro 1951, 51)

> Weep no more, dear José.—for though I die,
> To die is not to perish. Your father I have been,
> Impossible that I won't be so forever.

Notes

INTRODUCTION

1. Kenneth J. Andrien (1998) provides an illuminating contextualization of the *Noticias secretas* at a point of confluence between three sources of contemporaneous discourses of protest and reform: indigenous voices, local reform-minded American elites, and Enlightenment thinkers in Spain.

2. This and all translations in prose and verse are my own, unless otherwise noted.

3. See, for instance, Quesnay's essays "Fermiers" and "Grains" (1969, 159–92 and 193–249, respectively). For representative texts in economic theory from colonial Spanish America, see Chiaramonte 1979.

4. The understanding of transatlantic trade is itself undergoing revision. John R. Fisher's detailed account of commerce (1998) in the aftermath of the Free Trade Ordinance of 1778, which builds upon his own prior research (1981, see also Malamud and Pérez 1988), indicates that the 1780s and 1790s were a boom time for both metropolis and colonies with regard to imports and exports, even if the rapidly increasing volume of trade did not lead to a substantial increase in the industrialization of the Peninsula, as reformists had hoped (Fisher 1998, 460–61). It was not the continuing mercantilist spirit and consequent restrictions of the new Bourbon economic policy, therefore, but rather war with Britain and the blockade of the port at Cadiz that brought on a commercial crisis for imperial trade. Much as in the analysis of Juan and Ulloa, according to Fisher, American capital was not content to remain idle while waiting for Spanish merchant vessels to run the British blockade. Instead, the colonial administration in America, citing the danger of local unrest caused by the economic disruption, urged the crown to grant permission for the ships of neutral countries to enter American ports, and turned a blind eye to that and other forms of contraband trade until the permission was granted in November of 1797, and thereafter. The permission was revoked in 1799, but when hostilities with Britain resumed in 1804, "the cash-starved crown itself," writes Fisher, "began deliberately to undermine the 1778 mercantilist principles by its decision to promote the widespread sale of contracts for neutral expeditions to Spanish America from ports in both the United States and northern Europe" (469). Whether in conjunction with the crown or against imperial designs and interests, there existed a state of de facto free trade in American ports from 1797 to the end of the wars of Independence, by Fisher's account. Hence, he concludes, "with the possible exception of the case of the Río de la Plata, the quest for free trade cannot be seen as a dominant factor in determining the political attitudes of Spanish Americans toward the crisis of the Spanish monarchy in 1808–1810" (1998, 479).

5. The preeminent literary text of the period relating the routes of interior commerce is Carrió de la Vandera's *El lazarillo de ciegos caminantes* (1776); see the

376

indispensable study by Karen Stolley (1992). See also Hill 1996, an essay especially germane to my interest in contraband trade in eighteenth-century Peru. Hill frames her discussion with a consideration of Juan and Ulloa, and she also devotes attention to the polymath poet Pedro de Peralta Barnuevo, whose work will be taken up in the next chapter.

6. I refer to Pedro Henríquez Ureña's theory of literary historiography as set forth in his "Caminos de nuestra historia literaria" (1978), originally published 1925 and so long before the realization of his theoretical position in the masterful achievement of his *Literary Currents in Hispanic America* (1945). In "Caminos" Henríquez Ureña warns, "It is a noble desire, but a grave error, when one wishes to do history, to attempt to remember all of the heroes" (1978, 46). Against the flaw of critical hubris, then, he recalls: "With sacrifices and even the greatest of injustices is how the classical constellations are constructed in all literatures"; and in this light, he concludes: "The literary history of Spanish America ought to be written on the basis of just a few central names [unos cuantos nombres centrales]: Bello, Sarmiento, Montalvo, Martí, Darío, Rodó" (47). As would be the case with any critical canon, this list of "central names" could be easily be expanded: the Quiché poets of the *Popol Vuh*, El Inca Garcilaso, Sor Juana, Heredia. . . . The point, however, is not to quibble over the selections of Henríquez Ureña—on the contrary, his short list is richly instructive—but rather to propose that if there have been no eighteenth-century names deemed central to the history of Spanish American letters, and only one figure, Andrés Bello, in the nineteenth century prior to *modernismo*, there is all the more reason to inspect the social margins. For the "greatest injustices" are not strictly literary, and the process of canonization, as feminist criticism in particular has taught, replicates broader patterns of cultural hegemony. In the case of Spanish America, the social groups most affected are the indigenous peoples, whose literary practices, especially in the realm of oral culture, have been omitted, almost by definition, from the lists of central names; "their study," it has long been held, "is not the responsibility of literary historians, but rather of anthropologists or folklorists," as Martín Lienhard (1991, 30) notes in his sustained effort to reclaim a place within the institution of literature (see also Segala 1991). Angel Rama (1984b), too, writing in a different context, has remarked upon the need for literary studies of Spanish America to be more cognizant of anthropology, and I will turn in that direction on occasion in the effort to expand reading beyond "central names" (for another interdisciplinary model, see historian James Lockhart's approach [1992] to Nahuatl poetry). A fuller rapprochment of the two disciplines is achieved under the cultural studies model, which puts a strictly literary history into question. (See for instance, such discussions as Easthope 1991 and Beverley 1994; and for a wide-ranging review of theoretical challenges to literary history, Perkins 1992.) But inasmuch as Spanish American poetic texts of the eighteenth and early nineteenth century are often an as yet unreached destination rather than a familiar point of departure, I have not pursued the cultural studies course here.

7. Although I believe that few would contest the assertion that Spanish American poetry, and indeed all genres, from the early eighteenth to the mid-nineteenth century have received sparse critical attention in comparison with twentieth-century letters, modernismo and, in the current generation, colonial studies, the many citations throughout my study bear witness to a tradition of critical and editorial

labors in the field. For an overview, see the pertinent chapters of volume 1 of González Echeverría and Pupo-Walker 1996.

8. Silver quotes the expression "an absent romanticism" from Virgil Nemoianu (1984, 39), whom he follows closely in his proposal of Spanish Romanticism as "Spanish Biedermeier" (Silver 1994, 298).

9. James Mandrell (1991), who does find a strong romanticism in Espronceda's *El estudiante de Salamanca*, argues that the crux of that identification is to be found in eighteenth-century theoretical discussions of the sublime that underwrote contemporary and subsequent poetry. He underlines, for instance, the use of the term "sublime" by Juan Meléndez Valdés, with clear echoes from the theoretical texts of the moment—principally Burke and Kant, for the purposes of his essay, though Silver (1994, 295) and McVay (1994, 34–35) make useful reference to Hugh Blair. In this light, he observes that in Meléndez's "La noche y la soledad" (1779), "the poet, in confronting the celestial image and, by extension, his own death, confesses himself to be fearful of this idea, and the poem ends with a decadent reaction, the abandonment of the original project and the proposal of a new reading of [Young's] *Night Thoughts*" (Mandrell 1991, 303). The "decadent reaction" might otherwise be termed Biedermeier, following Silver. A fuller understanding of the reserve of Meléndez, the best poet in the language in the eighteenth century, calls for further study, particularly since his influence is felt on both sides of the Atlantic. I will return to this point. As for Peninsular letters, Meléndez's "real fears" before epiphany have a notable effect upon Quintana, who, in turn, exerts his own influence upon Spanish American poetry, its difficult relations to the sublime and its struggles with modernity.

10. As Mabel Moraña (1997) has remarked, nineteenth-century studies constitute a burgeoning field in Spanish American literary and cultural criticism, buoyed by new developments in the understanding of nationalism, particularly as viewed through the lens of postcolonialism. This renewed interest, however, has concentrated on prose, led by Doris Sommer's magisterial and highly influential *Foundational Fictions* (1991). The same may be said of eighteenth century studies. Perhaps the greatest change in the field since the time of the publication of *Los hijos del limo* has been in research devoted to Enlightenment science in Spanish America. See Soto Arango et al. 1995 for bibliographical orientation and chapter 1, note 12, below. For the state of research at the time of the publication of *Los hijos del limo*, see Lanning 1956, Whitaker 1961 and Aldridge 1971; and on eighteenth-century Spain, Herr 1958 and Sarrailh 1964. But again, poetry has not shared equally either with respect to textual analyses nor to the kind of overarching critical reorientation introduced by Pratt (1992), for instance, in the work that I cited at the outset. Hence, as concerns poetry, Silver's hearkening back to Paz gives an accurate sense of the continuing predominance of his views for the entire period under study here.

11. For the full elaboration of Alonso's argument see *The Burden of Modernity* (Alonso 1998).

12. Hence, Alonso's ironic swerve in his title away from Bateson's "burden of the past." Alonso himself refers to such a swerve as "Lucretian *clinamen*" (C. Alonso 1996, 235) at the conclusion of his essay, though the reference itself is rather a case of transumptive allusion (an early, distant source substituted for a more proximate, anxiety-producing one). The transumed middle term, between

Alonso and Lucretius, as between myself and Paz, is Harold Bloom. Here, Alonso's version of the anxiety of influence: "For the Spanish American text the *clinamen* represents both the search for and the impossible rhetorical predicament of discursive authority" (C. Alonso 1996, 235). See Bloom (1973, 14) for the appropriation of *clinamen* from Lucretius.

13. Alvaro Fernández Bravo (1997) brings theoretical clarity to the preeminence of temporal frontiers over political geography in mid-nineteenth-century constructions of American identity. Alonso, for his part, suggests that the "radical ambivalence" (cf "this ambivalent project," Fernández Bravo 1997, 144) of American identity plays itself out textually as a virtual temporality: "If we conceive of the double movement at the core of every Spanish American text as a displacement toward modernity, 'followed' by a recoil from it, for example, we can metaphorically project a temporal dimension onto every oeuvre. Each Spanish American work would then possess an internal 'chronology' that may or may not be consonant with the developments or currents in a proposed larger frame of cultural history" (C. Alonso 1996, 231).

14. Unfortunately, Vásquez Santa Ana does not provide a concrete date of composition for the *corrido* that would allow one to insert it with precision into the history of the revolutionary process.

15. Richmond F. Brown's study (1995) of the commercial career of Juan Fermín de Aycinena (1729–96) in Guatemala provides a picture of the political economy in which Bergaño y Villegas lived. Two points germane to the discussion of the poem may be underlined: first, Aycinena accumulated vast wealth and power through trade, a success that depended upon an extensive network of communication both with Spain and with agents of the *casa Aycinena* in the Americas (Brown lists Oaxaca, Acapulco, Mexico City, Havana, Callao and Lima along with numerous places in Central America, 1995, 427); and second, much as Bergano y Villegas leads the reader to expect, Aycinena did not dedicate the gains of commerce to the development of local industry to a significant degree (the general pattern, according to Fisher 1998, in Spain no less than in the colonies).

16. Writing from a different point of view, Carl Becker (1932) long since proposed that the Heavenly City of the *philosophes* resembled the idealizations of the medieval church rather more closely than the philosophes themselves imagined and more so, too, than appears in a historiography inclined to see modernity as a rupture without a counterbalancing tradition. Becker's influential book was soon challenged (see Rockwood, 1958), but, I am suggesting, Bergaño y Villegas's comment on the suppression of knowledge by political authority provides grounds for reopening the question in relation to an analysis of the institutions of power.

17. "I'll serve as a whetstone which, though it cannot cut of itself, can sharpen iron. Though I write nothing, I'll teach the business and duty of a writer" (Horace 1936, 407).

18. Walter Benjmain explicated his decision to devote himself to the study of the minor poets of the long-neglected German baroque drama by asserting: "It is one thing to incarnate a form, it is quite a different thing to give its characteristic expression. Whereas the former is the business of the poetic elect, the latter is often done incomparably more distinctly in the laborious efforts of minor writers" (1977, 58). I will not avoid the relatively central names of Spanish American poetry in the eighteenth and nineteenth centuries, but by considering the examples

of "minor poets," and by reading their "minor poems" attentively, I will seek to fill out the contours of the forms of modernity that more familiar figures incarnate. Henríquez Ureña's theory of central names subscribes, ultimately, to "the illusion that a combination of the —basically impossible—double task of historical reconstruction and aesthetic judgment is still possible" (Gumbrecht 1987, 237)—or that it ever was. With that illusion unmasked, the two tasks separate, and I choose the path of reconstructing the characteristic expression of a culture.

19. On the revolutionary character of Borunda's thesis as expressed by Fray Servando, see Lafaye 1977, Jara 1989 and Bénassy-Berling 1993. Lezama's discussion of Fray Servando as the transitional figure par excellence in the shift from the Baroque to Romanticism in Spanish America (1977, 328–34) is important in itself and also an antecedent to Reinaldo Arenas's novel based on Fray Servando's exploits, *El mundo alucinante* (1969).

20. Lluch and Argemí (1984) have studied the impact of the economic ideas of the French physiocrats in eighteenth and early nineteenth century Spain. Of special importance to my own study, Lluch (1984) identified the first Spanish-language translator of Quesnay's *Maximes générales* as the Argentine Manuel Belgrano (1770–1820) in the years before he emerged as one of the founding fathers of the new republic. See also Belgrano 1979.

21. See Freud 1957 and Abraham and Torok 1994. See the *diálogo crítico* dedicated to the work of Abraham and Torok, including Eduardo González 1988 and Bush 1988. For a broader introduction to Abraham and Torok's understanding of melancholia in the context of their associated concepts of "cryptic mourning" see Rand 1994. I have sought to introduce Abraham and Torok's work more generally, including a comparison to Lacanian psychoanalytic theory, within the context of Hispanic literary criticism in Bush 1993. An excellent essay in the field of nineteenth-century Spanish American letters by Susan Rotker (1997), though articulated through a different psychoanalytic orientation (i.e. André Green's discussion of narcissism) is nevertheless extremely close to Abraham and Torok's conception of the vicissitudes of mourning and the consequent transmission of ever-renewed *encubrimiento*. (A caution, however: Rotker's use of the verb "to incorporate" is unrelated to Abraham and Torok's key term.) Finally, the concepts of mourning and melancholia receive rich theoretical elaboration in relation to Spanish American letters in Eduardo González's *The Monstered Self* 1992. González's work focuses on twentieth-century prose fiction, so that the mediations necessary to enunciate clearly the dialogue between my study and his would carry me too far afield from my immediate context. Nevertheless, *The Monstered Self* remains, I hope, an implicit and ever-present interlocutor of my text.

22. Scholarship devoted to the preromanticism of the Salamanca school whose generations include Cadalso (and, collaterally, Jovellanos), Meléndez Valdés, Cienfuegos and Quintana, has reestablished their place in the course of Spanish literary history. See, for example, Sebold 1974, Derozier 1978, Polt 1987 and for a general introduction to the period, Arce 1981. The great divide between Peninsular and Spanish American studies, however, continues to obscure their significance for the poets under study here, except for customary comments on their baleful influence. It will be part of my task to attempt to bridge that gap

23. With respect to intergenerational transmission, Abraham and Torok's revisions of Freud may also be taken as a more precise psychoanalytical model for

Bloom's map of misreading (see Bloom 1973 and 1975), which orients my approach to the dialectical balance of rupture and continuity.

24. After a generation of listening to the Lacanian *Nom-du-Père*, which relegates the mother, at best, to Kristeva's prelinguistic semiotic *chora*, it is refreshing to read Abraham and Torok assertion that "without the constant assistance of *a mother endowed with language*, introjection could not take place" (1994, 128, emphasis added).

25. The primary text of Freud's analysis of the Wolf Man was originally published in 1918 as "From the History of an Infantile Neurosis" (Freud 1955–74, vol. 17). The case reopened by Abraham and Torok in *The Wolf Man's magic word* (1986).

26. Leopoldo Zea undertakes to define "history in Latin American consciousness," as he puts it, in terms of much the same alternative; "To count on the past, or to erase it definitively" (1978, 209) is one of many formulations by which he seeks to illuminate the contest of conservative and liberal projects for an independent America at the base of the fratricidal history of the nineteenth century. That dichotomy opened, he contends, because of an obstruction in the path of historical consciousness as it was developing in the West (and, I would add, defining modernity), which, for Zea, was the path of Hegelian *Aufhebung*, understood as "the absorption, the assimilation of the past so that the same does not come back to be repeated" (165). The obstacle was that the colonial era—"the only history with which these people could count" (165)—was conceived by the independence movements as foreign to America and so rejected, rather than overcome.

27. On the relation of bureaucracy to modernity, see Weber 1958, and especially his remarks on Roman law in modern European states (217).

28. See Jovellanos's own "Informe" of 1783 on burial practices (1956). For a general review of the topic see Ariès 1977, esp. 389–99 and 468–550.

29. In all events the field has been too long dominated by the late colonialist posture of Marcelino Menéndez y Pelayo, whose anthology (1895) remains, I believe, the most extensive and widely available collection of premodernista Spanish American poetry. Menéndez y Pelayo at once gathers a great many texts and annuls them by arguing consistently that Spanish American poetry is derivative of Peninsular models, and as such, a superfluous appendix to Peninsular literary history. The argument is facilitated by Menéndez y Pelayo's editorial decision to exclude living poets, which obviates the question of the originality of Darío.

30. See Bloom's critique (1975, 50) of Derrida (1967).

31. Luis (1990) makes the point throughout his study of the antislavery narrative that the economic advantages of slavery took precedence over the political advantages of independence for the Cuban sugar planters. The firm foundation of the extensive literature on the Cuban sugar industry and slavery is Moreno Fraginals 1976; I would also highlight Benítez-Rojo 1989. Here I cite a concordant passage by Agnes I. Lugo-Ortiz, whose passionate denunciation considers slavery in relation to modernity: "Slavery, backbone of the plantation, would be the unbridgeable abyss for the execution of an expansively modern design of society, the greatest economic dilemma of the sugar elite throughout the first half of the nineteenth century, its straightjacket in political terms and the most profound fracture of any approach whatsoever to a national will" (1997, 54). From this, Lugo-Ortiz concludes that slavery "constituted the hardest limit in the very heart of the

modernizing project advanced by the most critical and enlightened factions of the sugar oligarchy, its most pointed zone of impossibility" (54). The counter-example of the contemporaneous slaveholding and rapidly modernizing United States, however, suggests, rather, that the general project of modernization, like its instance in the strikingly modern nineteenth-century Cuban sugar industry, enabled slavery by dint of its characteristic instrumental reason.

32. See also Edmond Cros's analysis (1985) of Lizardi's *El periquillo sarniento* (1816), a text that Benítez-Rojo (1996) adds to the list of foundational fictions. Cros addresses the projectional poetics by underlining the testamentary structure of the narrative. "This new family," Cros writes, referring to the social formation constituted by the transmission of testaments, "is to have a cellular structure turned towards the future. From this point of view, Periquillo's father's pieces of advice, which Periquillo takes up, are destined to build up his children's future, and to settle on them this middle welfare that squares with the political project of liberalism" (Cros 1985, 101). Like Sommer, Cros points to illegitimacy as the problem to which the projectional vision responds, although he associates that problem with the genre of the picaresque, rather than the history of the Conquest. But still earlier, and still in prose, the genre of biography was emerging, as Lugo-Ortiz brilliantly argues, in the same projectional mold. Looking at Cuba at the end of the eighteenth century, she sees biography as a form of "monumental" historical consciousness, in Nietzsche's terms, with self-conscious ideological aims: "it is a matter of reorganizing the new subject of power in a double *genealogical* task: father/gestor of his children, father/gestor of his society" (Lugo-Ortiz 1997, 53). On the other side, while a tradition of poetry in the projectional mold may be developing throughout the eighteenth and nineteenth centuries, as I shall discuss, the projectional project in poetry is institutionalized in the anthologies that followed, often very closely, upon the establishment of the new nations, as Achugar (1997) demonstrates in careful detail. Denominating those collections as "the 'poetic foundation' of the Nation-State" and "*parnasos fundacionales*"(15), Achugar explains that "they are articulated with the past in the sense that they modify it, but above all they project themselves towards the future" (18). See also C. Alonso's remark: "for the tenets of the myth of futurity that the cultural foundation of the new countries rested on, and that had been especially effective in the anticolonial struggle against 'backward' Spain, harmonized rather than conflicted with the narrative of modernity that sustained the legitimacy and prestige of metropolitan rule" (1996, 228).

33. The exception to the current described by Henríquez Ureña and the most compelling literary history of Spanish American poetry of the nineteenth century is Oscar Rivera-Rodas. For his reading of the dialogue of Bello and Heredia, see Rivera-Rodas 1988, 15–71.

CHAPTER 1: RELIGIOUS PERSUASIONS

1. In addition to Salvatierra's account, Dawson's Book Shop of Los Angeles has published an extensive set of translations of related texts in the Baja California Travels Series. The missions to Baja California may be set into the broader context of the late stages of the Conquest as they developed at the geographical edges of

colonial Spanish America by consulting Guy and Sheridan (1998) and especially Deeds (1998), which considers missions and indigenous resistance in northern Mexico.

2. See R. Gutiérrez 1991 for a discussion of corn mythology.

3. Godzich and Spaddacini's illuminating discussion of the institutionalization of literature in Spain (1987) points in the direction of needed research in Spanish America, where similar processes may be discerned at a somewhat later date. They focus on the insertion of literature into a market economy, which is to say that their understanding of an instituionalized literature is already that of a modern literature. Older practices of letters were organized institutionally as well; the aristocratic academia was one such institution. For the period of the anonymous nun, see J. Williams 1995. For the end of the eighteenth century, see the suggestive introductory pages in Haidt (1995, 477–78) on the circulation of erotic manuscripts in eighteenth-century Spain and thereafter her discussion of the related phenomenon of exhibiting art in private *gabinetes*.

4. Recent theoretical discussion concerning the "neobaroque" sensibility in mid- and late-twentieth-century Spanish American literature has generally stressed much the opposite. The most brilliant contributor to that discussion, Cuban novelist Severo Sarduy, consistently stressed the volatility of baroque rhetoric as it skids along the redoubtable course of its excessive figurations, ever expressing the instability of desire, especially in *Barroco* (Sarduy 1974). However, in a less familiar essay devoted to his mentor, the neobaroque poet par excellence, José Lezama Lima, Sarduy asserts that *"Lezama fija"* [Lezama fixes] (Sarduy 1969, 65). He goes on to cite the corroborating testimony of Octavio Paz and to stress, for his own part, the importance of Lezama's collection *La fijeza* in his baroque aesthetic.

5. See McKnight 1997, 22–24, including her citation of Cascardi 1992. I would also highlight Gumbrecht 1997 as another important source for McKnight's illuminating discussion of subjectivity.

6. Madre Castillo's most recent editor, Dario Achury Valanzuela enumerates a variety of "modes of citation" in his introduction to her *Obras completas* (Castillo 1968 clx-clxiii), among which the most frequent is "enlace" ("stringing together," without the pejorative sense of the English): the linking of different passages from a single biblical book (Achury Valanzuela 1968, clxii). Although he identifies sources from Deuteronomy and Psalms in "Deliquios," the preponderant transcriptions are drawn from the Song of Songs—Achury Valanzuela identifies thirteen (see notes to "Afecto 46" in Castillo 1968, 2:124–25).

7. I recall here Abrams (Abrams 1953) influential distinction between the mirror and the lamp.

8. See McKnight's alternative translation and her commentary (1997, 172–77).

9. The verses quoted above, "Tan suave . . . el corazón mismo," is the only stanza in the first section of the poem for which Achury Valanzuela adduces no concrete referents, biblical or otherwise.

10. See Achury Valenzuela's explanation in Castillo 1968, 2:493–95.

11. See also Cáceres Romero 1987, 176–77 or Lara 1947, 180–81 for the original Quechua.

12. Peralta's many critics are in general agreement on both points of this assessment, that is the displeaure of the text, and yet the enduring importance of this

and other works. Peralta's most devoted contemporary reader, Jerry M. Williams remarks: "The literary merit of the poem is far overshadowed by its abundant and informative notes" (1998, 239). See as well Eva M. Kahiluoto Rudat (1985, 38), who registers her assent to the comment by Irving A. Leonard that the verse is "soporific." On the other hand, each of these critics have drawn attention to Peralta's crucial role in introducing Enlightenment ideas to America. As concerns *Lima fundada*, Peralta's positive contribution has been emphasized by focusing attention on his prologue (Kahiluoto Rudat 1985 and Hill 1994), which Kahiluoto Rudat, moreover, has reprinted (Peralta 1985). I will refer to the pagination of the 1863 edition, for consistency with my references to the verse; Mazzotti (1996) has stressed the importance of *editio princeps* of 1732, which, unfortunately, I have not been able to consult.

13. Ruth Hill's erudite and penetrating study of Peralta's prologue is especially pertinent here. The framework of the tripartite division of late-baroque authors into Scholastics, Catholic humanists and Catholic radicals (Hill 1994, 129) is itself a valuable counterweight to the broad tendency to equate modernity with secularization. More specifically, Hill works through those different positions in relation to historiography. Her cogent observations merit citation at some length:

> Peralta was greatly concerned that the historical events of *Lima fundada* not be misunderstood. Thus he provided the reader with footnotes that explicate his use of figures and separate *historia* and *fabula*. Freely-willed, human actions were "accidents" in the Aristotelian sense, not essences—not capable of being true or false. History came out of the demonstrative branch of classical rhetoric, which dealt with the verisimilar and the probable. Geometry, and the *exactly* true or false, had nothing to do with it. As epideictic discourse flowing from a Catholic pen, history was expected to praise those who loved God and to vituperate others who did not." (135).

14. José Antonio Mazzotti (1996) offers an excellent study of *Lima fundada*, delineating its "poética de la nación" in the context of other epic poems from the same milieu around the turn of the eighteenth century. Among many valuable insights centering on his reading of what I refer to as the love idyll and its aftermath in the denouement of the poem, I would underline the intertextual debate that he discerns between the poem and El Inca Garcilaso's *Comentarios reales*, as an expression of a "Peruvian national dualism" (Mazzotti 1996, 70). His argument that as early as Peralta's epic, the foundational fictions of "la conciencia criolla" were responding to a " 'conciencia mestiza' " (70), enhances and expands Sommer's views. As concerns the development of my own discussion, that contest may been seen as further evidence of the manner in which the Conquest remained an ongoing project at the beginning of the eighteenth century, and not only at the geographical borders of the empire in Baja California, but also in the very centers of viceregal power. In addition, as I will suggest in the next chapter, the cultural imposition that results from the contest between Lima and Cuzco (i.e. of Peralta and Garcilaso) is expressive of a paradigm by which the hegemony of the metropolis over the colonies was reproduced within the colonies between different localities.

15. Born in Spain, Barco Centenera (1544–1605) lived much of his life in Argentina, his poem *La Argentina* was first published 1602.

16. Mutis's own writings (see Mutis 1957–58 and 1982), like those of many

of his scientific peers working under Spanish auspices, languished for nearly two centuries without scholarly attention. As noted already, the situation has changed significantly since the time of Paz's *Los hijos del limo* (1974), and Pratt 1992 has been cited at the head of a renewed theoretical interest. The period of the Spanish bicentennial celebration of the reign of Carlos III in particular saw the publication of important research, which, taken as a whole, provides a greatly expanded picture of the Hispanic Enlightenment; e.g. on Mutis, see Chenu 1988, and more broadly, the special issue of the *Revista de Indias* (Del Pino Díaz 1987). See also the closely related publications of Madrid's Real Jardín Bótanico (e.g. *La botánica en la expedición Malaspina* 1989) and the Colección Theatrum Naturae under the auspices of the Centro Superior de Investigaciones Científicas in Madrid and of the Instituto de Cooperación Hispanoamericana, the latter under the heading of the quincentennary commemoration (e.g. *La América Española en la época de las Luces* 1988 and Berruezo León 1989). Finally, I make note of Norman E. Whitten's "Afro-Creoles on the Frontier" (1995), although the essay focuses upon the late twentieth century, the discussion of Afro-Americans as explorers opens a suggestive critical perspective for the earlier period under study here.

17. I adopt the punctuation of Barrera Vásquez 1965, 62.

18. My remarks on these texts and others in indigenous languages noted in this study are based on the work of their translators. Personal limitations in this area, however, are merely contingent. The place of the Latin-language poets of the Jesuit exile has always been assured in Spanish American literary history, even for those who depend upon translations. The other classical languages of the Americas have their literatures, and these too demand their place. See my related remarks in the introduction (note 6).

19. I stress the question of dating the texts, since it is my intention to abide within the chronological parameters of this study and so to adduce indigenous texts contemporaneous—as well as one may reasonably conjecture—to the Spanish-language poetry under consideration. Thus, while important works of scholarship have elucidated precontact poetry, paving the way for its inclusion in the curriculum of Spanish American literature (e.g. the pertinent section of de la Campa and Chang-Rodríguez 1985), that interest does not often extend to the eighteenth century. The hiatus is closed in the twentieth century by anthropologists working in contemporary indigenous communities and recording texts extant in the oral culture. But the gap left open for the period under study here—as though the indigenous communities either ceased to exist altogether or at least ceased to compose and to recite their own texts between the early colonial period and the twentieth century—conforms to the ideological masterplot of the Conquest that persisted and prevailed in eighteenth-century Spanish American letters and that is under discussion here, both in its propagation and the critical responses that it provoked.

20. Gary H. Gossen notes challenges that have been posed to the all-encompassing breadth of the assertion as regards Quiché literature and particularly the *Popol Vuh* (Gossen 1985, 87), but he reports on the ubiquity of the same fundamental device in Tzotzil literature (a Mayan language), where "pairing of ideas and phrases—semantic and syntactic couplets—is as common to Tzotzil language use as corn is to their diet" (87). As for the *Popol Vuh* itself, it is well to recall two cardinal moments: the production of the manuscript in a Quiché version transcribed into the European alphabet by Dominican friar Francisco Ximénez in Chi-

chicastenango between 1701 and 1703; and the reemergence of the text through its publication by Carl Scherzer in Vienna in 1837 and, more influentially, by Etienne Brasseur de Bourbourg in Paris in 1861.

21. The concept of transculturation was introduced by Fernando Ortiz in 1940 (1978, esp. 92–97) and developed as a an efficacious analytical instrument, rooted in a local perspective, by Rama (1982b) and Pratt (1992).

22. J. M. Gutiérrez first discovered Aguirre's verse in manuscript and published it with an appreciative critical study in his *Estudios bibliográficos y críticos* (1865). A long period of limited attention was rectified by Cevallos Candau (1983) and the valuable introduction to Rodríguez Castelo 1984.

23. Compare Sor Juana: "Deténte, sombra, de mi bien esquivo" ["Hold, shade, of my fleeting treasure"] (Juana Inés de la Cruz 1975, 309).

24. Aguirre begins the twenty-fifth octava real with an open allusion to the master, as Rodríguez Castelo has remarked (Rodriguez Castelo 1984, lxvi): "Era del año la estación florida" ["It was the flowery season of the year"] (Góngora 1972, 634) rewritten as "Era del año la estación lluviosa" ["It was the rainy season of the year"], a transposition made for the climate of Guayaquil, according to Cevallos Candau (1983, 70).

25. I recall here a remark by McKnight from her discussion of the self-limiting controls internalized by Madre Castillo: "The threat felt by a male hierarchy from the self-confidence that might bolster female authority is also displaced, in discourse, onto the individual's soul, which risks burning in hell for its sin of pride. In accordance with this ideology, Madre Castillo must balance her expressive self with humble denunciation in the *Vida*" (McKnight 1997, 163–64). The Jesuit Aguirre cannot advocate pride, but as a member of the male hierarchy (e.g. the institutional differences between Jesuits and Poor Clares) his figurative displacement here is onto Luzbel, who may revel in his pride in hell, precisely because that is all that is left to his irredeemable soul.

26. For a general introduction to the figures of the Jesuit exile, see Batllori 1966 and for Mexican Jesuits, Kerson 1989.

27. In addition to the studies cited in the preceding note, see Kerson's discussion (Kerson 1984) of Abad in relation to an important mentor among the Mexican Jesuits, José Rafael Campoy (1727–77). Both are presented as enlightened, liberal and progressive within the limits of religious orthodoxy, though Kerson indicates that Abad was the "less radically innovative" of the two (141). I note that Kerson's assertion of the preeminence of the Mexican Jesuits as promoters of the Enlightenment in Spanish America may be qualified by the preceding discussion of Peralta. And of course, there were other purveyors of Latin (see, for example, Carbón Sierra 1998). For a further study of Abad, see Mauricio Beuchot's detailed research (Beuchot 1992) on Abad's commentary on Aristotle's *De Anima*.

CHAPTER 2. THE ROAD TO INDEPENDENCE

1. For bibliographic information on the Enlightenment expeditionaries, see chapter one, note 16.

2. Francisco de las Barras de Aragón [1952, 516] has speculated that the impe-

cunious results of Mopox's exorbitant life at court created a personal need to replenish his wealth in Cuba, thus motivating the expedition.

3. I refer once again to the reinvigoration of a tired critical term by Marshall Brown (1991).

4. Although I will make several references to Ludmer's *El género gauchesco* (1988) in the text, these citations do not constitute sufficient recognition of what is the finest scholarly work dedicated to Spanish American poetry of any sort from the whole period under study here. Because my own historical boundaries are drawn to focus attention on the most neglected periods, deliberately leaving out of account the culminating point of the well-studied gauchesca poetry, Hernández's *Martín Fierro* and the *Vuelta*, I am unable to engage directly the whole of Ludmer's argument, to which, nevertheless, I am greatly endebted. Amidst the rich and extensive bibliography dedicated to the *gauchesca*, I would also signal Rama 1982a.

5. See Olivera-Williams 1986 for a discussion of the *gauchesca* focusing on the question of its addressee.

6. I cite from Regenos's translation in Landívar 1948.

7. See the passages compared by Fernández Valenzuela 1974, 22–23.

8. Landívar's able expositor, Arnold Kerson, though little given to psychoanalytic interpretations, registers the peculiarity of this climax to the "miniature epic" of the Jorullo episode when he comments, "It is almost as if the nostalgic longing of the poet for Jorullo had produced the tremor in Bologna" (Kerson 1990, 156)— *almost, as if* the uncanny forced itself upon his reading despite his better judgment. I myself invoke the psychoanalytic categories discussed above in the introduction at this point in order to enhance the all but inevitable reference to the nostalgia of the exiled Jesuits. See Browning (1985), for a study of the *Rusticatio* that carries beyond the discussion of nostalgia—still the tonic note of Juan Durán Luzio's brief notice (1991) on the publication of a new Spanish-Latin bilngual and critical edition by Faustino Chamorro González. By setting Landívar's poem within the eighteenth-century "dispute of the New World," studied in detail by Antonello Gerbi (1973), and the place of Guatemala in trans-Atlantic indigo trade, Browning offers a reading of the *Rusticatio* as a *discurso de economía política* with direct bearing upon the world of Bergaño y Villegas' *silva* a generation later. In this regard, see also López Marroquín 1994, 246–47.

9. On the allegory of the beavers, see Kerson 1976, 370 and Durán Luzio 1991, 594, n. 8.

10. Compare, for example, an anonymous satirist writing in *El Tizón Republicano* (Santiago de Chile, 19 May 1823). The poet sets aside very much the same figure that would come to occupy Sanfuentes's attention, as a type from a by-gone day, no longer to be found with his three-cornered hat, "Ni el libro de la gran genealogía/Cuelga hoy de la cintura" ["Nor does the book of the grand genealogy/ Hang today at his side"] (Feliú Cruz 1962, 249). But the target of poetic reprimand remains the figure of the reactionary, updated for republican times. Or, in short, satire takes aim at any "necio fanatismo/Para contradecir todo lo nuevo" ["stupid fanaticism/For contradicting all that is new"] (251).

11. For an account of that misogynist current, see Johnson 1983, 87–114. See also Johnson's valuable study of colonial satire (1993, conveniently condensed in 1994).

12. Matos Moctezuma is unable to discover firm dates for Meso Mónica. For Vasconcelos he cites the dates 1722–34 to 1760, provided by Nicolás León, to which he raises a critical challenge (Matos Moctezuma 1980, 18). The relay involving Quevedo, Father López, Mónica and Vasconscelos points to a process in the formation of popular culture that reverses the vector traced by Ludmer by which material crosses into the realm of the literary from below its threshold. The line between diffusion and original composition, furthermore, can blur to such a degree that folk culture can invent a local poet to whom verses generated elsewhere may become attached. Such is the case, according to Matos Moctezuma (28–32), with *El Negrito Poeta Mexicano*, author of six texts by Quevedo (Pierre Menard rewrote only one), three more by Meso Mónica, and several others of, at best, shared attribution.

13. Noting demographic information on the population of late eighteenth-century Lima, Daniel Reedy asserts that it "comes as no surprise" (Reedy 1987, 47) that disempowered groups are thus represented; but this is so, I would interject, only because Reedy himself has taken the previous step of opening critical attention to a poet composing his verse beyond the bounds of elite print culture. See also Stafford 1991.

14. Castillo's well-to-do black thus recalls the uses of satire of the slave, in keeping with William D. Piersen's illuminating discussion. Piersen (1977, 27) cites the contemporary witness J. G. F. Wurdemann in mid-nineteenth-century slave-holding Cuba: "in their native dialects ridicule their owners before their faces enjoying with much glee their happy ignorance of the burthen of their songs." Wurdeman himself continues: "Their African drums are then heard far and near, and their sonorous sounds, now falling, now rising on the air, seem like the summons to a general insurrection" (Wurdeman 1844, 84).

15. See Meehan and Cull (1984) for further biographical information on Teralla.

16. See Rivera de Alvarez and Alvarez Nazario 1982, 60.

17. For an excellent study of Meléndez's eroticism, see Haidt 1995. On Meléndez and the history of the Anacreontic mode in Spain, see especially Polt 1979 and more recently, Wright 1987. Saenz (1989) brings attention to a less frequent topic, Meléndez's romances as a mode of what I am calling the persistence of the baroque.

18. For a recent overview of the Independence movements, including extensive bibliographical information, see Hamnett (1997). Among the many sources, one might consult the following for a broad, Panamerican perspective: the revised second edition of Kinsbruner (1994), Domínguez (1980); and Rodríguez O. (1998).

19. Peralta is by no means a necessary filter between Olmedo and the Greco-Roman classics. Olmedo includes a note to the text of "Victoria de Junín" acknowledging Pindar (Olmedo 1947, 125, n. 3); and Henríquez Ureña (1963, 105) pointed out a direct borrowing from Horace at the outset of the poem. In addition, Olmedo himself made reference to the Cumean sibyl from Aeneid 6 in his elegy "En la muerte de doña María Antonia de Borbón, Princesa de Austria" of 1807. Nevertheless, Peralta remains a possible model for recourse to Virgil's prophecy to resolve a chronological difficulty while remaining consistent to a particular ideological interpretation of the relation of present to past—though the ideological position of *Lima fundada* is reversed in "Victoria de Junín." A literary history more attentive to the internal commerce of Spanish American poetry would be more concerned with such possibilities.

20. I am endebted to my friend and colleague Andrew Davison for his insights into the discrepancies between narrow expectations of a secularized modernity and the "alternative modernities"—he takes the phrase from Charles Taylor—that he finds in his research on Turkey and that also characterize the history of Spanish America. See Davison's discussion of revivalism and secularism in the modern state (Davison 1998). His remarks are crucial to the elucidation of the points brought forth in the passage to follow on the nature of modern devotional poetry. Note that Leopoldo Zea argues that the distinctive feature of Iberian and Ibero-American identities, vis-à-vis the modern history of Europe, was precisely the religious vocation of its imperial project (Zea 1970, 209–56). Zea expresses the distinction, however, not as an alternative modernity, but as an exclusion from modernity that informs the historical consciousness of Spanish America: "the tormented consciousness of being formed by peoples that are located already on the margins of history" (209). For a thorough discussion of the process of the secularization of Hispanic culture in the context of broader developments in the West, see Gutiérrez Girardot (Gutiérrez Girardot 1983, 77–157); his attention to the "sacralization of the world" that took place simultaneously with Weberian disenchantment ("desmiraculización") offers a more nuanced view of the process of secularization than the monolithic modernity, with no alternatives, contested by Davison. Finally, I note a strikingly similar, though independent formulation of "alternative modernities" in María Albin's observations concerning religious rhetoric in the work of Gómez de Avellaneda, a poet whom I will consider in some detail in chapter 5. Albín writes of "un proyecto alternativo de progreso," "an alternative project of progress based on Christian morality that counters those formulated by the modernizing statesmen of Latin America, especially the civilizing project of Sarmiento" (Albín 1995, 76).

21. This collection has been noticed previously as the setting of the elegies by Lafinur discussed in the introduction. See Achugar 1997 and González Echevarría 1996 (esp. 13–14) for discussion of anthologies in the history of Latin American literary historiography.

22. Moraña's thought-provoking discussion (1997) of the temporal dimensions of Bolívar's Pan American vision make his "Mi delirio sobre el Chimborazo" a closer parallel to Luca's prophetic moment. Her focus on the switchpoint between "delirium and reason" may be enhanced by reference to Ilie 1995.

CHAPTER 3. CONSTITUTIONAL DIALOGUES

1. On the policy and the historical reality of free trade, see Pérez Herrero 1992, 227–306, and Fisher (1981 and 1998) as well as Introduction, note 2).

2. One might compare Sarduy, reflecting on a later revolution from the perspective of the threshold of postmodernism, offering a figural reading of Castro's victory to wind history in the shroud of a hallucinatory snowstorm in "La entrada de Cristo en la Habana" section of *De donde son los cantantes* (Mexico 1967). The snowstorm would cover over the past, leaving a blank space, like Bolivar's deserts, upon which to create and record an unencumbered revolutionary future.

3. Compare Melville's national epic to the north, *Moby Dick*, which begins, "Call me Ishmael" (Melville 1976, 3).

4. The denomination "constitutional dialogue" and the correlated notion of "constituting America" are intended to recall and to contest Henríquez Ureña's influential and illuminating heading for the period under study in this second part of my own work, as a "declaration of cultural independence," a phrase more narrowly applied thereafter to Bello's *silvas americanas* as the programatic statement of that declaration. I might offer a hasty sketch of the differences between Henríquez Ureña's view of the literary currents of the time and my own approach by further noting that I use the term "the genre" here in the sense of Ludmer's designation of poesía gauchesca as the *tratado de la patria* in a dialogue, whose interlocutor is Sarmiento's *Facundo*. The "constitutional genre" shares with the gauchesca a propensity toward dialogic forms, as I will argue presently, driven by the same impulse to include previously marginalized voices in the debate of and about (Ludmer's polyvalent *de*) the nations in formation. The democractic impulse, however, is thwarted in the main literary currents, no less than the political sphere, and the genre of the contitutional dialogue tends ultimately to serve the restrictive, exclusionary ends of a conservative ideology. Likewise, in the debate of and about the tratado de la patria in Argentina, *Facundo* wins out over the gauchesca.

5. To set Lizardi's political fiction in the context of political history of Mexico, see Reyes Heroles (1982, especially vol. 1). Antonio Colomer Viadel (1990) considers constitutionalism from the period of the independence movements to the twentieth century with a pan American breadth. In theoretical terms, I am greatly endebted to Bartolomé Clavero (Clavero 1991).

6. Lizardi is one of the few writers of the early nineteenth century who might be called a central name in Spanish American literary history, primarily because his *El periquillo sarniento* (Mexico 1816) is generally considered the first Spanish American novel. In consequence, his novelistic production has received frequent and valuable critical commentary. For an introduction to Lizardi's novels, see Benítez-Rojo (1996), a discussion that relates *El periquillo sarniento* to Sommer's concept of foundational fiction. For my present purposes, namely the reading of the constitutional dialogue of the Payo and Sacristán, the excellent contribution of Jean Franco (1983) to the understanding of Lizardi is of special importance due to its thorough contextualization of *El Periquillo sarniento* within the body of his own journalistic prose and that of his contemporaries.

7. On the intermission from work and the implications that the countryside is the place of labor, see Viveros (1994), who draws upon Landívar's *Rusticatio* for evidence of the abundant leisure activities of rural society in eighteenth-century Mexico. Although Viveros argues for the relativity—"a sort of eventual democracy between dispossed and powerful" (229)—that one has learned to associate with the carnivalesque world of popular festivities from Bakhtin, it is by no means simply jolly, as Bakhtin's utopian would have suggested: "important elements of the amusements of the Mexican countryside of the eighteenth century," writes Viveros, "were the festive spirit, attractive appearance, belligerance, skill, temerity and cruel violence" (235).

8. Franco (1983) is concerned throughout her essay with the work ethic in relation to such topics as the Enlightenment valorization of reason, the impact of the latter on the speech genres (e.g. the dialog form) and "writing as a form of work" (15), and irrational breaches in labor (see the section, "La interrupción como táctica disciplinaria," 26–30), all of which bear upon my analysis.

9. See Raffi-Béroud 1992 for another consideration of Lizardi's concern for semiotics.

10. For a discussion of the manner in which colonialist language infiltrated post-independence discourse, see Vogeley (1993).

11. I follow Victoria Reifler Bricker (1981) closely in her historical analysis, and cite her translations. See also Newson (1987, 255–332) for a detailed study of cultural change in the indigenous populations in what is now Nicaragua in the period 1720–1821.

12. With this last phrase I allude to Sergio Serulnikov's (1996) penetrating historical analysis of "ambivalent rituals of justice" in the context of a rebellion of the Aymara communities of northern Potosí between 1777 and 1780. Serulnikov explains:

> The analysis of law and legal discourse is one of the critical means for understanding the languages of authority and consensus that cemented colonial society. Chayanta [i.e. the local community] records, however, suggest that Spanish justice could become, under certain circumstances, *a theater not only of resistance but also of counter hegemony.*" (Serulnikov 1996, 194; italics added)

Serulnikov further asserts, "Doubtless, the administration of the king's justice in the the Indian towns stands out as one of the fundamental forms of public theater. Paradoxically, however, political insurgency in northern Potosí was expressed through the mimicry, rather than the dismissal, of such rituals" (221). For a compelling meditation on that paradox, which appears as well in Anastasio Tzul's costume, see Taussig 1993 and for further discussion of art and resistance, see Gisbert 1992.

13. Reference to the material experience of imprisonment of Lizardi's Periquillo provides a telling contrast to the incorporeal disquisitions of the Payo and Sacristán.

14. Compare Lizardi's vagos in the dialogue of Payo and Sacristán and Franco's remarks on "la novela leperesca" 1983, 18–20.

15. I translate Ludmer's tratado as "tract" (rather than "tractate") to emphasize the relation, in the gauchesca (especially *Martín Fierro*) and in her study of it, between writing and land. In this combined sense of tract, the gauchesca pertains to the discourse of geography, as did Lizardi's dialog, with its concerns for the working of the rural landscape and the city as politico-legal textbook. If the gauchesca begins as a type of the genre of the constitutional dialogue, that dialogue in turn is rooted in the geography of the Enlightenment expeditionaries. The same trajectory carries forward into the twentieth century in the *novela de la tierra*, and has its antecedents in the "geographical discourses" of the first period of discovery and conquest, as studied by Mignolo (1994).

16. I refer to the moment when Fierro returns across the border and, recalling the death of his friend Cruz among the indigenas, he buries his body in absentia by kissing the ground (see esp. J. Hernández 1961, 347–48 [vv. 1531–38]. Holding to the chronological parameters of this study, I resist the temptation to undertake an analysis of the text.

17. Cabrera declares that the version she collects forms part of a tradition "more than three centuries old" (L. Cabrera 1984, 44); hence I speculate, as elsewhere with respect to poetry in oral culture, that some variant or close analog of the

undated verse "Alabanzas dedicadas a la eficacísima Oración de la Piedra Imán" (45–47) may be considered extant ca. 1823.

18. Taken as a Caliban, Blandengue will of course have his literary heirs. See Fernández Retamar (1972), above all, singing Blandengue's song in defiance of the *gaucho bueno* Rodó (1967), a counterpoint of cultural critics that has sparked enormous interest in current intellectual debate (e.g. Aronna 1999, who reinserts Rodo's *Ariel* into the epochal discourse of the body, and hence provides the groundwork upon which one might trace a trajectory back to the gauchesca in Ludmer's explication of the *usos del cuerpo*).

19. The D'Harcourts give "tenter, essayer, s'efforcer" ["to try, attempt, strive"] for "watekani" [D'Harcourt 1925, 309, n. 1], although they translate "j'étais t'épiant" [literally, "I was spying on you, on the lookout for you"] in this context.

20. I translate from the D'Harcourts' French version.

21. The only two poems published in its pages prior to J. F. de M's "Poesía" were an elegiac sonnet in memory of Meléndez Valdés, originally printed in the *Minerva Francesa*, and an ode by Meléndez himself.

CHAPTER 4. HESITANT STEP

1. See also Arturo Uslar Pietri's narrative fragment "La isla de Robinson" and his early essay on Rodríguez (Uslar Pietri 1996, 363–70 and 446–64, respectively). Two recent essays by Susan Rotker (1993, 1996) are valuable in distinguishing Rodríguez's egalitarian ideology from the discourses of power that come to be institutionalized in the postindependence era.

2. During his sojourn in Cuba, Fernández de Madrid would almost certainly have been acquainted with the poetry of Zequeira, and the latter's oft-anthologized "Oda a la piña" might well stand as an early and disappointing effort, though Vitier (1970, 47–50) sees it as a foundational text for Cuban poetry. A similar status for the history of Argentine letters is attributed to another attempt at the "descriptive genre," Manuel Lavardén's "Oda al Paraná," closer in spirit to Peralta's intermittent descriptive passages than to the nature poetry of the nineteenth century in Bello's wake. As for the poem's foundational status, note that the chronological parameters of the *Lira argentina* were stretched to include it. The great exception to Fernández de Madrid's general condemnation of early efforts at descriptive poetry in Spanish American literature, if not in Spanish, is Landívar's *Rusticatio mexicana*, as discussed in chapter 2, section 2.

3. This incident may well have been one of the brushes with death to which Fernández de Madrid would refer in the "Poesía" in the *Aguila Mexicano* the following year, discussed in the preceding chapter.

4. See Godzich and Spadaccini 1987 and 1994, for a discussion of these issues in relation to Peninsular letters.

5. Still a friend to *filósofos rancios*, or as Rodríguez would have it, courtiers without a crowned king, the print culture has demonstrated itself to be the conservative heir of the colonial *letrado*. One finds an effort, a century and a half since *El Broquel* of Oaxaca to invert the self-same process, that is to ally the printed book to oral culture by way of the artifice of the *pasquín* in Augusto Roa Bastos's

Yo el Supremo (1974). See also A. González (1993) for a broad and insightful discussion of the place of journalism in this trajectory.

6. For contributions to the vast scholarship on Bello that concentrate on his poetry see, in addition to Araya 1982, Rodríguez Fernández 1972, and more recently, Gomes 1998.

7. The poem was included in the anthology *Poetisas americanas*, edited by José Domingo Cortés and published in 1875. Although the anthology stands outside the chronological boundaries of the present study, I would draw attention to it as a valuable source for the study of women poets.

8. Whereas Durán Luzio adduces concrete textual antecedents in Bello's translation of Humboldt to almost all of the language of the lyric interlude of the "Alocución," he provides no such equivalent to the "tardo, incierto paso." As this break in the progress of poetry and the poetry of progress is crucial to my argument, I cite here at some length Durán Luzio's comments on these verses:

> One last incitement emanating from the text of [Humboldt] for Bello the reader-translator-poet situates this relation on the borderline of a problem that touches upon poetic creation in general; Humboldt concludes thus his reflections on the landscape [in the area of Cumaná]: ". . . like distant voices that were calling to us from the other side of the Atlantic, and whose magic power was transporting us from one hemisphere to the other. Maravlous mobility of the imagination of man, eternal source of our pleasures and our pains!" In this conclusion there are no allusions to the disadvantaged condition of a being far from its homeland; there is only a moving evocation of what is distant and gratitude for the versatility of the imagination. . . . Andrés Bello impregnates that evocation with the tone of his sufferings and with the hope that the crossing would provide him, imagining himself in his native Caracas.

Durán Luzio then quotes the four verses "¡Oh si ya . . . el tardo incierto paso," and adds the following remark: "It was not the Aragua . . . that was going to provide him, several years later, that longed for lovely bank, but the Mapocho; not his native Venezuela, but Chile, his second homeland, saw the movement of his 'tardo incierto paso' " (1987, 150–51). The uncertain step contradicts Humboldt's conception of the uninhibited mobility of the imagination. Thus, finding no precedent for the image in Bello's translation of the *Voyage*, Durán Luzio removes it from the context of the enunciation of the poem, i.e. the travails of Bello's London sojourn, which he suggests might otherwise explain the difference in tone from Humboldt (though Humboldt, too, is a "being far from its homeland"). In situating the "tardo incierto paso" on the far side of the ocean crossing and in the comfort of Bello's second home, he reads the image in the Humboldtian mold: a step of certainty, of progress, after all. Having acknowledged the Humboldtian pretext, the uncharacteristic uncertainty remains to be explained, and it is to that task that I devote the following discussion.

9. The best sources of biographical information on Heredia remain González del Valle 1938 and García Garófalo y Mesa 1945.

10. By way of contrast to Heredia's silence, one may recall Bello's interpolation, in the less flexible mode of translation, of his own grief over his daughter's death into his version of a poem by Hugo (Bello 1979, 90–97).

11. The subsequent rise of the evening star—"Y de Venus la estrella solitaria" ["And of Venus the solitary star"] (Heredia 1940, 2:151)—resonates equally with another avatar of Queztalcoatl in the person of his dark twin, Xólotl, together the

double aspect of Venus as morning and evening star. I add that the rising of Venus places the text in the line of poetry dedicated to the interstitial moment examined by Hartman (1975) and exemplified, as I have discussed above, by Meléndez Valdés. I am suggesting, however, that the pre-Colombian setting of the *Cholulteca pirámide*, its associated mythology in the career of Quetzalcoatl, and its place along the route of the Conquest conjoin to create a very different *Abendland* than that envisioned while looking westward from Meléndez's Spain or Collins's England.

12. Note that much as in Heredia's poem, Heredia the father is incorporated in Martí's thunderous rhetorical climax in the recollection of "su infancia gloriosa" in Venezuela. The poet was indeed a child there, but the glory, as Bello explained, was that of his father the magistrate. See the father's *Memorias,* J. F. Heredia 1986.

13. Mapping a unified trajectory that begins with Heredia's original composition at Cholula in 1820, includes the writing of "Niágara" in 1824, and ends with the augmented version of the Cholula poem of 1832, "En una tempestad" of September 1822 (as dated in J. M. Heredia 1940, 2:210) becomes the crucial point in the poetic project corresponding to Bloom's central dialectical restitution: the "heaping up" of repression (Bloom 1976, 24). For rather different approaches to the poems in recent critical studies, see Hamilton 1994 and Beaupied 1997.

14. On Minerva, see the first volume of Ilie 1995. Note also that Heredia would soon come to edit a journal in Toluca under that name (see J. M. Heredia 1972).

15. Critics frequently note that despite his championing of classicism against the insurgent romanticism of Sarmiento in their Chilean debate, Bello was himself attracted to the romantics late in life. His work as translator of Hugo is often cited as a case in point. I would add that Heredia returns to the dialogue as well. Bello's late "El incendio de la Compañía" surveys a "vasta ruina"[vast ruin] (Bello 1979, 59) that may be read fruitfully in conjunction with Heredia's Cholula poem.

CHAPTER 5. TAKING ROOT

1. For an introduction to that group, see Weinberg 1993.

2. Echeverría would have known "A M. Alphonse de L" from Hugo's *Odes et Ballades,* first published in Ladvocat, France in 1826.

3. See also the scene of overhearing that initiates Echeverría's "La guitarra" (1951, 477).

4. For a lively example of burlesque, consider the following excerpt from the parodic "Sermón" composed collaboratively by the Guatelmalans María Josefa García Granados (1796–1848) and José Batres Montufar (1809–44):

> Para evitar los males de que os hablo,
> escuchad las palabras de San Pablo:
> Mortales; fornicad, joded sin pena
> que la salud sin esto nunca es buena (Villacorta 1971, 163)

> To avoid the ills I related to you all,
> listen closely to these words of Saint Paul:
> Mortals, fornicate, screw to your heart's content,
> otherwise your health ain't worth one red cent.

See Berry-Bravo 1997, 175–78.
   5. See also Brotherston 1997, 256–65.
   6. I recall Bloom:

the meaning of a poem can only be a poem, but *another poem—a poem not itself*. And not a poem chosen with total arbitrariness, but any central poem by an indubitable precursor, even if the ephebe *never read* that poem. Source study is wholly irrelevant here; we are dealing with primal words, but antithetical meanings, and an ephebe's best misinterpretation may well be of poems he has never read. (1973, 70)

   7. In December of 1820 Iturbide's wars had not yet concluded.
   8. "La cautiva" continues to receive critical attention, e.g. Lagmanovich 1979, 25–26, Agüero 1983, Mattalia 1990 (47–59) and Premat 1993, 138–41.
   9. Susan Migden Socolow (1992) devotes considerable attention to the recuperation of captives by Rosas. On the figure of the captive, especially the captive woman, see also Haberly 1978, Lagmanovich 1979, Frederick 1980, and Rotker 1997, all of which at least touch upon Echeverría.
   10. I will again resist the temptation to follow the trajectory in Argentine poetry that leads to *Martín Fierro*, which belongs to a distinct historical moment beyond the boundaries of this study. I refer the reader once more to Ludmer's outstanding study of the gauchesca (1988) and her briefer overview (1996).
   11. The term is of course no novelty in and of itself, though perhaps it needs be added to the "key points" on Raymond Williams "map" of modernity (the terms "industry, democracy, class, art, and culture," R. Williams 1963, 13)
   12. On *Facundo*, see Goodrich 1996, and Shumway 1991 for a contextualization of Sarmiento's work in Argentine intellectual history. The excellent collection of essays edited by Halperin-Donghi and Jaksic 1994 provides broad coverage of Sarmiento's career.
   13. Compare Echeverría's critique, "liberty is me" (1940b, 146).
   14. On *Sab* in an antiabolitionist and a feminist frame, see Luis 1990 and Kirkpatrick 1989, respectively, as well as Jerome Branche's cogent critique (1998) of liberal readings of the novel.
   15. Cabrera and Zaldívar's collection (1981) marks an important turning point in the renewal of critical interest beyond *Sab*. Beth Miller's essay (1983) proved especially influential. See also Fontanella 1981 and Guerra 1985 and, more recently, Evelyn Picón Garfield's detailed account of Gómez de Avellaneda's role as editor (1992) and Raúl Ianes 1997 on Gómez de Avellaneda as a travel writer. Deyermond and Miller 1981 and Kirkpatrick 1992 have commented on the process of editing Gómez de Avellaneda's work; in the following discussion I will refer to the BAE edition of 1974.
   16. Recall McKnight's analysis of the sin of pride as it impinged upon the development and expression of subjectivity in Madre Castillo, discussed in chapter 2.
   17. I follow Manzano's punctuation in the translation, but do not attempt to reproduce his irregular orthography. See Luis (1994) on the intervention of editors and translators who have regularized Manzano's spelling and grammar.
   18. Amla is of course a transparent anagrama of *alma* [soul]: see the editorial note to "El deposorio en sueño," Gómez de Avellaneda 1974, n. 18, 312–13.
   19. I have already cited Albin 1995 in this regard; see also Alzaga 1990.

20. Gómez de Avellaneda underlined the quoted passage and added a note to the poem indicating the source of the citation.

21. See Trachtenberg 1979, 55.

CONCLUSION

1. I would signal two collections of critical essays by Gutérrez that I have heretofore mentioned in passing, which are of special relevance to my study as a whole: *Estudios biográficos y críticos sobre algunos poetas sud-americanos anteriores al siglo XIX* (1865) and *Los poetas de la Revolución* (1941). I have already had occasion in the preceding chapter to discuss in more detail his contribution to the formation of the Asociación de Mayo. Gutiérrez was the subject of a nineteenth-century monograph by Zinny (1878) and an important essay by Rodó (1967). Auza (1995) has recently renewed attention to Gutiérrez's work as an editor, focusing on his preparation of the *Obras poéticas de Olmedo* (1848).

2. I refer once again to Achugar's excellent study (1997) of postindependence national anthologies. In the case of *América poética*, of course, it is not an individual national identity, but rather the foundation of America as a whole that is in question.

3. See Achugar's remarks on public festivities in celebration of independence (1997, 25–28) for a suggestion of a direction for research beyond the print culture parallel to my interests in indigenous and Spanish-language oral poetry in the preceding chapters.

4. Gutiérrez provides what biographical and bibliographical information he can in his introductions to the selections of each poet in the anthology. In many cases his information is sparse and hardly supplemented by later critics. It is nevertheless precisely the "minor poets," in Benjamin's sense of the characteristic expression of their age, that make up the focus of my reading of *América poética*, since the relatively central names have been discussed in previous chapters.

5. I have found no current scholarship on Berro beyond the information available in national literary histories (e.g. Carvalho Neto 1965, 177–80). The same is true in the case of each of the poets to be discussed hereafter, with the exceptions noted.

6. I reiterate that here, as throughout, I do not pursue a history of styles; "El azahar" is indeed a "Flor sencilla," in Berro's words (J. M. Gutiérrez 1846, 97), in terms of diction and syntax.

7. I follow the orthography of *América poética*. Plácido has played a major role in Cuban literary history, receiving consistent critical attention. Vera M. Kutzinski's insightful comparative study (1990) includes comprehensive bibliographical information. See also Luis 1990, 113–15; Vitier 1970, 90–100 and Lezama 1965, 2.276–97 for a selection of poems.

8. Gutiérrez establishes Maitín's place in the national print culture by noting the following: "[Maitín] gave two dramas to the press in 1835 and 1838"; reviews of his literary work appeared in local journals; and he received "permission and license to print a collection of his poetry" (J. M. Gutiérrez 1846, 503).

9. Gutiérrez also includes other satires by Fernández de Madrid, light verse, a fine *costumbrista* scene in "A mi bañadera," his *Rosas*, his translations of Delille,

and, closer now to the concerns of my own discussion, "La noche de luna," a poem as crucial to the formation of Heredia as it was to Maitín. In short, Gutiérrez finds a diverse poetry which calls out for more extensive study; Fernández de Madrid ought to be a central name in the history of Spanish American poetry in the period embraced by *América poética.*

10. Heredia's "A Bolívar" was originally published in the Mexican journal *El Amigo del Pueblo*, 1828. It was reprinted in the *Poesías* of 1832, the edition unavailable to Gutiérrez, according to his bibliographical note in the anthology (J. M. Gutiérrez 1846, 286). Of relevance to the discussion in the preceding chapter of Echeverría's access to Heredia's poetry, I note that Gutiérrez had a version of the Cholula poem that extended beyond the 1820 composition as published in the *Poesías* of 1825, including the dream vision of human sacrifice, but without the final stanza as published in 1832.

11. On the traditional iconography of melancholia, see Klibansky, et al. 1964.

12. The haunted house of poetry, where the ghosts-in-life incorporate (enact, demetaphorize) a death not their own, is a legacy of nineteenth-century poetic melancholia among whose heirs are the *casas tomadas* of twentieth-century prose fiction. It is here, at last, that my work can anticipate an intersection with Eduardo González's deeply challenging and invigorating discussion of melancholia and related topics in *The Monstered Self* (1992).

13. The question of language as a marker of national identity was a crucial topic throughout Spanish-speaking America in the nineteenth century; for a critical discussion, see Niño-Murcia 1997.

Bibliography

Abad, Diego José. 1974. *Poema heróico*. Ed. and intro. Benjamín Fernández Valenzuela. Mexico City: Universidad Nacional Autónoma de México, Dirección General de Publicaciones.

Abraham, Nicolas. 1978. Notes du séminaire sur l'unité duelle et le fantôme (1974–75). In *L'écorce et le noyau*, ed. Nicolas Abraham and Maria Torok. La Philosophie en effet. Anasémies II. Paris: Aubier-Flammarion.

Abraham, Nicolas, and Maria Torok. 1986. *The Wolf Man's magic word: A cryptonymy*. Trans. Nicholas Rand. Foreward Jacques Derrida. Theory and History of Literature 37. Minneapolis: University of Minnesota Press.

———. 1994. *The shell and the kernel: Renewals of psychoanalysis*. vol. 1, ed., trans., intro. Nicholas T. Rand. Chicago: University of Chicago Press.

Abrams, M. H. 1953. *The mirror and the lamp: Romantic theory and the critical tradition*. Oxford: Oxford University Press.

———. The correspondent breeze: A romantic metaphor. In *The correspondent breeze, essays in English romanticism*. Foreward Jack Stillinger. New York: Norton.

Achugar, Hugo. 1997. Parnasos fundacionales: Letra, nación y estado en el siglo XIX. *Revista Iberoamericana* 63, no. 178–79: 13–31.

Achury Valenzuela, Darío. 1968. Introducción. In Castillo 1968.

Agüero, Eduardo de. 1983. El paisaje como adversario en *La cautiva*, *Cuadernos de ALDEEU* 1, 202–3: 157–74.

Aguirre, Juan Bautista. 1984. Obras selectas. In *Letras de la Audiencia de Quito (período jesuita)*, ed. Hernán Rodríguez Castelo. Biblioteca de Ayacucho 112. Caracas: Biblioteca de Ayacucho.

Alberdi, Juan Bautista. 1940. Doble armonía entre el objeto de esta institución, con una exigencia de nuestro desarrollo social: Y de esta institución con otra general del espíritu humano. In Echeverría 1940.

Albin, María C. 1995. *Album cubano* de Gómez de Avellaneda: la esfera pública y la crítica a la modernidad. *Cincinnati Romance Review* 14: 73–79.

Alcina Franch, José. 1988. *El descubrimiento científico de América*. Autores, Textos y Temas: Antropología 16. Barcelona: Anthropos.

Aldridge, A. Owen. 1971. *The Ibero-American Enlightenment*. Urbana: University of Illinois Press.

Alegre, Javier. 1941. *Memorias para la historia de la provincia que tuvo la Compañía de Jesús en Nueva España*. 2 vols. Ed. J. Jijón y Caamaño. Mexico: Librería de Porrúa Hmos.

Alegría, Fernando. 1954. *La poesía chilena, orígenes y desarrollo del siglo XVI al XIX*. Berkeley: University of California Press.

Alonso, Carlos J. 1994. *Rama y sus retoños*: Figuring the Nineteenth Century in Latin America. *Revista de Estudios Hispánicos* 28:283–92.

———. 1998. The burden of modernity. *Modern Language Quarterly* 57, no. 2:227–35.

———. 1998. *The burden of modernity: The rhetoric of cultural discourse in Spanish America*. New York: Oxford University Press.

Alonso, Martín. 1958. *Enciclopedia del idioma*. 3 vols. Madrid: Aguilar.

Alzaga, Florinda. 1990. La poesía religiosa de la Avellaneda: una dimensión olvidada. *Monographic Review/Revista monográfica* 6: 192–210.

La América española en la época de las luces. Tradición-innovación-representaciones (coloquio franco-éspañol, Maison des Pays Ibériques, Burdeos, 18–20 septiembre 1986). 1988. Madrid: Ediciones de Cultura Hispánica.

Amigo del filósofo rancio. 1834. Verses in *Broquel de las costumbres:* 128.

Anderson, Benedict. 1983. *Imagined communities: Reflections on the origin and spread of nationalism*. London: Verso.

Andrien, Kenneth J. 1998. The *Noticias secretas de América* and the construction of a governing ideology for the Spanish American empire," *Colonial Latin American Review* 7, no 2: 175–92.

Anuncio: *Poesías de D. J. M. Heredia*. 1823. *Revisor Político y Literario* (Havana) 13 (March 31): 5–8.

Arango y Parreño, Francisco de. 1979. Informe del síndico en el expediente instruido por el Consulado de La Habana sobre los medios que conviene proponer para sacar la agricultura y comercio de la Isla del apuro en que se hallan. In Chiaramonte 1979.

Araya, Guillermo. 1982. América en la poesía de Andrés Bello. *Homenaje a Andrés Bello en el bicentenario de su nacimiento, 1781–1981*. Diálogos hispánicos de Amsterdam 3. Amsterdam: Rodopi.

Arce, Joaquín. 1981. *La poesía del siglo ilustrado*. Madrid: Alhambra.

Arenas, Reynaldo [sic]. 1969. *El mundo alucinante (una novela de adventuras)*. Mexico: Diógenes.

Ariès, Philippe. 1977. *L'homme devant la mort*. Paris: Seuil.

Aronna, Michael. 1999. "Pueblos enfermos": *The discourse of illness in the turn-of-the-century Spanish and Latin American essay*. North Carolina Studies in Romance Languages and Literatures 262. Chapel Hill, NC: UNC Department of Romance Languages.

Arrom, José Juan. 1971. Mitos taínos en las letras de Cuba, Santo Domingo y México. *Certidumbre de América: estudios, folklore y cultura*. 2nd ed. Madrid: Gredos.

Auza, Néstor Tomás. 1995. Juan María Gutiérrez, editor de las *Obras poeticas* de Olmedo. *Boletín de la Academia Argentina de Letras* 60, no. 237–38: 229–43.

Bakhtin, Mikhail. 1984. *Rabelais and his world*. Trans. Hélène Iswolsky. Bloomington: Indiana University Press.

———. 1986. The *Bildungsroman* and its significance in the history of realism (towards a historical typology of the novel). In *Speech genres and other late Essays.* Trans. Vern W. McGee, ed. Caryl Emerson and Michael Holquist. Austin: University of Texas Press.

Ballou, Maturin M. 1854. *History of Cuba, or, notes of a traveller in the tropics. Being a political, historical, and statistical account of the island, from its first discovery to the present time.* Philadelphia: Lippincott, Grambo.

Baralt, Rafael Maria. 1939. *Resumen de la historia de Venezuela desde el descubrimiento de su territorio por los castellanos en el siglo XV, hasta el año de 1797, ordenado y compuesto por Rafael María Baralt: Ha cooperado a él en la parte relativa a las guerras de la conquista de la Costa Firme el señor Ramón Díaz, el cual le ha añadido los apéndices.* Brussels/Paris: Desclée/de Brouwer.

Barcia, Pedro Luis. 1982. *La lira Argentina o colección de las piezas poéticas dadas a luz en Buenos Aires durante la guerra de su independencia.* Reprint, Biblioteca de la Academia Argentina de las Letras. Serie Clásicos Argentinos, vol. 15. Buenos Aires: Academia Argentina de Letras.

Barco, Miguel del. 1981. *Ethnology and linguistics of Baja California.* Trans. Froylán Tiscareño, intro. Miguel León-Portilla. Baja California Travels Series 44. Los Angeles: Dawson's Book Shop.

Barnola, Pedro P, ed. 1935. *Las cien mejores poesías líricas venezolanas.* Caracas: Casa de especialidades.

Barras de Aragón, Francisco de las. 1952. Notas y documentos de la expedición del Conde de Mompox a la isla de Cuba. *Anuario de Estudios Americanos* 9: 513–48.

Barreiro, Jesús. 1933. Documentos relativos a la expedición del Conde de Mopox a la Isla de Cuba, durante los años 1796 a 1802, publicados ahora por vez primera. *Revista de la Academica de Ciencias exactas, físico-químicas y naturales* 30: 107–21.

Barrera Vásquez, Alfredo, ed. and trans. 1965. *El libro de los cantares de Dzitbalché.* Serie Investigaciones 9. Mexico: Instituto Nacional de Antopología.

Battlori, Miguel. 1966. *La cultura hispano-italiana de los jesuitas expulsos: Españoles-hispanoamericanos-filipinos, 1767–1814.* Madrid: Gredos.

Baudrillard, Jean. 1976. *L'échange symbolique et la mort.* NRF. Paris: Gallimard.

Beaupied, Aida M. 1997. Lo bello y lo sublime en dos poemas de José María Heredia. *Revista de Estudios Hispánicos* 31, no. 1: 3–23.

Becker, Carl L. 1932. *The heavenly city of the eighteenth century philosophers.* New Haven: Yale University Press.

Bedregal, Yolanda. 1991. *Antología de la poesía boliviana.* Cochabamba: Editorial "Los amigos del Libro" Werner Guttentag.

Belgrano, Manuel. Medios generales de fomentar la agricultura, animar la industria y proteger el comercio en un país agricultor. In Chiaramonte 1979.

Bello, Andrés. 1972. Consideraciones sobre la naturaleza, por Virey. In *Biblioteca Americana o miscelánea de literatura, artes y ciencia,* ed. Rafael Caldea. Caracas: Edicíon de la Presidencia de la República en homenaje al VI Congreso de la Asociacíon de Academias de la Lengua.

———. 1979. *Obra literaria.* Ed. and intro. Pedro Grases, Biblioteca Ayacucho.

Bénassy-Berling, Marie-Cécile. 1993. De Sigüenza y Góngora (XVIIe s.) à Fray Servando Teresa de Mier (XVIIIe-XIXe s.): vision de l'indien par le créole et enjeu politique." In *Les représentations de l'autre dans l'espace ibérique et ibéro-américain (II) (perspective diachronique). Actes du colloque organisé à la Sorbonne par le Grimesrep les 19, 20 et 21 mars 1992*, ed. Augustin Redondo. Paris: Presses de la Sorbonne Nouvelle.

Benítez-Rojo, Antonio. 1989. *La isla que se repite: El Caribe y la perspectiva posmoderna.* Hanover, NH: Ediciones del Norte.

———. 1996. Joaquín Fernández de Lizardi and the emergence of the Spanish American novel as national project. *Modern Language Quarterly* 57, no. 2: 325–39.

Benjamin, Walter. 1977. *The origin of German tragic drama.* Trans. John Osborne, intro. George Steiner. London: NLB.

Bergaño y Villegas, Simón. 1959. *Poemas.* Colección Letras de Guatemala. Guatemala: Revista de Guatemala.

Bernal, Ignacio. 1980. *A history of Mexican archaeology: The vanished civilizations of middle America.* Trans. Ruth Malet. London: Thames and Hudson.

Berruezo León, María Teresa. 1989. *La lucha de Hispanoamérica por su independencia en Inglaterra, 1800–1850.* Madrid: Ediciones de Cultura Hispánica.

Berry-Bravo, Judy. 1997. La irreverencia de dos poetas Guatemaltecas: María Josefa García Granados y Romelia Alarcón Folgar. *Instituto Literario y Cultural Hispánico* 15, no. 28–29: 175–84.

Beuchot, Maurcio. 1992. Una pieza de historia de la psicología: El *De Anima*, de Diego José Abad (México, siglo XVIII). *Dieciocho* 15, no. 1–2: 202–14.

Beverley, John. 1993. By Lacan : From literature to cultural studies. In *Against Literature.* Minneapolis: University of Minnesota Press.

Blondo y Zavala, Agustín. 1800. Fomento de Matanzas. April 1. MS 559, 17 fols. Museo Naval, Madrid.

———. 1802. Proyecto para habitar el Puerto de Mariel. April 2. MS 553, 7 fols. Museo Naval, Madrid.

Bloom, Harold. 1973. *The anxiety of influence: A theory of poetry.* New York: Oxford University Press.

———. 1975. *A map of misreading.* New York: Oxford University Press.

———. 1976. *Poetry and repression: Revisionism from Blake to Stevens.* New Haven: Yale University Press.

Bolívar, Simón. 1929. *Cartas del libertador.* 10 vols. Ed. Vicente Lecuna. Caracas: Lit. y Tip. del Comercio.

———. 1976. *Doctrina del Libertador.* Ed. Manuel Pérez Vila, intro. Augusto Mijares. Biblioteca Ayacucho 1. Caracas: Biblioteca Ayacucho.

Borges, Jorge Luis, and Adolfo Bioy Casares, eds. 1955. *Poesía gauchesca.* 2 vols. Biblioteca Americana. Literatura Moderna. Mexico: Fondo de Cultura Económica.

Borunda, Ignacio. 1898. *Clave general de jeroglíficos americanos.* Rome: Jean Pascal Scotti.

La bótanica en la expedición Malaspina, 1789–1794: Pabellón Villanueva, Real Jardín Botánico, Oct.–Nov. 1989. Colección "Encuentros." Madrid: Turner.

Branche, Jerome. 1998. Ennobling Savagery? Sentimentalism and the Subaltern in *Sab. Afro-Hispanic Review* 17, no. 2: 12–23.

Bribón, El. 1793. Letter to the Editor. *Papel Periódico* (Havana) 43 (May 30): 169–70.

Bricker, Victoria Reifler. 1973. *Ritual humor in highland Chiapas.* Austin: University of Texas Press.

———. 1981. *The Indian Christ, the Indian king: The historical substrate of Maya myth and ritual.* Austin: University of Texas Press.

Brotherston, Gordon. 1992. *La America indigena en su literatura: Los libros del cuarto mundo.* Intro. Miguel Leon-Portilla, trans. Teresa Ortega Guerrero y Monica Utrilla. Mexico City: Fondo de Cultura Económica.

Brown, Marshall. 1991. *Preromanticism.* Stanford, CA: Stanford University Press.

Brown, Richmond F. 1995. Profits, prestige, and persistence: Juan Fermín de Aycinena and the spirit of enterprise in the kingdom of Guatemala. *Hispanic American Historical Review* 75, no. 3: 405–40.

Browning, John. 1985. Rafael Landívar's *Rusticatio Mexicana*: Natural history and political subversion. *Ideologies and literature,* nueva época 1, no. 3: 10–30.

Bush, Andrew. 1988. Presentación. *Revista de Estudios Hispánicos* 22, no. 3: 87–92.

———. 1993. The Phantom of Montilla. In *Quixotic desire: Psychoanalytic perspectives on Cervantes,* ed. Ruth Anthony El Saffar and Diana de Armas Wilson. Ithaca: Cornell University Press.

Byron, George Gordon. 1855. *The poetical words of Lord Byron.* New York: Appleton.

Cabrera, Lydia. 1984. *La medicina popular de Cuba: Médicos de antaño, curanderos, santeros y paleros de hogaño.* Miami: Ultra Graphic.

Cabrera, Rosa M., and Gladys B. Zaldívar, eds. 1981. *Homenaje a Gertrudis Gómez de Avellaneda: Memorias del simposio en el centenario de su muerte.* Miami: Ediciones Universal.

Cáceres Romero, Adolfo. 1987. *Nueva historia de la literatura Boliviana.* Vol. 1. *Literatures aborígenas (Aimara-Quecha-Callawaya-Guariní).* La Paz-Cochabamba, Bolivia: Editorial los Amigos del País.

Cadalso, José. 1987. *Autobiografía: Noches lúgubres.* Ed. Manuel Camarero. Clásicos Castalia 165. Madrid: Castalia.

Calero y Moreira, Jacinto ("Hesperióphylo"). 1964a. Autoridades legales y canónicas, que prohiben los entierros eclesiásticos. 20 February 1791. *Mercurio Peruano* 15. Edición facsimilar. Lima: Biblioteca Nacional del Perú.

———. 1964b. Erección de un Campo-Santo en la villa de Tarma, y otro en el pueblo de Late. 27 January 1791. *Mercurio Peruano* 8. Edición facsimilar. Lima: Biblioteca Nacional del Perú.

———. 1964c. Examen histórico-filosófico de la diversas costumbres que ha habido en el Mundo relativamente á los entierros. 13 February 1791. *Mercurio Peruano* 13. Edición facsimilar. Lima: Biblioteca Nacional del Perú.

————. 1964d. Idea general del Perú. 2 January 1791. *Mercurio Peruano* 1. Edición facsimilar. Lima: Biblioteca Nacional del Perú.

————. 1964e. *Prospecto/del papel periódico intitulado Mercurio Peruano de historia, literatura, y noticias públicas, que á nombre de una/sociedad de Amantes del Pais, y como uno de ellos promete dar á luz Don Jacinto Calero y Mo/reira* 1790. Edición facsimilar. Lima: Biblioteca Nacional del Perú.

————. 1964f. Razones físicas, que reprueban la costumbre de enterrar en las iglesias" (February 17, 1791). *Mercurio Peruano* 14. Edición facsimilar. Lima: Biblioteca Nacional del Perú, 1.124–30.

Calvo y O-Farrill, Nicolás. 1795. *Memoria sobre los medios que convendría adoptar para que tuviese la Havana los caminos necesarios: Presentada al Consulado por la diputación que con este objeto nombró, Y escrita por el sr. consiliario D. Nicolás Calvo y O-Farrill.* Havana: Imprenta de la Capitanía General.

Carbón Sierra, Amaury B. 1998. Varela, latinista. *Cuadernos americanos* 12 nueva época no. 2: 70–76.

Carilla, Emilio, ed. 1979. *Poesía de la independencia.* Biblioteca de Ayacucho 59. Caracas: Ayacucho.

Carnero, Guillermo. 1983. *La cara oscura del siglo de las luces.* Madrid: Cátedra.

Caro, José Eusebio. 1951. *Antología: Verso y prosa.* Biblioteca Popular de Cultura Colombiana. Bogota: Editorial Iqueima.

Carpio Muñoz, Juan Guillermo. 1976. *El yaraví arequipeño: Un estudio histórico-social y un cancionero.* Arequipa, Peru: La Colmena.

Carrillo Rámirez, Salomón. 1960. *El poeta Villegas, precursor de la independencia de Centroamérica.* Guatemala: Ministerio de Educación Pública.

Carrión, Alejandro. 1988. *Los poetas quiteños de "El ocioso en Faenza."* Quito. Banco Central del Ecuador.

Carrizo, Juan Alfonso. 1937. *Cancionero popular de Tucumán.* 2 vols. Buenos Aires: A. Baiocco.

Carullo, Sylvia G. 1985. Una aproximación a la poesía afro-argentina de la época de Juan Manuel de Rosas. *Afro-Hispanic Review,* 15–22.

Carvalho Neto, Paulo de. 1965. *El negro uruguayo hasta la abolición.* Quito: Editorial Universitaria.

Cascardi, Anthony J. 1992. Afterword: The Subject of Control. In *Culture and Control in Counter-Reformation Spain,* eds. Anne J. Cruz and Mary Elizabeth Perry. Minneapolis: University of Minnesota Press.

Castañeda Paganini, Ricardo. 1946. *Las ruinas de Palenque: Su descubrimiento y primeras exploraciones en el siglo XVIII.* Guatemala: C. A.

Castillo, Francisca Josefa de la Concepción de. 1968. *Obras completas de la Madre Francisca Josefa de la Concepción de Castillo, según fiel transcripción de los manuscritos originales que se conservan en la Biblioteca Luis-Angel Arango.* 2 vols. Ed. Darío Achury Valenzuela. Bogotá: Talleres Gráficos del Banco de la República.

Castillo Andraca y Tamayo, Francisco del. 1948. *Obras de fray Francisco del Castillo Andraca y Tamayo.* Intro. and notes, Rubén Vargas Ugarte. S. J. Clásicos Peruanos 2. Lima: Editorial Studium.

Castro, Americo. 1977. The Historical "We." In *An idea of history: Selected essays of Americo Castro*. Ed. Stephen Gilman and Edmund L. King. Columbus: Ohio State University Press.

Certeau, Michel de. 1975. *L'écriture de l'histoire*. Paris: Gallimard.

Cervantes Saavedra, Miguel de. 1968. *Don Quijote de la Mancha*, ed. Martin de Riquer. Barcelona: Editorial Juventud.

Cevallos Candau, Francisco J. 1983. *Juan Bautista Aguirre y el barroco colonial*. Colección Temas y formas de la literatura 3. Madrid: EDI-6.

Cevallos Candau, Francisco J., Jeffrey A. Cole, Nina M. Scott, and Nicomedes Suárez-Araúz, eds. 1994. *Coded encounters: Writing, gender, and ethnicity in colonial Latin America*. Amherst: University of Massachusetts.

Charlot, Jean. 1962. *Mexican art and the academy of San Carlos, 1785–1915*. Texas Pan American Series. Austin: University of Texas Press.

Chénier, André. 1958. *Oeuvres complètes*. Ed. Gérard Walter. Biblioteque de la Pléiade 57. Paris: Gallimard.

Chenu, Jeanne. 1988. Desde la tierra hacia las estrellas: Búsqueda científica e identidad cultural en Nueva Granada. In *La América española en la epoca de la luces*. 1988.

Chiaramonte, José Carlos. ed. 1979. *Pensamiento de la ilustración: Economía y sociedad iberoamericanas en el siglo XVIII*. Biblioteca Ayacucho 51. Caracas: Biblioteca Ayacucho.

Civrieux, Marc de. 1980. *Watunna: An Orinoco creation cycle*. Ed. and trans. David M. Guss. San Francisco: North Point Press.

Clavero, Bernardo. 1991. *Razón de estado, razón de individuo, razón de historia*. Historia de la Sociedad Política. Madrid: Centro de Estudios Constitucionales.

Colomer Viadel, Antonio. 1990. *Introducción al constitucionalismo iberoamericano*. Instituto de Cooperación Iberoamericana, Quinto Centenario. Madrid: Ediciones de Cultura Hispánica.

Cooke, Michael G. 1979. *Acts of inclusion: Studies bearing on an elementary theory of romanticism*. New Haven: Yale University Press.

Cortés, José Domingo, ed. 1875. *Poetisas americanas: Ramillete poético del bello sexo hispano-americano*. Paris and Mexico: Librería de A. Bouret e hijos.

Cos, José María. 1984. Prospecto al *Ilustrador Nacional*. *Guía de Forasteros* 2, no. 7: 4–5.

Cros, Edmond. 1985. The values of liberalism in *El Periquillo Sarniento*. *Sociocriticism* 1, 2:85–109.

Danero, E. M. S., ed. 1953. *Antología gaucha*. Santa Fe, Argentina: Castellví.

Davison, Andrew. 1998. *Secularism and revivalism in Turkey: A hermeneutic reconsideration*. Yale Studies in Hermeneutics. New Haven: Yale University Press.

Deeds, Susan M. 1998. Indigenous rebellions on the northern Mexican mission frontier: From first-generation to later colonial responses. In Guy and Sheridan 1998.

de la Campa, Antonio R., and Raquel Chang-Rodríguez. 1985. *Poesía hispanoamericana colonial: Historia y antología*. Madrid: Alhambra.

Delille, Jacques Montanier. 1859. Les jardins. *Oeuvres complètes de J. Delille.* Notes. Parseval-Grandmaison, de Féletz, de Choiseul-Gouffier, Aimé-Martin, Descuret. Paris: Firmin Didot.

Del Pino Díaz, Fermín, ed. 1987. *Revista de Indias* 180.

Dérozier, Albert. 1978. *Manuel José Quintana y el nacimiento del liberalismo en España.* Trans. Manuel Moya. Madrid: Turner.

Derrida, Jacques. 1967. Freud et la scène de l'écriture. In *L'écriture et la différence.* Paris: Seuil.

Deustua, José. 1994. Routes, roads, and silver trade in Cerro de Pasco, 1820–1860: The internal market in nineteenth-century Peru. *Hispanic American Historical Review* 74, no. 1: 1–31.

Deyermond, Alan, and Beth Miller. 1981. On editing the poetry of Avellaneda. In *Studia Hispanica in Honour of Rodolfo Cardona.* Austin/Madrid: Cátedra.

D'Harcourt, R. and M. 1925. *La musique des Incas et ses survivances (texte).* Paris: Librairie orientaliste Paul Geuthner.

Discurso sobre el fomento de la industria popular de Orden de S. M. y del Consejo. 1988. Crisol 51. Madrid: Aguilar.

Dolorosa métrica espreción del Sitio, y entrega de la Havana, dirigida a N. C. Monarca el Sr. Dn. Carlos Tercero qe. Gue. 1960. *Revista de la Biblioteca Nacional 'José Martí'* 2, no. 1–4: 35–40.

Dölz-Blackburn, Inés. 1984. *Origen y desarrollo de la poesía tradicional y popular chilena desde la conquista hasta el presente.* Santiago, Chile: Nasciemento.

Domínguez, Jorge I. 1980. *Insurrection or loyalty: The breakdown of the Spanish American empire.* Cambridge: Harvard University Press.

Durán, Agustín. 1877. *Romancero general.* DAE 10:1. Madrid: Rivadeynera.

Durán Luzio, Juan. 1987. Alexander von Humboldt y Andrés Bello: Etapas hacia una relación textual. *Escritura* 12, no. 23–24: 139–52.

———. 1991. A propósito de una nueva edición bilingue de la *Rusticatio Mexicana,* de Rafael Landívar. *Revista Iberoamericana* 155–56: 591–96.

Easthope, Antony. 1991. *Literary into cultural studies.* London: Routledge.

Echeverría, Esteban. 1940. *Dogma socialista.* Intro. Alberto Palcos. Biblioteca de Autores Nacionales y Extranjeros referente a la República Argentina 2. La Plata: Universidad Nacional de La Plata.

———. 1951. *Obras completas de Esteban Echeverría.* Ed. Juan María Gutiérrez. Colección Argentoria 1. Buenos Aires: Antonio Zamora.

———. 1967. Epílogo a *Los consuelos.* In *La cautiva, El matadero y otros escritos,* ed. Noé Jitrik. Capítulo 9. Buenos Aires: Centro Editorial de América Latina.

Edmonson, Munro S. 1982. The songs of Dzitbalche: A literary commentary. *Tlalocan* 9: 173–208.

———. 1985. Quiche literature. In *Supplement to the handbook of Middle American Indians,* ed. Victoria Reifler Bricker. Vol. 3. *Literatures,* ed. Munro S. Edmondson, Patricia A. Andrews. Austin: University of Texas Press.

Edmunson, Munro S., and Victoria R. Bricker. 1985. Yucatecan Mayan literature. In *supplement to the handbook of Middle American Indians,* gen. ed. Victoria

Reifler Bricker. Vol. 3, *Literatures*, ed. Munro S. Edmondson and Patricia A. Andrews. Austin: University of Texas Press.

Feijóo, Benito Jerónimo. 1928. Entierros prematuros. *Obras IV: Cartas eruditas.* Clásicos castellanos 85. Madrid: Ediciones de "La Lectura."

Feliú Cruz, Guillermo. 1962. *Colección de antiguos periódicos chilenos: El Cosmopolita.-El diario de la convención.-El observador Chileno.-El Tizón Republicano.-El clamor de la patria-apéndice; correspondencia entre la junta gubernativa y el mariscal de campo don Ramón Freire, 1822–1823.* Santiago de Chile: Ediciones de la Biblioteca Nacional.

Ferenczi, Sandor. 1980. On the definition of introjection. *Final contributions to the problems and methods of psycho-analysis.* Trans. Eric Masbach et al., ed. Michael Balint. Brunner/Mazel Classics in Psychoanalysis 6. New York: Brunner/Mazel.

Fernández Bravo, Alvaro. 1997. La frontera portátil: Nación y temporalidad en Lastarria y Sarmiento. *Revista Iberoamericana* 63, no. 178–79: 141–47.

Fernández de Lizardi, José Joaquín. 1940. Constitución política de una república imaginaria. 1825 Reprint, *El Pensador Mexicano.* Biblioteca del estudiante universitario 15. Mexico: Ediciones de la Universidad Nacional Autónoma.

Fernández de Madrid. José. 1822. *Poesías del ciudadano Dr. José Fernández de Madrid.* Vol. 1. Havana: Impr. Fraternal de los Díaz de Castro.

———. 1823. Poesía. *La aguila mexicana* 23 (7 May): 91–92.

Fernández Retamar, Roberto. 1972. *Calibán: Apuntes sobre la cultura de nuestra América.* Mexico: Diógenes.

Fernández Valenzuela, Benjamín. 1924. Introducción, *Poema heróico*, Diego José Abad. Ed. and intro. Benjamín Fernández Valenzuela. Mexico City: Universidad Nacional Autónoma de México, Dirección General de Publicaciones.

Filantrópico. 1822. Letter to *El impertérrito constitucional* (Havana): 1–8.

Fisher, John. 1981. Imperial "Free Trade" and the Hispanic economy, 1778–1796. *Journal of Latin American Studies* 13, no. 1: 21–56.

———. 1998. Commerce and imperial decline: Spanish trade with Spanish America, 1797–1820. *Journal of Latin American Studies* 30: 459–79.

Flores, Angel. 1966. *The literature of Spanish America.* Vol. 1. The colonial period. New York: Las Américas.

Fontanella, Lee. 1981. Mystical diction and imagery in Gómez de Avellaneda and Carolina Coronado. *Latin American Literary Review* 19: 47–55.

Fornaris, José, and Joaquin Lorenzo Luaces, directors, and José Socorro León, ed. 1858. *Cuba poética: Coleccion escogida de las composiciones en verso de los poetas cubanos desde Zequeira hasta nuestros días.* Havana: Imprenta y papelería de la viuda de Barcina.

Foucault, Michel. 1975. *Surveiller et punir: Naissance de la prison.* Paris: Gallimard.

Franco, Jean. 1983. La heterogeneidad peligrosa: Escritura y control social en vísperas de la independencia mexicana. *Hispamérica* 34–35: 3–34.

Frederick, Bonnie. 1980. Reading the warning: The reader and the image of the captive woman. *Chasqui* 18, no. 2: 3–11.

Freud, Sigmund. 1953–74. *The standard edition of the complete psychological works of Sigmund Freud.* 24 vols. Trans. and ed. James Strachey with Anna Freud, Alix Strachey and Alan Tyson. London: Hogarth Press.

Gallegos, Rómulo. 1976. *Doña Bárbara: Obras completas.* Vol. 1. Madrid: Aguilar.

García del Río, Juan. 1972. Prospecto. In *Biblioteca Americana, o miscelánea de literatura, artes y ciencias,* ed. Rafael Caldea. Caracas: Edición de la Presidencia de la República en homenage al VI Congreso de la Asociación de Academias de la Lengua. 1972.

García Garófalo y Mesa, Manuel. 1945. *Vida de José María Heredia en México, 1825–1839.* Mexico City: Ediciones Botas.

Garrigó, Roque E. 1929. *Historia documentada de la conspiración de los Soles y Rayos de Bolívar.* 2 vols. Havana: Imprenta "El Siglo XX."

Gerbi, Antonello. 1973. *The dispute of the new world: The history of a polemic, 1750–1900.* Trans. Jeremy Hoyle. Pittsburgh: University of Pittsburgh Press.

Gilbert, Sandra M., and Susan Gubar. 1979. *The madwoman in the attic: The woman writer and the nineteenth-century literary imagination.* New Haven: Yale University Press.

Gisbert, Teresa. 1992. Art and resistance in the Andean world, trans. Laura Giefer. In *American images and the legacy of columbus,* eds. René Jara and Nicholas Spadaccini. Hispanic Issues 9. Minneapolis: University of Minnesota Press.

Godzich, Wlad, Nicholas Spadaccini. 1987. Introduction: From discourse to literature. In *The instutionalization of literature in Spain.* Hispanic Issues 1. Minneapolis: Prisma Institute.

———. 1994. Popular culture and Spanish literary history. In *The culture of literacy.* Cambridge: Harvard University Press.

Gomes, Miguel. 1998. Las *Silvas americanas* de Andrés Bello: Una relectura genealógica. *Hispanic Review* 66: 181–96.

Gómez de Avellaneda, Gertrudis. 1974. *Obras de doña Gertrudis Gómez de Avellaneda.* Ed. José María Castro y Calvo. Vol. 1. Biblioteca de Autores Españoles 272. Madrid: Atlas.

Gómez Marín, Manuel. 1981. *Obras castellanas y latinas en verso y prosa.* Intro. and trans. Jesús Yhmoff Cabrera. Mexico City: Biblioteca Enciclopédica del Estado de México.

Gomis Blanco, Alberto. 1987. Sessé y la expedición de Mopox a Cuba. *La Real Expedición botánica a Nueva España, 1787–1803.* Madrid: Real Jardín Botánico/CSIC.

Góngora y Argote, Luis de. 1972. *Obras completas.* Eds. Juan Mille y Giménez and Isabel Mille y Giménez. Madrid: Aguilar.

González [Pérez], Aníbal. 1983. *La crónica modernista.* Madrid: Porrúa Turranzas.

———. 1993. *Journalism and the development of Spanish American narrative.* Cambridge: Cambridge University Press.

González, Eduardo. 1988. Informe: Sergei Pankeiev (alias *el hombre de los lobos*), inmortal reiterado y por fin descubierto. *Revista de Estudios Hispánicos* 22, no. 3: 109–25.

———. 1992. *The monstered self: Narratives of death and performance in Latin American fiction.* Durham: Duke University Press.

González Casanova, Pablo. 1958. *La literatura perseguida en la crisis de la colonia.* Mexico: El Colegio de México.

González del Valle, Francisco. 1938. *Cronología herediana, 1803–1839.* Publicación de la Secretaria de Educación. Dirección de Cultura. Havana: Montalvo y Cárdenas.

González Echevarría, Roberto. 1976. José Arrom, autor de la *Relación acerca de las antigüedades de los Indios* (picaresca e historia). In *Relecturas: Estudios de literatura cubana.* Caracas: Monte Avila.

———. 1983. *Isla a su vuelo fugitiva.* Madrid: José Porrúa Turranzas.

———. 1996. A brief history of the history of Spanish American Literature. In González Echevarría and Pupo-Walker 1996.

González Echevarría, Roberto, and Enrique Pupo-Walker, eds. 1996. *The Cambridge history of Latin American literature.* Vol. 1. *Discovery to modernism.* Cambridge: Cambridge University Press.

Goodrich, Diana Sorenson. 1996. *Facundo and the construction of Argentine culture.* Austin: University of Texas.

Gossen, Gary H. 1985. Tzotzil literature. In *Supplement to the handbook of Middle American Indians*, gen. ed. Victoria Reifler Bricker. Vol. 3, *Literatures*, ed. Munro S. Edmondson, Patricia A. Andrews. Austin: University of Texas Press.

Gray, Thomas. 1966. *The complete poems of Thomas Gray, English, Latin and Greek.* Ed. H. W. Starr and J. R. Hendrickson. Oxford: Clarendon Press.

———. 1807. *The Works of Thomas Gray.* 2 vols. London: Vernor, Hood and Sharpe.

Griffith, Reginald Harvey. 1920. The progress pieces of the eighteenth century. *Texas Review* 5: 218–33.

Guerra, Lucía. 1985. Estrategias femeninas en la elaboración del sujeto romántico en la obra de Gertrudis Gómez de Avellaneda. *Revista Iberoamericana* 51, no. 132–133: 707–22.

Gumbrecht, Hans Ulrich. 1987. Censorship and the creation of heroes in the discourse of literary history. In *The institutionalization of literature in Spain,* eds. Godzich and Spadaccini, Hispanic Issues 1. Minneapolis: Prisma Institute.

———. 1992. Sign conceptions in European everyday culture between Renaissance and early nineteenth century." In *Semiotik: Ein Handbuch zu den zeichentheoretischen Grundlagen vom Natur und Kultur*, ed. R. Posner, K. Robering, and T. A. Sebeok. Berlin: Walter de Gruyter.

Guss, David M. 1989. *To weave and to sing: art, symbol, and narrative in the South American rain forest.* Berkeley: University of California Press.

Gutiérrez González, Gregorio and Epifanio Mejía. 1926. *Gregorio y Epifanio: Sus mejores versos.* Lima: Editora popular americana, 1926.

Gutiérrez, Juan María. 1865. *Estudios biográficos y críticos sobre algunos poetas sud-americanos anteriores al siglo XIX.* Buenos Aires: Imprenta del Siglo.

———. 1940a. Fisonomía del saber español: Cual deba ser entre nosotros. Echeverría 1940.

————. 1940b. Noticias biográficas sobre don Esteban Echeverría. In Echeverría 1940.

————. 1941. *Los poetas de la Revolución*. Buenos Aires: Academia Argentina de Letras.

————. 1951. "Advertencia." In Echeverrría 1951.

————, ed. 1846. *América poética: Coleccion escojida de composiciones en verso, escritos por americanos en el presente siglo: Parte lírica*. Valparaíso: Imprenta del Mercurio.

Gutiérrez, Ramón A. 1991. *When Jesus came, the corn mothers went away: Marriage, sexuality, and power in New Mexico, 1500–1846*. Stanford: Stanford University Press.

Gutiérrez Giradot, Rafael. 1974. Pedro Henríquez Ureña y la historiografía literaria latinoamericana. In *Literatura y praxis en América Latina*, Fernando Alegría, Gutiérrez Giradot, Noé Jitrik, Angel Rama and Marta Traba. Colección Letra Viva. Caracas: Monte Avila.

————. 1978. Pedro Henríquez Ureña. In *La utopía de América*, eds. Gutiérrez Giradot and Angel Rama, prolog Gutiérrez Giradot. Biblioteca Ayacucho 37. Caracas: Biblioteca Ayacucho.

————. 1982. Andrés Bello y la filosofía. In *Homenage a Andrés Bello en el bicentenario de su nacimiento, 1781–1981*. Diálogos Hispánicos de Amsterdam 3. Amsterdam: Roldopi.

————. 1983. *Modernismo*. Barcelona: Montesinos.

Guy, Donna J., and Thomas E. Sheridan, eds. 1998. *Contested ground: Comparative frontiers on the northern and southern edges of the Spanish empire*. The Southwestern Series. Tucson: University of Arizona Press.

Haberly, David. 1978. Captives and infidels: The figure of the *cautiva* in Argentine literature. *The American Hispanist 4*.

Haidt, Rebecca. 1995. *Los besos de amor* and *La maja desnuda*: The fascination of the senses in the *ilustración*. *Revista de Estudios Hispánicos* 29, no. 3: 477–503.

Halperin-Donghi, Tulio, and Ivan Jaksic, eds. 1994. *Sarmiento: Author of a nation*. Berkeley: University of California Press.

Hamilton, James F. 1994. The hero's journey to Niagara in Chateaubriand and Heredia, French and Cuban exiles. *Romance Quarterly* 41, no. 2: 71–78.

Hamnett, Brian R. 1997. Process and pattern: A re-examination of the Ibero-American independence movements, 1808–1826. *Journal of Latin American Studies* 29: 279–328.

Hartman, Geoffrey H. 1978. *Beyond Formalism: Literary Essay, 1958–1970*. New Haven: Yale University Press.

————. 1975. Evening star and evening land. *The fate of reading and other essays*. Chicago: University of Chicago Press.

Heath, Shirley Brice. 1972. *Telling tongues, language policy in Mexico, colony to nation*. New York: Teachers College Press.

Hechavarría O'Gavan, Prudencio de. 1879. *Sátira contra la predilección del derecho romano en nuestras aulas y tribunales*. Madrid: Imprenta de la Revista de Legislación.

Henríquez Ureña, Pedro. 1963. *Literary currents in Hispanic America*. 1945. New York: Russell and Russell.

———. 1978. *La utopía de América*. Eds. Rafael Gutiérrez Giradot and Angel Rama, prolog Gutiérrez Giradot. Biblioteca Ayacucho 37. Caracas: Biblioteca Ayacucho.

Heredia, José Francisco. 1986. *Memorias del Regente*. Caracas: Academia Nacional de la Historia.

Heredia, José María. 1819. Remitido. *Noticioso general* (Mexico) 578 (Sept. 13): 3.

———. 1823. A D. D. D., desde el campo. *Revisor Político y Literario* (Havana) 56 (July 9): 5–8.

———. 1946. *Poesías completas: Homenaje de la Ciudad de la Habana en el Centenario de la muerte de Heredia, 1839–1939*. 2 vols. Colección histórica cubana y americana 3. Havana: Municipio de la Habana.

———. 1972. *Minerva, periódico literario*. Ed. María del Carmen Ruiz Castañeda. Mexico: UNAM, Dirección General de Publicaciones.

Hernández, José. 1961. *Martín Fierro*. Ed. Carlos Alberto Leumann. Buenos Aires: Angel Estrada.

Hernández de Alba, Guillermo, and Guillermo Hernández Peñalosa, eds. 1982. *Poemas en alabanza de los defensores de Cartagena de Indias en 1741*. Publicaciones del Instituto Caro y Cuervo 50. Bogota: Instituto Caro y Cuervo.

Herr, Richard. 1958. *The eighteenth-century revolution in Spain*. Princeton: Princeton University Press.

Hill, Ruth. 1994. Between reason and piety: *Inventio* and verisimilitude in Pedro de Peralta's Prologue to *Lima fundada*, 1732. *Dieciocho* 17, no. 2: 129–41.

———. 1996. Churchmen, statesmen, smugglers *extraordinaires*: The prodigious 4 P's from Lima. *Indiana Journal of Hispanic Literatures* 8: 96–109.

Hollier, Dennis. 1993. On literature considered as a dead language. *Modern Language Quarterly* 54, no. 1: 21–29.

Horace. 1936. *The complete works of Horace*. Ed. Caspar J. Kraemer, New York: Modern Library, Random House.

Hugo, Victor. 1857. *Oeuvres complètes de Victor Hugo*. 18 vols. Paris: Alexandre Houssiaux.

———. 1867. Préface to *Théâtre*. Vol 1, *Cromwell*. Paris: Librairie de L. Hachette.

Hunt, Eva. 1977. *The transformation of the hummingbird: Cultural roots of a Zinacantecan mythical poem*. Ithaca: Cornell University Press.

Hyslop, John. 1984. *The Inka road system*. Studies in Archaeology. Orlando: Academic Press/Harcourt Brace Janovich.

Ianes, Raúl. 1997. La esfericidad del papel: Gertrudis Gómez de Avellaneda, La Condesa de Merlín, y la literatura de viajes. *Revista Iberoamericana* 68, no. 178–79: 209–18.

Ilie, Paul. 1995. *The age of Minerva*. 2 vols. Philadelphia: University of Pennsylvania Press.

Irisarri, Antonio José de. 1867. *Poesías satíricas y burlescas*. New York: Hallet.

J. V. 1823. Al R. P. Fr. Manuel Navarrete, celebérrimo poeta americano. *La aguila mexicana* 209 (9 Nov.): 4.

Jara, René. 1988. The inscription of Creole consciousness: Fray Servando de Mier, trans. Alma Bishop-Jara. In *1492–1992: re-discovering colonial writing*, ed. Jara and Nicholas Spadaccini. Hispanic Issues 4. Minneapolis: University of Minnesota Press.

Johnson, Julie Greer. 1983. *Women in colonial Spanish American literature: Literary images*. Contributions in Women's Studies 43. Westport, CT: Greenwood.

———. 1993. *Satire in colonial Spanish America: Turning the new world upside down*. Foreward, Daniel R. Reedy. Texas Pan American Series. Austin: University of Texas Press.

———. 1994. Satire and eighteenth-century colonial Spanish-American society. In Cevallos Candau, et al. 1994.

Jovellanos, Gaspar Melchor de. 1956. Informe sobre la disciplina eclesiástica antigua y moderna relativa al lugar de las sepulturas, 1783. In *Obras*. BAE 87. Madrid: Real Academia Española.

———. Discurso académico en su recepción a la Real Academia de la Historia: Sobre la necesidad de unir al estudio de la legislación el de nuestra historia. In *Obras en prosa,* ed. José Caso González. 3rd. ed. Madrid: Castalia.

Juan, Jorge, and Antonio de Ulloa. 1985. *Noticias secretas de América.* 2 vols. 1826 Reprint, Madrid: Fernández de Oviedo.

Juana, Inés de la Cruz. 1975. *Obras completas*. Mexico: Porrúa.

Kahiluoto Rudat, Eva M. 1985. Lo clásico y lo barroco en la obra literaria de Peralta Barnuevo. *Dieciocho* 8, no. 1: 31–42.

——— 1991. The spirit of intellectual independence in the writings of enlightened Creoles. *Dieciocho* 14, no. 1–2: 80–91.

Kernan, Alvin. 1982. *The imaginary library: An essay on literature and society*. Princeton: Princeton University Press.

———. 1987. *Printing technology, letters and Samuel Johnson*. Princeton: Princeton University Press.

Kerson, Arnold L. 1976. El concepto de utopía de Rafael Landívar en la *Rusticatio Mexicana, Revista Iberoamericana* 96–97.

———. 1984. José Rafael Campoy and Diego José Abad: Two enlightened figures of eighteenth-century Mexico. *Dieciocho* 7, no. 2: 130–45.

———. 1986. Rafael Landívar's *Rusticatio Mexicana* and the enlightenment in America. In *Acta conventus neo-Latini sanctandreani: Proceedings of the fifth international congress of neo-Latin studies. Saint Andrews 24 August to 1 September 1982*, ed. I. D. McFarlane. Medieval and Renaissance Texts and Studies 38. Binghamton, NY: Medieval and Renaissance Texts and Studies.

———. 1988. Enlightened thought in Diego José Abad's *De deo, deoque homine heroica*. In *Acta conventus neo-Latini guelpherbytani: Proceedings of the sixth international congress of neo-Latin studies, Wolfenbüttel 12 August to 16 August 1985*, eds. Stella P. Revard, Fidel Rädel and Mario A. Di Cesare. Medieval and Renaissance Texts and Studies 53. Binghamton, NY: Medieval and Renaissance Texts and Studies.

———. 1989. Los latinistas mexicanos del siglo XVIII. *Actas del IX congreso de la asociación internacional de hispanistas: 18–23 agosto 1986, Berlín.* Frankfurt am Main: Vervuert.

———. 1990. The heroic mode in Rafael Landívar's *Rusticatio Mexicana. Dieciocho* 13, no. 1–2: 149–64.

Kino, Eusebio Francisco. 1969. *First from the gulf to the Pacific: The diary of the Kino-Atondo peninsular expedition, December 14, 1684-January 13, 1685.* Baja California Travels Series 16. Trans. and ed. W. Michael Mathes. Los Angeles: Dawson's Book Shop.

Kinsbruner, Jay. 1994. *Independence in Spanish America: Civil wars, revolutions and underdevelopment.* 2nd ed. Diálogos. Albuquerque: University of New Mexico Press.

Kirkpatrick, Susan. 1988. Spanish romanticism. In *Romanticism in national context,* ed. Roy Porter and Mikuláš Teich. Cambridge: Cambridge University Press.

———. 1989. *Las románticas: Women writers and subjectivity in Spain, 1835–1850.* Berkeley: University of California Press.

———. 1997. Toward a feminist textual criticism: Thoughts on editing the work of Coronado and Avellaneda. In *The Politics of Editing,* eds. Nicholas Spadaccini and Jenaro Talens. Hispanic Issues 8. Minneapolis: University of Minnesota Press.

Klibansky, Raymond, Erwin Panofsky, and Fritz Saxl. 1964. *Saturn and melancholy: Studies in the history of natural philosophy, religion and art.* London: Nelson.

Kutzinski, Vera M. 1990. Unseasonal flowers: Nature and history in Plácido and Jean Toomer. *Yale Journal of Criticism* 3, no. 2: 153–79.

Lafaye, Jacques. 1977. *Quetzalcoatl y Guadalupe: La formación de la conciencia nacional.* Trans. Ida Vitale, preface Octavio Paz. Mexico: Fondo de cultura económica.

Lagmanovich, David. 1979. Tres cautivas: Echeverría, Ascasubi, Hernández. *Chasqui* 8, no. 3: 24–33.

Lamartine, Alphonse de. 1968. *Méditations.* Ed. Fernand Letessier. Paris: Garnier.

Landívar, Rafael. 1948. Rafael Landívar's *Rusticatio Mexicana* (Mexican country scenes). Latin text, intro. and trans. Graydon W. Regenos. *Philological and Documentary Studies* 1, 5.

Lanning, John Tate. 1956. *The eighteenth-century Enlightenment in the University of San Carlos de Guatemala.* Ithaca: Cornell University Press.

Lara, Jesús. 1947. *La poesía quechua.* Mexico: Fondo de cultura económica.

Lemaur, Felix, and Francisco Lemaur. 1798a. Discurso sobre el proyecto de una poblacion en la Bahia de Jagua. 30 July 30. Museo Naval (Madrid) MS 552. 63 fols.

———. 1798b. Ynforme sobre los caminos de la Ysla de Cuba dado al Señor Conde de Mopox (Havana, 24 November). Museo Naval (Madrid) MS 561. 107 folios.

León y Gama, Antonio de. 1832. *Descripción histórica y cronológica de las dos piedras, que con ocasion del nuevo empedrado que se esta formando en la plaza principal de Mexico, se hallaron en ella el año de 1790.* 1792. Reprint, 2nd augmented ed., ed. Carlos María de Bustamante. Mexico: Imprenta del Ciudadano Alejandro Valdés.

Leonard, Irving A. 1933. A great savant of colonial Peru: Don Pedro de Peralta. *Philological Quarterly* 12: 54–72.

Lerdo de Tejada, Luis. 1985. *México en 1856: Comercio exterior de México desde la conquista hasta hoy.* Colección Rescate. Xalapa, Mexico: Universidad Veracruzana.

Lezama Lima, José. 1965. *Antología de la poesía cubana.* 3 vols. Havana: Consejo Nacional de Cultura.

———. 1977. *Obras completas. vol. 2: Ensayos. Cuentos.* Mexico: Aguilar.

Lienhard, Martín. 1991. *La voz y su huella. Escritura y conflicto étnico-social en América Latina, 1492–1988.* Serie Rama 510. Hanover, NH: Ediciones del Norte.

Llaguno, Eugenio de. 1796. Carta al Príncipe de la Paz. (16 October). Museo Naval (Madrid) MS 2240, doc. 16, fol 57.

Lluch, Ernst. 1984. Manuel Belgrano, introductor de la fisiocracia en el área de la lengua castellana. In Lluch and Argemí 1984.

Lluch, Ernst, and Lluis Argemí. 1984. *Agronomía y fisiocracia en España, 1750–1820.* Valencia: Institución Alfonso el Magnánimo/Institució Valencia d'Etudis i Investigació.

Lockhart, James. 1992. *The Nahuas after the conquest: A social and cultural history of the Indians of central Mexico, sixteenth through eighteenth centuries.* Stanford: Stanford University Press.

López Marroquín, Rubén. 1994. Rafael Landívar, poeta cronista de América. *Cuadernos americanos* nueva época 47: 242–51.

López Prieto, Adolfo. 1881. *Parnaso cubano.* Havana.

Lozoya, Xavier. 1984. *Plantas y luces en México: La Real Expedicíon Científico a Nueva España (1787–1803).* Barcelona: Ediciones del Serbal.

Ludmer, Josefina. 1988. *El género gauchesco: Un tratado sobre la patria.* Buenos Aires: Sudamericana.

———. 1996. The gaucho genre. In González Echevarría and Pupo-Walker 1996.

Lugo-Ortiz, Agnes I. 1997. Figuraciones del sujeto moderno: biografía, plantación y muerte al albor del siglo XIX cubano. *Revista Iberoamericana* 63, no. 178–79: 47–60.

Luis, William. 1990. *Literary bondage: Slavery in Cuban narrative.* Austin: University of Texas Press.

———. 1994. Nicolás Azcárate's antislavery notebook and the unpublished poems of the slave Juan Francisco Manzano. *Revista de Estudios Hispánicos* 28, no. 3: 331–46.

MacLeod, Murdo J. 1984. Aspects of the internal economy of colonial Spanish America: Labour, taxation, distribution and exchange. In *The Cambridge history of Latin America*, ed. Leslie Bethell. vol. 2, *Colonial Latin America*. Cambridge: Cambridge University Press.

Malamud, Carlos and Pedro Pérez. 1988. El reglamento de comercio libre en

España y América: Principales problemas interpretativos. In *La América española en la epoca de las luces* 1988.

Mañach, Jorge. 1957. Heredia y el romanticismo. *Cuadernos hispanoamericanos* 86: 195–220.

Mandrell, James. 1991. The literary sublime in Spain: Meléndez Valdés and Espronceda. *MLN* 106: 294–313.

Manzano, Juan Francisco. 1970. *Autobiografía, cartas y versos Havana 1937. Poesías completas de Plácido (Paris 1862)*, Gabriel de la Concepción Valdés. Nendeln: Kraus Reprint.

Maravall, José Antonio. 1986. *Culture of the baroque: Analysis of a historical structure*. Trans. Terry Cochrane. Theory and History of Literature 25. Minneapolis: University of Minnesota Press

———. 1991. *Estudios de la historia del pensamiento español (siglo XVIII)*. Ed. María Carmen Iglesias. Madrid: Mondadori.

Martí, José. 1940. Discurso pronunciado en Hardman Hall, Nueva York, el 30 de noviembre de 1889. In J. M. Heredia 1940.

Martínez Baeza, Sergio. 1985. La introducción de la imprenta en le nuevo mundo: Los primeros impresos americanos, 1535–1810. *Atenea* 451: 81–98.

Matos Moctezuma, Eduardo. 1980. *El Negrito Poeta mexicano y el dominicano: ¿Realidad o fantasía?* Mexico: Porrúa.

Mattalia, Sonia. 1990. Estética romántica, estética modernista: Contrapuntos de una 'visión' americana. In *Pensamiento crítico y crítica de la cultura en Hispanoamérica*, Ana Pizarro, Sonia Mattalia, Francisco J. López Alfonso and José Carlos Rovira. Instituto de Cultura Juan Gil-Albert.

Mazzotti, José Antonio. 1996. *Sólo la proporción es la que canta*: Poética de la nación y épica criolla en la Lima del XVIII. *Revista de crítica literaria latinoamericana* 22, no. 43–44: 59–75.

McKnight, Kathryn Joy. 1997. *The mystic of Tunja: The writings of Madre Castillo, 1671–1742*. Amherst: University of Massachusetts Press.

McVay, Jr., Ted E. 1994. The sublime aesthetic in the poetry of José María Heredia. *Dieciocho* 17, no. 1: 33–41.

Meehan, Thomas C., and John T. Cull. 1984. El poeta de las adivinanzas: Esteban de Terralla y Landa. *Revista de crítica literaria latinoamericana* 19: 127–57.

Meléndez Valdés, Juan. 1988. *Poesías selectas: La lira de marfil*. Eds. J. H. R. Polt and Georges Demerson. Clásicos Castalia 108. Madrid: Castalia.

Melgar, Mariano. 1971. *Poesías completas*. Eds. Aurelio Miró Quesada, Estuardo Núñez, Antonio Cornejo Polar, Enrique Aguirre and Raúl Bueno Chavez. Clásicos peruanos 1. Lima: Academia peruana de la lengua.

Melville, Herman. 1976. *Moby Dick or, the whale*. Eds. Harison Hayford and Hershel Parker. New York: Norton.

Memorial dirigida á Carlos III por las señoras de la Habana en 25 de agosto de 1762. 1982. *Revista de Cuba* 12: 161–67.

Menéndez Pidal, Ramón. *Los romances de América y otros estudios*. Madrid: Espasa-Calpe.

———. 1975. *Flor nueva de romances viejos*. Madrid: Espasa-Calpe.

Menéndez y Pelayo, Marcelino. 1895. *Antología de poetas hispano-americanos*. 4 vols. Madrid: Sucesores de Rivadeneyra.

Mier, Servando Teresa de. 1981. *Obras completas: El heterodoxo guadalupano*. 2 vols. Ed. and intro. Edmundo O'Gorman. Nueva Biblioteca Mexicana 81. Mexico: Universidad Nacional Autónoma de México.

Mignolo, Walter. 1994. The moveable center: Geographical discourses and territoriality during the expansion of the Spanish empire. In Cevallos Candau, et al. 1994.

Miller, Beth. 1983. Gertrudis the great: Avellaneda, nineteenth-century feminist. In Miller, ed. *Women in Hispanic literature: Icons and fallen idols*. Berkeley: University of California Press, 1983. 201–14.

Minguet, Charles. 1988. Del Dorado a la leyenda negra; de la leyenda negra al caos primitivo: La América hispánica en el siglo de las luces. *La América española en la época de la luces* 1988.

Miquel y Vergés, J. M. 1946. *La independencia mexicana y la prensa insurgente*. Mexico: El Colegio de México.

Miranda, Francisco de. 1938. *Archivo del general Miranda*. 24 vols. Caracas: Tipografía Americana.

Miranda José, and Pablo González Casanova, eds. 1953. *Sátira anónima del siglo XVIII*. Letras mexicanas. Mexico: Fondo de cultura económica.

Miró, Rodrigo. 1974. *Itinerario de la poesía en Panamá, 1502–1974*. Panama: Editorial Universitario.

Monge, José María, Manuel M. Sama, and Antonio Ruíz Quiñones, eds. 1879. *Poetas Puerto-Riqueños: Producciones en verso, escogidas y coleccionadas*. Prolog J. M. Monge. Mayaguez: Martín Fernández.

Monteagudo, Bernardo. 1974. Diálogo entre Atawallpa y Fernando VII en los campos eliseos. In *El "Diálogo" de Bernardo Monteagudo: Estudio literario seguido del texto de dicho diálogo*. Carlos Castañón Barrientos La Paz: Universo.

Mopox, Joaquín de Santa Cruz y Cárdenas, Conde de San Juan de Jaruco y de. 1797. Informe sobre el modo de fomentar è instruir con utilidad del Rey, del Estado y de la juventud à aquellos naturales. (15 November). Museo Naval (Madrid) MS 2240, doc. 52, fols. 232–35.

———1798a. Carta a Francisco Saavedra. (2 July). Museo Naval (Madrid) MS 1578, doc. 11, fols. 41–47.

———. 1798b. Carta a Francisco de Saavedra. (2 July). Museo Naval (Madrid) MS 2241, doc. 15, fols. 44–48.

———. 1798c. Descripción de Guantánamo. (30 October copied 5 March 1801). Museo Naval (Madrid) MS 554, Cuaderno 5.

———. Carta a Godoy. (no date). Museo Naval (Madrid) MS 2240 doc. 42.

Moraña, Mabel. 1997. Ilustración y delirio en la construcción nacional, o las fronteras de la ciudad letrada. *Latin American Literary Review* 25, no. 50: 31–45.

Moreno Fraginals, Manuel. 1976. *The sugarmill: The socio-economic complex of sugar in Cuba, 1760–1860*. Trans. Cedric Belfrage. New York: Monthly Review Press.

Mörner, Magnus. 1984. The rural economy and society of colonial Spanish South

America. In *The Cambridge history of Latin America,* ed. Leslie Bethell, vol. 3 *Colonial Latin America.* Cambridge: Cambridge University Press.

Muller, John P., and William J. Richardson, eds. 1988. *The purloined Poe: Lacan, Derrida and psychoanalytic reading.* Baltimore: The Johns Hopkins University Press.

Munariz, José Luis. 1822. *Compendio de las lecciones sobre la retórica y bellas letras de Hugo Blair.* 2nd ed. Madrid: Ibarra, Impresor de Cámara de S. M.

Mutis, José Celestino. 1957–58. *Diario de observaciones de José Celestino Mutis, 1760–1790.* Ed. Guillermo Hernández de Alba. Bogota: Editorial Minerva.

———. 1982. *Pensamiento científico y filosófico de José Celestino Mutis.* Ed. Guillermo Hernández de Alba. Bogota: Fondo Cultural Cafetero.

Navarrete, Manuel. 1939. *Poesías profanas.* Biblioteca del estudiante universitario 7. Mexico: Ediciones del a Universidad Nacional Autónoma.

Nemoianu, Virgil. 1984. *The taming of romanticism: European literature and the age of Biedermeier.* Cambridge, MA: Harvard University Press.

Newson, Linda A. 1987. *Indian survival in colonial Nicaragua.* Norman: University of Oklahoma Press.

Niño-Murcia, Mercedes. 1997. Ideología lingüística hispanoamericana en el siglo XIX: Chile, 1840–1880. *Hispanic Linguistics* 9, no. 1: 100–42.

Nitzsche, Jane Chance. 1975. *The genius figure in antiquity and the middle ages.* New York: Columbia University Press.

Noriega, Julio E. 1991. Wallparrimachi: Transición y problematización en la poesía quechua. *Revista de crítica literaria latinoamericana* 133: 209–25.

Oakeshott, Michael. 1983. Three essays on history. In *On history and other essays.* Oxford: Basil Blackwell.

Ochoa, Anastasio María. 1828. *Poesías de un mexicano.* Vol. 1. New York: Lanuza, Mendía.

Olivera-Williams, María Rosa. 1986. *La poesía gauchesca: De Bartolomé Hidalgo a José Hernández: respuesta estética y condicionamiento social.* Xalapa: Centro de Investigaciones Lingüístico-Literarias, Instituto de Investigaciones Humanísticas, Universidad de Veracruz.

Olmedo, José Joaquín. 1947. *Poesías completas.* Ed. Aurelio Espinosa Pólit. S. I. Biblioteca Americana. Literatura Moderna Poesía. Mexico: Fondo de Cultura Económica.

O'Phelan, Scarlett. 1988. *Un siglo de rebeliones anticoloniales. Perú y Bolivia 1700–1783.* Cuzco: Centro de estudios andinos Bartolomé de las Casas.

Ortiz, Fernando. 1947. *El huracán, su mitología y sus símbolos.* Mexico: Fondo de cultura económica.

———. 1978. *Contrapunteo cubano del tabaco y el azucar.* 1940. Reprint, Biblioteca Ayacucho 42. Caracas: Biblioteca Ayacucho.

Palés Matos, Luis. 1974. *Tuntún de pasa y grifería: poemas afroantillanos.* San Juan, Puerto Rico: Biblioteca de autores puertorriqueños.

Palma, Ricardo. 1980. *Tradiciones peruanas.* Ed. Raimundo Lazo. Mexico: Porrua.

Pané, Ramón. 1974. *"Relación acerca de las antigüedades de los Indios:" El primer tratado escrito en América*. New version with notes, map and appendices by José Juan Arrom. Mexico: Siglo XXI.

Paulson, Ronald. 1971. *Satire: modern essays in criticism*. Englewood Cliffs, NJ: Prentice-Hall.

Paz, Octavio. 1974. *Los hijos del limo: Del romanticismo a la vanguardia*. Biblioteca breve. Barcelona, Seix Barral.

Peñalosa, Joaquín Antonio. 1988. *Letras virreinales de San Luis Potosí*. San Luis Potosí: Universidad Autónoma de San Luis Potosí.

Peralta Barnuevo, Pedro de. 1863. *Lima fundada o Conquista del Peru, poema heroico en que se decanta toda la historia del descubrimiento y sujecion de sus provincias por D. Francisco Pizarro Marqués de los Atabillos, ínclito y primer gobernador de este vasto imperio*. 1732. Reprint Colección de documentos literarios del Perú, Manuel de Odriozola, ed. Vol. 1. Lima: Establecimiento de tipografía y encuadernación de Aurelio Alfaro.

———. 1985. Lima fundada o Conquista del Perú, prólogo. Notes, Eva M. Kahilouto Rudat, *Dieciocho* 8, no. 1: 43–62

Perdices Blas, Luis. 1993. *Pablo de Olavide (1725–1803) el ilustrado*. Madrid: Editorial Complutense.

Pérez Bonalde, Juan Antonio. 1880. *Ritmos*. New York: n.p.

Pérez de Riva, Juan. 1977. Antonio del Valle Hernández, ¿el primer demógrafo cubano? In Valle Hernández 1977.

Pérez Firmat, Gustavo. 1985. La palabra invisible: Manuel de Zequeira y Arango en la literatura cubana. *Crítica Hispánica* 7, no. 1: 65–73.

Pérez Herrero, Pedro. 1992. *Comercio y mercados en América Latina colonial*. Colección realidades Americanas. Madrid: MAPFRE.

Perkins, David. 1992. *Is literary history possible?* Baltimore: The Johns Hopkins University Press.

Pichardo, Esteban. 1836. *Diccionario provincial de voces cubanos*. Matanzas: Imprenta de la Real Marina.

Picón Garfield, Evelyn. 1992. Periodical literature for women in mid-nineteenth century Cuba: The case of Gertrudis Gómez de Avellaneda's *Album Cubano de lo bueno y lo bello*. *Studies in Latin American Popular Culture* 11: 13–28.

Piersen, William D. 1977. Puttin' down ole massa: African satire in the new world. In *African Folklore in the New World*, ed. Daniel Crowley. Austin: University of Texas Press.

Polt, John H. R. 1979. La imitación anacreóntica en Meléndez Valdés. *Hispanic Review* 47: 193–206.

———. 1987. *Batilo: Estudios sobre la evolución estilística de Meléndez Valdés*. University of California Publications in Modern Philology 119. Textos y estudios del siglo XVIII 15. Berkeley: University of California Press/Oviedo: Centro de Estudios del Siglo XVIII.

Pratt, Mary Louise. 1992. *Imperial eyes: Travel writing and transculturation*. London: Routledge.

Premat, Julio. 1993. Quelques orgies argentines. Les fêtes indiennes, de *La cautiva* à *El entenado*. In *Les représentations de l'autre dans l'espace ibérique et ibéro-*

américain (II) (perspective diachronique): Actes du colloque organisé à la Sorbonne par le GRIMESREP les 19, 20 et 21 mars 1992, ed. Augustin Redondo. Paris: Presses de la Sorbonne Nouvelle.

Quesnay, François. 1969. *Oeuvres économiques et philosophiques*. Ed. Auguste Oncken. Research and Source Works Series 395. Selected Essays in History, Economics and Social Science 101. New York: Burt Franklin.

Quiñones Keber, Eloise. 1996. Humboldt and Aztec art. *Colonial Latin American Review* 5, no. 2: 277–97.

Quintana, Juan Nepomuceno. 1796. Carta al Príncipe de la Paz. (18 November). Museo Naval (Madrid) MS 2240, doc. 24, fols. 111–12.

———. 1798. El governador de Cuba: Propone los medios mas faciles que considera para el fomento de esta parte oriental de su mando, sin mayor gravamen del Real Erario." (28 May). (2 July 1798). Museo Naval (Madrid) MS 2240, doc. 16, fols. 58–70.

Quintana, Manuel José. 1898. *Obras completas*. Biblioteca de autores españoles 19. Madrid: Hernando.

———. *Poesías completas*. Ed. intro., and notes Albert Dérozier. Clásicos Castalia 16. Madrid: Castalia.

Rabinal achí: Tragedia danzada de los quiches de Rabinal. 1944. Adaptation José Antonio Villacorta. Buenos Aires: Editorial Nova.

Raffi-Béroud, Catherine. 1992. Semiotización del poder político: El teatro de Fernández de Lizarrdi, 1776–1827. In *Actas del IV simposio internacional de la Asociación Española de Semiótica. Celebrado en Sevilla, 3–5 de diciembre, 1990. Describir, inventar, transcribir el mundo*. Vol 1, Biblioteca Filológica Hispana 9. Madrid: Visor.

Rama, Angel. 1982a. *Los gauchipolíticos rioplatenses*. Buenos Aires: Centro Editor de America Latina.

———. 1982b. *Transculturación narrativa en América Latina*. Mexico: Siglo Veintiuno.

———. 1984a. *La ciudad letrada*. Hanover, NH: Ediciones del Norte.

———. La literatura en su marco antropológico. *Cuadernos hispanoamericanos* 407: 95–101.

Ramis, Pompeyo. 1984. *La razón filosófico-jurídica de la Independencia*. Estudios y monografias y ensayos 48. Caracas: Biblioteca de la Academia Nacional de Historia.

Rand, Nicholas. 1994. New perspectives in metapsychology: Cryptic mourning and secret love, editor's note. In Abraham and Torok, 1994.

Randolph, Mary Claire. 1971. The structural design of the formal verse satire. 1942. Reprint: *Satire: Modern essays in criticism*. ed. Ronald Paulson. Englewood Cliffs, NJ: Prentice-Hall.

Reedy, Daniel R. 1987. El ciego de la Merced: A blind poet's view of popular culture in eighteenth-century Lima. In *In retrospect: Essays on Latin American literature (In memory of Willis Knapp Jones)*, ed. Elizabeth S. Rogers and Timothy J. Rogers. York, SC: Spanish Literature Publications.

Reyes Heroles, Jesús. 1982. *El liberalismo mexicano.* Mexico: Fondo de cultura económica. 3 vols.

Rivera de Alvarez, Josefina, and Manuel Alvarez Nazario. 1982. *Antología general de la literatura puertorriqueña: Prosa-verso-teatro.* Vol. 1. *Desde los orígenes hasta el realismo y naturalismo.* Madrid: Ediciones Partenón.

Rivera-Rodas, Oscar. 1988. *La poesía hispanoamericana del siglo XIX: Del romanticismo al modernismo.* Madrid: Alhambra.

Roa Bastos, Augusto. 1974. *Yo el Supremo.* Buenos Aires: Siglo XXI Argentina.

Rockwood, Raymond O., ed. 1958. *Carl Becker's heavenly city revisited.* Ithaca: Cornell University Press.

Rodó, José Enrique. 1967. In *Obras completas.* Ed. Emil Rodríguez Monegal. Madrid: Aguilar.

Rodríguez, Simón. 1954–58. *Escritos.* 3 vols. Comp. Pedro Grases. Prolog by Arturo Uslar Pietri. Edición comemorativa del centenario de la muerte del maestro del Libertador. Caracas: Imprenta Nacional.

Rodríguez Castelo, Hernán, ed. 1984. *Letras de la audiencia de quito (período jesuita).* Biblioteca de Ayacucho 112. Caracas: Biblioteca de Ayacucho.

Rodríguez Fernández, Mario. 1981. Bello, el poeta. *Atenea* (Chile) 443–44: 41–52.

Rodríguez O., Jaime E. 1996. *La independencia de América.* Mexico: Fondo de cultura económica.

Rotker, Susana. 1996. Nation and mockery: The oppositional writings of Simón Rodríguez. Trans. Sophia McClennen Expósito, *Modern Language Quarterly* 57, no. 2: 253–67.

———. 1997. Lucía Miranda: Negación y violencia del origen. *Revista Iberoamericana* 63, no. 178–79: 115–27

———. 1993. Simón Rodríguez: Utopía y transgresión. *Casa de las Américas* 33, 9: 51–57.

Rubio, Darío. 1975. *La anarquía del lenguaje en la América Española.* 2 vols. Mexico: Confederación regional obrera mexicana.

Sacks, Peter M. 1975. *The English elegy, studies in the genre from Spenser to Yeats.* Baltimore: The Johns Hopkins University Press.

Saenz, Pilar. 1989. Revitalización en la poesía ilustrada: El romance en la poesía de Meléndez Valdés. *Dieciocho* 12, no. 1: 34–44.

Saínz, Enrique. 1983. *La literatura cubana de 1700 a 1790.* Havana: Editorial Letras cubanas.

Salas de Lecuna, Yolanda. 1987. *Bolívar y la historia en la conciencia popular.* With the collaboration of Norma González Vitoria and Ronny Velásquez. Caracas: Universidad Simón Bolívar/Instituto de Altos Estudios de América Latina.

Salgado, María. 1991. *Ut pictura poesis* y el autorretrato de Olmedo. *Dieciocho* 19, no. 2: 181–90.

Salvatierra, S. J., Juan María de. 1971. *Selected letters about lower California.* Ed. and trans. Ernest J. Burrus, S. J. Baja California Travels Series 25. Los Angeles: Dawson's Book Shop.

Sánchez, Luis Alberto. 1921. *Historia de la literatura peruana.* Vol. 1:*Los poetas de la colonia.* Lima: Ciudad de Lima.

Sanfuentes, Salvador. 1921. *Obras escogidas de d. Salvador Sanfuentes*. Edición de la Academia Chilena. Santiago de Chile: Imprenta Universitaria.

Sarduy, Severo. 1969. Dispersión (Falsas notas/homenaje a Lezama). In *Escrito sobre un cuerpo: Ensayos de crítica*. Buenos Aires: Sudamericana.

————. 1974. *Barroco*. Buenos Aires: Sudamericana.

Sarrailh, Jean. 1964. *L'Espagne éclairée de la seconde moitié du XVIIIᵉ siècle*. Paris: Klincksieck.

Sastre, Marcos. 1940. Ojeada filosófica sobre el estado presente y la suerte futura de la nación arjentina. In Echeverría 1940.

Schama, Simon. 1995. *Landscape and memory*. London: Harper/Collins.

Sebold, Russell P. 1974. *Cadalso, el primer romántico 'europeo' de España*. Biblioteca románica hispánica, estudios y ensayos 215. Madrid: Gredos.

Segala, Amos. 1991. Textología nahuatl y nuevas interpretaciones. *Revista iberoamericana* 155–56: 649–55.

Semprat Assadourien, Carlos. 1983. *El sistema de la economía colonial: El mercado interior: Regiones y espacio económica*. Mexico: Nueva Imagen.

Serulnikov, Sergio. 1996. Disputed images of colonialism: Spanish rule and Indian subversion in northern Potosí, 1777–1780. *Hispanic American Historical Review* 76, no. 2: 189–226.

Shelley, Percy Bysshe. 1951. *Selected poetry and prose*. Ed. Carlos Baker. New York: Modern Library, Random House.

Shklovsky, Victor. 1990. *Theory of prose*. Trans. Benjamin Sher. Elmwood Park, IL: Dalkey Archive Press.

Shumway, Nicolas. 1991. *The invention of Argentina*. Berkeley: University of California Press.

Silver, Philip W. 1994. Towards a revisionary theory of Spanish romanticism. *Revista de Estudios Hispánicos* 28: 293–302.

Smith, Adam. 1961. *An inquiry into the nature and causes of the wealth of nations*. 2 vols. Ed. Edwin Cannan. London: Methuen.

Socolow, Susan Migden. 1992. Spanish captives in Indian societies: Cultural contact along the Argentine frontier, 1600–1835. *Hispanic American Historical Review* 72, no. 1: 73–100.

Soler Cañas, Luis. 1958. *Negros, gauchos y compadres en el cancionero de la Federación, 1830–1848*. Instituto de Investigaciones Históricas Juan Manuel Rosas. Buenos Aires: Ediciones Theoría.

Sommer, Doris. 1991. *Foundational fictions: The national romances of Latin America*. Berkeley: University of California Press.

Soto Arango, Diana, Miguel Angel Puig-Samper, and Luis Carlos Arboleda, eds. 1995. *La Ilustración en América Colonial*. Colección Actas. Aranjuez: Consejo Superior de Investigaciones Científicas/Doce Calles/Colciencias.

Sotos Serrano, Carmen. 1984. *Flora y fauna cubanas del siglo XVIII. Los dibujos de la expedición del Conde de Mopox, 1796–1802*. Madrid: Turner.

Safford, Frank. 1991. Race, integration, and progress: Elite attitudes and the Indian in Colombia, 1750–1870. *Hispanic American History Review* 71, 1: 1–33.

Stafford, Barbara Maria. 1984. *Voyage into substance: Art, science, nature, and the illustrated travel account, 1760–1840.* Cambridge, MA: MIT Press.

Stolley, Karen. 1992. *El lazarillo de ciegos caminantes: Un itinerario crítico.* Hanover: Ediciones del Norte.

Stone, Cynthia Leigh. 1994. Rewriting indigenous traditions: The burial ceremony of the *cazonci, Colonial Latin American Review* 3, no. 1–2: 87–114.

Szuchman, Mark D., ed. 1989. *The middle period in Latin America: Values and attitudes in the seventeenth–nineteenth centuries.* Boulder: Lynne Rienner.

Taussig, Michael. 1993. *Mimesis and alterity: A particular history of the senses.* London: Routledge.

Teresa de Jesús. 1985. *Las moradas.* Austral 89. Madrid: Espasa-Calpe.

Terralla Landa, Esteban. 1978. *Lima por dentro y fuera.* Ed. Alan Soons. Exeter Hispanic Texts. Exeter: University of Exeter.

Testimonios de la época emancipadora. 1961. Intro. Arturo Uslar Pietri. Caracas: Academia Nacional de la Historia.

Tirry y Lacy, Juan. 1797. Descripcíon de la Ysla de Pinos. Museo Naval (Madrid) MS 560 bis. 53 fols.

Tomlinson, Janis A. 1992. *Goya in the twilight of Enlightenment.* New Haven: Yale University Press.

Toussaint, Manuel. 1967. *Colonial art in Mexico.* Trans. and ed. Elizabeth Wilder Weisman. Texas Pan American Series. Austin and London: University of Texas Press.

Trachtenberg, Alan. 1979. *Brooklyn Bridge: Fact and symbol.* 2nd ed. Chicago: University of Chicago Press.

Unánue, Hipólito ("Aristio"). 1964. Rasgos inéditos de los escritores peruanos, 28 April 1791. Vol. 1. *Mercurio Peruano* 34. Edición facsimilar. Lima: Biblioteca Nacional del Perú.

Urbina, Luis G., Pedro Henríquez Ureña, and Nicolás Rangel. 1985. *Antología del centenario: Estudio documentado de la literatura mexicana durante el primer siglo de independencia, 1800–1821.* 1910. Reprint, Mexico: Porrúa.

Uslar Pietri, Arturo. 1996. *La invención de América mestiza.* Ed. Gustavo Luis Carrera. Colección Tierra Firme. Mexico: Fondo de cultura económica.

Valderrama, Adolfo. 1912. Bosquejo histórico de la poesía chilena. 1866. Reprint in *Obras escogidas en prosa de Adolfo Valderrama,* ed. Enrique Nercasseau y Morán. Colección Biblioteca de escritores de Chile 8. Santiago de Chile: Imprenta Barcelona.

Valle Hernández, Antonio del. 1977. *Sucinta noticia de la situación presente de esta colonia, 1800.* Havana: Editorial de Ciencias Sociales.

van Tieghem, Paul. 1970. *La poésie de la nuit et des tombeaux en Europe au XVIIIe siècle.* 1921. Reprint, Geneva: Slatkine Reprints.

Vargas Tejeda, Luis. 1857. *Poesías.* Bogota: Imprenta de Ortiz.

Vargas Ugarte, Rubén, S. J., ed. 1951. *Nuestro romancero.* Clásicos Peruanos 4. Lima: n.p.

Vázquez Santa Ana, Higinio, ed. 1925. *Canciones, cantares y corridos mexicanos.* Vol. 2. Mexico: n.p.

Villacorta G., Jorge Luis. 1971. *María Josefa García Granados: Su vida, su obra, su correspondencia, sus papeles, en la leyenda, en el teatro*. Guatemala: Editorial José de Pineda Ibarra.

Vitier, Cintio. 1970. *Lo cubano en la poesía*. Havana: Instituto del Libro.

Vitoria, Francisco de. 1963. *Las relecciones de Indis y De jure belli*. Ed. Javier Malagón Barceló. Washington: Unión Panamericana.

Viveros, Germán. 1994. Diversiones campiranas en el Libro XV de la *Rusticatio Mexicana*. *Cuadernos americanos*, nueva época 47: 227–35.

Vogeley, Nancy. 1993. Colonial discourse in a postcolonial context: Nineteenth-century Mexico. *Colonial Latin American Review* 2, no. 1–2: 189–212.

Weber, Max. 1958. Bureaucracy. In *Max Weber: Essays in sociology*, ed. and intro. H. H. Gerth and C. Wright Mills. New York: Oxford University Press, 1958.

Weinberg, Félix. 1993. El salón literario de 1837 y los comienzos del romanticismo en el Plata. In *Cinco siglos de literatura en la Argentina*, ed. Julio C. Díaz Usandivaras. Buenos Aires: Corregidor.

Whitaker, Arthur P., ed. 1961. *Latin America and the Enlightenment*. Ithaca: Great Seal Books/Cornell University Press.

Whitten, Jr., Norman E. 1995. Afro-Creoles on the frontier: Conquering the Ecuadorian Pacific lowlands. In *Slavery and beyond: The African impact on Latin America and the Caribbean*, ed. Darién J. Davis. Jaguar Books on Latin America 5. Wilmington: Scholarly Resources.

Wilbert, Johannes, and Karin Simoneau. 1991. *Folk literature of the Makka Indians*. Folk Literature of South American Indians. Los Angeles: UCLA Latin American Center Publications/University of California, Los Angeles.

Williams, Jerry M. 1995. Academic and literary culture in eighteenth-century Peru. *Colonial Latin American Review* 4, no. 1: 129–52.

———. 1998. Feijóo and Peralta Barnuevo: Two letters. *Dieciocho* 21, no. 1: 237–46.

Williams, Raymond. 1963. *Culture and society, 1780–1850*. Hammondsworth, Eng.: Penguin.

Wordsworth, William. 1904. *Wordsworth's complete poetical works*. Ed. Andrew J. George. The Cambridge Editions of the Poets. Cambridge: The Riverside Press.

Wordsworth, William, and Samuel T. Coleridge. 1965. *Lyrical ballads*. Ed. R. L. Brett and A. R. Jones. London: Methuen.

Wright, Eleanor. 1987. The anacreontic odes by Juan Meléndez Valdés: Archetypes and aesthetic form. *Dieciocho* 10, no. 1: 18–31.

[Wurdemann, J. C. F.] 1844. *Notes on Cuba, containing an account of its discovery and early history; a description of the face of the country, its population, resources, and wealth; its institutions, and the manners and customs of its inhabitants, with directions to travellers visiting the island*. Boston: James Munroe and Company.

Zavala, Iris M. 1988. The turn of the century lyric: Rubén Darío and the sign of the swan. In *The Crisis in Institutionalized Literature in Spain*, ed. Wlad God-

zich and Nicholas Spadaccini. Hispanic Issues 3. Minneapolis, MN: The Prisma
Institute.

———. *Colonialism and culture: Hispanic modernisms and the social imaginary*.
Bloomington: Indiana University Press.

Zea, Leopoldo. 1970. *América en la historia*. Colección Cimas de América.
Madrid: Ediciones de la Revista de Occidente.

———. 1978. *Filosofía de la historia americana*. Colección Tierra Firme. Mexico: Fondo de cultura económica.

Zequeira y Arango, Manuel Tiburcio de. 1964. *Poesías [por] Zequeira y Rubal-
cava*. Havana: Comisión Nacional de la UNESCO.

Zinny, Antonio. 1878. *Juan María Gutiérrez: Su vida y sus escritos*. Buenos Aires:
Imprenta y Librerías de Mayo.

Zorrilla de San Martín, Juan. 1984. *Tabaré*. Ed. Antonio Selvaja Cecín. Montevideo: Universidad de la República, Dirección General de Extensión Universitaria,
División Publicaciones y Ediciones.

Zum Felde, Alberto. 1954. *Indice crítico de la literatura latinoamericana: Los
ensayistas*. Mexico: Editorial Guaranía.

Index